*The 1912 Stockholm
Olympics*

The 1912 Stockholm Olympics

Essays on the Competitions, the People, the City

Edited by LEIF YTTERGREN *and*
HANS BOLLING

McFarland & Company, Inc., Publishers

Jefferson, North Carolina, and London

This is a translation of *Stockholmsolympiaden 1912:
Tävlingarna — Människorna — Staden*
(Stockholm: Stockholmia, 2012)

LIBRARY OF CONGRESS CATALOG ONLINE DATA

The 1912 Stockholm Olympics : essays on the competitions,
the people, the city / edited by Leif Yttergren and Hans Bolling.
p.   cm.
Includes bibliographical references and index.

ISBN 978-0-7864-7131-7

softcover : acid free paper ∞

1. Olympic Games (5th : 1912 : Stockholm, Sweden) — History.
2. Sports — Sweden — Stockholm — History — 20th century.
3. Olympics — History. I. Title.
GV7221912+ 2012   2012039199

BRITISH LIBRARY CATALOGUING DATA ARE AVAILABLE

On the cover: The opening ceremonies of the 5th
Olympic Games in Stockholm (Library of Congress)

Manufactured in the United States of America

*McFarland & Company, Inc., Publishers
Box 611, Jefferson, North Carolina 28640
www.mcfarlandpub.com*

Table of Contents

PREFACE 1

INTRODUCTION (*Hans Bolling* and *Leif Yttergren*) 2

Nothing New Under the Sun? Marketing the Stockholm Olympics
(*Per Andersson* and *Hans Kjellberg*) 27

Organizing the 1912 Games (*Therese Nordlund Edvinsson*) 57

The Jewel in the Olympic Crown: The Training Preparations and
Competitions in Athletics (*Leif Yttergren*) 75

Counts and Draymen: The Swedish Participants (*Leif Yttergren,
Hans Bolling* and *Ingemar Ekholm*) 95

Gender and Class: Women on the Swedish Squad (*Hans Bolling* and
Leif Yttergren) 115

Art and Sport: Different Worlds? The Art Competitions (*Patrik Steorn*) 137

Spectators at the Stockholm Games (*Mats Hellspong*) 154

Punch, Splendor and Patriotism: The Olympics Outside the Stadium
(*Hans Bolling*) 174

"A New Experience in Life": The Olympics and the General Debate
in the Swedish Daily Press (*Jan Lindroth*) 199

Patriotic Games as a Breakthrough for the Olympic Movement
(*Ansgar Molzberger*) 217

The Results of the Competitions: The 1912 Olympic Games
in Numbers (*Ingemar Ekholm*) 233

ABOUT THE CONTRIBUTORS 275

INDEX 277

Preface

Major events are considered to be important in the popularization and diffusion of sport; they are said to consolidate sport in the community and to be beneficial for businesses. Despite this, knowledge of what importance they really have had is, at best, fragmentary and the arguments put forward for and against hosting major sporting events are largely based on things other than facts.

As of July 6, 2012, a century has passed since the fifth Olympiad was inaugurated by King Gustaf V of Sweden at the Olympic Stadium in Stockholm. That is as good a reason as any to write about and research this unique event in Swedish sporting history. Despite a number of attempts by cities such as Östersund, Falun and Stockholm once more, no Swedish city has managed to repeat the feat of hosting the Olympic Games, either Summer or Winter Games.

One aim of this book is to deepen the understanding of the 1912 Stockholm Olympics by studying them from a range of perspectives and with authors from different scientific disciplines. The focus is not on purely sporting matters, on the sporting achievements: They have been well described during the century that has passed since Stockholm was the host, and what's more, there are others who are more adept at writing about these. Another aim of this volume is to shed light on the significance of the event for sport in Stockholm, Sweden, and the future of the Olympic movement, as well as on its effects on the society hosting the Games, not least the ever-current stadium issue in Stockholm. This history of the 1912 Olympic Games in Stockholm is more than an antiquarian account of a past event.

The 1912 Stockholm Olympics is a translation of *Stockholmsolympiaden 1912: Tävlingarna — människorna — staden*, published in Swedish by the city of Stockholm's publishing house, Stockholmia, in early spring 2012. We are very happy that this book about the greatest sporting event ever to be held in Stockholm has reached an international audience and is available to more than the approximately one and a half percent of the world's population that understands Swedish.

Assembling this collection demands teamwork. Therefore, we would like to thank the other authors in this book for an inspiring and effective cooperation. Also, we would like to thank David Grist, who has helped us with the translation from Swedish to English, and Anders Gullberg at Stockholmia for encouraging us to disseminate our findings to an international audience. Finally, we would like to thank the Swedish National Centre for Research in Sports, the Swedish School of Sport and Health Science (GIH), the Committee for Stockholm Research, King Gustaf VI Adolf's Foundation for Swedish Culture, the Royal Patriotic Society, Åke Wiberg's Foundation and Magn. Bergvalls Foundation, National Sports Museum, and Sweden's Central Association for the Promotion of Sport for their support of our research and for contributing to the production of the book.

Introduction

HANS BOLLING *and* LEIF YTTERGREN

May 28, 1909, is a special day in the history of Stockholm. It was then that the city was awarded the Summer Olympic Games of 1912. The decision was made at the session of the International Olympic Committee (IOC) in Berlin. Behind the successful application lay Viktor Balck's lobbying activities. Balck, often called "the father of Swedish sport," was the great ideologist of Swedish sport and an internationally well known sporting profile. He also knew Pierre de Coubertin, the man behind the modern Olympic Games and the founder of the IOC, which certainly contributed to the Games being held in the capital of Sweden.[1]

Researchers interested in the Stockholm Olympics are very fortunate. It is not only an incredibly interesting subject, but there are also an almost infinite number of sources. The Archive of the Stockholm Olympics in the National Archives in Stockholm comprises 23 meters of shelves in all. They contain the minutes of the large organization surrounding the Stockholm Olympic Games, applications for planning permission, correspondence, photographs, etc. The Archive's own collection of newspaper cuttings comprises 334 archive volumes. It is a real gold mine. Most of the essays in this book are based on this excellent archive. The only major gap in the archive is in respect of the art competitions, Concours d'Art, which were arranged for the first time in connection with the Olympic Games in Stockholm in 1912. However, these were not administrated from Stockholm but by the president of the IOC, Pierre de Coubertin.[2] Mention should also be made of the more than 1,000-page *V. Olympiaden. Officiell redogörelse för olympiska spelen i Stockholm 1912* (*The Fifth Olympiad: The Official Report of the Olympic Games of Stockholm 1912*, translated by Evert Adams Ray) which was published under the management of the journalist and sports official Erik Bergvall just one year after the Games. It contains all sorts of information and has been used a great deal. Moreover, press material has been made use of to a great extent. The Stockholm Olympic Games were a media event of large proportions and the newspapers and the daily, weekly and sports press wrote page after page about the Games. The well-organized archives of the IOC in Lausanne should also be mentioned. They also contain very important and rarely used information about the Stockholm Olympic Games.

The Olympic City of 1912

What kind of city was it that was elected to host the 1912 Olympic Games? The time after the turn of the century was turbulent in both Sweden and Stockholm. In 1905 the union between Sweden and Norway had been dissolved and revanchist currents were stirring among nationalist groups, primarily on the political right wing. Four years later the Great Strike took place, which beat the world record of that time with regard to the number of people participating. The right was opposed to the left, workers were opposed to employers, and day-to-day life was full of antagonism, and here sport, and not least the Stockholm Olympic Games, came to take on a moderating and unifying function.

A traffic jam outside the Olympic Stadium during the Olympic Games (*Den femte olympiaden i bild och ord,* p. 360).

Sweden was a country in the midst of change: the old aristocratic society and La Belle Époque met the new, more modern society that was willing to change, but the direction was not clear and the future was uncertain in this time of political and social instability. The same can be said of Stockholm. The city was in the midst of an intensive urbanization, industrialization and modernization period. In 1900 Stockholm had just over 300,000 inhabitants and twelve years later the population had increased to approximately 370,000.[3] The typical stone-built city was not sufficient for the increasing population and the new industries and workplaces. Suburbs began to be built, amongst other things in the form of exclusive suburbs of detached houses, which could be reached using rail transport.[4]

The city was growing and the politicians on the City Council in the Old Town were busy handling the changing city. Universal suffrage had not yet been introduced. Women did not have many of the rights that we today consider self-evident and were also without political influence after extension of the right to vote in 1909. In Council elections there was also a system of graded voting rights: the higher your income, the more votes you had. Furthermore, certain people were barred from voting, in particular those of lesser means in society.[5] What we would today call non–socialist parties therefore had a large majority over the social democrats on Stockholm's City Council. They were in general more positive towards sport than the social democrats at the beginning of the previous century, but despite this neither the question of sport nor that of the Olympic Games was a central part of the agenda in the time around 1912.[6]

Giving priority to sport and the building of sports venues on valuable Council land was not a consideration. It seems that the general view in those days was that it was needed for housing and workplaces and not for "silly sports." There was thus some skepticism on the part of the city to investing in a private leisure-time activity that demanded a lot of resources when other more basic needs required public support in the expansive city. The

Kungsträdgården in central Stockholm 1912. In the background are the Royal Palace and the Opera House (postcard, National Sports Museum).

Organizing Committee had applied for 100,000 kronor for the building of the Olympic Stadium, but only received half from the tight-fisted politicians on the Council.

There was also resistance in Parliament to using public resources for sport. When the decision to award Stockholm the Olympic Games was taken, sport in Sweden was not financed as it is today through State grants each year. This first occurred in 1913, and then on a relatively modest scale. This meant that the organizers could not count on getting support from that direction. However, Balck and others had good contacts with the Conservative government under Prime Minister Arvid Lindman, which was more favorably inclined to sport. In February 1908 the Lindman ministry had granted the Swedish sports movement permission to arrange a lottery (eight draws), the proceeds of which were to be used to support Swedish sport. Each draw was estimated to give a surplus of 200,000 kronor (in total 1,600,000 kronor) and the return on the capital would be used for the promotion of sport generally in Sweden.[7] A foundation had thereby been laid for public support of Swedish sport and for coming Olympic investments. What made the Games possible was thus the government's, and specially the royal family's, positive attitude and will to grant money, and to make State land available.

Financing of the Stockholm Games

The decision on where the Olympic Games of 1912 were to be held was thus made at the IOC's session in Berlin in May 1909. Stockholm had made its candidacy known at the IOC meeting in London in 1908. However, there was one other candidate city, Berlin, which after pressure on the part of Pierre de Coubertin had refrained from applying for the Games in 1908. It was understood that Berlin would therefore be allowed to organize the Games in 1912. However, the Germans had problems, above all with regard to constructing a stadium worthy of the Olympic Games. Furthermore, when the president of the German Olympic Committee died in 1909 the Germans decided to refrain from applying for the Games in 1912. When the IOC met in Berlin in 1909, Stockholm was thus the only candidate, but the choice was not, however, completely self-evident.

As the Games had been moved from the appointed organizing city in both 1904 (from Chicago to St. Louis) and 1908 (from Rome to London) the IOC wanted to have guarantees from the Swedish IOC delegates that the Games really could be arranged in Stockholm. However, the Swedish application was well prepared and well founded, with promises from the government to contribute to the financing of the Games.

Balck and Clarence von Rosen (Sweden's second IOC delegate) thereby managed to convince the IOC delegates that Stockholm really could manage to arrange the Olympic Games in 1912. Berlin was promised, in compensation, that they could host the Olympic Games in 1916, Games that never took place due to the First World War. Berlin had to wait until 1936 before the city was able to host the Olympic Games. According to Coubertin the question of where the 1912 Olympic Games were to be held was decided in favor of Stockholm as early as in London 1908.[8] It thus needed two strong and well-reputed figures in the international world of sport, Balck and von Rosen, for Stockholm to get the Olympic Games, which puts into perspective later unsuccessful Olympic applications on the part of Sweden. More can be read about the figures behind the Stockholm Olympics in Therese Nordlund Edvinsson's article "Organizing the 1912 Games."

Oddly enough, the main responsibility for securing the financial preconditions for organizing the Games fell on the shoulders of a single organization, Sweden's Central Association for the Promotion of Sport, which during the first decades of the twentieth century was the financially leading organization within Swedish sport and consisted of people from the elite in society.[9] Even before Stockholm had been awarded the Games, an investigation into the financing of the Games had been carried out. It presupposed that a relatively simple stadium would be constructed at the relatively newly opened athletic ground Östermalms IP (located in the borough Östermalm's eastern edges). The estimate of the cost of holding the Games was, however, on the low side, and on account of this the Central Association applied for permission to arrange an extra draw in the sports lottery so as to be able to finance the intended Games. When a confidential guarantee had been obtained from the government that the application would be positively received, Victor Balck was able to announce that Stockholm was prepared to organize the Olympic Games of 1912, in a somewhat reduced format.

The original intention within the Swedish organizing bodies was to organize Games that were as simple as possible. They wanted the Games to only comprise events that were available to people irrespective of social position or wealth. A definitive program for the Stockholm Olympic Games was not adopted before 1911. The fact that the decision on the program was made so late and that it was more extensive than what the organizers had first intended involved of course extra costs for the organizers.

In the first estimate for the Games, from May 1909, the total cost of holding the Games was estimated to be 315,000 kronor. The largest expense was the construction of a fairly simple stadium at Östermalms IP (235,000 kronor = Swedish Crowns). In February 1910 a new estimate was made. The total cost for holding the Games had then risen to 630,000 kronor. The place for where the stadium was to be constructed had been moved to Idrottsparken, Stockholm's main sports arena in the early 1900s and located in close proximity to Östermalms IP, due to uncertainty concerning the future use of the land in the area where Östermalms IP was situated.

Daily program for the swimming competitions, July 10, 1912 (National Sports Museum).

There was also a demand on the part of the government that the stadium to be constructed for the Games should be of a more permanent nature, which meant even higher costs. The cost for constructing such a stadium was estimated to be 715,000 kronor in March 1910. The total cost for holding the Games rose by almost 170 percent to 845,000 kronor in less than a year.

Of course, the revenues from just one extra draw in the sports lottery were not nearly enough to cover these costs. The organizers were forced, through the Board of the Central Association, to apply for permission for one further draw in the sports lottery and to use its so-called surplus funds to cover the costs of the Olympic Games. The total revenues from the two extraordinary lotteries and the surplus funds were estimated to amount to 815,000 kronor.

However, these cost estimates did not hold either. In September 1911 and May 1912 the Organizing Committee was forced to admit that its cost estimates were wrong and to ask for more money. Being a "financial guarantor" for the Games ended up costing the Central Association at least the entire surplus the sports lottery brought in as well as a further 100,000 kronor.

The Olympic Games thus ended up being much more expensive than what had been planned, just as has been the case for many Games to follow. In the first place, the construction of the Olympic Stadium cost far more than what had first been budgeted for. In the second place, the number of events was considerably more than what had been imagined at the outset. This led to a need for more arenas than the Olympic Stadium. In the third place the number of participants was greater than what had been initially imagined. The participants are studied in the essay "Counts and Draymen." Finally, the Organizing Committee also paid for the Swedish Olympic squad's comprehensive and costly preparations. It was important to have a squad that could do well against the tough competition: national honor was at stake and the preparations were meticulous, as Leif Yttergren shows in his essay "The Jewel in the Olympic Crown."

Prime Minister Arvid Lindman also commented on the financial outcome of the Stockholm Olympics. We can see from the notes in his diaries that he was not in the least surprised by the fact that the Olympic organization exceeded its budget time and time again:

> You would have a poor knowledge of sportsmen's "financial side" if you thought that it would remain there. It was not long before one more draw was needed and also held, but they then expressly promised that it would now be sufficient. No such thing! It was not long before they came back again and we had to help them with further funding.[10]

In all the Stockholm Olympics cost almost 2.5 million kronor (approximately 114 million kronor in the value of money in 2011[11]) to organize, including the building of the Olympic Stadium. This cost was thus covered largely by revenues from the sports lottery, and the second largest source of income was ticket sales, which brought in almost 850,000 kronor.[12]

Olympic Tickets

Ticket sales give every large sports organizer a headache, and this was also the case for those responsible for the 1912 Stockholm Olympic Games. It was not that easy for the general public interested in sport to come into possession of tickets for the Olympic competitions. The Olympic organizers were worried that the tickets would be the object of speculation and sold on the black market. It was therefore decided at an early stage that only multi-event passes would be sold in advance. Sales of tickets for individual events began on the day of the specific event. Most of the one-day tickets were thus sold on a cash basis at the Olympic Stadium's turnstiles, which meant that for the most popular competitions there were queues of several thousand people and subsequent dissatisfaction. The multi-event passes for the Olympic Stadium were also expensive, almost out of the reach of common salaried workers and must have excluded large parts of Stockholm's population from following the competitions live over several days. They cost 50, 75, 100 and 200 kronor. They cost 20, 30 and 50 kronor for the swimming competitions, 10 kronor for the fencing competitions, and 25 kronor for the tennis and soccer. The price for one-day tickets to the different arenas varied from 1 to 25 kronor. The tickets for the equestrian events at the Olympic Stadium cost 5, 10 or 20 kronor per day.[13]

This way of doing things naturally meant that a large amount of cash was handled at the Olympic Stadium. The estimates were that 100,000 kronor per day would be received in entrance fees during the so called Olympic week. To protect these revenues the Olympic organizers took out the first robbery insurance in Sweden. It covered both the employees who transported money and various valuable documents between the Olympic Stadium and different places in Stockholm, as well as all ticket sellers at the Olympic Stadium. Furthermore burglary insurance had been taken out for cash and valuable documents that were stored in the Olympic Stadium's cash office.[14]

The decision not to sell tickets for the cheaper places for the competitions at the Olympic Stadium in advance in order to prevent speculation can be said to have been successful. In any case, there never arose any black market selling of tickets to the Olympic Games at unreasonable prices. In the middle of the Olympic week the daily newspaper *Dagens Nyheter*, for example, had an instructive article on what to do to get a ticket for the Olympic competitions. It was claimed that it was not as difficult or expensive as many people seemed to imagine. Every reader of newspapers' advertising columns should have been aware that there were multi-event tickets on sale at a price which was at least 25 percent under what was charged by the Games' ticket office. These prices were what the people selling hoped to get for the tickets — there was thus room for bargaining.[15] It has been reported that people who had speculated on the tickets lost money.[16]

After the end of the Games a newspaper gave the Organizing Committee the blame for the Olympic Stadium's stands being empty so often. The Games were not a success from the point of view of the number of spectators, far from it. It was said to have been because of the way ticket sales were handled. It had been too complicated for interested spectators

V. OLYMPIADEN

OLYMPISKA SPELEN I STOCKHOLM 1912.
INTRÄDESBILJETT
FÖR

till samtliga täflingar, hvilka under tiden 1—19 juli 1912 äga rum i samband med Olympiska spelen i Stockholm.
Å Stadion gäller denna biljett till ORGANISATIONS-KOMMITTÉNS LOGE, **B** vänster öfre, ing. fr. Sturevägen.

Får ej öfverlåtas.

Pass that entitled the holder unlimited entrance to the Olympic Stadium and other competition venues (National Sports Museum).

to get hold of tickets.[17] More about the spectators at the Olympic Games can be found in Mats Hellspong's essay "Spectators at the Stockholm Games."

Bearing in mind the limited public interest in many of the Olympic competitions, it seems as if the difficulty in buying individual tickets in advance coupled with the prices put Stockholmers off. Even if it was possible to obtain tickets for the competitions at prices that should not have been outside the realm of possibility for workers—a worker earned 0.42 kronor an hour on average in 1912—it was difficult to come into possession of them.[18] From that point of view, the Games must have been socially exclusive and an activity for primarily the well-off, tourists and not least the true sports enthusiasts. The Olympic organization also had revenues from sales of programs and different kinds of rights.

The Olympic Organization

The decision in Berlin to award Stockholm the Olympic Games meant the start of feverish activity on the part of Balck and others. It was not just a question of getting all the venues ready but also of finding suitable people for organizing the Games. First and foremost, the central and powerful Organizing Committee, which came to be the hub in the work on the Games, was to be appointed.[19] Then a number of sections and special committees, 27 in all (see Table 1), also had to be appointed, who had the task of organizing on behalf of the Organizing Committee everything from competitions in different sports to entertainment activities for the spectators after the competitions had ended for the day,[20] as well as the marketing of the Games and of Sweden as a tourist country and Stockholm as a tourist city.[21]

Table 1. Sections and Special Committees Under the Organizing Committee for the Olympic Games in Stockholm 1912

Sections of the Organizing Committee:	Special Committees: Sports:	Others:
Executive committee	Athletics	Accommodation committee
Finance section	Tug-of-war	Advertisement committee
Medal and badge committee	Cycling	Building committee
Technical section	Equestrian events	Entertainments committee
Program section	Fencing	Press committee
	Soccer	Reception committee
	Gymnastics	
	Hunting	
	Modern Pentathlon	
	Mountain Climbing	
	Rowing	
	Shooting	
	Swimming	
	Tennis	
	Wrestling	
	Yachting	

Source: Bergvall (ed.): *V. Olympiaden* (1913), pp. 4 ff.

When the Olympic committee got under way with its work during the autumn of 1909, it did so with Coubertin's full support, who in Berlin made the following observation:

"Of all countries in the world, Sweden, at the present moment, possesses the best conditions necessary for organizing the Olympic Games [...] The Olympic Games of Stockholm are, even now, assured perfect success."[22] This would be by the organizers following the advice that he so generously gave them. Coubertin maintained very frequent correspondence with the organizers up until the Games. He urged them at an early stage not to repeat the way the London Olympic Games of 1908 were organized. The Games in Stockholm should instead "be kept more purely athletic; they must be more dignified, more discreet; more in accordance with classic and artistic requirements; more intimate, and above all less expensive."[23] Whether the Swedish organizers lived up to this, which as was stated above was also a Swedish aim initially, is doubtful. Much suggests the opposite. It was a question of showing off Sweden, Stockholm and Swedish sport from its very best side. National honor was at stake and then nothing was to be left to chance. It was a wholehearted effort on the part of the organizers and nationalism was an important driving force.

Coubertin and the IOC, however, exercised some influence over how the Stockholm Olympics was organized, but it was not as great as he perhaps would have wished. According to one of the leading newspapers the French Baron had tried to get "our Olympic working organizations to dance entirely after his tune," which "had always been met with firm resistance, which more than once during the past years has given him occasion to express his dissatisfaction with us by letter."[24]

Unlike several of its predecessors the Stockholm Olympics was a coordinated event. However, this did not prevent them from also lasting just over two and a half months, on and off. It is true that the majority of the competitions were held during the so-called Stadium week or Olympic week, from July 6 to July 15, which was thus 10 days. But the Games began as early as May 5 when the indoor tennis tournament was begun, and carried on until July 22 when the sailing competitions were completed.[25] However, the Games were not officially inaugurated until July 6 by King Gustaf V, by which time the competitions in tennis (covered courts and lawn), soccer and shooting had already finished (see Table 2).

Table 2. Some Important Dates

May 28, 1909: Stockholm was awarded the 1912 Olympic Games by the International Olympic Committee at its session in Berlin.
October 7, 1909: First meeting of the Organizing Committee.
June 1, 1912: The Olympic Stadium inaugurated by Gustaf V.
Saturday, July 6: Formal opening of the Games by King Gustaf V. Beginning of the Olympic week at the Olympic Stadium.
Monday, July 15: Medal ceremony for the events held during the Olympic week.[26]
Saturday, July 27: Closing of the Games at Hasselbacken restaurant.
Sunday, May 5–Sunday, May 12: tennis, covered courts.
Friday, June 28–Friday, July 5: tennis, lawn
Saturday, June 29–Friday, July 5: soccer
Saturday, June 29–Friday, July 5: shooting.
Saturday, July 6–Monday, July 15: wrestling.
Saturday, July 6–Monday, July 15: athletics, incl. tug-of-war.
Saturday, July 6–Tuesday, July 16: swimming and diving.
Saturday, July 6–Thursday, July 18: fencing.
Sunday, July 7: cycle race.
Sunday, July 7–Friday, July 12: modern pentathlon.
Monday, July 8–Friday, July 12: gymnastics.
Saturday, July 13–Wednesday, July 17: equestrian events.
Wednesday, July 17–Friday, July 19: rowing.
Saturday, July 20–Monday, July 22: sailing.

Gustaf V was Patron of the Games. The princes Gustaf Adolf, Carl and Wilhelm were also involved in the organization of the Games. Crown Prince Gustaf Adolf was a committed and active honorary chairman of the Organizing Committee for the Games, and Princes Carl and Wilhelm were the honorary chairmen of the committees for equestrianism and tennis. The royal family thus worked very hard for the Games and thereby gave legitimacy and status to the Stockholm Olympics.

A horse outside the Olympic Stadium in the winter of 1911-12 (photograph by Axel Malmström, SCIF photo collection).

When the Stockholm Olympics was summarized at the end of July 1912, the organizers were probably satisfied. The Games seem to have been a success both from an organizational and a sporting point of view. Nevertheless, there was some criticism of the Swedish organizers and judges by the foreign delegates and athletes, as can be seen in Ansgar Molzberger's essay "The 1912 Games: Patriotic Games as a Breakthrough for the Olympic Movement," which to some extent goes against the prevalent, primarily Swedish picture of the Sunshine Olympics.

The Olympic competitions were the largest so far, with 2,380 competitors from 27 nations representing all five continents, and according to the Swedish press the competitions had more than met the demands that could be made of a "modern" Olympic Games.[27]

They have thus gone down in history as the Sunshine Olympics or "the Swedish Masterpiece." The weather was really unusually good, with little rain and a lot of sunshine. The organizers were lucky. In June and August 1912 and in July 1911 and 1913 the weather was definitely much worse; it was colder and the rain poured at times. The average temperature during July 1912 was 18.3 degrees Celsius (65 degrees Fahrenheit), 2 degrees higher than in 1911 and 1913, and 4 and 3 degrees higher than in June and August 1912, respectively.[28] In August 1912 180.9 millimeters of rain fell, compared with 28.7 in July. Even in comparison with 1911 and 1913, July 1912 was a month without much rain.[29] July 1912 was truly a sunshine month.

In the competition between the participating nations, Sweden was also in top place, which according to the Olympic general Viktor Balck was "an honor so great that it can hardly be estimated at its true value."[30] Arvid Lindman, who at the time of the Games was the ex–Prime Minister, was of the same opinion, even if he also saw problems with the Swedish Olympic success:

> The Olympic Games were a complete success for Sweden and our sport. Strange as it may sound, I would have almost preferred that we had been No. 2 rather than No. 1, because we would then have made a greater effort and not had so much to risk at the coming Games in Berlin. Even though I am fully convinced of the judges' impartiality, the thought cannot be escaped that we were No. 1 maybe partly due to the fact that we had the advantage of competing in our own country. Be that as it may, the 5th Olympiad has conferred honor on the Swedish name.[31]

The Competition Venues

Olympic Games are usually associated with spectacular and costly sports venues and not least a discussion about the use of the venues after the Games. How did the organizers in Stockholm solve the difficult venue issue? A relevant point is that during this dynamic period in the history of Stockholm the interest in sport took off in a big way and sports facilities began to be set up around the city, mainly on land owned by the State. At the turn of the century there was only one large sports facility for athletics and other sports worth the name in Stockholm, Idrottsparken from 1896. At first the facility was dominated by a cycling track; track cycling was a particularly popular sport in Sweden during the 1890s, but soon interest died out in favor of road cycling. At the turn of the century there were more than 40,000 cycles registered in Stockholm. Of importance for sport in Stockholm was that in 1901 a soccer field was set up in the middle of Idrottsparken, which meant that soccer teams could move from the more provisional conditions. In the winter a skating track was set up for bandy players, skaters and others.[32]

Idrottsparken was followed by a few more facilities that were smaller in format during the first decade of the previous century, and at the beginning of 1912 there were four sports facilities in Stockholm.[33] Idrottsparken had gone the way of all flesh in the autumn of 1910, but was replaced during the Olympic year by a fifth, the arena of arenas: The Olympic Stadium.

How then could the organizers in just three years complete the number of arenas necessary to arrange the Olympic Games when neither the Parliament nor the city were especially enthusiastic? The answer is partly to be found in the land ownership situation in Stockholm. In the north east part of the city, Djurgården in a broad sense, the land belonged to the State and, as has been mentioned, the State, and not least the royal family, was considerably more positive to sport than the politicians on the City Council. As a map of the Olympic venues shows most of them were therefore in Djurgården, and even today there are a large number of sports venues around the Olympic Stadium area. It was, strictly speaking, only the stand for rowing (torn down after the Games) which was in the domain of the city. With the royal family and the military behind them, the Organizing Committee was able to commit wholeheartedly to the venues in Djurgården, which were supplemented by existing venues in the suburbs.[34]

The sports venue of greatest importance to the Olympic Games and Stockholm's future sporting life was without doubt the Olympic Stadium, which a century after the Games remains as a proud and particularly beautiful symbol of the 1912 Stockholm Olympics. It was also the only sports venue of a permanent nature that was constructed for the Olympic Games. It was apparent from the very moment that Stockholm was awarded the Games that it was necessary to build a new stadium for the Olympic Games. The main arena of the

The Olympic Stadium on its way to completion (SCIF photo collection).

The Olympic Stadium's architect, Torben Grut, shows the stadium to members of Parliament and the Olympic "general," Colonel Viktor Balck (front left) (photograph by Axel Malmström, SCIF photo collection).

Games had an almost ideal location. It was near the city's most elegant residential area and had good communications in the form of two tram lines that passed on two sides of the venue as well as a number of sports venues in close proximity.

Building a permanent stadium had not been part of the Olympic organizers' plans from the beginning. The idea was to construct a temporary stadium but after the intervention of the National Board of Public Planning the plans were changed. The Board, which was in charge of buildings and building under State management, did not accept the construction of a temporary stadium using state funds. They insisted on a permanent stone stadium, a stadium that after the Games should be state property. The organizers complied with this, to the great delight of sport in Stockholm.

The result was architect Torben Grut's ring-wall construction in red brick from Helsingborg, which stood ready for inauguration on June 1, 1912.[35] The athletics, wrestling and gymnastics competitions were held in the Olympic Stadium, as well as some of soccer games, the equestrian events, which were also held at the Cross Country Riding Club's course and Lindarängen racetrack, and the start and finish of the running element of the modern pentathlon, which otherwise was largely held at the Olympic arenas for each individual sport.

The Olympic Stadium was thus the venue that the organizers really committed to, but as the Olympic Stadium was located where Idrottsparken was already situated, there was no real change in Stockholm's total sporting topography. The Organizing Committee had also received offers of land for the construction of a stadium from two of the limited com-

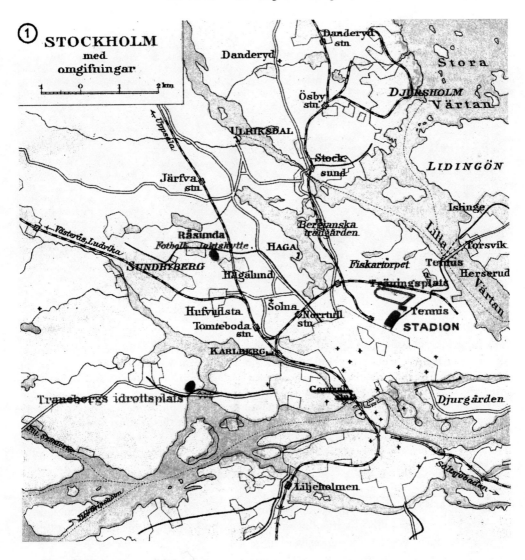

The location of the Olympic sporting venues in Stockholm. Östermalms IP (Östermalm Athletic Grounds), which had been constructed by the Central Association for the Promotion of Sports and inaugurated in 1906, had initially been intended as the location for the Olympic Stadium. Although ultimately no competitions were held there, the arena was done up and came to be used as a training facility for athletes before and during the Olympic Games. During 1911 the facility also gained a new neighbor when the Tennis Pavilion that had been constructed in the grounds of Idrottsparken was torn down and reconstructed, where it is still used for playing tennis. Outdoor courts were also laid, and these came to be used for the outdoor tennis competitions. The Tennis Pavilion, however, was not used for tennis during the Games, but for the fencing competitions instead. The indoor tennis tournament was played in another tennis hall in the area, the tennis hall from 1900 that was located on the hill north of the Olympic Stadium, where the new premises of the Swedish School of Sport and Health Sciences were built in the middle of the 1940s, a facility that was used as a restaurant during the Olympic week (National Sports Museum).

The Boathouse of the Stockholm Rowing Club during the Olympic competitions. The place that best met the demands that could be made of an Olympic rowing course was, according to the organizers, the stretch of water constituted by Djurgårdsbrunnsviken and Nybroviken, which had the advantages of offering calm water, being able to take large numbers of spectators and being situated close to the other Olympic venues. On the minus side was the indisputable fact that a straight rowing course could not be offered there: the organizers were forced to adapt the course to the natural conditions and the course turned before it passed under the Djurgårdsbron bridge on its way to the finish line at Nybroviken. Despite the central location the rowing competitions only attracted a few spectators (*Den femte olympiaden i bild och ord*, p. 258).

panies that exploited Stockholm's suburbs, but had declined these offers.[36] Companies that exploited Stockholm's suburbs often invested money in supporting sport in society, as sports venues were good publicity for an expanding society.[37]

The Olympic competitions were otherwise held in provisional or already existing arenas and in this way the costs could be kept down and above all the tight timetable could be kept to. Of the sports venues that were used at the Stockholm Olympics there are still, a century after the end of the Games, venues where sport is practiced. The other sports venues have at different points in time gone the way of all flesh: the rowing and swimming stadiums, and the shooting ranges, the racetrack, the tennis hall and the football facilities. The Stockholm Olympics did not thus mean any upswing in the number of sporting venues in Stockholm, with the important exception of the beautiful the Olympic Stadium.

The Previous Games: A Short Résumé

The Stockholm Olympic Games were not an isolated event and should of course be placed in a greater Olympic context. 1896 is generally seen as the year of the renaissance of the Olympic Games — the first modern Olympic Games were held then, with great pomp and ceremony, in the classic location of Athens. The painstaking historian will, however, make a small reservation and give an account of regional and local Olympic competitions at, for example, Chipping Camden and Much Wenlock in England, at Ramlösa outside Helsingborg and in Montreal in Canada, and even in Athens itself, from the beginning of the seventeenth century until the end of the nineteenth century.[38]

On June 23, 1894, the IOC was formed in Paris, made up of people who had been carefully selected by the French baron, Pierre de Coubertin. Of the twelve men, from as many countries, who were selected, Victor Balck was the only representative from the Nordic countries. What distinguished Coubertin's Olympic Games from the other attempts to recreate them was that he wanted to recreate them on an international basis and that he was aiming to create an international movement. Ever since the IOC was constituted its members primary task has been to designate a time and place for the Olympic Games and to constitute the senior management for these Games. The previous Games were more like irregular and recurring regional/national festivals.

The first modern Olympic Games were thus held in Athens in 1896. It was the largest event so far for the budding phenomenon of international competitive sport, with 246 participants, though with a clear majority of participants from the home nation.[39] The Games began on April 6 when the Greek King George I opened them and they came to an end

Competitive shooting at the Kaknäs shooting facility. Shooting comprised a number of disciplines that in many cases required separate shooting ranges. Most of the shooting competitions were held at Kaknäs in Northern Djurgården. The choice of shooting venues was simple for the organizers. Good ranges existed which could be used and they were relatively centrally located. The shooting ranges at Kaknäs had been built in 1890 and came to be used for rifle and army rifle competitions. New shooting ranges were also built next to the existing shooting ranges for miniature rifle, pistol and revolver competitions. Ranges were also needed for clay pigeon shooting and the running deer shooting events, the so-called game shooting competitions. Land for this was offered by a private company and the ranges were built in Solna. The Crown Prince's golf club had land at its disposal there, and agreed to make it available so that shooting ranges could be built (postcard, National Sports Museum).

nine days later. The sporting achievements, however, did not match the Greeks' enthusiasm for the Games. The Greeks tried to have the games permanently located in Greece, an idea which was launched every now and then, but in vain. Coubertin, who controlled the IOC with a steady hand, insisted that they should be held in different cities in different countries.

The second Olympic Games were held in Paris in 1900, not because the French had done exceptionally well in Athens, but because the French wanted to make use of the Games to attract people to the large World Fair that was held in the French capital at the turn of the century. The competitions were also included under the organizational umbrella of the World Fair and Coubertin and his allies had no influence over what form they were to take, which shows what limited power the IOC had at this time. Instead it was the French Sports Federation, Union des Sociétés Françaises de Sports Athlétiques (USFSA), that took on the task of organizing the Games, and the competitions were not even called Olympic by the organizers, who, on the contrary, avoided the name. In the press they came to be called international games, international championships, Paris championships and world championships, amongst other things. There were also professional championship competitions within the framework of the Paris exhibition.

The Games were a drawn out affair. They began on May 20 and continued, with many gaps, up until October 28, without either opening or closing ceremonies:

June 29, 1912. Germany–Austria (1–5) at Råsunda IP with just 560 spectators. Soccer, the only team sport apart from water polo at the Stockholm Olympics, was held at three arenas: the Olympic Stadium, Råsunda IP and Tranebergs IP. Råsunda IP was the first sports facility in the Stockholm area to have a grass pitch intended for soccer and had been built by the Swedish Football Association in 1910 to meet the need for soccer pitches created by soccer's increasing popularity. The Football Association bought the land the sports facility was built on for 37,000 kronor in 1909 and got 490 million kronor for it when the land was sold to a construction company 100 years later (postcard, National Sports Museum).

Tranebergs IP had been inaugurated as late as the autumn of 1911 and had room for 2,000 spectators. However, for Olympic soccer matches to be played there, certain improvements had to be made, as was the case with Råsunda (*V. Olympiaden,* p. 88).

Spectators at the harbor in Nynäshamn during the Olympic sailing competitions. When it was to be decided where the sailing competitions were to be held, the choice was between Gothenburg and Stockholm. The choice fell on Stockholm, which was, after all, the Olympic host. The Organizing Committee then gave the Royal Swedish Yacht Club the task of organizing the Olympic sailing competitions, and they were held at the Club's annual regatta. The water off Nynäshamn, south of Stockholm, was chosen for the Olympic sailing competitions. Spectators could get to Nynäshamn by train from Stockholm and the sailing competitions could be seen from land (*Den femte olympiaden i bild och ord*, p. 319).

Indeed, with Coubertin's resignation, the lack of IOC involvement, and the USFSA takeover, an interesting thesis could be advanced that the Olympic Games were not held in 1900, that they had been abandoned, that the movement had failed. This, of course, is not the official stance of the IOC, though it is certain that most competitors had no idea that they were competing in the IId Olympic Games. In 1912, the IOC attempted to sort out from the muddle which of the events and contests could be designated as "Olympic" sports and which winners would be placed on the Olympic roll.[40]

However, it is in Paris 1900 that we get the first Swedish gold medalists. A mixed Scandinavian team, with three Stockholmers and three Danes, won the tug-of-war against particularly limited competition. The tug-of-war team went to the final direct. Moreover, Ernst

The Olympic swimming course. There were many venues in Stockholm for swimming. Ström-badet was the leading one at the beginning of the twentieth century. The baths had three pools of different sizes, but the largest one was too short, only 33⅓ meters, for international swimming competitions. According to the statutes of the International Swimming Federation the pool had to be at least 100 meters long for competitions over 500 meters. A new swimming stadium thus had to be built for the Olympic Games. This was built at Djurgårdsbrunnsviken due to the desire to have geographically unified Games. The place chosen was considered to offer the greatest advantages not only with regard to communications but also with regard to constructing the provisional stand. In the autumn of 1910 the drawings for the new swimming stadium were ready. The Organizing Committee for the Games only wanted to grant funds for a stand that could hold 1,500 spectators, but the Swedish Swimming Federation wanted to have a stand with a capacity for 4,000 spectators. The solution was for three people in the building committee to give personal financial guarantees for the excess costs of 14,740 kronor. It was truly a risky undertaking. However, they never needed to pay any money, as the swimming competitions were very well attended and were a great financial success. The swimming pool looked different from today's standardized competitive pools. It was outdoors, measured all of 100 × 20 meters, and there were no lane lines. It was framed by floating rafts and outside the pool there was a 10 meter high diving board built on piles driven into the bottom. The water polo playing area was in the middle of the pool, with the goals hanging from lines (*Den femte olympiaden i bild och ord,* p. 242).

Fast finished third in the marathon. The star turn of the Swedish participants was, however, a purely display troop of 52 gymnasts. Swedish gymnastics was internationally well known and attracted interest even though there was absolutely no competitive element involved. Other sporting values than the purely competitive were obviously also appreciated by the general public.

The third Olympic Games were held in 1904 in St. Louis, Missouri, USA and were reminiscent of the Games in Paris regarding the lack of organization and their long duration. The sports competitions started on May 14 and went on until November 26, even if that part which is nowadays acknowledged to have contained Olympic competitions lasted from the beginning of July until the middle of November. These Games are considered by many historians to be the worst in the history of the Olympic movement. They had initially been awarded to Chicago, but were moved to St. Louis and once again drowned in an ongoing World Fair.[41]

The Games are today most famous, or most infamous, for the few days of competitions that were arranged for some so-called primitive peoples, the anthropology days. The reasons given for them were that "they aimed to constitute an interesting study of their sporting qualities in comparison to civilized peoples."[42] Sweden did not take part in the competitions in St. Louis and foreign participation was in general scant, mainly due to the long and costly journey.

In 1906 intercalary Olympic Games were held in Athens. The Greeks had got the IOC to accept, when the IOC had not wanted to allow Athens to host the Games forever, that Athens would hold the Games between the normal Games, starting in 1906. They were only held on this one occasion and a contributory factor to many finding them appealing was

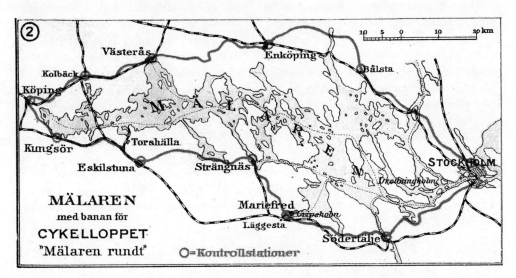

The cycling competition during the Games was held on the classic Swedish cycling route Round Lake Mälaren and did not require any special building work. The course was long compared to more modern distances: more than 315 kilometers. The start was just south of Stockholm, and the finish was at the Olympic Stadium. There were eleven checkpoints around the course and "at all crossroads, where mistakes can easily be made, there will be extra officials or notice-boards." The cycling competition was a trial of strength, with a winning time of 10 hours 42 minutes for the South African Rudolph Lewis (National Sports Museum).

that few European sportsmen had participated at St. Louis in 1904. Unlike the two previous Games they were also coordinated Games. They were opened by the participating nations marching into the stadium behind the flags of their respective nations.[43]

The intercalary Olympic Games in Athens 1906 also involved an international break-through for Swedish athletes. Their participation was a great success for the 32-man strong Swedish squad and they received considerable attention in the Swedish press. After their arrival home the Swedes were paid tribute to with a welcome-home party in Idrottsparken. Details about how many people went out to pay tribute to the Swedish Olympians vary, but Idrottsparken was full and people also gathered in the streets and on mounds in the neighborhood. The report in a newspaper of "maybe 20 thousand people" appears to be an exaggeration, however. According to the editor-in-chief of another newspaper, Karl Hilde-brand, the Swedish successes in Athens gave Sweden valuable prestige in the rest of the world after "the sad events of 1905."[44] Hildebrand is referring to the dissolution of the union with Norway, which had been traumatic for many Swedes, and sport had a compensatory function here. It allowed national honor to be restored, an idea that was also noticeable in the Games of 1912.

In 1908 the Olympic Games were held in London. The competitions were originally intended for Rome, which was not able to hold them, however. Instead it was London that organized the Games, despite little time to prepare.

A huge stadium, the White City Stadium, had been built as the mid-point of the Games and it housed a 603-meter long cycling track and a 536-meter long running track, and in the infield there was a swimming pool of 100 × 15 meters with a diving tower. It stood next to the venue for a large English-French exhibition.[45]

Like its predecessors the Games were held over an extended time. So that the program could be completed without any rush they were begun on April 27 with competitions in racquets (a game that is regarded as the direct model for squash) and went on until the end of the month of October when they were completed with the "winter sports": soccer, rugby, lacrosse, boxing, hockey and ice skating. However, the Games were not officially opened until July 13.[46]

It became clear in conjunction with the athletics competitions in London that there was a great need for common, internationally accepted rules. The Games came to be char-acterized by a bitter struggle between the British and the North Americans. They have gone down in history as the "Battle of Shepherd's Bush." The American squad, who adopted a strongly anti–English attitude, protested on every possible occasion, but seldom with any success, which meant that it became unpopular with the English spectators and the general public.[47] If lasting and friction-free sports exchanges between different countries were to come about and be kept alive, regulations that were acknowledged and accepted by everyone were necessary.

The Contents of the Book

The 1912 Stockholm Olympics consists of 11 essays. This has both its advantages and dis-advantages. On the plus side, it gives a great breadth of angles of approach and the essays can be read independent of each other. On the minus side, there is a certain risk that the book will sprawl and contain repetitions, which can be irritating for anyone reading the book from cover to cover. However, it is our belief and our hope that the advantages greatly outweigh the disadvantages.

Where the essays come in the volume is not random, however. There is a progression regarding the contents. The early essays deal with the preparations for the Games, then there follow essays about the sports held, the participants, the spectators and what else there was to do in connection with the sports competitions, and finally the book concludes with essays containing assessments of the Games. The book can be read from cover to cover, but as the essays stand firmly on their own legs, they can be enjoyed in any order that the reader finds appealing.

The book begins with "Nothing New Under the Sun? Marketing the Stockholm Olympics," by Per Andersson and Hans Kjellberg. They deal with the measures taken to market the Games and compare this with how marketing is seen today. This is followed by "Organizing the 1912 Games" by Therese Nordlund Edvinsson, who deals with the actions of the men behind the Games, for it was almost exclusively men that were involved.

The breakthrough of rational training under professional guidance is the subject of the next essay: how the Swedish sportsmen and sportswomen, above all those involved in athletics, trained and were prepared for their participation and how they succeeded. "The Jewel in the Olympic Crown. The Training Preparations and Competitions in Athletics" is by Leif Yttergren. Then follow two essays that deal with the Olympic participants. The first, "Counts and Draymen," deals with the Swedish participants at the Stockholm Olympics from a socio-economic perspective. The second, "Gender and Class," analyzes the Swedish sportswomen who in spite of everything were able to compete in the Games. Both are written by Hans Bolling and Leif Yttergren, the first with the help of Ingemar Ekholm.

The Stockholm Olympics were the first Olympic Games where there were not only competitions in physical but also in artistic sports. Patrik Steorn has taken a closer look at the art competitions in connection with the Games in the article "Art and Sport: Different Worlds?"

We then turn our gaze towards the audience and their behavior in the article "Spectators at the Stockholm Games," by Mats Hellspong.

Large sports events are seldom about sport alone. When the competitions are not in progress organizers, participants and spectators also need to be entertained with food, drink and various festivities. This aspect is given attention in Hans Bolling's essay "Punch, Splendor and Patriotism: The Olympics Outside the Stadium."

The last two essays in the book deal with how the Stockholm Olympics was received. First Jan Lindroth guides us in "'A New Experience in Life': The Olympics and the General Debate in the Swedish Daily Press" through the fierce and ideological debate in the press. Then Ansgar Molzberger takes on the Swedish Sunshine Olympics from a new, critical and international perspective in "Patriotic Games as a Breakthrough for the Olympic Movement." There were clearly certain dark sides — not everything was sunshine during the Games. The book ends with a summation of the results of the competitions and other facts about the Stockholm Olympics, presented by Ingemar Ekholm.

Notes

1. Höfer and Lennartz: *Im Dienst der Olympischen Idee* (2009), passim. In Berlin Balck was awarded the Olympic diploma by Coubertin, where he called him "der Gustav Adolf der Leibenskultur," with reference to the Swedish warrior king Gustavus Adolphus of the seventeenth century. Ibid., p. 36. On Balck, see Lindroth: *Idrott för kung och fosterland* (2007).

2. See also Patrik Steorn's essay on "Art and Sport — Different Worlds?"

3. http://www.usk.stockholm.se/histstat/arsfakta.asp?artal=1912 [April 10, 2011].

4. Johansson: *Stor-Stockholms bebyggelsehistoria* (1987), p.156 ff.

5. Voting rights: History. http://www04.sub.su.se:2054/rösträtt/historik, Nationalencyklopedin [April 14, 2011].

6. Lindroth: *Idrottens väg till folkrörelse* (1974), p. 295 f.

7. Ibid., p. 272 ff.

8. Coubertin: *Olympic Memoirs* (1997), p. 60.

9. What follows below on the financing of the Games is based on Bolling, unless otherwise stated: *Icke blott personliga insatser utan därjämte en riklig tillgång på penningar* (1996), section 3.2.

10. Lindman: *Dagboksanteckningar* (1972), p. 68.

11. www.scb.se/Pages/TableAndChart____33837.aspx, [January 13, 2012].

12. Bergvall (ed.), *V. Olympiaden* (1913), p. 38 f. Ticket revenues from the equestrian competitions are not included in the above sum. The total revenues from these competitions amounted to 123,540 kronor.

13. Bergvall, 1913, p. 26 ff. To convert the prices to the value of money in 2010, multiply the prices given by 45.

14. *Svenska Dagbladet,* June 9, 1912.

15. *Dagens Nyheter,* June 10, 1912, p. 7.

16. Hermelin and Peterson (ed.), *Den femte olympiaden* (1912), p. 356.

17. *Aftontidningen,* July 19, 1912.

18. Prado: "Nominal and Real Wages of Manufacturing Workers, 1860–2007" (2010), p. 511.

19. See Therese Nordlund Edvinsson's essay "Organizing the 1912 Games."

20. See Hans Bolling's essay "Punch, Splendor and Patriotism."

21. See Per Andersson and Hans Kjellberg's essay "Nothing New Under the Sun? Marketing the Stockholm Olympics."

22. Bergvall, *The Fifth Olympiad* (1913), p. 9.

23. Ibid.

24. *Dagens Nyheter,* June 21, 1912.

25. The Games were officially ended on July 27 by a closing party for the yachtsmen at Hasselbacken.

26. Athletics, tug-of-war, wrestling, fencing, modern pentathlon, swimming, shooting, gymnastics. The medal ceremonies for events outside the Olympic week were held at the respective competition venue. For cycling and sailing they were held at Hasselbacken restaurant.

27. Mallon and Widlund, *The 1912 Olympic Games* (2009), p. 29.

28. http://www.usk.stockholm.se/arsbok/Tabell%2044.htm [April 20, 2011].

29. http://www.usk.stockholm.se/arsbok/Tabell%2045.htm [April 20, 2011].

30. Balck, *Minnen* (1931), p. 156.

31. Lindman, 1972, p. 70 f.

32. Tjerneld, *Stockholmsliv* (1996), p. 110 f.

33. *Nordiskt Idrottslif,* September 29, 1911.

34. On the military in the Stockholm Olympics, see Gäfvert, "Militären och Stockholmsolympiaden" (Stockholm).

35. Ekberg: "Stockholms olympiastadion" (2000), p. 99.

36. National Archives: Stockholmsolympiaden 1912: Minutes of the Organizing Committee A I:1, the Organizing Committee, November 29, 1909, § 3.

37. Bolling; "Idrottsorten Saltsjöbaden" (2006), passim.

38. Eidmark: "Olympiska spelen" (1948), p. 1107 f. Widlund: "Olympiska spel 393–1895" (1987a), p. 16 ff.

39. Sylvén and Karlsson: *OS* (2008), p. 190. According to the authors, the number of competing nations varies between 12 and 14 depending on the source, which is due to the fact that many participants were citizens of a country other than where they lived.

40. Howell and Howell, "Paris 1900" (1996), p. 13.

41. Barnett, "St. Louis 1904" (1996), p. 18 ff.

42. Ringius, *Vägvisare genom olympiaderna* (1913), p. 30.

43. Lennartz, "Athens 1906" (1996), p. 27 f.

44. *Stockholms Dagblad; Stockholms-Tidningen; Svenska Dagbladet* May 15, 1908, and Bolling, "Saltsjöbadens IF sedan 1906" (2006), p. 53.

45. Ringius, 1913, p. 39.
46. Widlund, "Spelen 1896–1908" (1987b), p. 51.
47. Ibid., p. 53.

References

UNPUBLISHED SOURCES

Swedish National Archives: Stockholmsolympiaden 1912

ELECTRONIC SOURCES

www.usk.stockholm.se
www04.sub.su.se:2054
www.scb.se/

PERIODICALS AND NEWSPAPERS

Aftontidningen
Dagens Nyheter
Nordiskt Idrottslif
Olympiska Spelens tidning
Stockholms Dagblad
Stockholms-Tidningen
Svenska Dagbladet

PRINTED SOURCES

Balck, Viktor. *Minnen. II Mannaåren* (Stockholm 1931).
Barnett, Robert C. "St. Louis 1904," in Findling, John E., and Pelle, Kimberly D. (eds.), *Historical Dictionary of the Modern Olympic Movement* (Westport 1996).
Bergvall, Erik (ed.): *V. Olympiaden. Officiell redogörelse för olympiska spelen i Stockholm 1912* (Stockholm 1913).
Bolling, Hans: *Icke blott personliga insatser utan därjämte en riklig tillgång på penningar* (opublicerad rapport 1996).
_____. "Idrottsorten Saltsjöbaden" in Bolling, Hans (ed.), *Saltsjöbadens IF 100 år: Jubileumsboken* (Saltsjöbaden 2006).
_____. "Saltsjöbadens IF sedan 1906" in Bolling, Hans (ed.), *Saltsjöbadens IF 100 år: Jubileumsboken* (Saltsjöbaden 2006).
Coubertin, Pierre de: *Olympic Memoirs* (Lausanne 1997).
Eidmark, Henry: "Olympiska spelen," in *Sportens lilla jätte. Idrottsungdomens egen uppslagsbok* (Stockholm 1948).
Ekberg, Michael: "Stockholms olympiastadion," in *Bebyggelsehistorisk tidskrift* 40 (2000).
Gäfvert, Björn: "Militären och Stockholmsolympiaden," in Bo Lundström and Maria Gussarsson Wijk (eds.), *Den cyklande humanisten. Historiker, arkivman, stockholmare: en vänbok till Ulf Söderberg* (Stockholm 2009) pp. 173–185.
Hermelin, Sven, and Peterson, Erik (eds.): *Den femte olympiaden i Stockholm i bild och ord* (Stockholm 1912).
Höfer, Andreas, and Lennartz, Karl. *Im Dienst der Olympischen Idee: Die Berliner IOC-Session von 1909/Serving the Olympic Idea. The Berlin IOC Session of 1909* (Frankfurt am Main 1909).
Howell, Reet Ann, and Howell, Max L.: "Paris 1900," in Findling, John E., and Pelle, Kimberly D. (eds.), *Historical Dictionary of the Modern Olympic Movement* (Westport 1996).
Johansson, Ingemar: *Stor-Stockholms bebyggelsehistoria. Markpolitik, planering och byggande under sju sekel* (Stockholm 1987).
Lennartz, Karl: "Athens 1906," in Findling, John E., and Pelle, Kimberly D. (eds.), *Historical Dictionary of the Modern Olympic Movement* (Westport 1996).
Lindman, Arvid: *Dagboksanteckningar* (Stockholm 1972).

Lindroth, Jan: *Idrott för kung och fosterland. Den svenska idrottens fader Viktor Balck 1844–1928* (Stockholm 2007).

_____. *Idrottens väg till folkrörelse. Studier i svensk idrottsrörelse till 1915* (Uppsala 1974).

Mallon, Bill, and Widlund, Ture: *The 1912 Olympic Games: Results for All Competitors in All Events with Commentary* (Jefferson 2009).

Prado, Svante: "Nominal and Real Wages of Manufacturing Workers, 1860–2007" in Edvinsson, Rodney, et al. (eds.), *Historical Monetary and Financial Statistics for Sweden: Exchange Rates, Prices, and Wages, 1277–2008* (Stockholm 2010).

Ringius, Albert: *Vägvisare genom olympiaderna, med förord af hertigen af Vestergötland H.K.H: prins Carl* (Gothenburg 1913).

Sylvén, Sune, and Karlsson, Ove: *OS: Historia & statistik* (Stockholm 2008).

Tjerneld, Staffan: *Stockholmsliv: Hur vi bott och roat oss under 100 år. Första delen, norr om Strömmen* (Stockholm 1996).

Widlund, Ture: "Olympiska spel 393–1895" in *Sverige och OS: Sveriges olympiska kommitté 75 år* (Stockholm 1987a).

_____. "Spelen 1896–1908," in *Sverige och OS: Sveriges olympiska kommitté 75 år* (Stockholm 1987b).

William-Olsson, William: *Stockholms framtida utveckling Bilaga: Huvuddragen av Stockholms geografiska utveckling 1850–1930* (Stockholm 1984).

Nothing New Under the Sun?

Marketing the Stockholm Olympics

PER ANDERSSON *and* HANS KJELLBERG

Event marketing, both in the sense of using events as a marketing technique and the marketing of events, has been subject to considerable attention over the past two decades.[1] But the phenomenon itself is of course much older.[2] In this essay we offer an empirical study of event marketing as practiced a century ago. More specifically, we describe the marketing of the Olympic Games in Stockholm, 1912.

The study is based on the archive of the Organizing Committee for the Games, including its subcommittee for advertising. The material consists of the official report from the Games, the minutes from the meetings of the various bodies, including proposals and supporting documents, incoming and outgoing correspondence, official communications from the Organizing Committee, printed matter, newspaper clippings, etc. This rich material allows us to trace the various efforts made to market the Games in detail.

The study seeks to enrich our understanding of marketing as an area of expertise, which has recently attracted increasing scholarly attention, not least within the IMP community.[3] The event under study predates the emergence of the marketing discipline and the archive material does not suggest that the actors involved ever considered what they were doing to be "marketing."[4] Rather, they were creating publicity for the Olympic Games. One may thus question whether the Games were actually marketed.[5] On the other hand, the publicity dimension appears to be central to lay-understandings of marketing even today. Further, if we look at the concrete practices that the involved bodies and individuals engaged in, these bear much resemblance to what we would expect contemporary event marketers to engage in, i.e. contemplating event stakeholder management, partnerships and collaboration,[6] image-enhancement potential of events and their media coverage and how this might generate induced demand for e.g. a destination,[7] co-branding events and destinations,[8] the "leveraging" of events for additional benefits,[9] and the goal of generating a lasting event "legacy."[10] We suggest that by adopting a pragmatic approach, those who engage in (what we now consider to be) marketing are led to deal with certain task-related issues that remain more or less the same over time. The precise manner in which they attend to these issues, however, may differ over time.

We inquire into how the Games were marketed. We outline the specific practices involved in marketing the event, including what was done, who were engaged, which techniques were used, which resources were drawn upon, etc. Among other things, this mapping of marketing practices leads us to question the object being marketed: was the committee really marketing the Olympic Games, or were their efforts directed towards some other object, e.g. Sweden? In what ways did the marketing efforts contribute to stabilize this object? What were the organizers seeking to achieve through their marketing efforts? Here we seek to establish the ideas underpinning the observed practices. The activities related to the official poster for the Games are particularly interesting. The Organizing Committee was able to reach a decision on the design of the poster only after a prolonged process, in which two distinctly different values were contrasted (artistic merit vs. publicity effect). Second, the reception of the poster varied across countries around the world (perceived as artistic by some and obscene by others, explicitly banned in certain countries, etc.).

We strive to "write history forwards," i.e. we have tried to avoid letting our contemporary understanding of the phenomenon of marketing guide the account.[11] With the help of the source material we have instead followed the actors involved in order to capture their way of discussing the marketing of the Games.[12] Throughout the account we do, however, provide shorter comments, which relate to contemporary discourses on marketing. In the final discussion we take a comprehensive approach to these reflections and discuss how the marketing of the Stockholm Olympics appears in the light of today's understanding of the subject, but also how the practice described can enrich our understanding of marketing as a contemporary phenomenon. Thus the tension between current knowledge of marketing and the practices appearing in the archival material is used to understand both the historical course of events and to some extent contemporary marketing phenomena.[13]

Promotional Work Preceding the Games

The issues discussed by the Organizing Committee provide a first insight into the promotional work. Somewhat simplified we can say that an important part of the work during 1909 and 1910 was about organization. The Organizing Committee dedicated much time to establishing internal procedures and structures in which promotional issues were one of several specialty areas. In the autumn of 1910 members were recruited to the Advertising and Information Committee, and in early 1911 the decision was made to encourage the establishment of local advertising committees in foreign countries. However, attention was given as early as 1910 to advertising content and form. For example, the design of the official promotional poster was discussed at some ten meetings during 1910 and to an equal extent in 1911, when the design of the official advertising brochure of the Games was also thoroughly discussed. The promotional work in itself was a subject of discussion during the entire period though specific measures, such as distribution of printed matter, bill-posting and advertising, came up particularly during 1911 and 1912. The same goes for issues concerning contact with the press, tickets and ticket prices. During late 1911 and the spring of 1912 attention was given to the sales of souvenirs, photography and film rights during the Games, as well as various auxiliary arrangements, such as parties in connection with the Games.

Prerequisites for and Organization of Advertising Work

The supply of time and money set a framework for the advertising work. The dates for the Games set limits in time; in order for the advertising to successfully attract visitors to the Games it of course had to be done in reasonable time before the Games began. Available monetary resources in turn affected *what* could be done, although sometimes ways around the financial limits could be found.

The lack of resources for running the advertising work was something that was gradually brought to the fore during the preparations. When the finances were discussed in the autumn of 1910 nothing suggested an acute lack of resources. In December that year the Organizing Committee approved a number of advertising activities in principle, although a rough cost estimate was asked for. In the spring of 1911 the planning and preparations for the Games as well as the advertising work continued. As the details became clearer the expected costs rose as well. Several advertising proposals were discussed and approved, for example the printing of advertising brochures and advertising postcards for the Games.

The Finance Section investigated the financial situation during the summer and found serious problems: "Already a cursory summary of the expenses already approved and the ones which can certainly be expected shows that the assets in no way suffice to carry out the Games." The problem was primarily one of liquidity; it would simply not be possible to pay for the things required to carry out the Games. Another 285,000 Swedish kronor was required. The revenue from the Games would cover much of the deficit, but the prognosis was still a loss of about 100,000 kronor. To solve the problem the organizers tried to persuade "a number of people in a prominent economic position" to enter as creditors, but without success. The proposed general budget was approved on September 4, with the addition that the Finance Section needed the approval of the Organizing Committee for any essential divergences. In order to solve the liquidity issue no other way out was seen than asking the government for credit. To cover the expected loss the decision was made to go to the City of Stockholm for support, since the advertising for the Games "as good as exclusively is in the interest of the City of Stockholm."

The Finance Section's calculations regarding advertising expenses expected and incurred so far are summarized in Table 1. We can note that difficulties calculating costs for this type of project are not a new phenomenon. When it came to the construction of the Olympic Stadium the Finance Section's cost estimate from the autumn of 1910 landed at 715,000 kronor. The compilation of actual costs from January 1913 showed a cost of 1,188,000 kronor, an increase by 66 percent. As for the costs of advertising work the forecasting was even poorer. The estimate from summer 1911 indicated that total costs would be around 156,500 kronor (columns 1–3 in the table). The actual costs up until January 1913 were 306,000 kronor, an increase of over 95 percent. In the following passages we will examine in detail what this amount was used for.

Table 1. The Finance Section's Calculation of Advertising Costs at June 30, 1911, Estimate of Expenditure for Advertising Until June 30, 1912, and Actual Costs Until January 15, 1913

Account	1. Costs at June 30, 1911	2. Approved Grants Until June 30, 1912	3. Probable Expenses Beyond These	4. Costs Until January 15, 1913
Pstg./Tele./Adver.	2,665.80			60,160.75
Postage			7,500.00	
Telegrams			2,000.00	
Advertisements			1,000.00	
Poster/Advertising Account	3,472.41			106,527.22
Advertising		8,900.00	10,000.00	
The Advertising Brochure		11,000.00	2,000.00	
Translations			7,500.00	
Poster, Stamps, Freights			9,000.00	
Press Cuttings		500.00		
Medals and Diplomas	757.71	13,000.00		25,021.86
The Programs	734.71	14,000.00	17,500.00	70,878.31
Representation				43,400.44
Reception Party			10,000.00	
Final Banquet			10,000.00	
Dinner for Foreign Off. Repr.			5,000.00	
Various Rep. Exp.			10,000.00	
Sum	**7,630.63**	**47,400.00**	**101,500.00**	**305,988.58**

The precarious financial situation that became known in mid 1911 soon became apparent in the advertising work, for example in the circular letter which was sent to the Swedish consulates in September 1911:

> The now planned cooperation with the Swedish foreign consulates mainly concerns a *concentration* in the work for distributing the sales literature indicated above, so that this can be sent to and later on distributed from *one single address in one city.*... The Organizing Committee would, however, not be allowed to be caused any other costs than such originating from the sending of necessary sales literature from here.

In a corresponding letter expatriate Swedes were encouraged to work with the local consul in order to lower distribution costs. In connection with the major dispatches of advertising materials after New Year 1912 it was specifically pointed out that the Organizing Committee would not cover any distribution costs once the advertising materials had reached the consulates. In polite letters many offers, particularly from private persons, to participate in the advertising work against compensation were also turned down, for example:

> With reference to your offer through Colonel Balck to, against compensation for travel costs, give instructive lectures on the Olympic Games in various places in England, we hereby ask to inform you that the Organizing Committee — declaring their sympathy for the proposal — still have not considered themselves able to use it, due to the fact that the funds intended for advertising purposes are very limited.[14]

Offers of help also came from Swedish companies, usually asking for free tickets in return for their "voluntary" advertising work. Foreign companies also offered their services, such as advertising and/or billposting, often at heavily reduced prices. Most offers were kindly but firmly turned down referring to a lack of resources. But not all of them. Despite the limited budget making exceptions was in some cases seen as necessary, for example when it came to putting up posters in countries where this involved taxes and charges.

Despite certain exceptions the financial limits meant that the Organizing Committee had to rely primarily on non-profit advertising work. A large number of volunteers were successfully mobilized in the distribution of the advertising materials. By identifying the collaboration synergies of other organizations certain activities were carried out which the organizers could not have afforded on their own. Ultimately persuasion was of course required to convince companies and organizations do their bit. All in all, the limited budget required negotiation and persuasion, as well as creativity.

So how was the advertising work organized? According to the internal procedures approved by the Organizing Committee in May 1910 a specific *Advertising and Reception Section* was to be responsible for the arrangements around the Games (accommodation, travel, transport, food, etc.) while "matters concerning advertising, the press, correspondents in various places etc." were to be conducted by the Organizing Committee's secretariat. However, in November 1910 the decision was made to lay the responsibility of the advertising issues on a special *Advertising and Information Committee*. The committee had seven members at the most: the President of the Swedish Tourist Traffic Association R. Petre, the Organizing Committee's secretary Kristian Hellström, director C. L. Kornerup, "the official of Nordisk Resebureau in Stockholm" Edvin Molin, editor Gustaf Åsbrink, accountant Carl Hellberg, and director Nyman. In addition to organizing the home ground work the Organizing Committee in January 1910 decided to support the establishment of local advertising committees abroad. At least six such committees were formed (in London, Berlin, Paris, Marseille, Helsinki and Holland) and were important nodes for spreading information about the Games in each country. The difficult financial situation which ensued in 1911 also gave the Finance Section a substantial influence over what could be seen as justifiable advertising activities. In November it was decided that the members of the Finance Section were to be called to all of the Advertising Committee's meetings "to as far as possible accommodate the financial interests of the Organizing Committee."

How were the materials designed that were used by the Organizing Committee to promote the Games? Based on the register compiled by the Advertising Committee in 1912 we can identify four main categories of advertising materials:

1. Own printed matter — The general program, Special rules (in 13 sporting fields), Advertising brochures, Advertising posters, Advertising stamps
2. Other printed matter — Centralföreningen's yearbook, Excursions en Suède, Reisen in Schweden, Tours in Sweden, Holidays in Sweden, Views of Stockholm
3. Medals, marks — The prize medal of the Games, The steward and participant pin for the Games, The commemorative medal of the Games, The prize diploma of the Games
4. Photographs etc. — The Stadium, other sports arenas, The Organizing Committee's members and the secretariat, Lithograph of the Stadium, Sports postcards

Among these the first category appears to be the most important. The primary means of spreading information about the Games and gaining the interest of the public were no doubt the official poster, the advertising stamps with the same motif, the official information brochure, and the general program for the Games. The rules of the various sports served as an advertising channel above all in order to attract participants to the Games. When it comes to the degree of control over the design the first category of materials was largely influenced by the members of the Organizing Committee and the Advertising Committee, even though in many questions opinions differed. We have therefore chosen to focus on the design of these materials, particularly the poster and the brochure.

Events Leading Up to the Poster

The official account after the Games establishes that the poster regrettably was made available relatively late and that consequently it could not be exploited to the full.

> It is to be regretted that, in consequence of various circumstances, the poster was not in readiness earlier than 6 months before the Games as, for advertising purposes, it would have been of advantage to have had a greater amount of time available for its distribution, a task that now had to be performed in a very great hurry.[15]

What circumstances delayed the poster, then? We can establish that at least it wasn't poor planning. The Organizing Committee raised the question of an official poster as early as December 14, 1909, and decided to ask Ferdinand Boberg to come up with a proposal. Boberg declined, however, and recommended the artist Olle Hjortzberg instead. At the Organizing Committee's meeting on January 4, 1910, director Burman informed that Hjortzberg was willing to take on the task against remuneration of 500 kronor. The committee decided to accept the offer and in mid–February a first poster proposal was discussed. At the end of March a slightly revised version was discussed, but no decision was made. On July 11 Hjortzberg's proposal was accepted after being up for discussion a third time. On

July 25 the committee discussed in which format the poster should be printed, by whom and how many copies. So how is it then, that the poster was not available for distribution until 18 months later?

At the committee's meeting on August 8 it was decided to photograph the poster and send it to "appropriate publications" for advertising purposes. This was done, and the image of the poster was distributed in the media. The effect of this was not, however, as expected. On September 26 Colonel Balck informed that the Swedish Tourist Traffic Association was no longer willing to distribute the poster. They thought the poster was "for international reasons hardly appropriate for its purpose" since the placing of the flags "easily could be a cause of jealousy and thereby a bone of contention." Balck had also heard other criticism and suggested the rejection of Hjortzberg's poster and the developing of a new one. Two additional members, who had earlier supported Hjortzberg's proposal, now claimed that "the poster had never appealed to them." The poster question was remitted to the Advertising and Reception Section for further investigation.

Although this was hardly a desirable development from the perspective of the committee, it is still interesting to reflect on these events as part of a market communication process. By making the poster available through Swedish media, the committee appears to have created an effective pretest of the poster design, no doubt unintentionally. Such pretesting is today part of the standard toolkit for marketers to secure effective communications.[16] It is thus particularly interesting to note that this involuntary but "sharp" test seems to have had other qualities than contemporary methods to measure psychological and neurological effects of advertising exposure.[17] Although lacking the technical refinement of contemporary methods, the test proved much less myopic than these, and was able to pick up on issues that the organizers had not thought of.

In mid–October the Advertising and Reception Section suggested the organization of "a free contest for the obtaining of better proposals." The Organizing Committee decided to first explain the situation to Hjortzberg ("that the poster approved by the Committee had proved inappropriate for its purpose for political reasons") and ask him whether he would like to make a new proposal. Hjortzberg agreed and the committee decided to wait. At the following meeting, on November 14, signs of impatience were already starting to show: Hjortzberg was urged to submit his proposal by December 15 at the

The initially approved Olympic poster proposal by the artist Olle Hjortzberg July 11, 1910 (Stockholmsolympiaden 1912, Swedish National Archives).

latest. At the Organizing Committee's meeting on December 12 a committee of three members (Levin, von Rosen and Hellström) was appointed to express their opinion "on the sketch in question and the poster question in full." On January 23, 1911, the Organizing Committee accepted their proposal that Hjortzberg's new sketch should be rejected and a limited number of Swedish artists encouraged to come up with proposals for a new poster. The winner was to be granted an award of 500 SEK. It was also decided that the final settlement should take into consideration "not only the artistic value but also the suitability of the poster proposals from an advertising point of view."

When the time assigned for the contest expired the committee had received seven proposals "of which the Poster Committee did not consider any fit to be recommended for approval." Instead, voices were now raised suggesting Hjortzberg's proposal was not so bad. "In connection with this, Dr. Levin pointed out that Swedish artists had generally spoken favorably of Hjortzberg's poster proposal." Since additional artists were working on proposals, Thorsten Schonberg among others, the committee decided to wait. On May 8 the poster question was once again brought up for discussion.

After consulting with "a few called-in artists" a divided Poster Committee (von Rosen and Levin) now advocated Hjortzberg's proposal on condition that additional revisions were made. More specifically it was suggested: that the face of the figure in front should show "a Nordic model"; that the body should be made "more developed"; that "the male organs be more concealed"; and that the letterpress should be in white. The third member of the committee, Hellström, advocated Schonberg's proposal with the support of two members of the Advertising Committee, who considered it better for "advertising and athletic purposes." The crown prince, on the other hand, "undoubtedly advocated Hjortzberg's proposal, being the absolutely finest artistically." Von Rosen, Murray and Levin also expressed their support for Hjortzberg "from an artistic perspective," while Balck, Frestadius, af Sandeberg and Hellström preferred Schonberg's proposal, "particularly considering its value for athletic and advertising purposes." Finally it was agreed that both Hjortzberg and Schonberg should submit their revised proposals by May 31.

On June 27 it was time again. Both Hjortzberg and Schonberg had adjusted their proposals. Von Rosen and Levin once again advocated Hjortzberg, whom they considered "had further benefited from the accomplished revision." However, they still wanted to adjust the proposal through "the widening of the intersecting ribbon and the lightening of the blue color of the Swedish flag." The proposal was supported by several speakers who considered it "unquestionably the finest artistically," and in addition that it had "great advertising properties." Moreover, the permanent undersecretary Murray argued that Hjortzberg had already been paid and that unnecessary costs could thus be avoided. Levin added that Hjortzberg would hardly be interested in designing the diploma if his poster was once again rejected. Balck, Hellström and af Sandberg, however, still considered Schonberg's proposal better "not only athletically but also for advertising purposes." After the discussion was concluded "a decision of 3 votes to 2 was made to finally accept the artist Olle Hjortzberg's revised proposal for the advertising poster." Schonberg did not come away entirely empty-handed: The Organizing Committee decided to buy the proposal for 300 kronor against the committee's right to "regard it as their property."

These events prompt a reflection on the tension between artistic and commercial values, which has been subject to considerable discussion within marketing. In a classic article Elisabeth Hirschman argued that a marketing perspective was less suitable for artistic production due to the import of personal values and social norms in the production process.[18] More recently, the need to balance commercial and artistic values has been emphasized, i.e. securing that artistic values are not crowded out by commercial ones.[19] It is therefore interesting to note how the committee, seemingly without major difficulties, was able to mix different values in their decision, attending to both aesthetic, political, social and practical concerns (Nordic type, developed body, placement of flags, concealed organs, text in white, Hjortzberg already paid, etc.).

The official Olympic advertising poster by the artist Olle Hjortzberg (*V. Olympiaden,* p. 93).

At the meeting on August 7 the Organizing Committee decided to print 50,000 copies of the advertising poster. To facilitate distribution the poster was to be printed in several editions, with writing in different languages. The poster was eventually printed in 16 languages (Swedish, English, French, German, Russian, Italian, Turkish, Japanese, Spanish, Finnish, Dutch, Hungarian, Chinese, Greek, Portuguese and Bohemian). After Hjortzberg had made the final adjustments the members of the committee could study a first trial print in mid–October. Collaterally, the committee had applied to the Patent and Registration department for reproduction protection and negotiated an agreement for sole reproduction rights with Östberg & Lenhardtson AB. With this, the discussion passed on to how the poster would best be distributed (see the following passage).

In addition to the various editions of the poster, a miniature of the motif was also printed as an advertising stamp. It had been looked into whether it was possible to decrease the size of the poster and make it into an advertising stamp as early as the summer of 1910 and in September 1911 an agreement was made with Centraltryckeriet for the printing of advertising stamps in 16 languages. The stamps proved very popular, amongst others with stamp collectors worldwide. As a result of the great demand a number of additional orders for stamps were placed in the winter 1911-1912 and in total almost 4.8 million stamps were printed.

The Advertising Brochure

In April 1911 the Advertising and Information Committee suggested that a specific advertising brochure should be produced "with the purpose of spreading knowledge of the upcoming Olympic Games in Sweden and abroad." The production of two editions was suggested: one popular edition for distribution to "private persons, magazines, Olympic Committees and leading athletic organizations abroad, travel agencies, Swedish foreign consuls" (a total of 75,000 copies divided among Swedish, English, French, German and Russian), and one deluxe edition in a larger format for distribution to "reigning royal houses and heads of State" and for setting out in hotels, banks and shipping companies (2,000 copies in each language). The brochure was meant to appeal to a wider target audience than those interested in sports and was to contain detailed information on the Games, maps of Stockholm, views from places worth seeing, pictures from Swedish sporting life in the various events to be held at the Games, sports illustrations by Torsten Schonberg, water sport pictures by the marine painter Alfred Johansson, and the general program of the Olympic Games. The cost for producing the brochures was estimated to be 16,000 kronor, a price the Finance Section considered very high but still justifiable as the brochure was "quite an inevitable factor in the advertising work of the Games." In order to keep costs down it was suggested that the edition be halved and that a second printing be done if required.

The proposal was postponed by the Organizing Committee for further investigation and so that the special committees would be able to deliver material on Swedish sporting life. Preceding the meeting on May 8 director Sigfrid Edström, later IOC-president, suggested that the deluxe edition was unnecessary and should be cancelled to cut costs. The committee's decision was to produce only the simpler edition, to cancel the Russian edition, and to not print a greater first edition "than could be considered necessary."

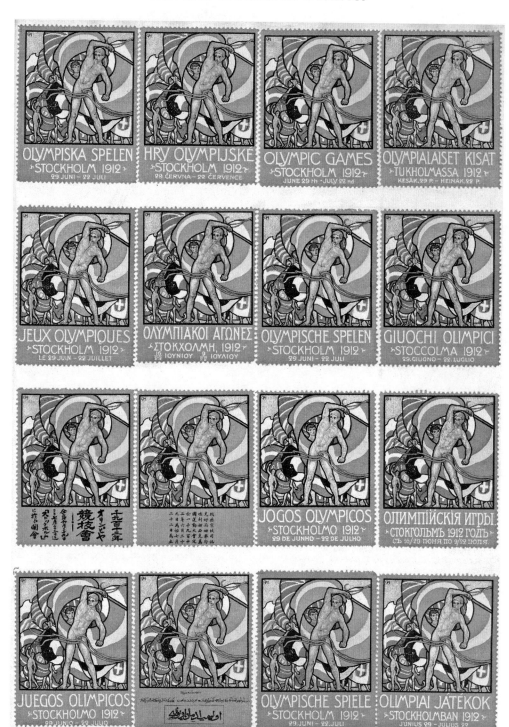

The advertising stamps for the Olympic Games in all 16 editions (National Sports Museum).

After the summer the special committees still had not delivered any material on Swedish sporting life. Referring to the stretched economy, director Edström suggested printing "merely a simple information brochure." Secretary Hellström pointed out that a decision had already been made and that the Advertising Committee had produced the necessary illustrations and that it would therefore "be unacceptable to change the character of the brochure." The Advertising Committee reacted strongly to the proposal, which was regarded as a "vote of no confidence." Most special committees delivered their articles on the sports during the latter part of August and the Organizing Committee decided to let the work proceed. At the beginning of November the contents of the brochure were discussed and Balck took on editing the texts before the brochure was translated. Another question of detail in the brochures was discussed at the end of November, namely the information on travel routes that was to be included in each edition. There were two suggestions: that all the brochures regardless of language should have the same content and therefore include information on "*all major routes* from European capitals" or that each edition should contain information on "the main routes *from the country whose language the brochure was printed in*." The Organizing Committee followed the Advertising Committee's recommendations and chose the first alternative despite the fact that this involved a certain increase in costs (four to five extra pages).

After being pressured by the Advertising Committee at the beginning of December — "when it is of utmost importance that the distribution of advertising printed matter commences" — the Organizing Committee decided to submit the brochure for printing on December 11. The estimated cost for the brochure was now 20,000 kronor, despite the restrictions placed upon the original proposal. But the brochure was to be further delayed: the proof was discussed at the meeting on January 16, 1912, and the members of the committee were asked to leave their comments by January 19. On February 6 Edström informed that the brochure had now been submitted for printing by the executive committee after the "remarks received had been tried in due order" But there were still divergent opinions and Levin, Linnér and Murray made reservations against the publication of the brochure "as this, such as it now is, for its purpose is less satisfactory, and the costs that its publication involves are designed to cause concern." When it came to the costs the delay of the brochure in itself involved a significant cost as it could not be co-distributed with posters and stamps but had to be sent separately.

Even though there were critics, the brochure seems to have been well received, so well that more copies and more variants of it were distributed than originally intended. According to the official account more than 245,000 brochures were printed, i.e. more than three times the number first planned. Moreover, in Finland the local Advertising Committee took on producing a shorter Finnish version.

The Committee first gathered on January 10, 1912, and decided to firstly produce a Finnish edition of the brochure of the Games, the cost of which the Organizing Committee declared to be incontestable. A total of 632 Finnish marks were collected through printed subscription lists, and 387 Finnish marks of this sum came from the vice consulates, besides which interested firms, with two Finnish and one North Swedish steamship companies in the forefront, subscribed 975 Finnish marks for 13 advertisements. The brochure was a shortened and revised translation of the Swedish one with the majority of its pictures, for which the line cuts were received free of charge from Stockholm. Fifteen thousand copies of the brochure were printed and sent out as a supplement to Helsinkin Sanomat's mail edition in the country. The funds were not sufficient for anything else, and it simply had to be enough. Distributing the brochure within Helsinki was considered less necessary, as the Finnish general public in the capital were also well informed of the Games.[20]

At the end of March 1912 the German Advertising Committee also proposed that a shortened version of the brochure be printed due to the great interest. The cost of an edition of 30,000 was estimated to be 1,695 kronor. The Finance Section approved the proposal, but the Organizing Committee still chose to limit the edition to 15,000.

Spreading the Advertising Materials

How were the advertising materials spread across the world? Customs and stamp duties in certain countries, local boycotts (of the poster), technical problems with the translation, and a limited budget for the physical distribution were some of the challenges the Advertising Committee faced. The necessity of advertising abroad had already been discussed in December 1910, when the Advertising and Information Committee established that "billposting is efficient but in most cases costs a lot of money" but that "it must, however, under any circumstances be used." By mobilizing a great number of, often voluntary, contacts the information about the Games was spread to organizations and the public in Sweden and abroad. Middlemen seeing opportunities to be helped in their own marketing (tourist and travel agencies for example) also offered their support. For long distance transport a number of very important sponsors were acquired in shipping companies and steamship companies, which offered free freight of packages to foreign ports.[21]

The efforts of travel agents and transport companies to associate themselves with, and piggyback on the Olympic Games can be seen as a version of contemporary "co-branding."[22] Most of these efforts presented benefits to both parties; e.g. travel and tickets to the Games became a combined offer benefiting both parties. In some cases one party unlawfully sought to exploit the other, a scenario known as "ambush marketing" in contemporary lingo. 100 years later, this represents one of the major problems that the organizers of the London Olympics are trying to counteract.[23]

The physical handling of the advertising materials required moving the business from the General Secretariat to more spacious premises at Freys Express, where an Olympics office was set up. Between September 1911 and June 1912 over 31,000 postal packages containing advertising materials were sent from that office. In total, 88,350 large posters, over 30,000 small posters, 4.7 million advertising stamps, and 245,000 advertising brochures were sent to all over the world. Moreover, rules and programs, tourist information, a "Commemorative book of Stockholm," plans of the marathon course, information on trials and information for stewards were sent. The distribution of these materials was essential in the work of informing about the Games, and its foundation was the Advertising Committee's collaboration with a very great number of various middlemen.

The Advertising Committee's tight budget involved obvious limitations on how information about the Games could be distributed. Thanks to a massive use of middlemen, spreading information about the Olympics was still successful within Sweden. An extensive network of individuals, companies and organizations was mobilized as distribution channels for "direct advertising" for the Olympics. On several occasions from 1910 to the beginning/opening of the Games in 1912 letters were sent to a great number of organizations with the purpose of informing and interesting the public, and mobilizing active athletes for the various events. Behind the efforts, high ambitions and expectations on those who would represent the country at the Games emerge.

The extent of the information campaign indicates a will to reach the entire population. At the same time, active athletes were to be informed via schools and educational organizations, clubs and sports facilities. The advertising work became a means of creating national unity around the upcoming Olympics. Among the organizations contacted by mail for the spreading of information about the Olympics were:

- The Army and the Navy
- Embassies and consulates
- Public libraries, reading rooms
- News agencies
- Adult education institutions
- Commercial schools and institutions
- Hotels, boarding houses, restaurants
- Sports grounds
- Railways
- Booksellers, stationers, music dealers
- Private, political, professional & youth clubs
- Art and music institutions
- Higher educational institutions
- Travel agencies, the tourist association's representative
- Shipping companies, steamship companies
- Athletic outfitters, swimming and tennis establishments
- Technical institutions and schools
- Universities, colleges, higher institutions

Many of the organizations became important local marketers and served as nodes for spreading information to the public and to active athletes. An example is the great number of *booksellers* contacted, in total more than 180 all over Sweden. These were important middlemen in two ways. They were essential contacts in spreading information about the Olympics, for example to local athletic associations. But they were also in many cases essential contacts for tourists, especially in places where no travel agencies or tourist associations were represented. This is where Swedish and foreign tourists came not just to inform themselves about local sights, but also for information on other tourist attractions, for example in the capital Stockholm. The booksellers often collaborated with the two major tourist associations and distributed their brochures and information materials. While the bookseller could provide information on the upcoming Olympics he could also inform about travel to the capital. The booksellers' significance is reflected in the intensive correspondence between these and the Advertising Committee during the winter and spring of 1912. Many booksellers sent letters with inquiries about more materials due to the great demand from tourists.

In the Stockholm area a large number of local companies were also mobilized. For example, in a mailing in the winter of 1912 one large poster and three small ones were sent to about 200 stores, 125 hair salons, 125 wine stores and to selected businessmen and private persons in Stockholm. Mailings were sent also to a great number of service companies in the area: restaurants and cafés, companies handling vending machines, hotels and boarding houses, etc. A picture emerges of a Stockholm where as good as every shop window and available wall had an Olympic poster.

Other strategically important middlemen in Sweden were the country's railway companies and the shipping companies and steamship companies serving Swedish ports. In these, the Advertising Committee saw potential strategic positioning of the advertising. The railways, shipping companies and steamship companies had access to important centers for both Swedish and foreign travelers, and advertising there would mean exposure to a large number of passengers. The Advertising Committee sent special letters with inquiries to the railway companies in Sweden and to stations officers and stations managers at selected stations in the country, for example Trelleborg, with its important boat service to and from Sassnitz.

In the contacts with the railway companies, the Advertising Committee encountered certain rules and demands established by the National Railways Board for billposting, among other things. For example, there could only be one (smaller) poster in each carriage. Despite these rules advertising companies also saw possibilities of exposure via railways and shipping companies. For example, Williams Affischerings Aktiebolag and its representative Hjalmar Troilius offered to perform advertising for the Advertising Committee within the country. For 500 kronor the company offered, for a period of three months, to "put up posters in railway stations, advertise on the back of State railway tickets, advertise in Svenska Kommunikationer, advertise in all the country's newspapers through Svenska Tidningsagenturen." The Advertising Committee, however, chose to try to influence these middlemen on their own, probably because of the limited budget, among other things through pointing out various synergies from advertising cooperation. The railway companies, but above all the shipping companies and the steamship companies also became important middlemen for spreading information abroad.

Boats and terminals belonging to shipping companies with connections to Sweden and Scandinavia were important both for billposting and for further distribution of advertising materials. Via mailings to representatives for the Swedish and foreign companies it was seen to it that their passengers were informed about the Games. For example, the Swedish representative for English Allen Line received a request to spread advertising materials and answered that he had sent on materials to the sister companies in Canada as well. These in turn sent requests for more materials "so that they could be used in sending letters from the Minneapolis Office which is the center of the Scandinavia district in the USA." Similar proposals came from the general agent for the American & Dominion lines, Sam Larsson in Gothenburg: "The only [additional] thing that possibly can be done to benefit traffic to the Games would be distributing programs and printed matter to tourists and travelers who usually change their money in my office in great numbers." The correspondence continued and Larsson suggested that the advertising materials for the Games should be complemented with "the brochure 'Tours in Sweden,' to be handed out simultaneously to the Swedes in America and the Americans." Larsson also asked for more advertising materials.

> [The A&D lines in England] wish a whole lot of English circulars and programs as well as sign posters, which they intend to spread in America in order to attract the Americans' attention to the Games in Stockholm, naturally for the purpose of selling many tickets from New York to Stockholm for the Lines ... be sent as soon as possible on behalf of the Companies as they consider it is time to start spreading them.... During the exhibition in Stockholm in 1897 I believe I got around 5,000 for America.... Through my Lines, I can spread tens of thousands of advertisements and know that in 1897 the American Line did a great amount of work in America in order to attract people to the Stockholm exhibition and that thousands of Americans then came through these advertisements.

In the letter the importance of right *timing* for the advertising is indicated. This recurs in several letters from voluntary advertising collaborators. In a letter to Kristian Hellström on March 18, 1912, Erik Sjöstedt in France points out: "it is my opinion that this advertising should not be introduced until May, for otherwise it will be too early and will be forgotten." The part about the design of the advertising suggested that the Advertising Committee was aware of the importance of timing and worried that the delay of the poster and the brochure would have a negative impact on the advertising.

To some extent it can be said that what was lost in time was made up for in volume. The number of shipping companies mobilized increased, as did the letters with ideas on synergies in the marketing. For example, the representative of the Cunard and Allen Lines, Axel Lagergren, called attention to the great amount of distribution which could be done through their ships "calling at Quebec–Montreal, Halifax, St. John, Portland, Boston, New York, Philadelphia and various South American and Mediterranean ports."

Many Swedes also served as middlemen for continued distribution to foreign countries. In the archive material there are several notes on people who have visited the secretariat asking for advertising materials. Especially important were the individuals assigned the task of representing remote countries in Sweden, often located in Stockholm. Important were also a number of locally situated contacts in Sweden, representing big countries but not officially connected to the embassies.[24] These individuals with their networks among Swedes and Swedish organizations in and outside the country played an important part in the continued spreading of information. Then there was the extensive correspondence and distribution of advertising materials to the major foreign legations in Stockholm.[25] Many foreign legations also asked for more materials, for example an official at the Argentinean consulate who wanted to spread information "to my friends in Germany and England." These middlemen in Sweden became essential in something that we would call "word-of-mouth," "buzz" or "viral marketing" today, i.e. an attempt to use interpersonal relations to spread an at least partially commercial message.[26] Despite the lack of internet, Facebook and e-mail, social networks served an important purpose in spreading information about the Olympics from these contacts in Sweden and out into the world.

On the list of important Swedish middlemen are also a very large number of businessmen and companies. (The correspondence suggests that the businesswomen were few, except in certain trading and service related business.) Many of these were proactive, i.e. they sent requests to the Advertising Committee for advertising materials to spread on to business contacts, colleagues, customers and suppliers both in Sweden and abroad. A typical example is a letter from Razo Fabrikerna in Stockholm: "Hereby we most respectfully permit ourselves to ask, whether we on our cartons and packing boxes may place the mark of the Olympic Games. As our make is exported everywhere, it will surely be great advertising for the Games."

Director Gustaf Berg at Aktiebolaget Lux exemplifies the international social networks which were mobilized and through which information about the Games was spread. During his business trips in the US Berg had come into contact with consul A.E. Johnson, who was also the director of the Scandinavian–American Line, which had requested the committee's advertising materials: "Naturally, Consul Johnson takes great interest in conveying as many passengers as possible with their Line and will, I presume, probably do a lot of advertising himself, but it seems to me that it would be beneficial for You to accept Consul Johnson's offer."

Many Swedish export and import companies sent advertising about the Games to their business contacts abroad, which was much appreciated by the Advertising Committee. Of great help in the distribution were also the export associations, which had important channels to businessmen and companies. Sveriges Allmänna Exportförening kept advertising materials in stock and distributed them to Swedish commerce scholars as well as other counterparts abroad.

In planning the advertising work the idea of "the importance of effective and systematic advertising work in foreign countries" recurred. Already in the first newsletters sent out in November 1910 an attempt was made to map out the foreign middlemen who could be mobilized for the advertising work, above all consulates, expatriate Swedes (especially Swedes in the United States), Swedish clubs, Swedish magazines and the foreign press. However, the most important middlemen abroad were the Swedish consulates. The limited budget called for an effective organization and the Ministry for Foreign Affairs was contacted early on to investigate the possibility of using the consulates. The financial issues observed during the summer of 1911 later strengthened the consulates' significance. The result was that the consulates and Swedish legations were designated central nodes for spreading information internationally. Moreover, to enable spreading information to as many as possible, the Organizing Committee asked the Ministry for Foreign Affairs for help with obtaining exemption from duty for the advertising items.

As mentioned earlier, six local advertising committees (London, Berlin, Paris, Marseille, Helsinki, and Holland) were formed, and the consulates played an important part here as well. The Dutch committee included the consuls in both Amsterdam and Rotterdam as well as the woman president for The Swedish–Dutch Association, Thérèse Boon. In other countries designated staff, usually at the consulate, attended to the work. In larger countries with several consulates one responsible consulate was appointed — for example the New York consulate for spreading information in the US and Canada. The matter of exemption from duty was most easily handled by sending the materials from Sweden to a consulate for further distribution from there. Part of the preparatory work was also sending inquiries to the American consulates about whom the advertising materials should be sent to: "railway stations, hotels, boarding houses, restaurants, clubs, tourist-offices, steamship agents and forwarding agencies, banks, companies and commercial firms, athletic outfitters, bath- and tennis establishments, booksellers and stationers, doctors, solicitors and other professional men, schools, private persons etc."

In September 1911 newsletters were sent to 254 Swedish consulates in English and to 240 consuls in Swedish. The letters informed about what preparations were being made in Stockholm for the advertising work and what materials were being developed: photographs, tourist literature, advertising postcards, advertising poster, advertising stamp and advertising brochure. The consulates were "pepped up" and prepared, and their central role in the advertising was explained (see quote above). Foreign consulates in Stockholm were also contacted in the preparatory work for the advertising, for example the American General Consulate that was asked to help in the work of "achieving effective advertising." Help was asked for with regard to completing the lists of news agencies, press cutting offices, daily and illustrated magazines, sports papers, and Swedish clubs in the United States. As a continuation of the letters to consulates and legations, a great number of letters to individual expatriate Swedes, Swedish magazines (69 in 18 countries), Swedish clubs (251 in 18 countries), and foreign correspondents for the major Swedish newspapers, were sent in October 1911.

During the autumn of 1911 the Organizing Committee also contacted Swedish and foreign shipping companies and travel organizers to procure carriage freight paid for the upcoming advertising mailings. Then, during January, February and March 1912 the circular letters were followed by mailings of posters, stamps and brochures, first to all the Swedish consulates, and then to expatriate Swedes, businessmen, hotels and travel agencies, Swedish and Scandinavian magazines abroad, foreign correspondents for Swedish magazines, the foreign representatives of the tourist association, etc. In response, the Advertising Committee received a large number of requests for more materials. Letters came as early as January 1912 saying that more materials had to be sent as soon as possible in order to be of any use. The tone in some letters was in fact a bit dejected, for example from the Scandinavia Travel Bureau in New York, which regretted that "only ten brochures have been received — like a drop in a bucket of water" as there were over 3,000 agents all across the country through which they wanted to distribute the advertising materials. The requests for more advertising materials from foreign countries continued to stream in during the spring, also via Swedish companies, which passed on requests from foreign partners. The Scandinavian tourist agencies in the United States also contacted the Advertising Committee for materials and information about the Games. Mobilizing people with a Swedish connection had paid off. Many were willing to spread the message about the upcoming Games in Stockholm.

Distribution via the consulates was supplemented by direct mailings and various forms of cooperation. Posters were sent to over 2,200 hotels in 30 countries. In January 1912 programs for the Olympics and advertising materials were also sent to 812 tourist offices in 38 countries. The same month it was decided to do joint advertising with the Swedish Tourist Traffic Association in "the London underground railways" to further "increase the number of visiting foreigners." In exchange for £25 each "two posters would be put up at every station, one with advertising for Sweden as a tourist destination and one Olympic poster." The local advertising committee in London considered the billposting to be "very desirable from an advertising perspective" and supported the proposal along with the Finance Section. During the spring of 1912 the Organizing Committee also sent requests to and received offers/estimates concerning advertising from several Belgian and French billboard companies with local poster monopolies in various cities. Despite the fact that many offers were heavily discounted the committee declined most of them with reference to their limited budget. In Paris, however, a firm was hired for putting up posters in stations and major boulevards.[27]

Distribution abroad was also made easier by the agreements made with government-owned and private railway companies in Europe, for example in Germany, Belgium, Holland, France and England. Of the over 30,000 mini-posters sent out from Stockholm most went to these railway companies, which saw an opportunity to raise awareness of their own companies. In letters from the Swedish representative of a Dutch train company, it is described that "the Dutch state railways would be prepared to have our posters put up in all stations, however only provided that we in turn display the company's prospectus and that a couple of its posters are conspicuously placed either outside or in a generally frequented room in the stadium." In Berlin an agreement with a major bookseller and newsstand chain was managed, which made it possible to distribute 5,000 copies of the smaller poster throughout the city.

How The Advertising for the Games Was Received

The Advertising Committee was worried that the delay in the advertising materials would have a negative impact on the spreading of information. But the problems they faced were not only connected to the time available. The official account once again: "[T]he result being that the poster somewhat failed in its object in certain districts, as in some cases a disinclination was shown to exhibit it, this adding very considerably to the difficulty of properly and thoroughly advertising the Games."[28]

It did not take many weeks after the first posters were sent out before the Organizing

Committee started getting signals that the poster was not being received in the best possible way. On February 27 Victor Balck informed that "the poster of the Olympic Games in several places abroad has been made the subject of criticism and that permission for putting it up in hotels and similar places has not been granted in several cases, which is likely to make the advertising work harder." Because this was second-hand information it was decided to let the matter rest. On March 4 director Burman gave a personal report to the executive committee based on observations he had made during a trip through Europe. In Berlin the poster had been put up in the Swedish travel agency as well as in the hotel, while Cook's travel agencies in Paris and Nice had not "bothered" to put it up. Another travel agency in Paris "had no knowledge about the Games" but had "four different Norwegian advertising brochures." In Burman's account there was nothing that suggested that the poster in itself was a problem. Two weeks later, however, the committee received concrete information on just that.

> The day before yesterday the confiscation of one of the Olympic Games' advertising posters was finally in the entire Dutch press. It is said to have happened in Oeffelt, a small place in Holland. The poster was hanging in the waiting room and the Mayor considered it most indecent. This confiscation of the poster should be great advertising for the Games, because it is publicly spoken of in the country. The Olympic Committee ought to send its thanks to Mr. Mayor in Oeffelt. Here in Holland the new law on morality is much laughed at, so the press does not let any opportunities they get to make fun of it go by.[29]

Similar signals about the poster's unsuitability come from other countries during the spring. In April, A. von Strussenfelt writes "I regret to inform you that the French in general, at least in this part of the country, have the impression that the poster is 'indecent.' Several have for this reason absolutely refused to put it up." In China the poster was altogether prohibited as it was considered "offensive to Chinese ideas of decency."

Is any advertising good advertising? The letter from Therése Boon highlights a classic issue in marketing.[30] If the objective of billposting was to raise awareness of the Games, which is arguably a central objective in contemporary advertising, it is quite possible that the controversies the poster caused contributed positively.[31] At the same time we can establish that the result in some places was that the poster was never put up, which could hardly be said to create attention. There is no exact information about how widely spread the discontent with the poster was. What we can establish is that the Organizing Committee in the Dutch case seems to have succeeded in something that has received a great deal of attention as a potentially successful strategy in modern marketing literature: benefiting from contemporary cultural tensions.[32] The motif of the poster seems to have connected with current tension in Dutch society concerning what should be regarded as indecent.

Advertising and PR

Even though budget limitations put a stop to large-scale advertising campaigns for the Games, ways to use the press in the advertising work were still found. Despite the fact that the main channel for spreading information was the network of middlemen described in the previous passage, the mass media was also used. As early as in the spring of 1911 there were advertisements in Svenska Utlandstidningen with the headline "Appeal to Swedes in foreign countries!" stressing the importance of the upcoming Games for Sweden as a sports and tourist nation and from a business point of view. During the autumn, more adverts were placed. The purpose was simple: mobilize as many as possible with a connection to Sweden to promote the Games. In February 1912 an appeal was also made in the magazine *Svensk Export*:

> To Swedish businessmen! Considering the utmost importance of effective and systematically arranged advertising work in foreign countries for the upcoming Olympic Games we hereby urge businessmen travelling to foreign countries to support us in this respect through taking with them and — possibly in collaboration with the Swedish consulates, which have taken over the main distribution for the cities respectively — appropriately distributing the program of the Games and brochures, published in the Swedish, English, French and German languages, as well as the Advertising Stamp and particularly the Advertising Poster, which have later been printed in 16 languages.

The only foreign newspaper which had advertisements for the Games was the continental edition of the Daily Mail. Firstly, it was agreed that the Games should be mentioned in the Swedish Tourist Traffic Association's adverts in the paper during the summer of 1911. Secondly, an advert for the Games occurred 15 times during the autumn of 1911 and the spring of 1912. Part of these deals were also a promise that the paper would regularly publish shorter items on the Olympic Games.

The modest advertising in the daily press was supplemented by free adverts placed in a number of publications aimed at foreign tourists. Most important were the Tourist Traffic Association's guidebooks in English, German, French and Russian, of which more than 500,000 copies were printed in total during 1911 and 1912. Free advertising in Tulebolagen's tourist guide "Holidays in Sweden" was also achieved. In both cases the Organizing Committee also received several thousands of copies for their own distribution (and thus advertising for the publishers).

Another attempt at advertising via the press was made in France, where Erik Sjöstedt during the spring of 1912 negotiated with Club Alpin and Touring Club about distributing advertising cards for the Games with their magazines. However, these efforts do not seem to have resulted in any advertisements.

In the countries hosting Olympic Games the countries' own media usually take great interest in following how the media in other countries describe and analyze the Games. Stockholm 1912 was not an exception. The Swedish press regularly informed its readers of how foreign magazines reported on the Games, particularly the many positive accounts which appeared at regular intervals in foreign papers. During 1911 and 1912 both the Swedish and foreign press wrote a great number of articles about the Games. Proof of this are for example the press cuttings which the Organizing Committee subscribed to in order to follow

---

OLYMPIC GAMES of STOCKHOLM 1912
JUNE 29th—JULY 22nd.

Postal Address: OLYMPISKA SPELEN, STOCKHOLM.

Advertisement for the Olympic Games in the *Daily Mail* during the autumn of 1911 and the spring of 1912 (*V. Olympiaden*, p. 255).

what was written about the Games. In the official account it is said that the amount of press cuttings spoke for themselves about how successful the spreading of information had been: in total the clippings filled 325 volumes of 100 pages each. Furthermore, few foreign papers had missed describing the Stockholm Games in one or more articles.

The plans for advertising activities from December 1910 included two activities directed at the press: "the arranging of a prize competition in a major English newspaper" (for tickets) and "journal advertising." The daily papers in Sweden, the foreign press, the sports press and other types of publications also became important PR channels that were canvassed in order to spread information about the Games. During the autumn of 1910 the general consulates in Sweden were asked to supply the Advertising Committee with lists of news agencies, press cutting offices, daily and illustrated magazines, and sports papers.

The first real contact with the foreign press was taken in September 1911 when the complete general program was sent out to 1,608 daily papers and illustrated magazines in 41 countries, 402 sports papers in 37 countries, 145 news agencies in 32 countries, 37 press illustration agencies in 17 countries, and 69 Swedish papers abroad in 6 countries. In February 1912 all the papers were contacted once again, this time with the finished advertising brochure. Information intended for publishing was sent out at regular intervals. It could be about the rules for various sports, sports photos from the various Olympic events, the Swedish Olympic organization's current work, printed advertising materials, advertising stamps, photos of the poster, the prize diploma, the commemorative medals, photos of the new Stadium and other locations where events were going to take place, and pictures from Stockholm taken by the King's court photographer Oscar Halldin.

The Stockholm Games in the Foreign Press

Many of these photos and illustrations were published, often attracting wide coverage in the foreign press. The daily press and the sports papers were canvassed particularly intensely in the countries which had local advertising committees. An example is *Le Temps* in Paris (under the editorship of Erik Sjöstedt who belonged to the local French advertising committee), which during the spring of 1912 had a special issue on Sweden, of which over 60,000 copies were printed. The issue contained portraits of the royal family, short illustrated articles on Swedish politics, Swedish industries and the Swedish economy, combined with illustrated items about the upcoming Olympic Games. In Finland 15,000 copies of the translated brochure were distributed as a supplement to *Helsinkin Sanomat*.

Similarly, a special Sweden issue with information about the Games was developed in collaboration with the German magazine *Welt auf Reisen*. The Swedish papers in the United States were also a great support. The Advertising Committee had already carefully prepared them with letters in October 1911: "to make the Games the subject of as many articles as possible in the columns of your paper." In March 1912 these papers were contacted once more, now with the request to mobilize Swedish–American athletes in the U.S., get them to train and also to represent Sweden in the upcoming Games.

The immediate correspondence between the Advertising Committee and the editorial offices of foreign papers increased during the spring, for example in connection with the mailing of the advertising brochure. The editorial offices of many of the Swedish–American and American papers sent laudatory words to the Advertising Committee: "When it comes to advertising I think that You at home in Sweden need not take a back seat to the Americans"[33]; "As a general rule I may say that the press here is quite favorably disposed and obliging and many articles with content advantageous to Sweden have been included in several newspapers"[34]; The posters have done a roaring trade"[35]; "Your pamphlet with reference to the Olympic Games received and I wish to congratulate your committee on its magnificent work. Everything that your association has done seems to surpass anything that has ever been done in previous Olympiads. I wish you success."[36]

The correspondence with foreign papers indicates that the brochure was a success: "The careful regard for details shown by Kristian Hellström, secretary of the Swedish Olympic Committee, is reassuring to all who are interested in the Games. His letters to James E. Sullivan, secretary of the AAU show the most painstaking considerations and planning."[37]

The foreign press took great interest in the purely athletic aspects, as in the rules and regulations. It was considered an important opportunity to mobilize their own potential participants for the Games:

> All eyes are on Stockholm: In every quarter of America great interest is taken. At no period in time in the history of track and field in the United States has there been so much excitement shown as at the present time. In every quarter of the country where there is practice of track and field sport has been established has there been nothing but talks of the Olympic struggle next summer, and nearly every man with pretensions to first class has already begun to train for the tryouts.[38]

The positive PR the Games received in foreign papers was usually connected to much praise about how the rules in the various events were handled. It was described how the organization handled differences between countries and how rules were explained and analyzed, as well as how decisions on new rules were made.

In Swedish papers the advertising work that was being done throughout the world was also noted in positive terms. An item on "the advertising work abroad for the Olympic Games" described the marketing work being done by athletes and consulates in Russia in very positive tones. Similarly, one article described Austrian contentment with the Swedish preparations for the Games. Austrians visiting Sweden before the Games were also reported to have seen the colorful poster all the way from Vienna to Stockholm. And in the Austrian paper *Morgen* the upcoming Games, Swedish athletes and the Swedish Olympic committee's work were described:

> Only a few nations are in the position to, for the accomplishment of such a giant task as the Olympic Games, draw up such an ensemble of experienced and capable sportsmen. And if this time the Olympic Games give sporting life in the entire world a strong incentive, then Sweden and its Olympic committee can indeed take great credit for that.

On February 17, 1912, one newspaper reported under the heading "Beautiful words on the work of the Olympic Organizing Committee" on a positive article in the Danish paper *Riget*. The Danish article emphasized particularly that "the Swedes deserve much praise for their preparatory work" and that "the rules for most of the Games are so well worked out that all of them with some modification could serve as standard rules."

The articles in the foreign press increased in number right before and during the Games, but continued after the Games as well, as expressed in Thérèse Boon's letter to the committee on October 26, 1912:

> The representatives for the Dutch press have also in their correspondence from the Olympic Games especially pointed out how excellent the organization of it all was on all occasions, and how *just* the Swedish jury was. The praise for Sweden, its people, nature, industries, art,

sports etc. at the time of the Olympic Games has not been without effect in Holland. Within sports circles conferences were held and in newspapers articles were written, in which Sweden was pointed out as a model for sport [...] The praise for our beautiful language gave cause for many to enroll in the Swedish–Netherlands Association for lessons in Swedish, and all of this has delighted us Swedes in Holland indescribably.

Organizing Press Contacts and Handling the Press on Site

During the autumn of 1911 the need to deal with the Swedish and foreign press which was expected to come to Stockholm and report from the Games was discussed. A special Press Committee was formed and given responsibility for the contacts with the Swedish and foreign press before and during the Games. The committee comprised a chairman and ten members, of which five were appointed by the Publicist club and represented major Swedish newspapers.

The Press Committee was immediately put in charge of many small and great issues. These included decisions on the number of press seats at the Olympic Stadium, the number of press tickets, the issuing of press badges, decisions on the drawing of direct telegraph and telephone lines to the press stand at the Stadium, how the press on the spot should be gathered at editorial sites, sending out official invitations to the major news agencies in Europe, and how the Swedish daily and sports press should be informed regularly before the Games. In addition there was also the question of how to deal with the daily information that had to be spread during the Games about results etc. The result of the latter discussion was the decision to publish 30 copies of an "Olympic News" from June 17 to July 25 in both Swedish and English. This would be supplemented during the Games by *Dagens Nyheter's* publication of a similar so-called "Stadium-edition" in English. Some activities directed at the press had to be abandoned due to lack of resources, for example the plans to arrange travel throughout the country for the foreign press.

The Difficulty of Controlling What Is Written and Spread Through the Press

Not everything that was written about the Games in the foreign press was positive. A rumor spread in several foreign daily papers during the spring of 1912 that there were problems with accommodation in Stockholm. At the end of January, Consul-General Daniel Danielsson in London reported on information in the English press about limited accommodation in Stockholm. The cause is said to be that the German Olympic administration had gone to Stockholm to reconnoitre and found only 60 rooms for their 160 participants. To get around this problem plans were now openly being made to hire a steamship to accommodate the German team. In connection with this story a rumor arose about sky-high housing costs and a shortage of rooms, which during the spring spread in several European countries (Finland, Norway, Denmark and Holland among others) and circulated in the American press. The Advertising Committee tried to counteract the rumors via the consulates and the local advertising committees and through sending a clarification via the Swedish news agency. In his reflection over the advertising work in Finland J. Lilliehöök observes: "Above all any incorrect items on a shortage of accommodation and high prices must be carefully prevented: a single such item does nearly irreparable damage, for it spreads very swiftly and the audience is predisposed to believe it but overlooks the disclaimer, if one comes."[39]

Other Marketing Activities

During the spring of 1911 the Organizing Committee discussed various auxiliary activities for the Games. It concerned the sales of a variety of souvenirs, restaurant and entertainment activities, prize competitions, photo and film activities and the compilation of various commemorative books. Another marketing-related activity, which caused much discussion, was setting the ticket prices and different forms of subscriptions and multi-event passes, and free tickets.

In October 1911 the Organizing Committee came to an agreement with Granbergs Konstindustri AB about the production and selling of official "view postcards." The company Östberg & Lenhardtsons AB was given the rights for the reproduction of the poster and the advertising stamp, medals and marks, stadium pictures and metal souvenirs, "...and the sales thereof within the Stadium." Plans and rights for sales stands on Valhallavägen were developed for merchandising and for information etc. Åhlén & Åkerlund in Gothenburg obtained the rights for printing and selling commemorative books from the Games. In this connection, the rights for photography and cinematography were thoroughly discussed. Complications concerning photography rights during the Games arose, and complaints about the limitations came from foreign papers. There were also uncertainties regarding photos in commemorative books. The whole photo issue was later left to the Finance Section. When it came to film rights it was suggested during the planning that these should be advertised in foreign papers. An agreement was made with Svensk-Amerikanska Filmkompaniet, but it was also discussed that the Organizing Committee should own the rights and later leave the film work to a Swedish film syndicate. Deciding on this in good time was considered important in order to give the filmmakers time to familiarize themselves with all the different sports. However, the film adventure was on the point of failing completely since the film company suspended payments before any films had been received. In 1913, the Organizing Committee was forced to buy up the footage they were entitled to according to the contract.

Like the Organizing Committee, many private operators in Sweden and abroad saw business opportunities in various forms of *merchandising*. The closer the Games came the more obvious the competition from unauthorized suppliers of souvenirs became. In January 1912 the Organizing Committee established that "lots of metal objects, bearing the name of the Olympic Games, are daily imported from abroad" and because of this demanded information from the Customs Department on how this flow could be stopped. Above we noted that the organizers of the London Olympics actively sought to handle this problem. The problem is not only one of guarding the financial interests of the organizers, but equally one of protecting the official sponsors. What appears to have been an unexpected, minor side effect in 1912 has become a major issue 100 years later. Considerable effort is now spent on counteracting brand infringements before and during Olympic Games (as well as other types of events).

Another important marketing activity was how visitors and participants were taken care of outside the Olympic sports program. The Organizing Committee discussed different possibilities to enlarge and strengthen the visitors' experiences from the Games and Stockholm. In October 1911 it was decided to set up a special Entertainments Committee, with representatives from suitable institutions in Stockholm. During the planning many suggestions on activities were discussed: opera and theatrical performances, cinema shows of the day's Olympic events, excursions on Lake Mälaren and Saltsjön, popular festivals and open-air theatres, for example at Skansen, a flower parade in connection with a riding festival, a display by Svenska Folkdansens Vänner at the Opera and the Olympic Stadium, a procession of singers through the city concluding at the Olympic Stadium, air displays arranged by Aeronautiska Sällskapet, arranging various visits to museums, and showing the sights of Stockholm with trained guides with a good knowledge of languages. Some proposals were realized others not, see also the essay "Punch, Splendor and Patriotism."

What Was Marketed?

What was it that the Advertising Committee and other involved bodies and individuals in Sweden were really marketing? Was it something besides the actual Games? It was obvious that the advertising for the Games had had an effect. The Stockholm Games were the first Games with participants from six continents and many said that the Games thereby became a worldwide event for the first time. Twenty-seven nations and over 2,500 participants came to Stockholm, which can be compared to the 260 participants from 14 countries who had participated in Athens 16 years earlier. The organization of the Games thereby strengthened the image of Sweden as a good arranger of major events. It was also apparent that great awareness of the event had successfully been created in Sweden, among athletes and the public. The Swedish team was the largest with almost 500 people and the Swedes did very well.

Besides marketing the Games themselves interest was also successfully created in the various events, athletes, the rules of the events and in the so-called Olympic spirit. Another indirect consequence was increased interest in and an altered view of sports among Swedish politicians. Primarily the Stockholm Games were financed via the sports lottery, but after the success at the Games the Swedish Parliament became friendlier towards sports. When the Parliament gathered in 1913, the first annual government grant for sports was approved (100,000 Swedish kronor) and ever since Swedish sport has enjoyed government grants. The advertising for the Games can therefore be said to have acted as advertising for Swedish sports over a broad spectrum.

The work put into gathering, compiling and developing the rules for the different sports became a very important part in the information and communication work and attracted much attention. Everyone was generally content with the rules during the Games. The organizers had worked hard to construct modern rules. It would turn out at coming international congresses that this work had paid off; the Stockholm organization's rules were approved to a great extent by the different special federations.

The world press was also interested in the Games. The Stockholm Games attracted a great number of journalists: 445 journalists were accredited, of whom 229 were foreign. Besides attracting attention to the various events these journalists highlighted individual athletes and sporting occurrences. The American James Thorpe became the most well-known athlete at the Games. After easy victories in both the pentathlon and decathlon King Gustaf V called him "the greatest athlete in the world" at the prize ceremony. After his successes in Stockholm Thorpe became something of a national hero in the United States. In 1913 he was stripped of his Olympic gold medals for violation of the amateur rules. In connection with the marathon great attention was paid to a tragic event: the Portuguese Francisco Lazaro collapsed due to dehydration and died at Serafimersjukhuset the following day. However, the most talked about event during the marathon was "the Japanese who disappeared." Shizo Kanakuri dropped out of the race close to Tureberg where he rested in a garden and let his hosts serve him refreshments. The competition officials never found out that he had dropped out and only 55 years later could Kanakuri finish the race and come into the Olympic Stadium during a visit to Stockholm.

In conclusion, the purpose of the Stockholm Games was also to market Sweden as a tourist country. At least that was something that was often pointed out in the arguments supporting advertising, especially in the attempts to mobilize volunteers in the advertising work. We have established that the marketing of the Games, of Sweden as a tourist country, of specific sights in Sweden, of Swedish culture, and of Swedish and foreign travel and transportation companies overlapped and that this created certain synergies. The tourist aspect of the Games was important, even if tourism during and immediately after the Games was not overwhelming. Despite some disappointment in the number of tourists visiting during the Games, it was expected that the advertising would have an effect in the years following the Games.

> The travel agencies are of the opinion that the immense advertising done in and for and through the Olympic Games last year for Sweden all over the world, will not take effect until this year. Regarding the stream of visitors, last summer was a great disappointment to many. However, as you will recall, the experienced tourist guides had already warned in advance about too high expectations. Experience has shown that the real tourist avoids countries and places where exhibitions and similar price raising events are taking place. He does not avoid them solely because of the extra costs, but also because he wants to see and study the country and people as they normally appear. However, the immense advertising has surely not been a waste of effort. It has attracted attention to our country's existence among millions of tourists who may never before have given us a thought.[40]

To some extent, the same also applied to Swedish companies, above all the major Swedish export companies, which could profit by being associated with the Stockholm Games. The ability to use the Olympic effect for economic purposes was both local in Stockholm and more general.

How Were the Stockholm Olympics Marketed?

As noted by way of introduction, the Stockholm Olympics were not marketed; there is nothing that suggests a coherent understanding of the activities we have described as "marketing." But what was done still stands out as surprisingly modern, with many examples of contemporary marketing practices. Marketing something like the Olympic Games is of course in many ways different from marketing a new dairy product or a new service. Today, we speak of "event marketing," through different types of arrangements.

Today, "event marketers" are expected to dedicate themselves to various image-enhancing activities, to create greater interest in the city, region or country where the event is going to take place, via press and press contacts.[41] In organizing the Stockholm Olympics, this was an essential activity for the Advertising Committee. To create a strong brand and give the Games, Stockholm and Sweden a clear, positive image it was considered important to supply the Swedish and foreign press with information regularly throughout the entire preparation process. At the same time, we saw how difficult it was to control these processes.

The rumor in the foreign press about accommodation problems in Stockholm proved to be very hard to stop once it began spreading. Just as we would expect from organizers today, certain attempts at "crisis management" were made through denying the information in direct communication with the press.[42]

In the marketing of the Games we saw several examples of so-called "co-branding," i.e. that the advertising for the Games was connected with advertising for other offers, for example advertising for Sweden as a tourist country in general (joint advertising with the Tourist Association), and advertising for travel to Stockholm (advertisements in the travel organizers' publications).[43] The companies' use of the so-called advertising stamp on their business mailings is another example. The phenomenon is of course based on the idea that joint communication can have a positive effect for both parties. In the advertising work we also saw examples of trying to make other parties see the "leverage" of the Games, for example the argument that the advertising for the Games was of such great use to the City of Stockholm that the city should cover the expected loss.[44]

The Olympic organization also devoted much time to activities with the purpose of creating strong "experiences" for the audience and participants, experiences which would generate lasting memories and "heritage" from the 1912 Stockholm Olympics. In "event marketing," the importance of creating a lasting heritage from the event is often pointed out.[45] The Organizing Committee worked hard to develop souvenirs and memorabilia of different kinds, so-called "merchandising." The purpose of these objects and of all the auxiliary events organized in connection with the Games seems to have been to enhance "the experience" of the Games (so-called "experience marketing").[46] The heritage from the Games, including the picture of "the sunshine Olympics," was not only a result of the fortunate weather. The organizers' efforts very much contributed to the experiences, which built this positive picture not only of the Games but also of Stockholm as a destination and of Sweden as a tourist country.

The picture of the marketing of the Stockholm Olympics that we have described also gives reason for some reflections regarding marketing as a contemporary phenomenon. A first such insight is how marketers can use current values as a "sounding board" for their messages. Here, we are thinking about how both the Swedish population and the expatriate Swedes were successfully mobilized through striking a note of national unity. That the national and the Nordic were important was clear, for example, in the demand that the face of the prominent figure in the official poster should show a "Nordic type." The Swedish–Norwegian union's dissolution may of course have contributed to creating fertile ground for national rhetoric, something that was suggested by the observation that a French travel agency actually had "four Norwegian advertising brochures."

A second insight is about the energy that was devoted to the distribution of the advertising. In today's communication society it is easy to take such distribution for granted; almost everyone has the opportunity to inform themselves, but that does not mean that they do it. The importance of recruiting good spokespersons has been noted previously, for example in research on innovations,[47] and lately marketers have used "buzzadors," i.e. users who recommend products to acquaintances against compensation.[48] In marketing the Stockholm Olympics the scant resources forced direct contact with a very large number of potential spokespersons. Even though not all of these took initiatives to spread the message, many did. The result was a spreading of the word through personal contacts rather than anonymous media. The weakness of such a strategy is of course that it can result in the message being spread in relatively limited circles.

Notes

1. E.g. Cunningham and Taylor, "Event Marketing" (1995); Hoyle, *Event Marketing* (2002) and Getz: "Event Tourism" (2008).

2. Zauhar, "Historical Perspectives on Sport Tourism" (2003).

3. Araujo, et al., *Reconnecting Marketing to Markets* (2010); Zwick and Cayla, *Inside Marketing* (2011); Hagberg and Kjellberg: "Who Performs Marketing?" (2010); Barrey, et al.: "Designer, packager et merchandiser" (2000); Geiger and Finch, "Industrial sales people as market actors" (2009), and Simakova and Neyland: "Marketing Mobile Futures" (2008).

4. Shaw and Jones: "A History of Schools of Marketing Thought" (2005).

5. At roughly the same time as the planning started for the Olympic Games in Stockholm, the first university courses in marketing were developed in the United States. The first books and articles on the subject that employed the term "marketing" were also published during the following decade, e.g. Weld, *The Marketing of Farm Products* (1916); Weld, "Marketing Functions and Mercantile Organization" (1917); Duncan: *Marketing: Its Problems and methods* (1920), and Ivey, *Principles of Marketing* (1921).

6. Getz, et al.: "Festival Stakeholder Roles" (2007).

7. Smith, "Spotlight Events, Media Relations, and Place Promotion" (2005).

8. Chalip and Costa, "Building Sport Event Tourism into the Destination Brand" (2006).

9. O'Brien, "Event Business Leveraging" (2006).

10. Ritchie, "Turning 16 Days into 16 Years through Olympic Legacies" (2000).

11. Nilsson, *Banker i brytningstid* (1981).

12. The paper is based on the official repository of the Organizing Committee for the Olympic Games in Stockholm kept by the Swedish National Archives: National Archives: Stockholmsolympiaden 1912: Organizing Committee A 1:1–6, and National Archives: Stockholmsolympiaden 1912: Documents of the Advertising Committee Ö I j: a–d.

13. Bloch, *The Historian's Craft* (1953).

14. Excerpt from a letter to Mr. Donald E. Kidd, Torstenssonsgatan in Stockholm, December 1911.

15. Bergvall (ed.), *The Fifth Olympiad* (1913), p. 266.

16. Vanden Abeele and Butaye, "Pretesting the Effectiveness of Industrial Advertising" (1980), and Pieters and Wedel: "Pretesting Advertising" (2007).

17. Krishnan and Chakravarti, "Memory Measures for Pretesting Advertisements" (1999) and Schneider and Woolgar: "Technologies of Ironic Revelation: Enacting Consumers in Neuromarkets" (2012).

18. Hirschman, "Aesthetics, Ideologies and the Limits of the Marketing Concept" (1983).

19. Beverland, "Managing the Design Innovation — Brand Marketing Interface" (2005) and Eikhof and Haunschild, "For Art's Sake!" (2007).

20. Letter from J. Lilliehöök at the Finnish consulate to the Advertising Committee, in the autumn of 1912.

21. Among these were AB Svenska Ostasiatiska Co. (to China, Japan), Svenska Levant-Line (Mediterranean ports), Thos. Wilson Sons & Co. (London–Hull, Hull–North America), Stockholms Rederi AB Svea (Germany, Holland, Russia), Rederi AB Nordstjernan (South America), Finska Angfartygs AB (Finland and Russia), Ångfartygs AB Bore (Finland), Scandinavian–American Line (Copenhagen–New York), and AB Sandström, Stranne & Co. (Gothenburg–Cuba–Mexico).

22. E.g. Farrelly, Quester and Greyser, "Defending the Co-Branding Benefits of Sponsorship B2B Partnerships" (2005).

23. On June 21, 2010, *The Telegraph* reported: "London 2012 Olympics: International Olympic Committee to clampdown on ambush marketing…. The International Olympic Committee has said it is constantly on the look-out for any ambush marketing tactics that may be adopted at the London 2012 Olympic Games."

24. "The Foreign Powers' Consulates in Sweden" which were corresponded with were: Argentina, Bolivia, Brazil, Costa Rica, France, Guatemala, Honduras, Liberia, Monaco, Panama, Persia, Portugal, San Domingo, Belgium, Chile, Colombia, Cuba, Greece, Haiti, Italy, Mexico, Nicaragua, Paraguay, Peru, Salvador, Spain, Romania, Switzerland and Serbia.

25. The legations in Stockholm for Austria-Hungary, Belgium, England, France, Italy, Japan, the Netherlands, Portugal, Russia, Siam, Spain, Turkey, Germany, USA, Denmark, and Norway.

26. Kirby and Marsden *Connected Marketing: The Viral, Buzz and Word of Mouth Revolution* (2006).

27. The foreign correspondent for *Stockholms Dagblad* in France noted in a letter dated March 10, 1912: "concerning the widely discussed posting of the large poster on the walls of Paris, it should be noted that this costs considerable sums, in part due to the stamp tax on advertising, but particularly due to the high rents on advertising space. It is easy to demand posting on walls, in hotels and railroads, but easily forgotten at home that all such advertising in France (which is performed by specialized firms) is a matter of money."

28. Bergvall, 1913, p. 266.

29. Excerpt from letter Therése Boon to the Organizing Committee for the Stockholm Olympics, dated March 17, 1912.

30. Levy, "How New?" (2006).

31. Pieters and Wedel, "Pretesting Advertising" (2002).

32. Holt and Cameron, *Cultural Strategy* (2010).

33. *Svenska Nordwästern Spokane*, Washington, May 31, 1912).

34. From Boston, Mass.

35. Birger Lindh, *Svenska Kuriren*, Chicago.

36. *The Evening Bulletin*, Philadelphia, March 31, 1912)

37. *Journal Boston*, February 29, 1912.

38. Article in newspaper in Omaha, February 18, 1912.

39. Letter on July 10, 1913.

40. *Svenska Dagbladet*, April 12, 1913.

41. Smith, "Spotlight Events, Media Relations, and Place Promotion" (2005).

42. Coombs, *Ongoing Crisis Communication* (1999).

43. Chalip and Costa, 2006.

44. O'Brien, 2006.

45. Ritchie, 2000.

46. Pine and Gilmore, "Welcome to the Experience Economy," 1998.

47. Akrich, Callon, and Latour, "Key to Success in Innovation Part II" (2002).

48. See for example http://www.buzzadors.com/.

References

UNPUBLISHED SOURCES

Swedish National Archives: Stockholmsolympiaden 1912

ELECTRONIC SOURCES

www.buzzador.com

PERIODICALS AND NEWSPAPERS

Dagens Nyheter
The Evening Bulletin
Göteborgs-Posten
Journal Boston
Svenska Dagbladet
Svenska Kuriren
Svenska Nordwästern Spokane
The Telegraph

PRINT SOURCES

Akrich, Madeleine, Michel Callon, and Bruno Latour: "Key to Success in Innovation Part II: The Art of Choosing Good Spokespersons" in *International Journal of Innovation Management* 6 (2:2002), pp. 207–225.

Araujo, Luis, John H. Finch, and Hans Kjellberg (eds.), *Reconnecting Marketing to Markets* (Oxford, 2010).

Barrey, Sandrine, Franck Cochoy, and Sophie Dubuisson-Quellier. "Designer, packager et merchandiser:

trois professionnels pour une même scéne marchande" in *Sociologie du Travail* 42 (3:2000):457–482.

Bergvall, Erik (ed.): *The Fifth Olympiad: The Official Report of the Olympic Games of Stockholm 1912* (Stockholm, 1913).

Beverland, Michael B.: "Managing the Design Innovation — Brand Marketing Interface: Resolving the Tension between Artistic Creation and Commercial Imperatives" in *Journal of Product Innovation Management* 22 (2:2005), pp. 193–207.

Bloch, Marc: *The Historian's Craft* (New York, 1953).

Chalip, Laurence, and C. Costa: "Building Sport Event Tourism into the Destination Brand: Foundations for a General Theory," in H. Gibson (ed.), *Sport tourism: Concepts and Theories* (London, 2006).

Coombs, W. T: *Ongoing Crisis Communication: Planning, Managing, and Responding* (Thousand Oaks, 1999).

Cunningham, M.H., and S.F. Taylor: "Event Marketing: State of the Industry and Research Agenda" in *Festival Management and Event Tourism* 2 (3–4: 1995), pp. 123–137.

Duncan, C.S.: *Marketing: Its Problems and Methods* (New York, 1920).

Eikhof, Doris Ruth, and Axel Haunschild: "For Art's Sake! Artistic and Economic Logics in Creative Production" in *Journal of Organizational Behavior* 28 (5:2007), pp. 523–538.

Farrelly, Francis, Pascale Quester, and Stephen A. Greyser. "Defending the Co-Branding Benefits of Sponsorship B2B Partnerships: The Case of Ambush Marketing" in *Journal of Advertising Research* 45 (3:2005), pp. 339–348.

Geiger, Susi, and John H. Finch: "Industrial Sales People as Market Actors" in *Industrial Marketing Management* 38 (6:2009), pp. 608–617.

Getz, Donald: "Event Tourism: Definition, Evolution, and Research" in *Tourism Management* 29 (3:2008), pp. 403–428.

_____, Tommy Andersson, and Maria Larson: "Festival Stakeholder Roles: Concepts and Case Studies" in *Event Management* 10 (2/3:2007), p. 103–122.

Hagberg, Johan, and Hans Kjellberg: "Who Performs Marketing? Dimensions of Agential Variation in Market Practice" in *Industrial Marketing Management* 39 (7:2010), pp. 1028–1037.

Hirschman, Elizabeth C.: "Aesthetics, Ideologies and the Limits of the Marketing Concept" in *The Journal of Marketing* 47 (3:1983), pp. 45–55.

Holt, Douglas B., and Douglas Cameron: *Cultural Strategy: Using Innovative Ideologies to Build Breakthrough Brands* (Oxford, 2010).

Hoyle, Leonard H.: *Event Marketing: How to Successfully Promote Events, Festivals, Conventions, and Expositions* (New York, 2002).

Ivey, P.W.: *Principles of Marketing* (New York, 1921).

Kirby, Justin, and Paul Marsden (eds.): *Connected Marketing: The Viral, Buzz and Word of Mouth Revolution* (Oxford, 2006).

Krishnan, H. Shanker, and Dipankar Chakravarti: "Memory Measures for Pretesting Advertisements: An Integrative Conceptual Framework and a Diagnostic Template" in *Journal of Consumer Psychology* 8 (1:1999), pp. 1–37.

Levy, Sidney J.: "How New? How Dominant?" in R. Lusch and S. Vargo (eds.) *The Service-Dominant Logic of Marketing: Dialog, Debate, and Directions* (Armonk, 2006).

Nilsson, Göran B.: *Banker i brytningstid, A. O. Wallenberg i svensk bankpolitik 1850–1856* [*Banks in Changing Times: A. O. Wallenberg and the Swedish Banking Policy, 1850–1856*]. (Stockholm, 1981).

O'Brien, Danny: "Event Business Leveraging: The Sydney 2000 Olympic Games" in *Annals of Tourism Research* 33 (1:2006), pp. 240–261.

Pieters, Rik, and Michel Wedel: "Pretesting Advertising: Before the Rubber Hits the Road" in G. J. Tellis and T. Ambler (eds.), *The Sage Handbook of Advertising* (London, 2007).

Pine, B. Joseph II, and James H. Gilmore: "Welcome to the Experience Economy" in *Harvard Business Review* 76 (4:1998), pp. 97–105.

Ritchie, J.R. Brent: "Turning 16 Days into 16 Years Through Olympic Legacies" in *Event Management* 6 (2:2000), pp. 155–165.

Schneider, Tanja, and Steve Woolgar: "Technologies of Ironic Revelation: Enacting Consumers in Neuromarkets" in *Consumption Markets & Culture* (15:2012).

Shaw, Eric H., and D. G. Brian Jones: "A History of Schools of Marketing Thought" in *Marketing Theory* 5 (3:2005), pp. 239–281.

Simakova, Elena, and Daniel Neyland: "Marketing Mobile Futures: Assembling Constituencies and Creating Compelling Stories for an Emerging Technology" in *Marketing Theory* 8 (1:2008), pp. 91–116.

Smith, Michael F.: "Spotlight Events, Media Relations, and Place Promotion: A Case Study" in *Journal of Hospitality and Leisure Marketing* 12 (1/2:2005), pp. 115–134.

Vanden Abeele, P., and I. Butaye: "Pretesting the Effectiveness of Industrial Advertising" in *Industrial Marketing Management* 9 (1:1980), pp. 75–83.

Weld, Louis Dwight Harvell: "Marketing Functions and Mercantile Organization" in *American Economic Review* 7 (2:1917), pp. 306–18.

_____. *The Marketing of Farm Products* (New York, 1916).

Zauhar, John: "Historical Perspectives on Sport Tourism," in S. Hudson (ed.), *Sport and Adventure Tourism* (New York, 2003).

Zwick, Detlev, and Julien Cayla (eds.): *Inside Marketing: Practices, Ideologies, Devices* (Oxford, 2011).

Organizing the 1912 Games

Therese Nordlund Edvinsson

The 1912 Summer Olympics, officially known as the fifth Olympiad, were arranged in Stockholm, Sweden. The Games were associated with positive terms such as "the Sunshine Olympics," "the Happy Olympics," "the Swedish Masterpiece" and the first "Modern Olympics." It was a result of the unusually good Swedish weather throughout the competition. But the Olympics in Stockholm also put Sweden on the world map, in terms of becoming a successful model for future organizers. However, the work behind the scenes was easier said than done.[1]

This essay investigates the people behind the Games and their main preparations. How were the Olympic Games in Sweden organized? What were the difficulties and opportunities? Who were the men and women involved in this type of work? In order to answer these questions, this article focuses on the Swedish Organizing Committee, which was responsible for initiating the Olympic Games in Stockholm.

It was not until the end of the nineteenth century that the Swedish sports movement began to emerge. In a sporting calendar from 1894 229 sports clubs are listed in the country with about 21,000 athletes.[2] Researcher Eva Olofsson says that one cannot see sport as a mass movement in Sweden during the early 1900s, but rather as a "men's movement."[3] Women were seldom represented as athletes or board members. Sport was considered to be particularly a recreational form for the male elite. As sports historian Leif Yttergren pointed out, it was mainly men from the middle and upper classes who practiced sport in Stockholm.[4] Within the Swedish labor movement resistance against sport dominated, as it was associated with militarism and regarded as an upper class amusement. In addition, physical activities were believed to require discipline and education, a threat to the class struggle.[5]

The Swedish sports movement was initiated by the upper and middle classes. Not least, the National Sports Federation and the Central Association for the Promotion of Sport were dominated by industrialists, military officers and senior officials.[6] Colonel Viktor Balck (1844–1928) was a driving force behind the hosting of the Olympic Games in Sweden. He had been an original member of the International Olympic Committee (IOC) since 1894 and had established good contacts with the IOC president, Baron Pierre de Coubertin (1863–1937). In Sweden, Viktor Balck is often called "the father of Swedish sports." He combined a military profession with a career as a senior sports official. He founded the sports magazine *Tidning för Idrott* in 1881 and was the initiator of several sports clubs in Stockholm. However, Balck was not the only Swede on the IOC. Count Clarence von Rosen (1867–1955) also earned membership. Historian Jan Lindroth says that Viktor Balck contributed to the fact that the Olympic Games were arranged in Stockholm. The intention was to put Swedish interests in focus as a way of promoting the country through its sport.[7] Viktor Black's international networks enabled these plans. He also had a nationalist motive, where the aim was to win worldwide recognition. Critics argued that Sweden was far too remote and not sufficiently equipped to be awarded such a great competition.[8]

However, Viktor Balck was convinced that Stockholm could handle the enormous organizational work that was needed in order to arrange a competition of this caliber. In international terms, Sweden was at that time a rather anonymous country in the north. Some advantages were considered to favor Stockholm over Berlin, which also showed interest in hosting the Games. Sweden had hosted the Nordic Games on several occasions, an international sports event focused primarily on winter sports.[9] Another advantage was that Swedish athletes had performed well in previous Olympic Games. Moreover, de Coubertin, spoke in favor of Sweden as a host country. In a speech he revealed his high expectations when he guaranteed "perfect success," provided that Stockholm refrained from imitating the London Olympics in 1908. His recipe for success was to make it simple, dignified and intimate by pulling down costs and not creating an excessively large and unmanageable competition program.[10]

Organizing the Olympic Games in Stockholm demanded coordination, structure and resources. One problem was that both capital and a stadium were missing when Stockholm was planning for a possible Olympic Games. It led the leading figure Viktor Balck and his colleagues to establish a large organization where various people worked together in order to reach the final goal.

The Swedish Organizing Committee

According to previous research the Stockholm Olympics established an effective organization.[11] However, earlier research has not discussed why it was well organized or how it can be related to previous Games. The delegation in Stockholm was keen to make the Games successful. They felt that it was especially important that the judges were objective and fair. In prior Games, the judges were criticized for being biased.[12] Avery Brundage (1887–1975) was a contestant who represented the United States in the pentathlon and decathlon events. Later Brundage became eventually the IOC President. He felt that the event in Stockholm was characterized by precision and formal correctness.[13] Preparations for the Games began early in 1909 when the Swedish Organizing Committee (SOC) was established. The first meeting was held on October 7, 1909. The Committee consisted of three representatives and one deputy from the National Sports Federation and The Central Association for the Promotion of Sport. The Swedish Organizing Committee was responsible for the finances and general management. Over time it grew to 17 members, who were divided into the executive committee, finance section, program section, medal and badge section (reception section) and a technical section (see organization chart, introduction). All the sections had different work tasks. For example, the technical section was responsible for contest rules, amateur and disqualification issues and matters relating to judges, officials, coaches and sports equipment.[14] The finance division worked with support for various sports committees, travel expenses and the purchase of materials. They had overall responsibility for cost issues and legal matters. All sections were subordinate to the Organizing Committee and did not act independently. Sixteen special subcommittees were established for the various sports (for example swimming and shooting). In total there were about 187 members/commissioners.[15] Decisions taken in the special subcommittees would be "subject to the Organizing Committee, which had the final word and determination."[16] Four additional subcommittees worked with questions such as accommodation, recreation, advertising and reception of the media. They had 47 members.

The elected chairman of the Swedish Organizing Committee was president Viktor

Balck and industrialist J. Sigfrid Edström was vice president. The Swedish Crown Prince Gustaf Adolf was asked to become honorary president. The crown prince was genuinely interested in sports and was believed to have influence in important circles. Gustaf Adolf led the majority of the negotiations in the committee.[17] Initially, Nore Thisell acted as general secretary until May 1910, when Kristian Hellström accepted this duty. Other members were also elected to the committee, such as director Bernhard Burman, office manager Frits af Sandeberg and Captain Eric Frestadius. Doctor Astley Levin, Lieutenant Gustaf Gustafsson Uggla and Count Clarence von Rosen were deputy board members. Director Charles Dickson, merchant Frederick Löwenadler, undersecretary of State Walter Murray, Colonel Sven Hermelin, Captain and gentleman of the bedchamber Oscar Holtermann, the undersecretary of State Sigfrid Nathanel Linnér and the clerk/publisher Harald Sohlman were co-opted members.

Viktor Balck was very involved. Besides his membership on the Organizing Committee, he was also the chairman of three special subcommittees. In an article written by researcher Björn Gäfvert it emerges that military power was widespread among the subcommittees. Eleven of the sixteen subcommittees had a member of the Armed Forces as chairman, but with rather low ranks, such as captains and cavalry captains.[18]

Each member had specific assignments. For instance, Mr. Burman and Mr. af Sandeberg investigated the financial issues related to the committee's assets and payments.[19] Industrialist Sigfrid Edström (1870–1964) was a successful network builder and doors were opened wherever he went. His contacts with sportsmen all around the world favored the organizing of the Games in Stockholm. As an industrialist, he was knowledgeable and delegated to persons whom he perceived as competent. He was a professional manager at ASEA (today ABB) from 1903 to 1933 and chairman of the board from 1934 to 1949.[20] As a prominent

The Organizing Committee. Standing from left, Astley Levin, Erik Frestadius, Sven Hermelin, Kristian Hellström, Gustaf Uggla, Nore Thisell and Oscar Holtermann. Sitting from left, Bernhard Burman, Viktor Balck, Crown Prince Gustaf Adolf, Sigfrid Edström, Frits af Sandeberg and Sigfrid Linnér (postcard, National Sports Museum).

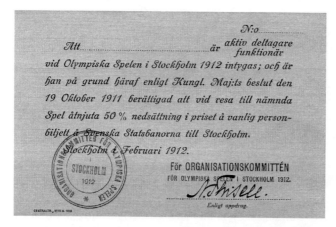

This card that gave the holder a 50 percent discount on the train journey to the Olympic Games (National Sports Museum).

Crown Prince Gustaf Adolf, left, in conversation with a correctly dressed official in the Olympic Stadium (SCIF photo collection).

figure in Swedish business, Edström can probably be best described as a "doer" and an entrepreneur who was one step ahead of everyone else. Outside the working group Edström was engaged in both industrial associations and clubs of various kinds. His sporting interest was extensive and he influenced both the Swedish and the international sports movement. Later he became the president of the IOC (1946–1952) and when he retired he was succeeded by his good friend Avery Brundage.[21]

Sigfrid Edström was also a driving force in recruiting Kristian Hellström (1880–1946) as the general secretary of the Swedish Organizing Committee. Hellström had a past as a prominent runner. Among other things, he won a bronze medal in the extra Games in Athens 1906. After the Games in Stockholm, Hellström became the General Secretary of the International Association of Athletics Federations (IAAF) from 1913 to 1914.

So, what had these gentlemen on the Swedish Organizing Committee in common? The majority belonged to the upper class or had a bourgeois background. Most of the members were middle-aged men, apart from 30-year-old Kristian Hellström, who was considered a young man in the group. Unlike the other members, he had been employed. In their professional lives, the majority of the members had senior positions in companies and other authorities. Several of the men had a past as an athlete at an elite level. Sigfrid Edström set the Scandinavian record for running 150 meters in a time of 16.4 seconds (the record was held during the years 1891 to 1907). Clarence von Rosen was considered one of Sweden's most popular horse riders. He also competed in various sports like bandy (which he was responsible for introducing to Sweden) and lawn tennis, among many others.[22]

According to the source material and newspaper articles, the national organization unit that planned the Olympics 1912 gradually expanded. They recruited technical organizers, volunteers, committee members, judges, starters, timekeepers, supervisors, and so on. Many people on the various subcommittees performed unpaid work and received no compensation for travel and meetings. The unpaid work was done on a large scale. Participants and officials were forced to pay for their own train tickets when they traveled. However, they could get a 50 percent discount on the train journey if they showed a special card.[23]

Each and every committee considered both large and small matters. One such matter was the creating of special uniforms for officials. The men who were volunteers at the swimming competition would wear a uniform "consisting of dark blue, double-striped jacket, white flannel trousers and a straw hat."[24] The clothes were delivered by the exclusive department store NK in Stockholm. Viktor Balck had previously been very critical about how Swedes were dressed on the international sports scene. In Athens 1906, the Swedish athletes did not participate in the march but stayed in the stands. This was because Balck complained about their outfit.[25] He also set high standards for officials in Stockholm. Those who did not measure up were deselected. The Organizing Committee was keen to recruit the "right" men in the right place. There was a common belief among the Swedish delegation that the nation would perform better than any previous host countries. Perhaps this attitude towards discipline and order was a result of Balck's military background.

The Financing of the Games

Arranging the Stockholm Olympics required a large amount of money.[26] Personal networks contributed to obtaining financial resources. Many people behind the Games were influential in a number of areas. Ticket revenues were also an important source of income. Several contracts were established with business corporations.[27] The Swedish government gave support by providing multiple sports lotteries for the benefit of the Games. A helping hand came from private donations to the various sporting disciplines.[28] A lot of money was spent making an extravagant event. For instance, the final cost of building an arena (Stockholm's Olympic Stadium, mostly called Stadion) for the competitions was 1,187,880 Swedish kronor.

Issues Addressed by the Organizing Committee

The Organizing Committee held a total of 90 meetings and special subcommittees nearly 386 meetings. Overall, the minutes of the meetings provide a good insight into the topics discussed. The preparations for the Games resulted in several investigations. The main issues were finances, competition rules and preparations for the Swedish athletes.[29] The aim was to create a viable Olympic schedule. The national committee presented a number of drafts before initiating the Games. On several occasions the IOC rejected the drafts presented by the Stockholm committee. During a session in Budapest in 1911 the IOC, however, approved the program of competitions. The Olympic program grew larger than they had originally thought, which resulted in even more work that demanded a solution.[30] On the Swedish side the elected members wanted to avoid a chaotic situation with too many sports on the program.[31] The leading committee agreed that winter sports would not be included in the Summer Olympics. Much effort was devoted to convincing the various sports federations to participate in the Games. The Swedish Rowing Federation did not at first enter the competition, but later changed their minds, provided that they would receive funding for a trainer during 1911 and 1912 and that the committee would pay for their boats and other necessary equipment. Members of the committee had different views on this issue. Frits af Sandeberg did not want rowing as a part of the Olympic program, as he thought that the Swedish sportsmen were not good enough. Viktor Balck believed that Swedish rowing deserved "encouragement." He also claimed that they could get financing from individuals.[32] The discussions among the committee members were at times very lively. Sometimes they disagreed on which sports would be represented at the Olympic Games.[33] Sigfrid Edström argued for example that football (soccer) should be included, while Balck was against it.[34] Doctor Astley Levin claimed that there were already enough sports in the Olympic schedule. Anyhow, Edström was confident and got support from representatives in Norway, England and France when he appeared at the IOC session in Luxembourg 1910.[35] Finally Edström got his way. In Stockholm 1912, it was the fourth time football (soccer) was on the Olympic schedule.

According to the protocols each and every member apparently worked methodically. They were keen to represent Swedish sport in a good light. However, some issues were more important in the discussions among the members. The minutes show that the members often discussed the question of the coach, who would be recruited, and how to introduce new talent to be trained. The Swedish committee requested special coaches from abroad. The Englishman Charles Hurley was appointed as coach of both the Swedish swimming and football (soccer) teams.[36] Another good example is the Swedish American coach Ernie Hjertberg who was recruited as a trainer for the Swedish athletes. Advertisements for a wrestling coach were inserted in the German sports magazine *Illustrierte Sportzeitung*.[37] Eventually, of the applicants, the Finn Ivar Toumisto was considered to be best qualified to train the Swedish team. He received a salary of 750 Swedish kronor a year.[38] The Organizing Committee was in constant contact with all the subcommittees. The issue of international or Swedish judges was a major discussion point. Each subcommittee had different views on the matter. The Wrestling Committee and the Fencing Committee preferred foreign judges, while the Athletics Committee suggested only Swedish judges.[39] When they finally took a decision, they suggested having only Swedish men as judges and officials. In special cases, foreign judges were appointed. Otherwise, there was an international jury present at some individual sports.[40]

Other issues that were aired among the members concerned more practical issues. For example, they discussed the planning of health care assistance, ticket arrangements and guards.[41] Technical issues were also discussed at board meetings. Before the swimming competitions the delegation wanted to put up a structure where the spectators could sit and watch the event. However, the sources reveal that they had to seek permission, which was quite complicated. They were asked to write letters to various Swedish authorities. In some cases the members' networks came to play a crucial role in the contacts with the authorities in the capital.

Viktor Balck appears in the protocol as an authoritarian and a conservative person. He had a clear idea of what was the best for the Games and wanted for example only to have male gymnasts in performances. Viktor Balck did not like the fact that the committee's ideas leaked to the media.[42] He did not want the press to monitor any questions before they were adopted and implemented by the Organizing Committee. Balck was also keen to enlist more deputy members and honorary members, something that the other members more or less wanted to prevent. For Balck, it seems to have been important to recruit more people to the delegation, only as an expression of loyal friendship or personal gratitude. He was eager that count Clarence von Rosen should be involved in committee work. The other members were less enthusiastic. Balck felt forced to explain why von Rosen should become a deputy member. He sent a special letter to the other committee members, in which he spoke in favor of von Rosen's merits. Clarence von Rosen had a strong reputation in international sport and through his position on the IOC had contributed so that Stockholm could arrange the Olympic Games. According to Balck, von Rosen always worked in favor "of Swedish sport." He also claimed in his letter that Clarence von Rosen had offered his "own cash" to enrich Swedish sport. Furthermore, he stated that von Rosen felt disappointed and "mistreated" when he had not been elected chairman. According to sources, Clarence von Rosen himself appeared to have struggled with feelings of alienation, when he felt that he had not received enough support for his efforts in the Swedish world of sport.[43]

Sigfrid Edström was not always keen to support Victor Balck's ideas, although he appreciated his opinions. Edström hesitated to appoint too many "honorary members," while the member Frits af Sandeberg was against such appointments for "reasons of principle." Balck insisted on recruiting merchant Frederick Löwenadler on the grounds that he had done so much for Swedish sport, particularly as a contributor to the rowing competitions.

The Swedish Reception Committee on board the S.S. *Finland,* home of the American Olympic troupe (*Den femte olympiaden i ord och bild,* p. 362).

The other members responded that they would prefer other qualifications than being a financier in order to become a member. Eventually, Viktor Balck was satisfied, when both von Rosen and Löwenadler became deputy and co-opted members, respectively.[44]

Subordination to the IOC

The Swedish Organizing Committee had to submit to the IOC on a range of issues. Therefore the committee had regular contact with international members and especially the President of the IOC, Baron Pierre de Coubertin, who kept a watchful eye on the Games. The committee in Stockholm was also forced to report "every fourteenth day" about how their work was progressing.[45] Beyond this, they also had to stay in contact with various committees in foreign countries. The IOC President Pierre de Coubertin sometimes sent letters to the organization in Stockholm, in which he put forward proposals. For example, he would not recommend the members in Stockholm to draw up rules for the decathlon, as he felt that the IOC would take over the matter.[46] Coubertin was also eager to make suggestions concerning the design of the Games. He wanted to institute awards for the best performance in game shooting, mountain climbing and air sports. The committee in Stockholm agreed to this, with the exception of air sports. Sigfrid Edström claimed that professional pilots should not get these types of awards.[47] The committee members in Stockholm were generally not afraid to express their views on various issues; on the contrary, the IOC made proposals on several occasions which were dismissed by the Organizing Committee. The English commissioner Theodore Cook suggested that Stockholm should use the London Olympia diploma as a template when giving awards to the athletes.[48] In Stockholm they had a few reservations and refused to support this opinion. The American professor William Sloane demanded that the competitions in Stockholm should be called off on Sundays for religious reasons.[49] However, no one from the Swedish delegation accepted this suggestion. The committee members thus acted with self-confidence and authority in most questions. There was no doubt that the people behind the Games in Stockholm wanted to implement their own ideas. The Swedes also criticized Pierre de Coubertin's idea of organizing "Concours d'art" (competitions in architecture, sculpture, painting, music and literature for unpublished works).[50] Coubertin insisted that sport was a way of educating men in both body and soul. He had a desire to combine art with sport, by including artistic competition.[51] The opposition from the Swedes was obvious; even Crown Prince Gustaf Adolf said that competitions in art were in appropriate. He received the support of several members. About thirty Swedish artists expressed negative views on this matter. On the whole, the artists felt that the idea of art combined with competition seemed ridiculous.[52] They suggested it was up to the IOC to initiate a competition for culture. Eventually, the competition of art was initiated. Surprisingly enough, Coubertin himself won a medal in literature when he competed under a pseudonym.

On the whole, the Organizing Committee in Stockholm had sole responsibility for organizing the Olympic Games. It was their task to fulfill their commitments and to coordinate all the bodies involved. The Swedish representatives also attended the IOC sessions in Luxembourg and Budapest, where they could argue for their lines of thought. The discussions at the international meetings were at times very heated. Viktor Balck often succeeded in convincing his critics.[53] Kristian Hellström recalled that Balck used rather drastic methods. At the session in Budapest 1911 Viktor Balck claimed that unless he got his way, Stockholm would decline to host the Games. According to press sources Coubertin immediately adapted after this threat.[54]

A Risk of Failure

The Swedish Organizing Committee's work has often been described as a model of efficiency. However, the Swedes struggled with bureaucratic devices that caused problems. The administration was the engine in the machinery, as they handled all the practical issues.[55] The man who led the secretariat was former sportsman Kristian Hellström. He applied for the post of General Secretary as he had good language skills in English and German. Hellström had a solid background as the head of the correspondence department at a Swedish trade office. He also mastered the art of stenography and typing. His main merit for claiming the new position was probably his post as Secretary of the sports club IF Sleipner 1897–1903, where he organized large sporting events with international athletes.[56] Hellström, however, hesitated a long time before accepting the new position as General Secretary. He even got as far as withdrawing his application, because he felt discouraged due to Viktor Balck's cynical criticism. For his part, Balck believed that none of the candidates for the secretarial position was "suitable." Balck believed that the work demanded authority. A General Secretary should, according to Balck, have solid experience and not be too young. He therefore suggested Baron Sven Hermelin as a possible General Secretary of the Swedish committee.[57] Edström was among those who supported Hellström. He became very annoyed about Hellström's weak behavior and wrote in a letter:

> You can also very well understand that I cannot personally be extremely satisfied with your actions. You apply for a job and then return your application, just when we have recruited you. I was really expecting some explanations from you, before this letter was written.[58]

Edström argued that Hellström had misunderstood the criticism. According to an employment contract Kristian Hellström accepted a salary of 5000 Swedish Crowns a year. As a part of the contract he was expected to work solely in accordance with the employer's instructions. This meant that he had to pay his own expenses to fund a three-month stay in France, to learn the French language and foreign sporting conditions.[59] Hellström had to learn all he could about international sports management before planning the Olympics.

My findings suggest that ongoing conflicts threatened the planning of the Games. In fact, the preparations before the Olympics in Stockholm were quite a struggle. For example, Kristian Hellström experienced that he was being used in a power struggle within the organization. As a loyal employee he was expected to behave like a puppet and do what the others wanted. Hellström had difficulties in accepting these special working conditions. Sigfrid Edström had noticed that Kristian Hellström could not handle the tasks. In a letter Edström wrote:

> Then I noticed with concern that Mr. Hellström had been a little nervous. I want with a few lines to warn Mr. Hellström to not overstrain yourself. You must every day take a proper walk. You have to eat regularly and you must not work more than a maximum of 9 hours per day. A man cannot cope with more than a certain quantum of work. When this quantum is used up your working capacity is as well. Now we will keep Mr. Hellström as our General Secretary during the whole Olympic Games and it is therefore absolutely important that you save yourself.[60]

The general secretary of the Organizing Committee, Kristian Hellström, at work in his office (*Den femte olympiaden i bild och ord*, p. 356).

However, Edström's supporting words did not comfort Kristian Hellström, who replied with a sense of anger. He questioned the direction of the Organizing Committee. He believed that the bureaucratic system was time consuming; yet again he was considering leaving the job. As a General Secretary, Hellström felt that it was impossible for a single person to keep up this "giant machinery" on his own. He tried to explain his workload for Edström:

> To watch over and deal with 12 special subcommittees and be present at their meetings, to be General Secretary for the Organizing Committee and two special subcommittees. In all, care for correspondence both within the country and with several dozen other countries, and write to all the Swedish people in these. To lead the press and promotional work, and superintend the training and also be obliged to take care of its administration, phone calls and visits from everywhere.[61]

Kristian Hellström criticized the fact that he was forced to write reports on his commitments to the committee every day. He feared that the Olympic Games in Stockholm would become a giant fiasco. Hellström felt constrained by the formal work process, even though he had by his own admission tried to follow the instructions from his employer. He claimed he needed more support to carry out the work in time. In addition, Hellström said that the work entailed irregular working hours. His private life had been suffering and he had to eat out each and every day, which was very expensive. Living abroad in France for language training had resulted in a private debt, which set him back about 1200 Swedish Crowns.[62]

How did the other members respond to this behavior? Hellström's criticism grated in the large and hierarchical organization. He found it difficult to assert himself in this assembly, according to the letters. But somehow Kristian Hellström managed to express his views in a way so that the other members of the head committee could meet some of his wishes. They let him hire an assistant, and expanded the other staff. However, one must remember that Hellström could not operate freely because he had signed a contract where he promised "to perform every task, the Organizing Committee requires him to do."[63] Nevertheless, Hellström completed the work as General Secretary. He was also the secretary responsible for the advertising committee and the committee for track and field athletics. He also had influence in the subcommittees for the tug of war, modern pentathlon and swimming. Furthermore, Hellström was a member of the subcommittees for recreation and accommodation. Sigfrid Edström must have been pleased with his efforts, since he took him to the International Association of Athletics Federations when it was founded in 1913. The relationship between Hellström and Balck seems to have been far more problematic. Correspondence shows that they were continually involved in different types of conflicts. Hellström did not always meet the management's desire for precision and efficiency. Viktor Balck, for example, wrote a letter to Hellström when the IOC president Pierre de Coubertin had been "cruelly insulted" by the Swedish secretariat, which had printed an article by Coubertin in a brochure on the Olympic Games. Instead of quoting the Baron, they had reduced Coubertin's own words to a brief summary. They had to publish his text in its entirety; otherwise the Games in Stockholm could lose its reputation, claimed Balck angrily.[64]

Nationalism and Masculinity

In studying the archive material dealing with the Stockholm Olympics, it is obvious that "men" were in focus when it concerned the Olympic organization, as well as the active athletes. Erik Bergvall (later a director for the Olympic Stadium in Stockholm), wrote in an article that the Games in Stockholm were conducted by "the men who strove and worked to make way for the Swedish sports movement."[65] Men's work in the Olympic Games often referred to nationalism. For example, they spoke about the "Swedes' sacrifice" and the ability to manage information, which was alleged to distinguish them from other ethnic groups. By emphasizing the "Swedish character" or the "Swedes'" characteristics, they put emphasis on the nation of Sweden.[66] Nationalism was at this time widespread, not at least as a result of the dissolution of the union with Norway in 1905. By being a successful nation in sports and an excellent host country, Sweden would gain prestige in the rest of the world. The symbolism of Swedishness was constructed in the encounter with other nations, where the interplay of "us vs. them" generated competition. National identity was expressed in the team outfit, banners and other symbols. Kristian Hellström felt that the Games brought "nationalist frenzy" to Sweden, as the country was finally united. Sweden was no longer a political power, but through sporting success the country could strengthen its national identity and create its own place on the world map. Sport was used as a tool to induce community feeling. There was a certain nationalist approach to sport, which Viktor Balck took notice of, in his eagerness to spread the sports movement's message. Jan Lindroth says that Viktor Balck advocated a tough line against Norway in conjunction with dissolution of the union. This can be seen in the light of his manhood ideals and Social Darwinism.[67] The dark side of nationalism encouraged patriotic passion and aggressive self-assertion. Some researchers have chosen to liken the sports movement to a metaphorical warfare between states.[68] By competing against other countries in international competitions, nationalism creates a symbolic expression where achievement and success become a way of defending one's own country.

Sporting activities often included a clear power dimension marked by gender, class and ethnicity. In research, masculinity has often been associated with the physically strong body associated with power sports. But masculinity must also be understood in a much broader context. According to sociologist Raewyn Connell hierarchies exist among males. This means that some "masculinities" are more idealized and dominant than others.[69] Early on, sport reproduced a particular masculinity, represented by the white, heterosexual middle-class man. At the Games in Stockholm, the ideal was a hard and martial masculinity. Viktor Balck was convinced that sport could foster and shape strong men, a kind of moral superiority, in which the white man was regarded as far superior to other races. The colored athletes were considered to represent the barbaric savage, according to the sources. In Stockholm 1912, American runners of Indian ancestry competed in the Games. Athletes with other ethnicity than white were highlighted in the Swedish media and often commented on with pronounced notions of race and national identity.[70] In connection with the Olympic Games in St. Louis 1904 prejudices about other races had flared up. The IOC President Pierre de Coubertin considered these Games a failure, and he made reference to African Americans who participated for the first time in the Games. According to Coubertin "primitive people" should not practice "European sports." Coubertin had a perception that people of different ethnic background were not ready for Olympic competitions at this level.[71] This could be viewed as an expression of racism, but also of elitism, which characterized the Olympics at this time, when nationalism promoted westernized sports.

The Role of Women

It was mainly men who ruled, led and organized work preparing for the Games in Stockholm. However, there were some women present at the Olympic Games at various levels. The minutes state that the Organizing Committee advertised for a female assistant at the pre-start in 1910.[72] A certain Miss Mörk was mentioned in the records. Who she really was and what type of administrative work she performed remains a mystery. Unfortunately the sources do not reveal much about her past. She received a salary of 1,800 Swedish crowns during the two years she was employed. This can be compared with General Secretary Kristian Hellström, who received 10,000 Swedish crowns during his two years of work.[73]

In contrast to the men, the women and their work behind the Games are almost completely forgotten. Their work was rarely mentioned in the reporting of the contemporary press. The reason for this strict gender division of labor was due to the fact that it was not considered appropriate that women should engage in sports. The board of directors' work was done mainly by men in Sweden. The role of women was quite the opposite. They were expected to adorn the males and act like hostesses, not organize and lead. In a list of officials some female names are named, not primarily as athletes, but as instructors and hostesses.[74] There are not many names, but it suggests, however, that some women were involved in the work behind the Olympic Games. They usually had professional occupations, such as certified physical training instructors and physicians. For example, Doctor Hedvig Malmström was mentioned as the leader of the gymnastics squad. In connection with her name specific hostesses for the ladies were also mentioned. Representing the category of swimming/water polo was Lisa Regnell, a successful swimmer during the Games. She also led "the women's shows."[75] In the professional sphere Regnell worked as a music teacher and organist. She figured as a "name" and nothing more in the sources, which indicates that men's and women's contributions to the Games were valued in different ways. The male athletes' performances were perceived generally as more significant. Erik Bergvall summed up the Games in Stockholm with the words: "Those memorable days in the stadium and on the swim course, our feelings of connectedness, male power, and courage and action lust."[76] The culture of the male body was celebrated in the competitions. Women's efforts were hardly mentioned. This interest in and admiration for male athletes can be referred to the concept of homosociality. It can be described as a social, non-sexual preference for members of one's own sex. As a theoretical concept, homosociality can for example explain why women become invisible, while some types of males are accepted.[77] In Stockholm 1912, male athletes got more attention than female athletes. The National Sports Federation made badges and medals with the inscription: "Male sport, an inheritance of the fathers," a confirmation of men's dominance and women's exclusion.[78] This was of course not questioned, but regarded as natural, since the majority of the competitions were dominated by males only. Women's partici-

pation in the Olympics was regarded with some suspicion. The resistance to female athletes was found in the Swedish organization, but perhaps above all in the IOC, where President Pierre de Coubertin stood opposed to female athletes. A letter to Kristian Hellström reveals that Coubertin "greatly regret[ted] the fact" that females participated in swimming and tennis in Stockholm.[79] However, female swimming and diving made their Olympic debut in 1912. Coubertin's thoughts were not unusual; in fact he was supported by the feminist Rose Scott (1847–1925), who argued that female swimmers could attract voyeurism.[80] The objectification and sexualization of women's bodies were considered to inhibit the competitions. Generally speaking, women were believed not to understand sports. Sadly, the elite men of Swedish society continued to argue that women should be reduced to passive and wistful spectators, who paid tribute to the male athletes.[81]

The Swedish diver Lisa Rignell on a promotional postcard before the Olympic Games (postcard, National Sports Museum).

What Was Crucial for the Games?

The Swedish newspapers and even parts of the international press afterwards praised the General Secretary Kristian Hellström's hard work to coordinate the various committees. A magazine wrote that Hellström "has time for everything, knows everyone and everything, is liked by all, and brings life and movement."[82] Others chose to admire Viktor Balck and his efforts behind the Olympic Games in Stockholm. The sources described Balck as an impressive man with an eye like a hawk. He demanded much of his co-workers, often in a fierce way. He was a long-time friend of Pierre de Coubertin, despite their 20 years age difference. The older Balck was a patriot who fought for the well-being of Sweden, by fostering and producing something he believed was Swedish. Coubertin on the other hand romanticized ancient Greece. Through the Olympics he made his dream come true, by reviving the ancient Games.

Another important person who helped to realize the Games was Sigfrid Edström, who truly had the ability to bring out the best in his co-workers. His social skills made him popular. With a combination of confidence and competence he used different tricks to get results. As a networking leader he was skillful and open-minded. Other sources refer to the fact that the Stockholm Olympics also had the blessing of the Swedish court thanks to Crown Prince Gustaf Adolf's dedicated sports interest. The Crown Prince had a special authority and expertise knowledge which were of great benefit to the organizational work.[83] King Gustaf V was honored as an official guardian of the Games.

However, just one individual cannot be responsible for the success in Stockholm 1912. The Games required intense work and collaboration between the people planning the event in detail. The impression one gets, while investigating the sources, is that it was primarily a question of several people working towards the same goal, which was to put Stockholm on the map. They also had a vision of promoting Sweden as a tourist destination. Sport was believed to offer a new view of Scandinavia and proved an economic boost to Sweden. As the host nation it hoped to show its achievements and success in the competitions.

The dynamics of the networks cannot be underestimated. It was important to know the "right" people, not least in order to push through decisions. The enthusiasm among the members of the Swedish Organizing Committee seems to have been instrumental in implementing the Games. Creativity and dedication were important. The members of committees often worked carefully and tirelessly before final decisions were made. Several members were also occupied with professional careers, but clearly a lot of time was still spent on building a broad organization. Some combinations appear to have been particularly crucial. Erik Bergvall emphasized the importance of the National Sports Federation in Sweden, which generated coordination. He argued that the Stockholm Olympics had the potential to succeed because sports management already had a solid organizational structure in Sweden.[84] The committee in Stockholm also had plenty of time to construct a general program for the competitions and inspired the subcommittees to develop early Olympic schedules. This meant that the individuals behind the Games managed to keep their deadlines. The Organizing Committee also prepared the Swedish athletes before the Games started.[85] The collaboration with the IOC was also crucial, particularly when the Swedes were required to report about the ongoing work. They managed to make an Olympic program in good time, translated into English, Swedish, German and French. In Stockholm, the committee established international networks. At the same time the committee would also take the initiative in various issues without having to constantly adapt to the IOC. However, bureaucratic problems tended to hamper the Swedish organization, when the division of work was sometimes uneven and unfair. Many people worked as volunteers. Overall, the Swedish committee members were authoritarian men who liked to give clear orders and be obeyed. No wonder it caused internal conflicts. Those who worked at the lower levels in the hierarchical organization were usually overlooked or endured a very heavy workload. The Stockholm Olympics were better structured than previous Olympic Games. They had probably learned from their predecessors' failures. Some technical innovations were also used in the Swedish Games. For instance, they introduced the first use of automatic timing devices for the track events, the photo finish and a public address system.

However, the Olympic Games in Sweden cannot only be remembered as a remarkable combination of effective work and smooth operation. The historian Christian Widholm claims that the Stockholm Olympics can be described as militarized and aggressive, as they were dominated by members of the Armed Forces and produced Swedish nationalism. He means that one should exercise caution and not try to idealize the Games in Stockholm.[86] Leading a big sporting event of this type was clearly a class issue. There was also gender-segregation, where women's efforts were neglected.

This essay complements previous research and has studied the preparations for the Stockholm Olympics conducted by the Swedish Organizing Committee, whose members played an immense part in creating the Games. However, the source material used confirms the picture of a socially homogeneous group of men who collaborated to host the Olympic Games in Stockholm, while people outside this group were made invisible.

Notes

1. A doctoral thesis has been published on what journalists wrote about sport during the Olympics. See Widholm, *Iscensättandet av Solskensolympiaden* (2008). Previous research has mainly focused on the events and the statistics. Sylvén and Karlsson, *OS* (2008). Gäfvert, "Militären och Stockholm-solympiaden" (2009).

2. Norberg, *Idrottens väg till folkhemmet* (2004), p. 64.

3. Olofsson, "Likhet och särart: Om kvinnors motstrategier i svensk idrottsrörelse" (1990), p. 7.

4. Yttergren, *Täflan är lifvet* (1996), p. 77–90.

5. Widholm (2008), p. 56.

6. Lindroth, "Den svenska idrottsrörelsen och lingianismen 1850–1914" (2002), p. 202.

7. Lindroth, *Idrott för kung och fosterland* (2007), pp. 100–101.

8. Bratt, *J. Sigfrid Edström* (1953), p. 270.

9. Sylvén and Karlsson (2008), p. 38.

10. Bergvall, *The Olympic Games of Stockholm 1912* (1913), p. 9.

11. Hamilton, "Stockholm 1912" (2004), p. 57. See also Gäfvert (2009).

12. Sylvén and Karlsson (2008), p. 39.

13. Sylvén and Karlsson (2008), p. 40.

14. Arbetsordning antagen vid sammanträde med organisationskommittén den 17 maj 1910 (Stockholm 1909). Stockholmsolympiaden 1912, National Archives. See also Gäfvert (2009), p. 175.

15. Bratt (1953), p. 271.

16. Arbetsordning antagen vid sammanträde med organisationskommittén den 17 maj 1910 (Stockholm 1909). Stockholmsolympiaden 1912, National Archives.

17. Originally, there were six members, two deputy members and seven co-opted members and one General Secretary. See Bergvall (1912), p. 42. Dr. Astley Levin became a member after Bernhard Burman's death in 1912. See lista över organisationskommittén för 1912 års olympiska spel. Stockholmsolympiaden 1912, National Archives.

18. Gäfvert (2009), p. 176.

19. Protokoll, fördt vid sammanträde den 14 december 1909 med Organisationskommittén för Olympiska Spelen i Stockholm 1912, Stockholmsolympiaden 1912, National Archives.

20. Bratt (1953), p. 271. According to K.A. Bratt, Edström could be described as a General during the preparations for the Olympics. Edström was also president of the Working Committee and a member of the Building Committee.

21. Nordlund Edvinsson, *Broderskap i näringslivet* (2010).

22. Clarence von Rosen was the initiator of the Nordic Games, 1901, 1905. Together with Viktor Balck, he founded Idrottsparken 1895–1896. Clarence von Rosen was the editor and publisher of the sports magazine *Ny Tidning för Idrott* and *Nordiskt Idrottslif* (1898). Clarence von Rosen is often described as the person who introduced bandy in Sweden. In later life he was associated with National Socialism.

23. Kristian Hellström March 27, 1912, Korrespondens 3:4, Kristian Hellströms arkiv, National Archives.

24. I maj 1912 skriver Kristian Hellström till Herrar funktionärer vid Olympiska spelens simtäflingar, Korrespondens 3:4, Kristian Hellströms arkiv, National Archives.

25. Till Svensk Idrotts hyllningsnummer, till Viktor Balcks minne på 100-årsdagen av hans födelse April 25, 1944, Korrespondens 3:5, Kristian Hellströms arkiv, National Archives.

26. Sylvén and Karlsson (2008), p. 39.

27. Sylvén and Karlsson (2008).

28. Hamilton (2004), p. 58.

29. Bergvall (1912), p. 20.

30. Bergvall (1912), p. 20–21.

31. Hamilton (2004), p. 58

32. Protokoll June 6, 1910. Stockholmsolympiaden 1912, National Archives.

33. There was disagreement as to whether participants in the equestrian events would have to bring their own horses or if they could borrow a horse in Sweden. At the Budapest session in 1911, they solved the issue by deciding that contestants would bring their own horses to the Games in Stockholm. Those contestants who had no horse would have to borrow a suitable one. *Aftontidningen* June 1, 1911.

34. Protokoll August 8, 1910. Stockholmsolympiaden 1912, National Archives.

35. Protokoll October, 10, 1910. Stockholmsolympiaden 1912, National Archives.

36. Protokoll July 11, 1910. Stockholmsolympiaden 1912, National Archives.

37. Protokoll August 8, 1910. Stockholmsolympiaden 1912, National Archives.

38. Protokoll January 9, 1911. Stockholmsolympiaden 1912, National Archives.

39. Protokoll May, 17, 1910. Stockholmsolympiaden 1912, National Archives.

40. Olympiska spelen i Stockholm 1912: program och allmänna bestämmelser (1912). Stockholmsolympiaden 1912, National Archives

41. Protokoll October 31, 1910. Stockholmsolympiaden 1912, National Archives.

42. Protokoll May 17, 1910. Stockholmsolympiaden 1912, National Archives.

43. Letter from V. Balck to the Swedish Organizing Committee March 26, 1910. Stockholmsolympiaden 1912, National Archives.

44. Protokoll August 8, 1910. Stockholmsolympiaden 1912, National Archives.

45. Protokoll January 26, 1910. Stockholmsolympiaden 1912, National Archives.

46. Skrivelse från P. Coubertin. Avskrift i protokoll January 9, 1911. Stockholmsolympiaden 1912, National Archives.

47. See for example protokoll February 20, 1911, protokoll March 18, 1911. Stockholmsolympiaden 1912, National Archives.

48. Protokoll January 9, 1911. Stockholmsolympiaden 1912, National Archives.

49. *Aftontidningen,* June 1, 1911.

50. Hamilton (2004), p. 59.

51. Coubertin, "Konsttävlingarna 1912" (2001), p. 105.

52. Protokoll January 23, 1911. Stockholmsolympiaden 1912, National Archives

53. Till Svensk Idrotts hyllningsnummer, till Viktor Balcks minne på 100-årsdagen av hans födelse April 25, 1944, Korrespondens 3:5, Kristian Hellströms arkiv, National Archives. Balck, von Rosen, Edström and Hellström participated in the sessions at various times.

54. *Aftontidningen* June 1, 1911.

55. Letter from E. Bergvall to K. Hellström November 11, 1909, Korrespondens 3:5, Kristian Hellströms arkiv, National Archives.

56. Letter from Kristian Hellström to the Swedish Organizing Committee for the Olympic Games in Stockholm 1912, dated November 12, 1909, Korrespondens 3:5, Kristian Hellströms arkiv, National Archives.

57. According to a letter signed Viktor Balck to the Swedish Organizing Committee for the Olympic Games in Stockholm, dated January 4, 1910, Stockholmsolympiaden 1912, National Archives.

58. Letter from J.S. Edström to K. Hellström January 2, 1910, Korrespondens 3:5, Kristian Hellströms arkiv, National Archives

59. Contract between the Swedish Organizing Committee and Kristian Hellström May 1, 1910, Korrespondens 3:5, Kristian Hellströms arkiv, National Archives.

60. Letter from J.S. Edström to K. Hellström January 27, 1911, Korrespondens 3:5, Kristian Hellströms arkiv, National Archives.

61. Letter from K. Hellström to J.S. Edström January 29, 1911, Korrespondens 3:5, Kristian Hellströms arkiv, National Archives.

62. Letter from K. Hellström to J.S. Edström January 29, 1911, Korrespondens 3:5, Kristian Hellströms arkiv, National Archives.

63. Arbetsdelning, antagen vid sammanträde med organisationskommittén den 17 maj 1910, Stockholmsolympiaden 1912, National Archives.

64. Letter from V. Balck to K. Hellström January 22, 1912, Korrespondens 3:5, Kristian Hellströms arkiv, National Archives.

65. Bergvall (1912), p. 39.

66. Bergvall (1912), p. 39.

67. Lindroth (2007), p. 156.

68. Hylland Eriksen, *Etnicitet och nationalism* (1993), p. 139.

69. Connell and Wood, "Globalization and Business Masculinities" (2005), pp. 347–364.

70. Widholm (2008), pp. 42, 178.

71. Matthews and Marshall, *St. Louis Olympics*, 1904 (2003), p. 8. See also Schantz, "Pierre de Coubertin's 'Civilizing Mission,'" p. 53 f. http://www.la84foundation.org/SportsLibrary/ISOR/isor2008h.pdf

72. Protokoll August 8, 1910. Stockholmsolympiaden 1912, National Archives.

73. Bilaga 3, Organisationskommittén för Olympiska Spelen i Stockholm 1912. Beslutade, men icke likviderade utgifter November 1, 1910. Stockholmsolympiaden 1912, National Archives.

74. A list containing names of certified physical training instructors: Louise von Bahr, Anna Lundberg, Maria Palmqvist, Sigrid Hellström, Signild Arpi. See Förteckning Täflingsfunktionärer, Olympiska spelen i Stockholm 1912 (1912). Stockholmsolympiaden 1912, National Archives.

75. Förteckning Täflingsfunktionärer, Olympiska spelen i Stockholm 1912 (1912). Stockholmsolympiaden 1912, National Archives. The Swedish females who competed in diving had a male coach, who gave them instructions.

76. Bergvall, "Olympiska spelen i Stockholm 1912" (1912), p. 1.

77. For the concept of homosociality, see a summary, with included research, in Nordlund Edvinsson (2010), pp. 21–23.

78. Låftman, "Svensk idrott," *Ord och bild*, 5 häftet, 1912.

79. Letter from P. Coubertin to K. Hellström, in *Olympism* (2000), p. 447.

80. Hamilton (2004), p. 59.

81. Widholm (2008), p. 172.

82. *Hemmet* nr 22, 1912. See also *SVD* February 2, 1910

83. Willebrand, "Olympiska spelen i Stockholm," p. 43.

84. Bergvall (1912), p. 39.

85. Bergvall (1912), p. 10–11.

86. Widholm (2008), p. 258–259.

References

UNPUBLISHED SOURCES

Swedish National Archives: Stockholmsolympiaden 1912
Kristian Hellström's archive

NEWSPAPERS AND MAGAZINES

Aftontidningen
Hemmet
Svenska Dagbladet

UNPUBLISHED

Schantz, Otto. "Pierre de Coubertin's 'Civilizing Mission,'" p. 53 f.
http://www.la84foundation.org/SportsLibrary/ISOR/isor2008h.pdf

PRINT SOURCES

Bergvall, Erik. *The Official Report of the Olympic Games of Stockholm 1912* (Stockholm 1913).
_____. "Olympiska spelen i Stockholm 1912": *Svenska Riksförbundets Årsbok* 1912.
Bratt, K.A. *J. Sigfrid Edström. En levnadsteckning* (Stockholm 1953).
Connell, Raewyn, and Julian Wood. "Globalization and Business Masculinities," *Men and Masculinities* (2005) 7:4, pp. 347–364.
Coubertin, Pierre de. "Konsttävlingarna 1912" in Jan Lindroth (ed.), *Pierre de Coubertin och den olympiska rörelsen. En idrottsfilosofs texter i urval* (Stockholm 2002) pp. 105–108.
_____. *Olympism: Selected Writings* in Norbert Müller (ed.) (Lausanne 2000).
Gävert, Björn. "Militären och Stockholmsolympiaden" in Bo Lundström and Maria Gussarsson Wijk (ed.), *Den cyklande humanisten. Historiker, arkivman, stockholmare: en vänbok till Ulf Söderberg* (Stockholm 2009) pp. 173–185.
Hamilton, Ulf. "Stockholm 1912" in John E. Findling and Kimberly D. Pelle (eds.), *Encyclopedia of the Modern Olympic Movement* (USA 2004), pp. 57–63.
Hylland Eriksen, Thomas. *Etnicitet och nationalism* (Nora 1998).
Lindroth, Jan. "Den svenska idrottsrörelsen och lingianismen 1850–1914" in K Arne Blom and Jan Lindroth (ed.), *Idrottens historia. Från antika arenor till modern massrörelse* (Stockholm 2002) pp. 180–224.
_____. *Idrott för kung och fosterland. Den svenska idrottens fader Viktor Balck 1844–1928* (Stockholm 2007).
Låftman, Sven. "Svensk idrott," *Ord och bild*, 5 häftet, 1912.
Matthews, George and Sandra Marshall. *St. Louis Olympics*, 1904 (Chicago 2003).
Norberg, Johan R. *Idrottens väg till folkhemmet. Studier i statlig idrottspolitik 1913–1970* (Stockholm 2004).
Nordlund Edvinsson, Therese. *Broderskap i näringslivet. En studie om homosocialitet i Kung Orres Jaktklubb 1890–1960* (Lund 2010).
Olofsson, Eva. "Likhet och särart: Om kvinnors motstrategier i svensk idrottsrörelse" in Eva Olofsson and Anita Wester-Wedman (eds.), *Kvinnorna och idrotten* (Stockholm 1990) pp. 7–16.
Sylvén, Sune, and Ove Karlsson. *OS. Historia och statistik* (Stockholm 2008).
Widholm, Christian. *Iscensättandet av Solskensolympiaden. Dagspressens konstruktion av föreställda gemenskaper vid Stockholmsolympiaden 1912* (Stockholm 2008).
Willebrand, R.F. v. "Olympiska spelen i Stockholm," *Finsk Tidskrift* (July–August 1912).
Yttergren, Leif. *Täflan är lifvet. Idrottens organisering och sportifiering i Stockholm 1860–1898* (Stockholm 1996).

The Jewel in the Olympic Crown

The Training Preparations and Competitions in Athletics

Leif Yttergren

For many sports lovers athletics is the sport that has the highest status in the modern Summer Olympic Games. Athletics is surrounded by a special aura in the Olympic Games and many of the great Olympic stars come from athletics. Names like Jim Thorpe, Jesse Owens, Wilma Rudolph, Bob Beamon, Abebe Bikila, Florence Griffith-Joyner and Carl Lewis are forever inscribed in the annals of Olympic history. It was also for the athletics competitions that Sweden's Central Association for the Promotion of Sport had the Stockholm Olympic Stadium built at a cost that was enormous at the time.[1] It was a magnificent arena, designed by the Swedish architect Torben Grut. It was also to the Olympic Stadium that the general public was drawn to watch athletics, though not nearly to the extent that was desired by the organizers. In all the competitions (mainly athletics) at the Olympic Stadium were watched by just over 226,000 spectators, which can be compared to the just over 48,000 who watched the swimming competitions, the second most popular spectator sport. The members of the special Athletics Committee bear witness to the status of athletics in the Stockholm Olympic Games.

It was composed of a number of prominent people who were well known by some in posterity, amongst others Viktor Balck (chairman), Kristian Hellström, Leopold Englund, Sven Låftman and Carl Oskar Löwenadler.[2] Less well known is the fact that the person carrying the Swedish flag at the Stockholm Olympic Games was an athlete, Robert Olsson, a 29-year-old hammer thrower from Gothenburg. There is thus reason to take a closer look at athletics during the 1912 Stockholm Olympic Games. More specifically, the training preparations and competitions will be analyzed on the basis of the following questions: What events were included in the Olympic program? How did the athletes train for the competitions? Were the competitions special in any way and what was the view of the Swedish performance after the Games?

Something that arouses interest and fascination in present-day observers of athletics at the Stockholm Olympic Games is the technical innovations that were brought in and the awareness of the great importance of information. For the first time in Olympic history an "automatic timing and photo finish device" was used in the running events. It was invented by a Swedish engineer, R. Carlstedt. The timing was not fully automatic, but the finish was timed manually by one timing official for each runner. The photo finish camera, which was also new, was not used particularly often. Only on one occasion, in the 1,500 meters final, was it necessary to separate the athletes finishing second and third by means of a photo finish. According to the official report the new technology was not affected by any mishaps but "worked completely satisfactorily."[3] So that the press and the general public could see the results immediately "three-sided noticeboards with hoisting devices" were used. The results of the different competitors were put up on these to the delight of the spectators,

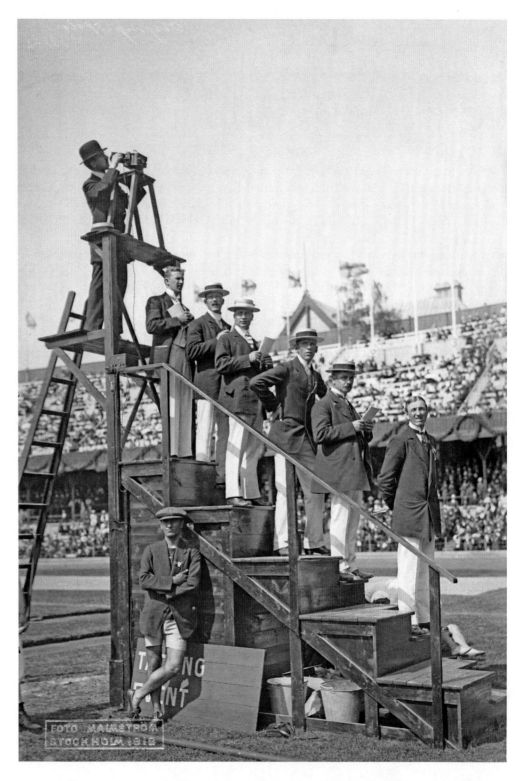

Timing officials and photographers (photograph by Axel Malmström, SCIF photo collection).

who could thereby follow the competitions before the age of modern loudspeaker technology.[4] The Stockholm Games were a model for coming Games in this area as well.

Contemporary Swedish Athletics

In 1912 athletics was an established sport in the ever more strongly budding sporting life of the Swedish capital. In terms of the number of people practicing the sport it was big from a quantitative point of view (in the statistics of the time wrestling and weightlifting were also included, oddly enough). Athletics was even the largest individual association sport in the country. Around 1912 approximately 75 percent of the National Sports Federation's associations had athletics in their programs and the sport thus had something of a special position in Swedish sporting life[5] (possibly in competition with Ling gymnastics, which dominated schools' sports education).

Athletics underwent a comprehensive and occasionally complicated organizational process at the beginning of the twentieth century. The Swedish Athletic Association was formed in 1895 and in 1903 became one of the associations in the newly formed Swedish Sports Confederation.[6] There was thus an organizational structure that was able to mobilize both human and financial resources for the rapidly growing athletics in Sweden, and these resources were activated for the 1912 Stockholm Olympic Games. Athletics attracted men with both power and money. In 1913 the International Association of Athletics Federations (IAAF) was founded, with the dynamic J. Sigfrid Edström as Chairman, a post he held until as late as 1946.[7] Edström later became IOC president (1946–1952). In his youth Edström was a good sprinter and athletics was close to his heart, and in his capacity as vice chairman of the mighty Organizing Committee he also had a central role in the organizing of the Stockholm Olympic Games.

Experience of international sports exchanges was, with a few exceptions, fairly limited among the Swedish athletes before the 1912 Games. For example, Sweden participated in the first Olympic Games in 1896 in Athens with just one participant, the athlete Henrik Sjöberg from Stockholm's Amateur Association. However, Swedish involvement gradually increased as interest in the Olympic Games increased in Sweden and abroad. The exception that confirms the rule is the Olympic Games in St. Louis, Missouri, in 1904, where no Swedes took part. The long and costly journey constituted the main obstacle.[8]

On the other hand, a real effort was made in connection with the "extra Olympic Games" in Athens in 1906 and Sweden took part with an athletics squad consisting of a dozen athletes. They were very successful and won all of 11 medals, whereby the country's position within the world of athletics was considerably strengthened. Sweden was the next best nation after the superpower of athletics, the USA. Several of the participants in the Swedish squad were all-round athletes, in the sense that they competed in several events, but the time when this was possible would soon be a thing of the past. Specialization in individual events was becoming stronger and stronger as competition increased and was necessary to be able to keep up with the international development of results and records. This was noticeable in the 1912 Stockholm Olympic Games and has continued ever since.

In the 1908 London Olympic Games the Swedish squad had more than doubled. In spite of this, successes were conspicuous by their absence and those taking part never reached their normal level, and on the whole the London Olympic Games were a big failure for Swedish athletics.[9] The performance was evaluated afterwards and the Athletic Association came to the conclusion that Swedish athletics must change strategy and direction in order to achieve success at the Olympic Games in Stockholm. It was decided to focus on three things:

- specialization in individual events at the expense of all-round ability
- intensification of training under the leadership of a competent trainer
- standardization of the rules and regulations.[10]

The Battle Over the Athletics Program

Determining the athletics program at the Stockholm Olympic Games was not without its problems. Two different views of the function and benefits of sport confronted each other. One of the views had its roots, to put it simply, in Ling gymnastics and the other in competitive sport. These different views came to characterize the discussion about what the program should look like and resulted in a number of compromises. Moreover, two demands were made. Firstly, that the athletics should be held for a total of eight days, that is to say a highly compressed program timewise. This demand was almost met: the competitions went on for ten days, between July 6 and July 15, the so-called Olympic week. Secondly, the events should be practiced in all the competing countries. This demand was not fully met either, and that will be discussed in a few pages. Furthermore, in the same Lingian spirit, the Swedish organizers were of the opinion that "a place of honor should be given to those sports that particularly demanded all-round training on the part of the athlete."[11]

The athletics competitions were thus begun on July 6 with throwing the javelin,

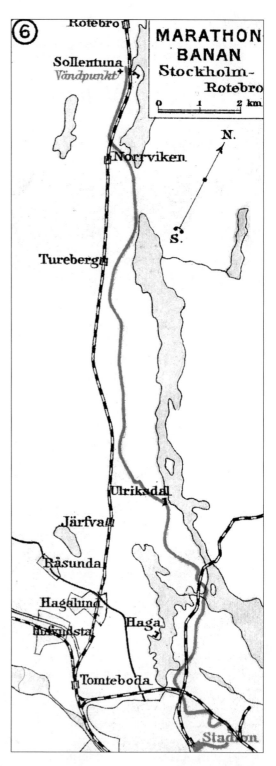

The Olympic marathon course (National Sports Museum).

best hand, and running 100 meters and came to an end with the relays on July 15. The much talked about marathon race on July 14 gathered a lot of spectators both in the Olympic Stadium and along the course.

To satisfy the demand for all-roundedness, the organizers decided to give priority to the pentathlon and decathlon, team events and throwing with both the left and the right hand in the throwing events. This Swedish passion for all-roundedness bore fruit in the hunt for medals. In the decathlon the Swedes Hugo Wieslander and Charles Lomberg managed to win the silver and bronze medals, respectively, after the outstanding American Jim Thorpe, who was hailed in the press: "America, the world, has never before had such an all-round sportsman."[12] Thorpe also won the pentathlon ahead of the Norwegian Ferdinand Bie and the American Jim Donahue. The pentathlon consisted of the long jump, javelin, 200 meters, discus and 1,500 meters. The event was taken away after the 1924 Paris Olympic Games.[13]

Events that were removed from the athletics program in Stockholm were, amongst others, "antique discus throwing." It was considered to be too difficult for the judges to assess, as other assessment criteria than the length of the throw were included. Furthermore, events where "the form" was a deciding factor in the assessment were rejected. At one stage it was thought that the "straddle jump" from gymnastics would be included, but the event was removed from the program as it was considered too "Scandinavian."[14] There was no discussion, to judge from the minutes, or in the media about whether women should be allowed to take part in athletics in the Stockholm Olympic Games. The exclusion of women was obviously self-evident and this was the case up until the Olympic Games in Amsterdam in 1928. Women continued to be excluded from longer running events up until the 1960s.[15]

What was the final athletics program then? It can be divided up into five different categories: running, jumping, throwing, combined events and walking.

Running:
  (a) individual: 100, 200, 400, 800, 1,500, 5,000 and 10,000 meters, marathon, 110 meters hurdles, cross country — approximately 12,000 meters.[16]
  (b) team: relay 4 × 100 meters, 4 × 400 meters, team event 3000 meters where each country could have five participants and the results of the best three were counted.
Jumping: high jump with and without a run-up, long jump with and without a run-up, triple jump and pole vault.
Throwing: Discus, both best hand and right and left hand, javelin (Swedish grip), both best hand and right and left hand, shot putt both best hand and left and right hand, hammer.
Combined events: pentathlon and decathlon.
Walking: 10,000 meters.[17]

Athletics Rules

After having agreed on the athletics program the laborious work of trying to achieve consensus regarding the rules for the competitions began. They were different from country to country and this caused dissension at international competitions. The organizing country clearly had the right of interpretation at the Olympic Games. One question that caused intense discussion was the apparently eternal controversy over how a false start should be judged in the sprint distances. Some demanded that those making a false start should be punished; others thought that it was wrong to punish, and this was also the decision, a decision that was considered to be a good one after the Games. Other questions that led to discussion were amongst other things the complex points system in the decathlon.[18]

After the Games the Swedish organizers received criticism from other countries because the athletics program had prioritized "Swedish interests." The critics had in mind here that in the spirit of Per Henrik Ling, the father of Swedish gymnastics, the throwing events were done with both the left and the right hand.[19] How did things go then in these competitions? Did the Swedes have an advantage? In throwing the javelin with both the left and right hand, the Finns Julius Saaristo, Valnö Siikaniemi and Urho Peltonen took a triple victory. In throwing the discus with both the right and the left hand the Finns Armas Taipale and Elmer Niklander took the gold and silver medals ahead of the Swede Emil Magnusson. However, in the shot put with both the right and left hand the USA managed to grab the first and second places before a Finnish shot putter. Obviously the Finnish representatives in particular benefited from the throwing events being both with the left and right hand, not the Swedes. There were also events in throwing the javelin, the shot put and throwing the discus with one's best hand and then there was no Nordic superiority. It is true that in the javelin, best hand, Eric Lemming from Gothenburg won with 60.64 meters, just before the Finn Saaristo and the Hungarian Miklos Kovács, but in the shot put the USA took a triple victory and in the discus the Finn Armas Taipale won ahead of the Americans Leslie Byrd and James Duncan.[20] The throwing competitions were clearly a success from the point of view of results. The Swedish sport leader Sven Hermelin writes in the book *Den femte olympiaden* that in the throwing competitions the results were "astounding," with many broken world records.

Konstantin Tsiclitiras of Greece, winner of the standing long jump at 3.37 meters (photograph by Axel Malmström, SCIF photo collection).

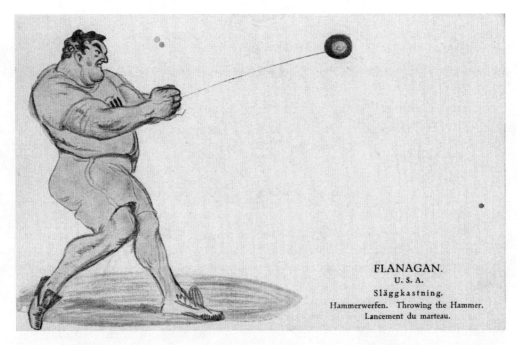

FLANAGAN.
U. S. A.
Släggkastning.
Hammerwerfen.   Throwing the Hammer.
Lancement du marteau.

Promotional postcard of Irish American hammer thrower John Flanagan, who had dominated the event since the late 1890s and won three Olympic gold medals (1900, 1904 and 1908) and set 15 world records. He did not, however, compete in Stockholm 1912 (postcard, National Sports Museum).

The rules and regulations for athletics comprised a total of ten pages, and these were distributed to every athlete in the form of a "book in waistcoat pocket format." The instructions for the marathon may serve to illustrate. What stands out for a present-day observer is both the doctor's examination just before the start and the fact that doping was obviously a problem even then. There were three paragraphs, of which the last one dealt with the drug issue:

(a) The marathon race will be held on the roads, starting and finishing in the Olympic Stadium.
(b) Every entry must be accompanied by a doctor's certificate regarding the entrant's state of health, and immediately before the start the participants are also obliged to undergo a doctor's examination performed by the Swedish Organizing Committee's official doctor, who will accept or reject the entrant's participation.
(c) Competitors may not — upon pain of immediate disqualification — either at the start or during the race take so-called drugs.[21]

The Athletes

As has been mentioned, athletics was easily the largest sport from the point of view of the number of people competing in the Stockholm Olympic Games and it interested many foreign athletes. Participants from 27 countries in all were attracted to the competitions. What is most striking is that the early Olympic Games were important for North America and above all European countries. There were only four countries from other parts of the world. They were Chile, Japan, South Africa and Australia, and they had relatively few participants.[22]

Countries taking part in athletics in the 1912 Olympic Games in Stockholm divided up by continent:

Europe: Austria, Hungary, Germany, Sweden, Great Britain, Serbia, Switzerland, Russia, Portugal, Norway, Luxembourg, Italy, Holland, Greece, France, Finland, Denmark, Bohemia, Belgium, Turkey, Iceland.
North and South America: USA, Chile, Canada.
Asia: Japan.
Oceania: Australasia (Australia and New Zealand competing together).
Africa: South Africa.

As far as the size of the athletics squads is concerned, Sweden, the USA and Great Britain were in a class of their own, with 118, 109 and 71 participants, respectively. Sweden's neighboring Nordic countries sent relatively small athletics squads: Norway 21, Finland 22 and Denmark 15.[23]

All of 841 athletes were entered for the athletics competitions, but of these only 556 started, or 66 percent. Many did not give notice that they were not going to turn up, which led to some odd situations. Thus there was just one lone runner who ran in the first heat of the 100 meters.[24] The 100 meters attracted the largest number of starters, with 79 runners, followed by the marathon with all of 68 participants and the 200 meters with 64. In most events the number of participants was decidedly lower. For example, there were 29 participants in the "high jump with a run-up," 24 in the javelin, best hand, and 22 in the triple jump.[25]

The powerful Organizing Committee really committed to athletics. They even looked for athletes among the many Swedes who had emigrated to the USA and who still had Swedish citizenship. The Swedish Americans could register via The Swedish Gymnastic and Athletic Union of America. The association organized qualifying competitions in the USA via "The Selection Committee for Swedish Americans for the Olympic Games in Stockholm in 1912." One of the Swedish Americans selected caused debate and irritation in the USA. The marathon runner Alexis Ahlgren was a member of an American sports association, which was considered inappropriate, even unpatriotic. He should have been in a Swedish American association, in the opinion of the person in charge in the USA. This person wrote to the secretary of the Athletics Committee and Organizing Committee, Kristin Hellström: "I am particularly familiar with his reprehensible manipulations out here, where he has been unpatriotic enough to represent American interests instead of those of his own country."[26]

Three Swedish Americans were selected in all in athletics. Swedish–Americans also took part in other sports, amongst other things in wrestling. The journey to Stockholm and other expenses were covered by collections made among Swedish Americans — a Swedish gymnastics association in New York, for example, collected money. The Organizing Committee overlooked Ahlgren's "unpatriotic" behavior and he was included in the Swedish squad. Together with another participant, John Eke, he left New York for Sweden on April 10, 1912.[27]

The Swedish Americans did well in the Games and well justified their presence in the old homeland. The "unpatriotic" Alexis Ahlgren was the only one of the three who did not win a medal. He took part in the marathon, but was forced to drop out in the record heat, a fate he shared with many other runners. Erik Almlöf, originally from Stockholm, finished third in the triple jump with the fine result of 14.17 meters. The third Swedish American, John Wictor Eke, represented a Stockholm club, but was born on the island of Öland. Eke won an individual bronze in cross country running and a gold in the team event.[28]

The Organizing Committee's commitment to athletics was also noticeable in the allocation of money to the various sports. Athletics was given high priority. It received money for trainers, training and materials far in excess of what the other sports received:

Table 1. Costs for Trainers and Participants (Training Costs) for Different Sports Before and During the Stockholm Olympic Games (Kronor)

Sport	Trainer (Salary and Traveling Expenses)	Participants
Athletics	35,666	32,894
Wrestling	10,040	5,933
Cycling	440	5,696
Football	2,838	10,006
Fencing	750	304
Tennis	1,950	519
Modern pentathlon	825	1,393
Rowing	716	12,790
Swimming	5,777	5,478

Source: Bergvall (ed.), *V. Olympiaden* (1913), pp. 41.

Training and Ernie Hjertberg

With the 1912 Stockholm Olympics approaching the stage was set for Swedish athletics' great revenge after the failure in London four years earlier. Decisive action was taken: national honor was at stake. The Athletics Committee not only recruited participants from home and abroad, but the athletics trainer was also to be a foreign force, someone who could lift the Swedish athletes to much longed-for heights.

The Athletics Committee began its work on January 27, 1910, two and a half years before the Olympic Games. The first task consisted of getting a foreign trainer for the Swedish squad. The Board of the committee thought that the Swedish athletes had done what they could, "but that a lot of work still remains before we are on the same level as the foremost sporting nations," and here the new trainer would fill a function.[29] Adverts were put in foreign sports magazines:

Trainer
The Swedish Olympic Council has decided to engage a fully efficient trainer for track and field events. Only those with expert knowledge and experience, and absolutely competent to supervise, advise and manage athletes need apply. The Trainer is anted during June–September 1910, May–September 1911, and April–July 1912.
Application stating conditions and all further particulars to be addressed to
Kristian Hellström
Organizing Committee for the 1912 Olympic Games in Stockholm,
Stockholm[30]

Many trainers replied in connection with the advertisement and finally the well-qualified Swedish American Ernie Hjertberg was chosen, and he thus became the first official "national trainer" in Swedish athletics.

After a good deal of negotiating the parties agreed on a contract. Under this contract Hjertberg would work for four months after his arrival in Sweden in 1910 and six months during 1911 and 1912. Hjertberg had a good reputation and was very aware of his value and charged accordingly. The Swedish officials were forced to accept his demands. Hjertberg received a particularly high monthly salary of 1,500 kronor,[31] which caused a number of reactions. The contract between Hjertberg and the Organizing Committee not only covered payments to Hjertberg. He also pledged on his "honor and faith" not to use Swedish sportsmen who took part in professional competitions. An exception was made for the successful runner John Svanberg and two other professional runners who lived and competed in the USA. Hjertberg had already trained them during his time in the USA. Furthermore, Hjertberg would be liable to pay damages of 20,000 kronor if he broke any paragraph in the contract.[32] The contract was renewed after some negotiations after each period of employment.[33]

Athletics was not alone in looking for training competence abroad. The Wrestling Committee, the Swimming Committee, the Football Committee and the Tennis Committee also decided to employ foreign trainers.[34] Employing Hjertberg and others can be seen as the first step in the professionalization of the Swedish trainer profession, a process that took on different expressions in different sports. It was thus not someone who was born yesterday that was employed, but a full-blooded professional who was both commercial and professional in everything he took on and therefore the expectations of and the demands on the Swedish athletes rose.

The Swedish–American athletic coach Ernie Hjertberg while he was still an active sportsman (National Sports Federation).

Hjertberg was born in 1868 and, like so many other Swedish emigrants, came from Småland. He had emigrated to the USA as a child with his parents and when he was young he was a good runner before he became a trainer in 1907 at the large New York Athletic Club.[35] He had trained many successful runners in the USA, among others John Svanberg after the latter had been declared a professional in Sweden. Svanberg then traveled to the USA to have a career as a professional runner, and he managed to do so. Hjertberg was thus not a completely unknown person in athletics circles in Sweden when he arrived together with his wife, Loretta, in Stockholm during the summer of 1910.

Hjertberg stayed in Sweden for just over 10 years. In connection with the Olympic Games in Antwerp in 1920 he left the Swedish squad while the Games were still in progress in protest against the bad discipline, which in his opinion was the cause of the bad results. He considered that he "could not be held accountable for the results achieved as long as the athletes did not obey him."[36] Hjertberg's actions were sensational and must be unique in Swedish athletics. Even the *New York Times* noted Hjertberg's defection.[37] After a while he returned to the USA, where he died in 1952 at the age of 84.

Training Preparations

Hjertberg was full of energy and threw himself wholeheartedly into the work after his arrival in Sweden. The question was how the Athletics Committee could best make use of the competence of the "demon trainer" and give as many as possible access to his training advice. The committee worked on several different solutions in this respect. Hjertberg held a great number of courses for athletes and officials and also wrote long articles, "Ernst Hjertberg's column," in the leading Swedish sport magazine *Idrottsbladet*, where he gave information on his training philosophy in detail. It is unclear whether Hjertberg wrote the articles himself. What is clear is that he preferred to correspond in English. It was probably the owner of *Idrottsbladet*, Bruno Söderblom, that translated Hjertberg's training advice into Swedish.[38] It appears that Hjertberg quickly gained a strong position in athletics in Sweden. Only a few contrasting alternatives to Hjertberg's training advice have been found and criticism was sparse.

The Swedish author Christian Lindstedt has written a most readable book on the history of the marathon, where the spectacular marathon race in Stockholm is given a lot of space. He points out that Hjertberg's training philosophy demanded "control and submission" on the part of the athletes. It was a question of getting into line and accepting Hjertberg's ideas. One person, probably the only one, who expressly did not obey Hjertberg's advice was the big Swedish favorite in the marathon, Sigge Jacobsson from Stockholm. As a rule he trained alone and extremely hard and entirely in his own way, which was in conflict with Hjertberg's leadership philosophy, where the trainer decided more or less everything, in accordance with the American model. It is true that Jacobsson received help from a cyclist to keep up the pace during training, but he otherwise kept apart from the other runners in the athletics squad. Jacobsson also refused to live in the special Sports Home for the athletes next to the Olympic Stadium.[39] Instead he chose to live and train in the Botkyrka area, south of Stockholm, and for this he demanded financial compensation from the Organizing Committee to cover his expenses.

Hjertberg of course reacted very negatively to Jacobsson's willfulness and apparently he even wished that Jacobsson would fail in the marathon race, something which also happened. It is true that he finished sixth and thereby was the best European, but this was not good enough for the expectant and demanding press. They had raised expectations with regard to Jacobsson and these were enormous. It was claimed that the failure was due to his equipment, amongst other things. He had run in new shoes, and these had given him

The best Swedish marathon runner, Sigge Jacobsson (no. 10) in Idrottsparken (postcard, National Sports Museum).

blisters.[40] After the Olympic Games Jacobsson had for different reasons to take a good deal of criticism in the press and he defended himself against Hjertberg and his training methods, amongst other things:

> I have not wished to submit myself to a training system that I have considered to be wrong. And that is why I must be punished. All that I asked of the committee so that I could go for a win was a pair of shoes in time. I did not even get that. Instead I am slandered and presented as a person without a sense of responsibility and honor.[41]

Hjertberg had his base in Stockholm, but also went out around the country to find talent for the coming Olympic Games and to spread his training philosophy to others. An assistant was employed in 1911 to relieve the burden on Hjertberg's shoulders, and this person came to work under Hjertberg for many years.[42]

Before the Stockholm Olympic Games the athletes were given two months off, December and January, before the hard training began in February 1912. At the same time the Organizing Committee managed to get the running and jumping tracks at two other large play grounds in Stockholm improved so as to optimize training opportunities, and most of the training of the Swedish athletics squad took place there. The Swedish athletes were able to begin training on the new tracks in the Olympic Stadium as early as in April.[43] So as to support the athletes and improve their performances and results and above all get them under Hjertberg's control, it was decided that the best athletes in the country would travel to Stockholm and live and train on the spot under the leadership of Hjertberg.[44]

As early as the month of April, almost three months before the inauguration of the Games, the Swedish athletes began to gather and to live in Stockholm at the so-called Sports Home. It was the newly built and became the Swedes' headquarters.[45] The training facilities were optimal. Furthermore, the Sports Home was right next to the Lill-Jansskogen woods, which were also very suitable for training, in particular for the cross country runners. The time up until the Olympic Games was characterized by the selected athletes training intensively and supplementing this with competitions at the weekends with the aim of further sharpening their form and above all getting "much needed competitive practice and self confidence."[46] The foreign athletes also used a play ground close to the Olympic Stadium for their training. Showers, massage benches and masseurs were at the disposal of the athletes.[47] Massage was an important part of Hjertberg's training system.

Nothing was left to chance by the organizers in the hunt to get the best athletes to participate. As early as at the end of 1911 the Organizing Committee had sent out a circular to the employers of the best athletes, asking whether they could be given leave as from April 1. According to the official account this request was very positively received. Athletes were as a rule compensated for loss of income after having approached the Organizing Committee by letter where they explained their difficult financial situation.[48] This financial compensation must have been a violation of the amateur regulations and of a considerably more serious nature than the breach of regulations that Jim Thorpe was disqualified for after the Games.

Relatively shortly before the Stockholm Games, just over a month, athletics qualifying competitions were held at the Olympic Stadium. A total of 243 athletes from 80 associations took part in the competitions. 118 athletes were selected for the Games. The qualifying competitions were very much a trial run both for the athletes and the officials before the coming Games. All of 44 runners took part in the qualifying race for the marathon and 26 in the 100 meters. So that athletes from outside Stockholm were financially able to take part, they received a 50 percent discount on the train journey.[49]

Hjertberg's Training Philosophy

What then was Hjertberg's training philosophy? What was his view of the different elements of training? Hjertberg based his philosophy on previous experience that he had obtained in the USA, his homeland and the leading country, but also on observation, the

Frederick Kelly, USA, winner of the 110 meter hurdles, July 12, 1912 (*V. Olympiaden*, p. 135).

so-called observation method, of other athletes and trainers' ideas and methods. Scientifically based training theory had not yet made a breakthrough and it would take several decades before science considered sport to be an interesting object of study. Information is given about Hjertberg's training philosophy in his *Handbok i friidrott* (Athletics Handbook) and the articles he wrote in *Idrottsbladet*. In the preface to the above-mentioned book Hjertberg emphasized that the aim of the book was to "contribute to raising our sport to a higher level." The book is divided up into three sections, where the first section takes up "training, massage, diet, sleep etc," the second mainly deals with the throwing events and the third sheds light on the running events. Hjertberg had a holistic view of training: everything had an impact on results and performance, even the athletes' behavior outside sport.[50]

Hjertberg was extremely thorough and paid attention to every detail. Choice of shoes, starting blocks, jumping pits and so on, everything was commented on and nothing was left to chance. As an example of Hjertberg's fixation with detail, it can be mentioned that in the summer before the Games he was worried about the shoes of the cross country runners, which he considered more or less inadequate. The Sport Magazine *Nordiskt Idrottslif* drew attention to this. It was pointed out that the cross country runners were the poorest athletes and therefore they could not afford to buy new shoes, which cost about 15 kronor. The newspaper therefore organized a collection which would go to purchasing shoes, not only for the cross country runners but also for all the athletes.[51]

What Hjertberg emphasized above all was the importance of systematic and regular training. The concept of rational training was the term that was in fashion. He said that serious training should be begun three months before the competitive season started. He hailed the principle of long-term and regular training rather than short-term and intensive training.[52] It was thus not enough to train hard on individual occasions before certain competitions.[53] The most important thing was that athletes trained every day: "During my stay in Stockholm now I want to see every athlete who has some thoughts about being able to participate in the Olympic Games out on Östermalms IP (Östermalms Athletic Ground) every day."[54]

A great problem for the athletes of the time (and now) that was commented on in a lively fashion in the press was the risk of "overtraining," a phenomenon whose cause is still a mystery. Unlike other "experts" Hjertberg thought that is was best cured by "exercise and bodily movement" and not by total rest, which was the most common recommendation.[55] According to Hjertberg overtraining arose when the athlete exceeded his maximum capability too many times. The consequence was then that he lost strength and stamina. And if the athlete neglected his diet and his sleep he was more subject to overtraining. Furthermore, overtraining expressed itself at its most extreme in the form of "unbearable tiredness," loss of weight and smaller and hard muscles.[56]

After training the athlete should immediately take a cold bath and then rub olive oil into his body to prevent the risk of catching a cold. However, no more than one bath per day should be taken. As has been mentioned, massage was praised to the skies by Hjertberg, primarily as a way of softening up the muscles and making the body warmer.[57]

Diet was important for athletes before big competitions such as the Olympic Games. Hjertberg had tested different types of diet and thought that it was difficult to prove whether a given diet was better or worse. He emphasized that the most important thing was not to set up general rules, but to adapt to the individual's situation and wishes.[58] Hjertberg was therefore not particularly specific in his dietary advice but recommended a varied diet that should include meat, vegetables, fruit and bread. However, care should be taken with spices, especially salt, fresh fruit and bread, as well as meat that contained a lot of fat. Rather surprisingly, Hjertberg thought that water should be drunk with great caution except when training hard and absolutely not before a competition. This is a method that Kenyan runners also apply 100 years later with great success and contrary to Western scientific research findings. Apparently experienced-based knowledge can sometimes be just as successful. Alcohol and smoking had to be avoided by all athletes; the runners in particular were not allowed to smoke.[59] Hjertberg also emphasized the moral aspect of training and sport. It kept youngsters away from "unhealthy pleasures and bad company," arguments that can be recognized from more recent times when the legitimacy of sport is to be defended by its representatives.

The mental aspects are a self-evident component of modern-day athletics training. Hjertberg also gives expression to thoughts touching on these aspects. The guiding stars were perseverance and self-confidence. It was thus a question of having "your nerves" under control. Hjertberg thought that you had to be a little nervous before a competition, but it was important that this nervousness was of the right kind, so that it did not affect the body and thereby performance negatively.[60]

The Athletics Competitions

How then did things go in the prestigious athletics competitions? Hardly surprisingly the superpower USA completely dominated, and then came Sweden, just ahead of the sensational upstart Finland. The USA won gold medals in the important distances 100 meters, 200 meters, 400 meters, 110 meters hurdles and 800 meters. In the 1,500 meters the Americans came second, third and fourth. The Swedes were remarkably weak in these much followed and popular running events. Only one Swede, Ernst Wide, came in among the top six — he was fifth in the 1,500 meters. This may have affected the way the press angled the Games. What is noticeable is the attention paid to the competitions at a national level. To judge from the press, the Stockholm Olympic Games appear to have been more of a competition between nations than between athletes.

Table 2. Inter-Nation Athletics Competition at the 1912 Stockholm Olympic Games

USA	80 points
Sweden	30 points
Finland	29 points
Great Britain	15 points
Canada	8 points

Source: Bergvall (ed.), *V. Olympiaden* (1913), p. 392.

In all the Swedish athletics squad consisted of 118 athletes and the Swedish success can be partly explained by the many participants that Sweden entered in each event. Travel costs prevented many countries from sending a large squad.[61] This apparently did not affect the USA, whose squad consisted of 109 athletes. The Finnish squad was considerably smaller, with only 22 athletes. The explanation given above may thus go some way to accounting for the performance of the Swedes, but not that of the Finns, whose relatively small squad, less than a quarter of the Swedish squad, was highly successful.[62] On the basis of the number of participants per event, the Swedish performance is questionable. *Svenska Dagbladet*, a daily Swedish newspaper, was positive to Hjertberg and his coaching, however: "Ernie Hjertberg, who seems to have mastered the difficult art of totally winning the hearts of all these young men during the time he has led their heavy training work."[63]

The athletics competitions themselves seem to have been a success, with many records, good results and fine competitions. The marathon was the big event of the Stockholm Olympic Games. Several sources witness to the tens of thousands of people who lined the course "several people deep" and that the Olympic Stadium was unusually well-filled: "Out on Valhallavägen thousands upon thousands gathered, and when there was no room over around the Olympic Stadium, the masses moved off to Östra station and out along the roads where the marathon runners would compete."[64]

The organizers had prepared in detail before the marathon, the highlight of the Games. There were special stations along the course where there were doctors, ambulances and medical facilities. The course had even been swept and watered to bind together the dust in the heat. All motor traffic was forbidden. The race was run in record heat and many runners were forced to drop out: "Medical staff and ambulances also worked hard to pick up the many competitors along the edge of the road who for different reasons had to drop out of the race."[65]

Many of the spectators had come to see the Swedish marathon runner and favorite Sigge Jacobsson: "If it is hot, Sigge Jacobsson in the marathon, for example, has every chance," wrote a newspaper.[66] Twelve Swedes in all started. Jacobsson and the other Swedes failed, however. As has been mentioned Jacobsson only finished sixth, to the great disappointment of the spectators and not least the newspapers. The South African Kennedy McArthur won ahead of fellow countryman Chris Gitsham in the impressive time of 2 hours 36 minutes. The bronze medal was captured by the American Gaston Strobino.[67]

The Athletics Competitions: A Success?

The picture of the Stockholm Olympic Games is incredibly positive in Swedish Olympic literature. There we find descriptions such as "success," "the Sunshine Olympiad," and "indisputable success," but the comments at the time and my own analysis bear witness to a more complex picture.[68] The importance and the consequences of the athletics competitions will be commented on below:

Spectators: Were the competitions a success from the point of view of the number of spectators? The Olympic Stadium held approximately 22,000 spectators and during most days when the athletics competitions were held spectators approximately numbered a modest 12,000, just over half full, in other words. An exception was the marathon, which had been given a lot of publicity in the newspapers, when all of 18,713 paying spectators had made their way to the Olympic Stadium. "Let us just win the marathon now. That will be the icing on the cake," wrote the newspaper *Svenska Dagbladet*. At the inauguration on July 6 only 13,653 had paid to attend.[69] Another newspaper, *Aftonbladet,* regretted that the seats "were so barely filled."[70] From a spectator point of view the Games left a great deal to be desired.

The athletics program: How was the program received? The official account regretted the lack of a predetermined standard program in athletics in the Olympic Games. If there had been one, the discussion over the program's choice of events would have been avoided, as would have the criticism concerning the favoring of "Swedish interests." Here the Stockholm Olympic Games led a move towards standardization and the removal of out-of-the-way events. After Stockholm the athletics program had a more modern design.

Rules and regulations: Regarding rules and regulations, the Organizing Committee had elected to depart from an earlier tradition that the organizing country's rules and regulations were to apply. At the Stockholm Olympic Games the organizers took into consideration the rules and regulations of several different countries, with the aim of creating internationally standardized rules and regulations. They were successful in this, to the great benefit of future organizers.

Participants: One point for discussion was how many participants per event were allowed to start from each country. In the Stockholm Olympic Games twelve athletes were allowed to start, which gave the organizing country and nearby nations a great advantage. There was a wish to reduce this number to six or eight in the future, which also happened, and the Stockholm Olympic Games were of importance for the future here as well.

The breakthrough of rational training: Those responsible for athletics realized before and after the Olympic Games the importance of rational training under professional leadership. Hjertberg was therefore allowed to continue.[71] It was decided as early as early as December 1912 to formalize the organization of the training and "The Swedish Athletic Association's Training Committee for the Olympic Games in Berlin 1916" was established. The Swedish Athletic Association thus began preparations for the Olympic Games all of four years before the Games in Berlin. Such an effort had never been made before and the Stockholm Olympic Games paved the way for a completely new way of viewing "rational" training.

Results: There are different opinions as to whether Hjertberg and those under his training were a success in the 1912 Stockholm Olympic Games. There were five Olympic gold medals in all: Erik Lemming in javelin, best hand, which according to newspaper *Stock-holms-Tidningen* "caused a storm of ecstasy"[72] and Gustaf "Topsy" Lindblom in the triple jump. The other gold medals were won in peripheral events such as the tug-of-war and the team cross country event. Cross country running, both in the team event and individually, proved to be one of Sweden's top events, with three medals. The gold in the decathlon was won by the Swede Hugo Wieslander after Jim Thorpe was disqualified. Some people had probably hoped for more gold medals bearing in mind the big effort which had been made over a long period of time and which had swallowed a lot of money. Many people had above all hoped for success in the more prestigious events such as the marathon, 100 meters, 400 meters, 800 meters and the 1,500 meters. At the same time the number of medals won was much greater in Stockholm than in the 1908 London Olympic Games. Fifteen medals were won, from a present-day perspective an almost inconceivable number.

Table 3. Swedish Medals in Athletics in the Olympic Games 1896–1912

Olympic City	Number of Medals
Athens 1896	0
Paris 1900	1 bronze
St. Louis 1904	0
London 1908	1 gold, 1 bronze
Stockholm 1912	5 gold, 5 silver, 5 bronze*

Source: http://www.friidrott.se/historik/internationellt/OS.aspx.

*In some literature a somewhat lower number of medals is given. The tug-of-war has been added here as well as the medals won after the disqualification of Jim Thorpe. See also the statistics essay.

Costs: It is debatable whether the Swedish successes stood in proportion to the large financial investment that was made on the part of the organizers. Several means of financing were used: amongst other things displays and concerts were arranged "for the benefit of the athletes' training." Another method that was applied was collecting money through so-called subscription lists: "The Athletics Committee ... therefore finds itself obliged to appeal to Swedish men and women to contribute to the costs associated with such training work, so that Sweden is able to honor its position among sporting nations at the V Olympiad."[73]

For example Count A. Wachtmeister donated 500 kronor to athletics training and received an effusive letter of thanks from the athletics committee: "We would like to express our most respectful thanks for the Count's extraordinary interest and for the wonderful financial contribution, which will most certainly be of great benefit to Sweden's sport." Otherwise the gifts were between 100 and 300 kronor according to a subscription list that has been preserved.[74]

However, it is clear that Hjertberg seems to have made an impression on those around him, primarily on those in charge within athletics and on the Organizing Committee, but the patrons of the time were obviously also impressed. Almost immediately after the Olympic Games the wealthy Swedish industrialists Axel Ax:son Johnson and Helge Ax:son Johnson donated 60,000 kronor, an enormous sum at the time, in order to guarantee Hjertberg's employment up until the Olympic Games in Berlin in 1916.[75] The ultimate aim was for Sweden to maintain and preferably strengthen its position as a strong sporting nation.[76]

Maybe the most important consequence of the Stockholm Olympic Games for athletics was the great mobilization of resources that also continued with unabated strength after the Olympic Games. It shows the strong forces and the spin-off effect that are set in motion in industry, among politicians and in the sports movement when an Olympic Games is organized at home irrespective of whether the Games are a success or not.

Notes

1. The exact cost was 1,187,879 kronor. Bergvall (ed.), *V. Olympiaden* (1913), p. 191 f, s. 41; for Torben Grut, see Ekberg, *Torben Grut* (2000).
2. Bergvall (1913), p. 299.
3. Bergvall (1913), p. 322.
4. Ibid., p. 317 f.
5. *Ett idrottssekel* (2002), p. 34.
6. Persson and Pettersson, *Svensk friidrott 100 år* (1995), p. 35 ff.
7. Ibid., p. 71 f.
8. Sylvén and Karlsson, *OS.* (2008), p. 22 f.
9. Persson and Pettersson (1995), p. 46 ff.
10. Ibid., p. 51 ff.
11. Ibid., p. 301.
12. *Olympiska spelens tidning*, no. 67.
13. Sylvén and Karlsson (2008), p. 274 ff.
14. Bergvall (1913), p. 300 f.
15. Helena Tolvhed. "Damolympiaden i Göteborg 1926 och det olympiska spelet kring kvinnlig friidrott" (2008), p. 93 ff.
16. Details of the length of the course vary greatly in the literature, from 8,000 meters to 12,000 meters.
17. Bergvall (1913), p. 301. On walking, see p. 362.
18. Ibid., p. 304.
19. Ibid., p.391.
20. Ibid., p. 370 ff. See also the results essay.

21. Bergvall (1913) p. 318 f, p. 959.

22. It should be pointed out here that in the official report Australia and New Zealand were counted as one country. A total of 24 participants came from Australia, 22 men and two women, and only three men from New Zealand.

23. Bergvall, 1913, p. 842.

24. Ibid., p. 842 f, *Dagens Nyheter,* July 7, 1912.

25. Bergvall (1913), p. 838.

26. Swedes abroad, roll: F035-30777, Archive of the Stockholm Olympiad, National Archives.

27. Ibid.

28. Bergvall (1913), p. 269.

29. Report of the Board of Directors 1912, Archive of the Swedish Athletic Association, National Archives.

30. Advertisement, Documents concerning training (FII:I), Archive of the 1912 Stockholm Olympiad, National Archives.

31. The sum of 1,321.25 kronor was also mentioned in the minutes.

32. Contract November 16, 1911, Documents concerning training (FII:3), Archive of the 1912 Stockholm Olympiad, National Archives.

33. Correspondence Hjertberg — Hellström November 1911, Documents concerning training (FII:II), Archive of the 1912 Stockholm Olympiad, National Archives.

34. Bergvall (1913), p. 265, 270.

35. *New York Times,* February 14, 1907.

36. *Dagens Nyheter,* August 19, 1920.

37. *New York Times,* August 19, 1920.

38. Ibid., August 8, 1910, August 12, 1910.

39. After the Olympic Games the Sports Home became Allmänna BB, and today it houses the Swedish Sports Confederation and several of its special federations.

40. Lindstedt (2005), p. 185 ff.

41. Ibid., p. 189.

42. *Nordiskt Idrottslif,* 53/1910; Bergvall (1913), p. 265.

43. Bergvall (1913), p. 267 f.

44. *Nordiskt Idrottslif,* 26/1910; 48/1910.

45. Bergvall (1913), p. 267 ff.

46. Ibid., p. 264 ff.

47. Ibid., p. 323.

48. See correspondence of different kinds, Documents concerning training, Archive of the Stockholm Olympiad, National Archives.

49. Letter to the gentlemen participants ... May 30, 1912; Program ... Documents concerning training (FII:6), Archive of the Stockholm Olympiad, National Archives.

50. Hjertberg, *Handbok i friidrott* (1911), Preface.

51. *Nordiskt Idrottslif,* 13/1912.

52. Ibid., p. 18 f.

53. *Nordiskt Idrottslif,* 38/1910.

54. *Idrottsbladet,* June 30, 1911.

55. *Nordiskt idrottsliv,* 42/1910. Hjertberg is not completely consistent, however. In other connections he makes the case for total rest.

56. *Idrottsbladet,* August 19, 1910.

57. Hjertberg (1911), p. 29 ff.

58. *Nordiskt idrottsliv,* 35/1910.

59. Hjertberg (1911), p. 39 ff.

60. Ibid., p. 7 ff.

61. Bergvall (1913), p. 391 f.

62. Ibid., p. 842.

63. *Svenska Dagbladet,* July 11, 1912, July 18, 1912.

64. Hermelin, Sven, *Den femte olympiaden* (1912), p. 130 f.

65. Bergvall (1913), p. 361. The Portuguese Lazaro died at the Serafimer Hospital due to the effects of the marathon race.

66. *Stockholms-Tidningen*, July 4, 1912.

67. Hermelin (1912), p. 130 f. It can be mentioned here by way of comparison that during the period 1972 to 2004 the winning time was about 2 hours, 10 minutes, in the Olympic marathon.

68. See for example *Sverige och OS* (1987), p. 56 ff.

69. Bergvall (1913) p. 44.

70. *Aftonbladet*, July 7, 1912.

71. *Olympiska spelens tidning*, no. 82.

72. *Stockholms-Tidningen*, July 8, 1912.

73. "Appeal," Documents concerning training (F II:5), Archive of the Stockholm Olympiad, National Archives.

74. *Svenska Dagbladet*, February 7, 1912; Letter to County Governor Count A. Wachmeister August 28, 1911; Appeal No. 1, Documents concerning training (FII:5), Archive of the Stockholm Olympiad, National Archives.

75. *Nordiskt Idrottslif*, 48/1912.

76. *Olympiska spelens tidning*, July 27, 1912.

References

UNPUBLISHED SOURCES

Swedish National Archives
Stockholmsolympiaden 1912
Svenska friidrottsförbundets arkiv (Archive of the Swedish Athletic Association)

PERIODICALS AND NEWSPAPERS

Aftonbladet
Dagens Nyheter
Idrottsbladet
New York Times
Nordiskt Idrottslif
Olympiska spelens tidning
Stockholms-Tidningen
Svenska Dagbladet

PRINT SOURCES

Bergvall, Erik (ed.). *V. Olympiaden. Officiell redogörelse för Olympiska Spelen i Stockholm 1912* (Stockholm 1913).

Ekberg, Michael. *Torben Grut. En arkitekt och hans ideal* (Göteborg 2000).

Hermelin, Sven. *Den femte olympiaden. Olympiska spelen i Stockholm 1912 i bild och ord* (Stockholm 1912).

Hjertberg, Ernest. *Handbok i friidrott.* (Stockholm 1911).

Jönsson, Åke. "100 år sedan Sverige fick OS," *Blå boken 2008.*

Lindroth, Jan. *Idrott för kung och fosterland. Den svenska idrottens fader. Viktor Balck 1844–1928* (Stockholm 2007).

Lindroth, Jan, and Johan R. Norberg (eds.). *Ett idrottssekel. Riksidrottsförbundet 1903–2003* (Stockholm 2002).

Lindstedt, Christian. *Mellan heroism och idioti. Opinionsstämningar och idédebatt kring maratonlöpningens etablering i Sverige* (Göteborg 2005).

Persson, Lennart K., and Thomas Pettersson. *Svensk friidrott 100 år* (Värnamo 1995).

Sverige och OS (Stockholm 1987).

Sylvén, Sune, and Ove Karlsson. *OS. Historia och siffror* (Stockholm 2008).

Tolvhed, Helena. "'Damolympiaden i Göteborg 1926 och det olympiska spelet kring kvinnlig friidrott," *Idrott, historia och samhälle 2008.*

Counts and Draymen

The Swedish Participants

LEIF YTTERGREN, HANS BOLLING
and INGEMAR EKHOLM

The question of which people been actively engaged in sport has always interested researchers. This means that we know a great deal about those who organized (the officials) and those who participated in sport (the members) and when and how modern sport spread in Sweden. The results are unequivocal. They show that the Swedish sports movement was, like in many other countries in the north-west part of Europe, initially above all a middle class and upper class movement, for young men and found mainly in major cities, often of an industrial nature.[1]

The participants in the Olympic Games in Stockholm have also attracted a good deal of interest. Bill Mallon's and Ture Widlund's ambitious study, *The 1912 Olympic Games*, takes pride of place. The authors give an account of all the participants in all the competitions. In German there is a simpler copy, *Die Spiele der V. Olympiade 1912 in Stockholm*, which contains, however, brief biographical details of the German participants in Stockholm.[2] A relatively unknown Swedish study in this connection is an investigation contained in the Swedish historian Hilding Johansson's essay "Idrotten och Samhället" (Sport and Society) published in connection with the Swedish Sports Confederation's 50th anniversary in 1953. In order to approach the question of the Swedish sports movement's social composition he investigates the social composition of Swedish Olympic squads from 1906 to 1952. Unfortunately Johansson does not report his sources in the article, which makes it impossible to return to his data at a later date. However, they show that the Swedish Olympic squad of 1912 was dominated by athletes from the middle and upper classes.[3]

The Swedish Olympic squad will be analyzed in detail below on the basis of the following questions: How were they entered? Where did the Swedish participants come from? What social background did they have and what was the age distribution in the Swedish squad?

The investigation goes both more deeply and more broadly into the participants at the Stockholm Olympic Games than previous investigations have done. Not only those who actually started but also all Swedes who were entered have been included in the study.[4]

Entering for the Games in Stockholm

This study is primarily based on a database of the Swedish Olympic participants that we created within the framework of the research project "The 1912 Stockholm Olympiad: The Competitions — The People — The City." It contains 1,236 items, of which the majority, 1,089, stem from the entry forms preserved in the Archive of the Stockholm Olympic Games in the National Archives. The Stockholm Games was the first Olympic Games at which everyone who wanted to participate was obliged to enter through their own national Olympic committees or, if no such committee existed, through some national sports association. At previous Games interested athletes had been able to enter on the spot, a system that could lead to great disorder and planning difficulties for the organizers when they did not know in advance the number of participants in the different events.

Four "private" entries by letter have been found in the general correspondence in the Archive of the Stockholm Olympic Games, that is to say athletes who wrote direct to the Organizing Committee or an association and put their services at the nation's disposal. These were Gustav F. Wass, who lived in Philadelphia, USA, who wanted to enter the marathon; Arno Almqvist, a Finnish soldier serving for the Russians who considered that he was qualified to take part in the 200 and 400 meters breaststroke; Hjalmar Johansson, who lived in England, who likewise entered for the swimming; and A. Genberg from Junsele who entered for the shooting. None of these people came to represent Sweden in the Stockholm Olympic Games. However, Arno Almqvist came to represent Russia.[5]

In all the Swedish Organizing Committee sent out around the world a quite incredible 61,800 entry forms in four languages: Swedish, German, English and French.[6] The forms that were returned are in most cases filled out in elegant and clear handwriting, but in some cases are hard to decipher. The personal details in the Swedish participants' entry forms are sometimes filled in by the athlete in question or by the person in charge at each special sports association. This means that the competitor's name may have been spelt in one way on the form while the signature has a different spelling.

The entry form was to be filled out on both the front and the back. On the front the formal conditions for being allowed to take part in the Olympic Games were stipulated and on the back there was a pre-printed page for the sport in question where the entry period was specified and where there were lines for: the competition (event within the sport), nation, the competitor's full name, date of birth, place of birth and date of naturalization.

No entry forms have been preserved in the archive for the rowing, fencing, sailing and equestrian events. The reason for them not being found there is unknown and can only the subject of speculation. However, these were sports where the participants came from a socially definitely more exclusive social milieu than the other participants. It was exclusively officers who took part in the equestrian events and fencing was also dominated by officers. The sailing competitions were organized as part of the annual regatta of the Royal Swedish Yacht Club and the Organizing Committee transferred full responsibility for organizing it to the Yacht Club.[7] Finally, in rowing there are entry forms for participants from the other nations preserved in the Archive of the Stockholm Olympic Games but strangely enough not for the Swedish participants. Rowing also had a somewhat exclusive social character, though not to the same extent as the equestrian events. Rowing's amateur rules excluded many potential participants (see the discussion on amateurism below). The Swedish Rowing Federation was also initially opposed to rowing being included in the Olympic program, which shows that the Olympic Games did not have the same status as today, when all sports fight tooth and nail to be a part of the Olympic program.[8]

A clear reminder that not all Olympic participants, however, were regarded as equal can be found in the official guidebook that was published before the Games, where the participants in the equestrian events were urged: "The following *royal personages and directors* (authorities) should be called on by foreign officers participating in the Olympic equestrian competitions (a visiting card should be taken)."[9]

Three of the sports were also held after the "official" Olympic week finished in the middle of July: the equestrian events in and around the Olympic Stadium, the sailing in the city of Nynäshamn, south-east of Stockholm and the rowing competitions in Stockholm.

Who Was Allowed to Take Part

The issue of who was to be allowed to compete in Stockholm in 1912 contained a number of questions to be answered before it was time to decide on the sporting competence of interested athletes: What sports were to be included in the Olympic program? Should women be given the opportunity of taking part? What athletes were entitled to take part (that is the question of their amateur status, which came up after the Olympic Games as well in connection with the disqualification of the American Jim Thorpe)? Which sports were to be in the Olympic program in Stockholm was far from self-evident. The Swedish organizers initially wanted to limit the program in Stockholm and during the IOC's session in Berlin in 1909 they proposed a program comprising only four sports: wrestling, athletics, gymnastics and swimming. The reasons behind the Swedish proposal were as follows:

> The normal program of the Olympic Games should principally comprise such competitions as could be completed during the course of a week, or at the most ten days, that is to say truly Olympic competitions, concentrated into a short period of time and thus not drawn out over a whole summer, or three quarters of a year, as was the case in both Paris and London. These competitions should mainly comprise events where anyone can take part and from which no one is excluded due to the cost of practicing them. They should also consist of such activities that are common to all civilized peoples and which do not give a definite advantage to some particular nationality which is particularly suited to that activity.
>
> An attempt should also to be made to limit the training of specialists, which may possibly kill the general interest in sport, as sport's goal should be to train all-round good, harmonious and developed men, with health, strength and courage as basic leading concepts. It is general physical and moral upbringing that should be the foundation of the Olympic Games. And it is on the basis of these principles that we now present our proposal for the normal program.[10]

George Patton of the United States and Jean de Mas Latrie of France in the modern pentathlon's fencing event. They finished fourth and second in the fencing event, and fifth and sixteenth in the overall standing. Modern pentathlon was a new sport at the Stockholm Olympics. Custom-made to fit military officers, it brought officers from ten countries to Stockholm (*Den femte olympiaden i bild och ord,* p. 330).

ENTRY FORM
FOR
MODERN PENTATHLON
(SUNDAY, JULY 7th—THURSDAY, JULY 11th, 1912.)

ENTRIES CLOSE JUNE 1st, 1912.

The Entry, therefore, must be in the hands of the Swedish Olympic Committee not later than 12 o'clock midnight between the 1 and 2 of June 1912.
Entries made later will not be accepted. (For exception, see Section 11 on the opposite side.)
For the Riding, horses may be provided by the competitors themselves or will, if desired, be supplied by the
Swedish Olympic Committee.
Competitors not providing horses themselves shall clearly state so in the Entry Form.

Entry shall be made in typed or other distinct Latin characters.

A separate form must be filled in by each competitor.

1. NATION which the competitor represents	United States
2. NAME of Competitor in full *(Write distinctly!)*	George S. Patton, Jr.
3. DATE of BIRTH	November 11 th 1885.
4. PLACE of BIRTH	San Gabriel, California, U.S.A.
5. Date of NATURALISATION (To be filled in if the competitor be not a natural-born subject or citizen of the "nation" he represents, but be qualified as a fully naturalised subject or citizen — See Section 6 of the General Regulations for the Olympic Games. —)	
6. State if you yourself will procure the HORSE	No.

Declaration to be signed by the competitor

I hereby declare that the above statements are correct, and that I am an amateur in accordance with the definitions laid down for the different branches of sport comprised in the Modern Pentathlon.
In addition, I engage to accept and observe the Rules, Regulations and Conditions for the Olympic Games of Stockholm 1912.
I also engage, in the event of my winning a Challenge Cup, to give the guarantee stipulated in Section 16 of the General Regulations for the Olympic Games.

Signature of Competitor:

George S Patton Jr

Declaration to be signed by the Olympic Committee of the country.

The following declaration must be signed by the Olympic Committee of the country.

We hereby declare that the above statements are correct to the best of our knowledge and belief, and we herewith nominate the competitor for the event mentioned above.

Signature

James E Sullivan

SECRETARY AMERICAN
OLYMPIC COMMITTEE

P. T. O.

George Patton's entry form for the modern pentathlon at the Olympic Games in Stockholm 1912. He became the best non–Swedish competitor in the modern pentathlon at the Stockholm Olympics with fifth place. During the Second World War Patton was very successful as military general (photograph by Emre Olgun, Swedish National Archives).

RODD

V. OLYMPIADEN

OLYMPISKA SPELEN
I STOCKHOLM 1912

□ ◆ □

ANMÄLNINGSBLANKETT

Denna blankett skall — noggrant ifylld — insändas af vederbörande lands
Olympiska Kommitté till den Svenska Organisationskommittén under adress:
OLYMPISKA SPELEN, STOCKHOLM.

Utdrag ur
Olympiska Spelens Allmänna Bestämmelser:

3. I Spelens täflingar äga endast amatörer deltaga.

6. Såsom »nation» i idrottslig bemärkelse anses hvarje land med egen representant i den Internationella Olympiska Kommittén eller, i händelse dylik representation saknas, hvarje land, som erkänts såsom »nation» vid närmast föregående Olympiska Spel, samt i öfrigt hvarje suverän stat, som icke ingår i statsförbund, äfvensom hvarje statsförbund under gemensam statschefs öfverhöghet.

Endast infödda eller naturaliserade undersåtar af en »nation» eller af den suveräna stat, hvaraf en »nation» bildar en del, äro berättigade att representera »nationen» i fråga vid de Olympiska Spelen.

7. Deltagares amatörskap i enlighet med för hvarje idrottsgren gällande bestämmelser skall garanteras af den organisation, som i hans eget land är ledande myndighet för den idrottsgren, i hvilken han ämnar täfla, eller — om dylik organisation ej finnes — af den därvarande Olympiska Kommittén.

8. Minimiåldern för deltagande i Spelen är 17 år, men kan undantag från denna regel medgifvas underårig person, hvars anmälan åtföljes af tillstyrkande läkarintyg.

10. Anmälan till deltagande i täflan skall göras *genom hvarje lands Olympiska Kommitté af den styrande organisationen för vederbörande idrottsgren* (eller, om dylik styrande organisation saknas, direkt genom den Olympiska Kommittén) *till den Svenska Organisationskommittén.*

11. Anmälan skall för att vinna afseende vara i den Svenska Organisationskommitténs händer före utgången af den för hvarje särskild idrottsgren fastställda anmälningstiden.

För icke europeiska länder utgår dock anmälningstiden först 8 dagar efter nämnda tidpunkt.

Telegrafisk anmälan godkännes icke.

12. Den Svenska Organisationskommittén förbehåller sig rätt att tillbakavisa anmälan utan skyldighet att angifva orsaken därtill.

Om så sker, kommer dock orsaken att konfidentiellt delgifvas vederbörande Olympiska Kommitté.

• • •

Entry form, rowing, front page (National Sports Museum).

The IOC and Pierre de Coubertin were not impressed by the Swedish proposal and presented several counter-proposals. The Olympic competitive program grew from the four sports that the Swedes had recommended to 13: wrestling, cycling, football, athletics, fencing, gymnastics, equestrian competitions, modern pentathlon, rowing, sailing, aquatics, shooting and tennis, with a total of 102 events, as well as art competitions and a few demonstration sports, amongst other things in Gotland's ball game *pärk* and Icelandic wrestling, *glima*. The Swedish organizing committee was only successful in its attempts to prevent track cycling, boxing, weightlifting and winter sports from being introduced into the Olympic competitive program in Stockholm.[11]

With the 1912 Olympic Games it was clear that power over the Olympic program had been transferred from the local organizing committees to the IOC. Ever since 1912 it has also been the IOC that has decided which sports are to be included in the Olympic program and the local organizing committees have to adapt to this.

Many influential sports officials at the beginning of the last century were negatively disposed to women doing sport in public. And at first the Swedish Organizing Committee also did not intend to let women participate. But they had to give in to external pressure and allowed women to compete in two sports: aquatics and tennis. In all, 53 women from ten nations competed in Stockholm, just over 2 percent of the total line-up.[12]

The third question regarding participation that the organizers had to decide on was: who was to be considered an amateur or a professional? Professional athletes were not eligible to take part in the Olympic Games.[13] The IOC was formed in 1894 at a congress in Paris that had been convened with a view to discussing the question of amateurism and it was only in the 1980s that the amateur regulations were abolished for the Olympic Games.

As there were no common international rules and regulations concerning what it meant to be an amateur in sport, the Organizing Committee had the delicate task of trying to draw up such rules and regulations. It proved to be unfeasible to create common amateur rules and regulations for all sports. The general amateur regulations that were finally drawn up only came to be fully applied in two of the sports: wrestling and athletics. They were as follows:

> An amateur is someone who has never
> > (a) competed for a money prize or for some financial gain or acquired any financial advantage whatsoever in the practicing of his/her sport
> > (b) competed with professionals
> > (c) taught in some sporting event against payment
> > (d) sold, pawned or exhibited against payment a prize won in a competition.[14]

The general amateur regulations came to serve as a norm for the drawing up of regulations in other events. These rules had very much the same wording and the same content, but with certain clarifications. In gymnastics, for example, the amateur rules were liberal: "gymnastics teachers and officials, even if they have received payment, are regarded as amateurs, however." In the equestrian events the problem of the participants' amateur status was solved by "[allowing] only gentlemen riders to compete," that is to say officers, "professionals are excluded." Swimmers serving in the Army or the Navy in their everyday life could also retain their amateur status even if they had competed against professionals, if it had been in a competition arranged by the Army or the Navy.[15]

In rowing, strongly influenced by the English rowing culture, they were not as accommodating towards those who through their work could be conceived as being able to gain some material advantage. There the rules clarified that in addition to people who had received payment, every sailor, fisherman or person who had made a living from rowing was considered to be a professional. On the other hand, it stated in the rowing rules that rowers could receive travel expenses through their club for competitions or displays. Finally, it was prescribed for shooting that an amateur was someone who had never been employed by a weapons company and specifically worked there with range finding for rifles and zeroing rifle scopes. However, using a firearm when serving in the Army was no obstacle to being classified as an amateur.[16] For sports where there were international federations, cycling, football and swimming, their own rules and regulations were used.

It can be seen from the clarifications of the amateur rules in the different sports that officers were a particularly privileged group. The advantages they had gained through the practicing of their profession did not disqualify them from taking part. This is maybe not so surprising given their strong position in sport, Swedish sport in general and sport in Stockholm in particular. Ten of the 14 chairmen of the organizing committees for the different sports were in the armed forces.[17]

The Swedish Olympic management took the amateur issue seriously. Professionalism was to be combated, which is witnessed by the contract written with the Swedish American athletics trainer Ernie Hjertberg in July 1910. There was a clause there where he undertook:

> on his honor and faith not to use until the end of the year 1912, either directly or indirectly, Swedish athletes in or for professional competitions, with the exception of Svanberg, Ljungström & Johansson. However, should he breach this clause, he undertakes to immediately pay to the Committee damages of twenty thousand (20,000) kronor.[18]

In connection with the amateur issue, it can also be noted that the committee for the equestrian events had well worked out plans to award money prizes at the Olympic equestrian events. The reason given for this was that it was so expensive to transport the animals. The committee had secured 25,000 kronor from individual donors and decided to give out the whole sum as prize money at the Games. However, this was forbidden by the IOC, which at its session in Luxembourg in 1910 decided that only medals and diplomas were to be awarded, which resulted in the members of the equestrian committee hurriedly visiting those in charge of the equestrian organizations in the major European countries to ensure that they would compete despite the fact that there would be no prize money. However, there was prize money at the Swedish qualification competitions before the Olympic Games: 20,000 kronor "donated by the Nobel brothers in Petersburg." However, the money was not paid before the Olympic competitions had come to an end.[19] It is nevertheless remarkable that the above is quite openly recorded in the official account.

It thus seems as if the amateur definition that was used within equestrianism aimed more to exclude competitors for social reasons than it was an aversion to financial gain in connection with practicing sport.

The above shows how complex the amateur issue was at this time, and what caused problems was not only the difficulty in agreeing on a common amateur definition but also the unwillingness to treat everyone alike in the class-segregated society at the turn of the century. It was a question of different forms of exclusion.

The Swedish Olympic Squad

There were thus a number of formal obstacles that limited the number of athletes at the Stockholm Olympic Games. But despite this the number of participants was higher than at any previous Olympic Games. According to the official account of the Games there were 4,281 athletes entered for the competitions. Of these 3,282 started, including 792 display gymnasts. A total of 76.7 percent of everyone entered thus started.

The number of participants entered in all events amounted to all of 7,367, but there were only 4,742 starters during the Games, which means that less than two-thirds of all planned starts actually happened. The largest shortfall was in athletics, where less than half of everyone entered to start actually started, 49.2 percent.[20] The reason for the great shortfall has not been commented on in the source material of the time but seems to have been taken for granted. The worst sinner when it came to not starting must have been the Swede Hugo Wieslander. He was entered in no less than ten events in athletics but started in only two: the pentathlon and the decathlon. He won a gold medal in the decathlon after Jim Thorpe had been disqualified.

The Swedish Olympic squad was easily the biggest, but its neighboring countries and the great powers of the day contributed with a large number of competitors.

Table 1. The Ten Largest Sports Squads in the Stockholm Olympic Games

Sweden	445
Great Britain	271
Norway	190
Germany	183
USA	174
Finland	164
Russia	159
Denmark	152
Hungary	123
France	109

Source: Mallon and Widlund (2009), pp. 56–57.

As can be seen in Table 1, ten nations sent more than 100 competitors to Stockholm. Other nations contributed with between one and 85 participants; Serbia, Japan, Turkey and Iceland sent two participants each and Switzerland just one.[21]

In the individual sports events each nation was entitled to enter twelve participants. The entry rules were different for the equestrian events, where the maximum number of participants was set at four riders in the cross country event and six riders each in dressage and jumping, and for tennis, with eight players per class. In rowing and sailing each nation was entitled to enter two boats.

Sweden entered participants in almost all events, with the exception of three gymnastics events, the 10,000 meters walking race and rowing, single sculler. In athletics the maximum number of participants were entered in 13 out of 26 events and almost the full number in most of the others.[22]

The fact that Sweden only took part in one gymnastics event, the team competition, Swedish system, should be understood in the light of the animosity that prevailed between the Swedish gymnastics, which was hostile to competition, and German Turnen, which was considerably more positive to competition. It would not be until the 1940s that the first Swedish championships were organized in individual gymnastics, which says a great deal about the strong position of Ling gymnastics in Sweden as an alternative to competitive sport. Gymnasts representing Sweden practiced Ling gymnastics and nothing else. The lack of representation in the walking race can be explained by the low status of the sport in Swe-

Ernest Webb of England, left, silver medalist, and Georg Goulding of Canada, the winner in the walking competition. Walking was one of the few events in which Sweden was not represented during the 1912 Olympic Games (*Den femte olympiaden 1 bild och ord,* p. 159).

den, which is clear from a statement made by the prominent sport leader Sigfrid Edström at one of the meetings of the Highest Board of the National Sports Federation: "Such silliness as there is in walking is unparalleled in the rest of the sporting world. We must fight so that walking is got rid of in international competitions."[23]

Two more events were conspicuous from a Swedish perspective: 110 meters hurdles in athletics and swimming's team event over 800 meters. There were no Swedish starters in these events, despite the fact that participants were entered, all of eleven in the hurdles race.

The Origin of the Olympic Participants and Club Membership

The 1,236 entries for the Games' competitions comprise 743 different individuals. For 729 of them there is information about where they were born. The athletes born in Sweden were from Råneå in the north to Trelleborg in the south and were divided among the different parts of Sweden. The majority were born in the south part of the country (670) while the sparsely populated north part only contributed with 48 athletes. Twelve of the Swedish entries were born abroad.[24] It is true that details about place of birth do not say everything about where the people in question grew up or where they lived when the Olympic Games were held in 1912. However, a picture of where they originate from is obtained.

We get a picture of where in the country sport at a high level was practiced at the time of the Stockholm Olympic Games if we study which clubs the athletes represented during the Games. Most of the 290 athletes for whom there is no club address, 233, are gymnasts, as a club address has only been registered for those gymnasts who were also part of the men's team competition squad, and individuals who never started, 47 in all.

A comparison per part of the country in accordance with what was done above regarding place of birth shows that 436 competed for clubs in the south part while just 17 athletes represented a club from the North.

A comparison between the associations that the Olympic participants represented and the distribution of the National Sports Federation's members cannot be done without certain adjustments to the material as several sports were not organized within the National Sports Federation at the time. When the Swedish Sports Confederation was formed to give Swedish sport a common main organization in 1903 the founders (amongst others Sigfrid Edström and Viktor Balck) had decided that its activities would focus on "gymnastics and sports which do not require material of an expensive nature and/or do not require common material, which is why sailing and equestrian events should not be included, and likewise the specially organized shooting movement cannot come into question here."[25]

In all there are 332 athletes practicing sports organized within the Swedish Sports Confederation in our database whose club membership we know. We thus find a relatively greater representation here as well clubs from the south part of the country than the actual distribution of athletes over the country would indicate.

With regard to which clubs were represented in 1912, Stockholm's dominance is obvious: all of 243 athletes, 53.6 percent, represented sports clubs from Stockholm and the surrounding area. This can be compared with the two other large cities in the country: Gothenburg contributed with 78 athletes and Malmoe with 33.

The clubs that were represented by most athletes at the Games were the Stockholm Swimming Club with 36 participants and the Royal Swedish Yacht Club with 23 participants. The Yacht Club's equivalent in Gothenburg had 16 participants and the two yacht clubs were the only associations that were represented in sailing. In addition, among the top clubs with regard to sending participants to the Games there are also several specialist associations, that is to say sports associations from whose name it can be concluded that they were only active in one sport, for example the Association for the Promotion of the Art of Fencing in Stockholm with 19 participants, Stockholm Sharpshooter Club with 17 participants and Stockholm Pistol Club with 15 participants. There were a striking number of marksmen representing Stockholm clubs.

In tennis 15 out of the 17 entrants represented the Royal Lawn Tennis Club of Stockholm. When a sport was dominated by representatives from one association it was almost always an association that was only active in one sport.

A large number of athletes in 1912 came from so-called category associations, which are associations for people with a certain professional or social position. It could be associations whose name points out a school, a regiment or a professional category. This type of sports association was more common before the First World War. In the years around 1910, 35 percent of the Swedish Sports Confederation's members came from two types of category associations: military associations and IFK associations, whose members primarily came from regiments and State schools, respectively.[26]

All of 14 different IFK clubs were represented at the Stockholm Olympic Games by a total of 43 members.[27] A total of 31 participants belonged to a military association and took part primarily in the military-influenced equestrian events, modern pentathlon and fencing. In the successful tug-of-war team seven of the eight gold medalists were from police force in Stockholm, and the eighth was from police force in Gothenburg. These were another

Swedish riflemen at Kaknäs. At the beginning of the twentieth century the sharpshooter movement was well established in the Swedish secondary schools (postcard, National Sports Museum).

The Swedish tug-of-war team (photograph by Axel Malmström, SCIF photo collection).

type of category association, which was linked to the workplace (compare company sports associations today). However, one of the medalists, Herbert Lindström, was not a policeman but a fisherman from Stockholm's outer archipelago and became a member of the association solely to be able to train with his team mates before the Games in Stockholm.[28]

The religiously colored and still active Swedish YMCA movement was also represented in the Olympic Games. It provided four of the gold medalists in the team gymnastics. It is hardly surprising that athletes from the YMCA movement were to be found among the gymnasts and not among the more competition-focused athletes, as this was more in harmony with the YMCA's early ideals.[29] The Stockholm club Hellas, which contributed with three swimmers and three athletes, could also be included among the religiously colored associations. The association had been formed in 1899 by the socially-minded priest Ernst Klefbeck and the members comprised a large number of his own confirmation candidates. At first it went under the name of The Pastor's Boys, but from 1912 was known as the Swimming and Athletics Club Hellas, which can be seen as an early example of Muscular-Christianity in Sweden.[30]

It could be argued that the very largest Swedish association at the Stockholm Olympic Games was the association created for the women's gymnastics display at the Games. The Women's Gymnastics Association for the Swedish Display was a temporary association that comprised all the 57 women display gymnasts who were entered. The gymnasts were, however, also members of local gymnastic associations all around Sweden so it is not a wholly correct conclusion, which would give the material an undeservedly large Stockholm bias. Nevertheless, the women taking part in competitive events give a strong Stockholm preponderance anyway, as 21 out of 23 participants represented clubs from the capital city.[31]

Athletes could also represent several different associations if they took part in more than one sport. For example, it may be mentioned that Eric Carlberg took part in three sports: shooting, modern pentathlon and fencing and represented three different Stockholm clubs. There are five further examples of people who represented more than one association, which means that the number of associations is greater than the number of individuals, but as it is entirely a question of Stockholm associations it has not affected the initial nationwide comparison. It has also contributed to giving individual Stockholm associations extra weight.

There is reason to be careful with regard to club membership as well. The dominance of the Stockholm associations was strengthened by the fact that athletes who we know did not live in the capital represented Stockholm clubs during the Games. The tennis player Ebba Hay, who lived in Jönköping, represented the Royal Lawn Tennis Club of Stockholm. The Swedish Americans who returned to their old homeland to participate also represented Swedish clubs at the Olympic Games.

It was not only in Sweden that efforts were made so that the nation would be as strongly represented as possible at the Olympic Games. Swedes living in the USA who were members of the Swedish Gymnastic and Athletic Union of America (SGA), whose chairman was the dentist William Borgström, set up a selection committee and held qualification competitions for Swedes living in the eastern parts of the USA. These activities were sanctioned by the Organizing Committee in Stockholm after above all Sigfrid Edström had spoken in support of the committee, which gained the impressive title of "The Selection Committee for Swedish Americans for the Olympic Games in Stockholm in 1912." The Organizing Committee set a limit, however. It was willing to allow the selected athletes to represent Sweden in Stockholm, but it was not willing to contribute with money for the Swedish American athletes' journey to Sweden. Funds were collected in America and six athletes were sent to Stockholm.[32]

Even if this survey of which clubs were represented at the Stockholm Olympic Games

The Swedish silver medal winning team at pistol shooting 50 meters. From left: Erik Boström, Georg de Laval, and twin brothers Wilhelm Carlberg and Eric Carlberg (postcard, National Sports Museum).

does not provide the whole truth about where the Swedish Olympic participants practiced most of their sport, it does give a good indication of where in the country competitive sport was strongest. Even if sport was not as specialized and advanced in 1912 as it became later, great sporting skill was necessary, acquired through long training in order to be able to qualify for the games in Stockholm. And the longer a sports association had existed, the greater the likelihood that it had the capacity to produce athletes who were good enough to be able to represent Sweden in the important sports competition that the Stockholm Olympic Games constituted for the Swedish sports officials.

Age of the Athletes

Details about age have been found for 729 individuals. In addition to those who competed in the Games, all the display gymnasts, reserves entered and those who did not start in the different events are included in the compilation.

The Swedish squad had an average age of just over 25. The majority of the participants were under 25 (425), while only 30 were over the age of 40 (see Table 2). Among those who were older there are few who can be said to have practiced demanding sports. On the contrary, they were sports that could be done even by those more advanced in years. They primarily did shooting, but the occasional individual was represented in sailing, riding and may be a trifle surprisingly in diving. The only participants over 40 who can be said to have practiced more physically demanding sports were Ebba Hay, 45, who took part in the mixed tennis indoors, and Louis Sparre, 48, who was a member of the épée team. However, we should be aware of the fact that the tennis of the time was considerably less physically demanding than modern-day tennis.

Table 2. Age of Swedes Entered for the 1912 Stockholm Olympic Games

Age	Number
Under 20	101
20–24	324
25–29	190
30–39	84
40–49	25
50 and older	5
Total	729

Source: Database, participants at the 1912 Stockholm Olympic Games.

It can be seen from the age distribution of the Swedish Olympic squad that sport at the beginning of the twentieth century was above all the domain of young men. In athletics,

In tennis the mixed-double pair of Sigrid Fick (1887–1979) and Gunnar Setterwall (1881–1928) won bronze and silver medals in the covered court and lawn-tennis events even though they only won one match (SCIF photo collection).

for example, only three out of 59 Swedish runners entered were over the age of 30, the sprinter Knut "Knatten" Lindberg who had his thirtieth birthday during the year and the two marathon runners Ivar Lundberg and Carl Nicanor Andersson. Knatten Lindberg was the early 20th century big Swedish star sprinter, with nine gold medals in the Swedish 100 meters championships and a member of the Swedish silver team in the 4 × 100 meters in 1912, but a sufficiently all-round sportsman to win the silver medal in the javelin at the extra Olympic Games in Athens in 1906 and five Swedish soccer championships with Örgryte IS. His Swedish record in the 100 meters from 1906, 10.6 seconds, lasted for 30 years. Of all the wrestlers and cyclists there was only one in each sport who had reached the age of 30.

By today's standards the football team was very young. The 33 players entered were between 18 and 27 years of age.

In aquatics only four of all the participants were over 30, and two of these were also over 40. All the women swimmers were under 20 and among the women divers we find that only five of the twelve participants were over the age of 20.

In tennis the women and the men participating differ. Overall the participants were between 20 and 45 years old. Oldest was Ebba Hay, who was 45. The female players had an average age of 33 and this is considerably higher than the average age of the male tennis players, which was 26. It should be mentioned here, however, that Ebba Hay raised the average age quite considerably — the next oldest was Ellen Brusewitz, who was just 33 years old.

The 28 fencers were relatively old, between 18 and 48 years old, with eight of them over 30. The average age was also high among the participants in the equestrian events, where ten of the 17 participants were over the age of 30 and the youngest was 23. Shooting had the oldest participants and the highest average age. Among the 64 marksmen, 18 were over 40 years old, and a further 28 were older than 30.

Sweden had the youngest and the oldest Olympic participants for both women and men. The oldest woman by far was the above-mentioned tennis player Ebba Hay, who was 45 years and 148 days old. The youngest woman was Greta Carlsson, who was 14 years and 2 days old when she competed in the 100 meters freestyle, followed by her fellow country-woman Märta Adlerz, 15 years and 97 days, who competed in the diving. The oldest male participant was Oscar Swahn who was 64 years and 257 days old when he shot at running deer. The youngest male participant was Åke Bergman, who was 16 years and 74 days old when he competed in the 100 meters backstroke, followed by the diver Gösta Sjöberg who was nearly two months older. Sweden was granted dispensation for several participants who

Oscar Swahn (1847–1927) was the oldest competitor at Stockholm in 1912 and also become a gold medalist as a member of the winning Swedish team in the running deer team event. He still is the oldest gold medalist in the Olympic history (postcard, National Sports Museum).

were under the age of 17 through a doctor's certificate, which was included on the entry form. In all six men, four of whom were Swedes, and seven women, three of whom were Swedes, took part who were under the age of 17.[33]

The events that had the oldest participants were above all those:

- which had been practiced for a long time in Sweden
- where physical status was not crucial for performance
- where the equipment was of great importance
- which were practiced by people of relatively high social status.

The Participants' Social Status

In his study of the 1912 Swedish Olympic participants, Hilding Johansson reported that the number of participants was 457. He divided them up into three social classes, as was typical at the time, and arrived at the following distribution: 19.0 percent in social group one (upper class), 19.7 percent in social group two (middle class), 13.8 percent in social group

Alfred Swahn (1879–1931) was the winner for running deer, single shoot, individual and team. He was the son of Oscar Swahn and a successful shooter (postcard, National Sports Museum).

three (working class), and for 47.5 percent there was no information about their occupation.[34] Unfortunately the entry forms provide no information about the titles of the Olympic participants. However, we have found titles for 271 of the participants, but the material has a very high concentration of participants from Stockholm and the surrounding area.

Instead of repeating Johansson's study — the results do not differ in any crucial way — the dominant occupations within the different sports will be very briefly commented on. Among the participants in athletics, football and aquatics we find above all workers, office workers, employees in the wholesale and retail trade, and in addition students and members of the armed forces. In wrestling and cycling we find a strong dominance of workers and craftsmen, but only a few titles have been found. The gymnastic squads had a clear middle class character, with above all white-collar workers and certified gymnastic instructors, office workers, members of the armed forces and students. Shooting is seen to have been the sport with the greatest social spread, where there participated clerks and managing directors, doctors and forest officers, people in the wholesale trade and craftsmen, engineers and students and so on, and of course a large group of members of the armed forces. The fencing squad was dominated by members of the armed forces, but in addition there were also independent professionals, amongst others the artist Count Louis Sparre. The equestrian competitions were, as has been seen above, a sport that only officers had access to and the modern pentathlon was also something that was for this group. Among the 19 yachtsmen for whom a title has been found, there are occupations such as lawyer, architect, engineer, dentist and tradesman, but also a definite worker: Jonas Jansson, an able-bodied seaman born in Norway. Within tennis we find the titles Mrs. and Miss among the women participants and middle-class occupations among the men. For the rowers as a group the material is so thin and straggly that it is not possible to say anything.

Wrestling and cycling were thus sports that were dominated by representatives from the working class while sailing and tennis had a pronounced upper class character. The pentathlon, fencing and the equestrian events also had an upper class character and they were the playgrounds of the so influential Swedish officers during the games in Stockholm. Within football, athletics and swimming we find above all athletes from the working and lower middle classes while shooting and gymnastics were the sports that crossed most barriers from a social point of view.

The social composition of the Swedish Olympic squad and the sports practiced by people coming from different social groups are largely consistent with previously made observations. In his study of Stockholm sport during the last decades of the nineteenth century Leif Yttergren shows that of the sports that were competed in during the Stockholm Olympic Games tennis and equestrian events were done by the upper social classes of society, gymnastics, swimming and fencing by the middle classes, and athletics and sports requiring strength by the working class. One sport, sailing, was practiced within all the social classes, while football, cycling and rowing were done within both the middle class and the working class.[35] Research into the sporting preferences of different social classes during the 20th century has not in any crucial way come to conclusions that change this picture, but rather confirms it.[36] Surprisingly enough, the continuity appears to be particularly strong in this question. Few events change their class affinity over time, which is remarkable given the democratization of society during the 20th century.

Summary

The Stockholm Olympic Games have gained attention as the first global Olympic Games. However, they were strongly dominated by athletes and sports officials from North-West Europe and North America, in other words the industrialized western world of the time. A total of 2,380 athletes from 27 countries competed. Of these 445 were Swedes, which was a record large squad for Sweden. Other countries that sent large squads to Stockholm were Great Britain, Norway, Germany and the USA. Non-European participation was otherwise low. South America was represented by Chile with 14 participants, Asia by Japan with two (it has not been possible to ascertain whether the two Turkish participants were from the Asian or the European part of the country), Africa by South Africa with 21 and Oceania by Australasia (Australia and New Zealand) with 24 participants. The Games were marketed intensively and an enormous number of entry forms were sent out around the world with a view to attracting competitors to Stockholm.

There was an ideological sporting dilemma for the organizers and it was the amateur issue. It was a question of keeping the Games free of non-amateurs at any price. However, the organizers had great problems in drawing up common and standardized amateur rules for all sports. Different sports had different views of the amateur issue, which resulted in different rules and regulations. There was clearly class thinking in several amateur regulations, where it was more a question of excluding the lower echelons of society from participating than of receiving money when doing sport.

It was not only the view of the amateur issue that was sport-specific. The choice of sport was intimately associated with the social status of the athlete. The choice of sport was thus a clear marker of class. The tennis players thus came from the upper class, whereas cyclists and wrestlers came from other social ranks. It is worth noting that the officers, who were so influential in Swedish sport in general, and in the Olympic organization in particular, had several sports within which they could themselves compete without having to compete with civilians with another, lower, class background than themselves.

There was a great age span in the Swedish squad: the youngest had just had her 14th birthday and the oldest was close to his 65th birthday. There were all of 30 athletes out of just over 700 who were 40, which is remarkably old in a modern-day perspective. The older participants went in for less physically strenuous sports such as shooting and equestrian events. A clear majority were in the 20 to 24 year old age range.

The number of women in the Swedish squad was small. There were only 23 in all who competed and they had to take part in tennis and aquatics. These were two sports of a completely different nature and they attracted women from completely different social ranks of society. The Stockholm Olympic Games were thus primarily something for young men from the middle and upper classes, far from the popular movement's ideal of sport for everyone.

As far as the geographic domicile of the participants is concerned, it did not reflect the demographic structure of the country either. The majority came from the south part of the country with a surprisingly strong Stockholm dominance in comparison with the distribution of athletes over the country.

Notes

1. Johansson, "Idrotten och samhället" (1953), p. 28 ff.; Janzon, *Manschettyrken, idrott och hälsa* (1978), Lindroth's *Idrottens väg till folkrörelse* (1974), and Yttergren's *Täflan är lifvet* (1996).
2. Mallon and Widlund, *The 1912 Olympic Games* (2009), and Lennartz, *Die Spiele der V. Olympiade 1912 in Stockholm* (2009).
3. Johansson, 1953, p. 38 f.
4. The entry forms for fencing, the equestrian events, rowing and sailing have not been found.
5. National Archives, Stockholm Olympiad 1912, Foreign correspondence of the secretariat E II:1, Swedes abroad.
6. Bergvall, 1913, p. 23.
7. Bergvall, 1913, p. 652 f.
8. National Archives, Stockholm Olympiad 1912, Minutes of the Organizing Committee A I:1, Organizing Committee April 25, § 16.
9. *Stockholm, Olympiska Spelens officiella vägvisare*, Gustaf Åsbrink (ed) (Stockholm, 1912), p. 67.
10. Uggla, *Olympiska spelen i Stockholm 1912* (1912), p. 120.
11. Most present-day compilations regarding the Stockholm Olympic Games give the number of sports competed in during the Games as 15, instead of the 13 above-mentioned sports. The difference lies in the fact that nowadays aquatics' different disciplines are counted as separate sports, which for the Stockholm Games gives three sports: swimming, diving and water polo instead of one: aquatics (Mallon and Widlund, 2009, p. 29). Two other sports/events that were in the competitive program in Stockholm in 1912 should be commented on: tug-of-war and walking. The tug-of-war was first included in the

athletics program, but in autumn 1911 a special committee was founded solely for the tug-of-war, in order to create interest in the tug-of-war in Sweden. This has led to the tug-of-war being considered as a sport in some compilations regarding the Stockholm Olympiad. However, when we talk about the number of sports at the Games we do not see the tug-of-war as one sport but as an event within athletics. Internationally, walking comes under the International Association of Athletics Federations but is organized in Sweden as a sport of its own. Walking is also seen below as an event within athletics and not as a sport.

12. See Bolling and Yttergren's "Gender and Class."

13. For a detailed treatment of the importance of the amateur issue in sport during above all the first half of the twentieth century, see Wikberg, *Amatör eller professionist?* (2005).

14. Bergvall, 1913, p. 87

15. Ibid., p. 87 ff.

16. Ibid, p. 88 f.

17. Lindroth, 1974, chapter 5, and Bergvall, 1913, p. 5 f.

18. National Archives: Stockholm Olympiad 1912: Minutes of the Organizing Committee A I:1, Organizing Committee August 8, 1912, Appendix 1. John Svanberg, Gösta Ljungström and Thure Johansson were runners who had become professional. John Svanberg, among other things the silver medalist in the marathon in Athens 1906, was Sweden's most popular runner during the first decade of the twentieth century and had been a professional since 1909. He then went off to the professional long-distance races in the USA where he had Ernie Hjertberg as a manager and was successful for a couple of years. Gösta Ljungström, the Swedish cross country champion in 1908, and Thure Johansson later followed in Svanberg's footsteps. *Nordisk familjeboks sportlexikon,* vol. 6 (1946), esp. 727 f; *Nordisk familjeboks sportlexikon,* vol. 5 (1943), esp. 146; Persson and Pettersson: *Svensk friidrott 100 år* (1995), p. 361.

19. National Archives, Stockholm Olympiad 1912, Minutes of the Organizing Committee A I:2, Organizing Committee April 24, 1911, § 32, Appendix 15, and Bergvall, 1913, p. 552.

20. Bergvall, 1913, p. 838 ff.

21. Mallon and Widlund, 2009, p. 56 f.

22. Otherwise Sweden made use of the entry rules as follows: Tug-of-war: 12, with eight in the team. Cycling: 17 including five reserves. Wrestling: From 10 to three competitors, depending on the weight class. Football: 11, plus 22 reserves. Fencing: 12 in épée, 11 in foil and 10 in sabre, and four plus three team reserves. Gymnastics, team competition: 59 entries, of whom 24 plus the carrier of the flag took part in the competition. Equestrian events: full in all events, including team. Tennis: full number in all events both indoor and outdoor except in women's singles. Modern pentathlon: twelve participants. Rowing: two boats in inrigged four and outrigged eight, one boat in outrigged four. Sailing: two boats in 6 m, 8 m and 10 m classes and one boat in 12 m class. Aquatics: 12 in plain high diving for both men and women and plain and variety diving combined diving for men, eight in springboard; three to eight in the different swimming events; seven plus eight reserves in water polo. Shooting: full number of participants in all events including team competitions.

23. Persson and Pettersson, 1995, p. 40.

24. Information from the entry forms should not, however, be seen as definitive evidence about where an athlete was born. It can be seen from the entry forms of John Eke, the Swedish American, that he was entered in three events: 5,000 and 10,000 m and cross country running. It can be seen in his entry forms that the place of birth could vary for one and the same person, even within the same sport. In the entry forms for track running it says that he was born in Högby on the island of Öland while in his entry for the cross country race his place of birth is given as Oxelösund in Sörmland. According to information in the Stockholm Register Office Archives John Eke (born as John Jonsson) was born in Högby, County of Kalmar, and has thus also been noted as an athlete born in Götaland.

25. Zander (ed.), *Svenska gymnastik- och idrottsföreningarnas riksförbund 1903–1928* (1928), p. 32.

26. Lindroth, *Från "sportfåneri" till massidrott* (1988), p. 77 ff.

27. Top came Stockholm nine, Gothenburg seven, Norrköping seven and Malmoe five. A further four participants came from State school associations that were not IFK associations.

28. Lennartz (2009), p. 302.

29. Lindroth (1988), p. 80.

30. Falk, Jan, et al., *Hellas* (1980), p. 1.

31. See "Gender and Clans."

32. National Archives, Stockholm Olympiad 1912, Foreign correspondence of the secretariat E II:1,

Swedes abroad. There is also information about two Swedish American wrestlers: K. Karlsson and Karl Johnson. *Dagens Nyheter*, June 17, 1912. See also "The Jewel in the Olympic Crown."
  33. Mallon and Widlund, 2009, p. 47ff.
  34. Johansson, 1953, p. 38.
  35. Yttergren, 1996, p. 108.
  36. Schelin: *Den ojämlika idrotten* (1985), p. 15 ff.

References

UNPUBLISHED SOURCES

Swedish National Archives: Stockholmsolympiaden 1912
Stockholm City Archives: Stockholm Register Office

ENCYCLOPEDIAS

Nordisk familjeboks sportlexikon 1–7 (Stockholm 1938–1949).

ELECTRONIC SOURCES

www.olympic.org
www.sok.se

PRINT SOURCES

Åsbrink, Gustaf (ed.). *Stockholm, Olympiska Spelens officiella vägvisare* (Stockholm, 1912).
Balck, Viktor. *Minnen. II Mannaåren* (Stockholm 1931).
Bergvall, Erik (ed.). *V. Olympiaden. Officiell redogörelse för olympiska spelen i Stockholm 1912* (Stockholm 1913).
Falk, Jan, Kjell Löfberg, and Sverker Tirén. *Hellas. Boken om en idrottsklubb* (Stockholm 1980).
Janzon, Bode. *Manschettyrken, idrott och hälsa. Studier kring idrottsrörelsen i Sverige särskilt Göteborg, intill 1900* (Göteborg 1978).
Johansson, Hilding. "Idrotten och samhället," *Svensk idrott. En ekonomisk, historisk och sociologisk undersökning* (Malmö 1953).
Lennartz, Karl. *Die Spiele der V. Olympiade 1912 in Stockholm* (Kassel 2009).
Lindroth, Jan. *Från "sportfåneri" till massidrott* (Stockholm 1988).
Lindroth, Jan. *Idrott för kung och fosterland. Viktor Balck den svenska idrottens fader* (Stockholm 2007).
Lindroth, Jan. *Idrottens väg till folkrörelse. Studier i svensk idrottsrörelse till 1915* (Uppsala 1974).
Mallon, Bill, and Ture Widlund. *The 1912 Olympic Games. Results for All Competitors in All Events, with Commentary* (Jefferson 2009).
McIntosh, PC. *Idrotten och samhället* (Stockholm 1969).
Persson, Lennart K., and Thomas Pettersson. *Svensk friidrott 100 år* (Stockholm 1995).
SCB. *Befolkningsutvecklingen under 250 år. Historisk statistik för Sverige* (Stockholm 1999).
Schelin, Bo. *Den ojämlika idrotten. Om idrottsstratifiering, idrottspreferens och val av idrott* (Lund, 1985).
Sylvén, Sune, and Ove Karlsson. *OS. Historia och statistik* (Stockholm 2008).
Uggla, Gustaf G:son. *Olympiska spelen i Stockholm 1912* (Stockholm, 1912).
Wikberg, Karin. *Amatör eller professionist? Studier rörande amatörfrågan i svensk tävlingsidrott 1903–1967* (Stockholm 2005).
Yttergren, Leif. *Täflan är lifvet. Idrottens organisering och sportifiering 1860–1898* (Stockholm 1996).
Zander, John (ed.). *Svenska gymnastik- och idrottsföreningarnas riksförbund 1903–1928. En minnesskrift* (Stockholm 1928).

Gender and Class

Women on the Swedish Squad

HANS BOLLING *and* LEIF YTTERGREN

> We have not sent women to the competitions, as we in America do not wish to see them doing sport in public. Both sport and they are better off if they practice sport at a distance from public curiosity.[1]

This statement made by the influential American sports official James E. Sullivan was by no means unique for sports officials at the beginning of the last century. He shared this negative attitude to women's competitive sport and women's participation in the Olympic Games with, amongst others, the president of the International Olympic Committee, Pierre de Coubertin, and Viktor Balck, president of the Organizing Committee for the Stockholm Olympiad in 1912. If women were to do sport, this was not to be done in public, particularly not as *competitive* athletes in the Olympic Games.[2]

Despite the opposition of several very influential sports officials to women competing, women did participate in the Stockholm Olympics, albeit only on a small scale. In all there were 53 women from ten nations competing in Stockholm in 1912. In addition, gymnastic squads from four countries, Norway, Denmark, Finland and Sweden, took part in the gymnastics display.[3]

The aim of this essay is to analyze the prevailing conditions for women competing in the Stockholm Olympic Games in 1912. In order to meet this aim, the inclusion of sports for women in the 1912 Olympic program will be discussed, the social background of the women in the Swedish Olympic squad analyzed and their training preparations discussed.

Source Material and Limitations

The source material is derived from different places. The article is largely based on information from a database on the Swedish participants in the Stockholm Olympics that we have created as part of our research project, "The 1912 Olympic Games in Stockholm: The Competitions — the Myths — the Consequences." In addition, the 1,117 pages of the official report, *The Fifth Olympiad: The Official Report of the Olympic Games of Stockholm 1912*, has been scrutinized. It was compiled by the sports journalist and sports official Erik Bergvall. Parts of the official Olympic archive have also been studied, primarily the minutes and correspondence of the large and powerful Organizing Committee, with Viktor Balck as its dynamic and strong president.

There is a clear gender aspect in the source material. It was men who wrote in the daily and sports press. It was also men who wrote the official report and it was also men who organized the Games in Stockholm, and finally it is now two men who are analyzing and writing about the women in the Games.

The main focus is on the two sports (aquatics and tennis) in which women were allowed to compete in the 1912 Olympic Games. We will touch on the social composition of the relatively large Swedish women's gymnastic squad, in all 48 gymnasts, which only took part in the Olympic display program, not the competitions.

Framework

The early history of the Olympic Games has been almost entirely about men: men who have taken part, men who have organized and men who have written about men's performances. This is not only due to a consciously exclusive choice of perspective but also to the fact that it was very difficult for women to gain access to the Olympic arena. The Olympic Games, like modern competitive sport in general, were quite simply created by men and for men.[4]

The Olympic Games and the IOC are thus what gender research usually calls homosocial environments, where men met, competed, socialized and not least created networks with other men. An example of this is that Avery Brundage, Sigfrid Edström and the German sports officials Carl Diem and Karl Ritter von Halt met during the Stockholm Olympic Games. After this they were close for several decades and were a considerable power factor within international top sport.[5] Men choose other like-minded men to socialize with, work with, and sit on boards with.[6] Women were, as we will show, excluded from this closed male environment. This was also true for many years to come in the IOC. It was only in 1981 that the first women were elected to the IOC.

Women's chances of participating in the Olympic Games were affected by the contemporary perception of the nature of women and simple but widespread ideas that women's physical frailty was something biologically predetermined. Most of the criticism and the loudest criticism of women who engaged in sport was aimed at those who willfully took part in physically demanding competitive activities, while more restrained physical activity such as gymnastics could be tolerated, supported by exercise and health arguments current at the time.

The practicing of sport of a competitive nature which was nevertheless accepted among women was also to a greater extent than its male equivalent a phenomenon reserved for the higher social classes. Further down the social scale physical activity was advocated almost exclusively as a preventive activity. What these women did in their leisure time was incorporated in a utilitarian system and was seen as an appendage to work. Physical activities that could be fitted into such a pattern were accepted for both women and men. However, when the activities threatened to become purely pleasure, the chances of taking part were considerably less for women than for men. This meant, for example, that the physiologically oriented and competition-free troop gymnastics was considered to suit women better than for example athletics and other more physically demanding competitive sports.[7]

The Women in the Stockholm Games

The 1912 Olympic organization was large. At the top of the hierarchy was the Organizing Committee for the 1912 Olympic Games, with Viktor Balck, often called "the father of Swedish sport," as the president and Crown Prince Gustaf Adolf as a committed and active honorary president. Under the committee there were five sections, with just over 30 members. None of these were women.

What, then, was the situation in the special committees, 22 in all, that were created for the running of the Games? Besides committees for the individual sports there were committees for the press, advertising, living quarters and so on. Each committee consisted of a handful of members. In all the different committees women were represented in only one, the one for tennis, where two women were members.[8] There were no women in the committees for the other two Olympic sports for women, swimming and gymnastics. Women were strongly underrepresented, even in the incredibly large team of officials, which was recorded in detail in the official report. They were to be found primarily as officials in the gymnastic displays, but also in swimming.[9] The organizing of the Olympic Games was clearly men's business.

The comprehensive program in Stockholm comprised 13 sports in all: athletics, wrestling, cycling, football, fencing, gymnastics, equestrian events, tennis, modern pentathlon, rowing, sailing, aquatics and shooting. All of these were open for participation by men and they consisted of 95 different events for men only and two where they competed together with women, in total 97 different events.[10]

Women could thus compete in two of the 13 sports: aquatics and tennis. Within these there were a total of seven events that they could compete in: the three aquatic events 100 meters freestyle, 4 × 100 meters team relay and plain high diving and the tennis events singles (indoors and outdoors) and mixed doubles (indoors and outdoors).

Most present-day compilations of the Olympic Games in Stockholm state that the number of sports that were competed in during the Games was 15, instead of the 13 above-mentioned sports. The difference arises from the fact that aquatics' different disciplines are nowadays counted as separate sports, which gives three sports for the Stockholm Games: swimming, diving and water polo instead of one, aquatics, and thus three sports where women could participate: swimming, diving and tennis.

It is worth noting that there were not any sports or events that were only designed and open for women to participate in, even if distance and length in some cases had been cut down when women were to compete, 4 × 100 meters in the team relay compared with 4 × 200 meters for men and the best of three sets in tennis compared with the best of five sets for men.[11]

Table 1. Men and Women at the Olympic Games in Stockholm in 1912

	Men	Women
Number	2,327	53
Nations	27	10
Sports	13	2
Events	97	7

Source: Mallon and Widlund, (2009), p. 57.

We can thus note that women's participation in the Olympic Games in Stockholm in 1912 was particularly limited. Out of a total of 2,380 competitors women constituted just 2.2 percent of those starting. Which countries then sent women to Stockholm? Table 2 shows that the participants were primarily from Northwest Europe. There was no nation that sent only women competitors. It can be noted that the USA and Canada had no women representatives at all, which was completely in line with the American sports official James E. Sullivan's view of women practicing sport in public settings. France's participation was limited to one woman tennis player.

Table 2. The Number of Women Per Nation
at the Olympic Games in Stockholm in 1912

Nation	Number
Sweden	23
United Kingdom	10
Austria	6
Germany	5
Australia	2
Finland	2
Norway	2
Belgium	1
Denmark	1
France	1
Total	53

Source: Mallon and Widlund (2009), pp. 56–57.

In the beginning the Swedish Organizing Committee had not intended to let women participate at all in the Olympic Games of 1912. Women's participation in the swimming competitions was accepted by the Organizing Committee only after pressure had been applied, mainly by the British. The British, who had a positive attitude to women's competitive swimming and were also successful, acted through the British Amateur Swimming Association, the British Olympic Association and the International Swimming Federation. The latter had been formed in the wake of the London Olympic Games in 1908 and remarkably enough had made women's competitive swimming one of its priorities. Success was obtained in getting the IOC to put pressure on the Organizing Committee to include women's aquatics in the Stockholm Olympic Games.[12]

However, the proposal to include women's tennis in the program came from the Swedish Tennis Association. When it was contacted in April 1910 by the Organizing Committee about arranging tennis competitions during the Olympic Games, a program was proposed that also contained events for women.[13] This program apparently did not stir up any criticism, but was accepted by those involved. Tennis for women had of course also been on the Olympic Games' program in 1900, 1906 and 1908. In 1908 in London there were two Swedish participants. Tennis was thus different from most other sports and had included women for a long time, even in competitive tennis. Wimbledon had introduced a women's class as early as 1884.[14]

The Organizing Committee, however, had to make a decision on whether women would be allowed to participate in one further sport in May 1912. It received an official letter from the British Olympic Committee asking whether women would be allowed to participate in the newly introduced sport the modern pentathlon. The committee decided to refer the letter to the committee for the modern pentathlon and to contact Pierre de Coubertin to find out his position on the matter.[15]

The committee for the modern pentathlon was negative to women's participation. A committee vote resulted in ten votes against and two votes for women's participation. Pierre de Coubertin for his part declared himself neutral on the matter. On the basis of the replies that had been received the Organizing Committee decided that women would not be allowed to participate in the modern pentathlon.[16] Given what research has shown about Coubertin's attitude to women's participation in the Olympic Games his reluctance to take up a position on the question can be regarded as somewhat surprising. However, his pronounced neutrality should not be seen as him not caring about the question of women's participation, but rather it seems that the previous decisions to allow women to participate in tennis and aquatics had made him somewhat resigned:

> I am personally opposed <u>to the admittance of ladies</u> as competitors in the Olympic Games. But as they are this time admitted as tennis players, swimmers etc. I do not see on what ground we should stand to refuse them in the Pentathlon. However I repeat that I greatly <u>regret the fact.</u> Therefore I leave it to you to decide and if you refuse or accept the engagement, I shall agree with you.[17]

What is more surprising is that a month and a half before the start of the competitions, there were two persons on the committee for the modern pentathlon who were positive to women participating, and this was a committee for which Viktor Balck was the president.

The two committee members who were for allowing women to compete in the modern pentathlon were the swimming official Erik Bergvall and the Olympic rider to be, Claes König.[18] It can be noted that women had to wait 88 years, until 2000, before they could compete in the modern pentathlon in the Olympic Games.

Women's participation was not self-evident in the gymnastic displays either. At first the organizers had thought that the Olympic gymnastics program would be limited to displays by troops of men. Viktor Balck spoke out strongly against displays by troops of women. He considered them unsuitable and to some extent contrary to the concept of the Olympic Games, and "all the displays in London seemed ridiculous."[19] However, the program was expanded after pressure from different quarters and finally came to include individual competitions and three different troop competitions for men and troop displays for men and women.[20]

In what follows the social

Swedish military officers were successful in the new Olympic sport modern pentathlon at Stockholm 1912. From left: the winner Gustaf Lilliehöök, fourth placed Åke Grönberg and the bronze medalist Georg de Laval (photograph by Axel Malmström, SCIF photo collection).

composition of the women's part of the Swedish Olympic squad will be studied from an event perspective, aquatics and tennis at an individual level and the gymnastics squad at an aggregation level. The women's training preparations will also be paid attention to and be compared with the men's.

The Swimmers' Social Composition

A total of 17 Swedish women took part in aquatics at the Stockholm Olympics of 1912: twelve in high diving and six in swimming. One of them was in both: Margareta "Greta" Johanson from Stockholm.

All the swimmers were under 20; the average age was 17. The oldest of them was 19-year-old Vera Thulin and the youngest was Greta Carlsson, who had her 14th birthday two days before she swam in the 100 meters heats. The other four were all born in 1895. Three of the swimmers were born in Stockholm and the others in Eskilstuna, Gothenburg and Uppsala.

Four out of the six swimmers competed for the leading swimming club in Stockholm, Stockholms kappsimningsklubb (SKK). The remainder represented Eskilstuna simsällskap and Göteborgs damers simklubb. The Gothenburg club, which was founded the same year, was Sweden's first club specially for women's swimming.[21] The swimmers were thus young and came from big towns and cities, where the sport was relatively well established, even as early as the beginning of the twentieth century.

As the swimmers were so young it is hardly surprising that none of them were married. Several of them worked despite their low age. Among the occupations mentioned we find two office clerks and a commercial clerk. The two swimmers who were not from Stockholm still went to school, however. Karin Lundgren graduated in 1914 from the Teacher Training College in Gothenburg and Greta Carlsson was still a pupil at the girls' high school at home in Eskilstuna at the time of the Olympic Games.[22]

Besides the six Swedes, 21 foreign swimmers participated in the competitions. They represented seven nations: the United Kingdom, Norway, Germany, Austria, Finland, Australia and Belgium. They had an average age of just under 20.[23] They were thus somewhat older than the Swedish swimmers. Only three nations besides Sweden, the United Kingdom, Germany and Austria, had sent enough swimmers to be able to take part in the team relay over 400 meters. The British women won easily and the Swedes came last.[24]

If we leave the swimmers and move on to the divers we find a similar pattern. Diving was a popular, and for women accepted, sports event in Stockholm during the first decades of the twentieth century. All twelve participants in the event represented SKK. Among the divers there were five who were older than 20 and the average age was 20, that is they were three years older than the swimmers. Lisa Regnell, 25, was the oldest of the divers and Märta Adlerz 15, was youngest. Nine of them were born in Stockholm and the others in Svealand: Kristinehamn, Uppsala and Västerås, but all of them lived in Stockholm at the time of the Olympic Games. Neither were any of the divers married at the time of the Games in Stockholm.

As the divers were older than the swimmers we also find that they had more qualified occupations. Lisa Regnell worked as a music teacher. She also had a more solid middle-class background than most of the swimmers and divers, as her father was the captain of a steamer. A study of twelve women swimmers and divers who were members of SKK shows that their

Margareta "Greta" Johanson, gold medal winner in the women's plain high diving at Stockholm 1912. She also competed in the swimming events but without success, eliminated in the first round in 100 meters and last out of four teams in the relay with Sweden (photograph by Theodor Modin, SCIF photo collection).

The winning English team in the women's 4 × 100 meter freestyle relay, in swimsuits: Isabella Moore, Jennie Fletcher, Annie Speirs and Irene Steer. Unknown, center (photograph by Theodor Modin, SCIF photo collection).

fathers largely belonged to the working class.[25] Among the other divers we also find occupations such as milliner, draughtsman and telephonist, but also a cleaner and the same type of occupations as amongst the swimmers.

A comparison with the foreign women participants cannot be made as there were only two who did not come from Sweden that took part in the competition: Isabelle White, United Kingdom, born 1894, and Hanny Kellner, Austria, born 1892.[26]

TRAINING PREPARATIONS

The Swedish organizers had worked hard on the Swedish sportsmen being able to perform well during the Games, preferably take lots of medals and thereby honor Sweden and cover the nation in glory. It may be worth remembering here that the President of the Organizing Committee of the Olympic Games, Viktor Balck, despite his involvement in international sport, amongst other things as a member of the IOC 1894–1920 and President of the International Skating Federation 1893–1925, was above all a strongly nationalistic-minded Swedish officer for who the overriding purpose of competing in international sport was to assert Swedish values.[27]

The training preparations, and not least the coaches, played a central role in this work. This could also be seen in aquatics, at least for the men. An English coach was employed as early as 1910, Charles Hurley, in order to improve the Swedish swimmers and divers. Similar, if not greater, efforts were made in other events as well, amongst other things in athletics and wrestling.

The coach who was imported from abroad was, however, only interested in the men's swimming and diving. There is nothing to indicate that he devoted time and energy to the women. In the official report the men's preparations are described very thoroughly and at great length while the women's training is only mentioned in two lines.[28] The training opportunities offered the women swimmers and divers were not on the same level as those offered the men. The men in the Olympic swimming committee were primarily interested in the men's preparations and the women's training was therefore insufficient. It focused above all on diving, which according to the conventions of the time was a suitable sport for women.[29]

However, in the winter of 1911/12 the women got the chance to begin to train indoors in Stockholm as part of the Olympic preparations. The women trained twice a week, on Sundays at one o' clock and on Tuesdays at eight, under the leadership of a Swedish coach. It can be noted that several participants, with only the odd exception, trained both diving and swimming, but that, as was seen above, only one of them qualified for the competitions in both events.

A large number of women had been selected for training and then selections were made from this training squad for the final squad. The decision to have the preparations run by SKK had consequences for the composition of the Swedish Olympic squad, as has been seen above — all the participants except for two represented the club. The swimming and diving selection trials were arranged by the Swedish Swimming Federation at the end of May/beginning of June 1912.[30]

The women swimmers' and divers' coming debut in the Games obviously aroused interest. In the magazine *Idun*, which was aimed at "the woman and the home," an account was given of how the training was carried out:

> The training goes like this: the participants dive five or so times from the diving board, after which they are subjected to extremely thorough criticism, and then they practice swimming (the same as the swimmers do these days, the so-called trudgeon) and finally they race one or two lengths.[31]

The most coherent effort to achieve success in swimming and diving for women seems to have been made by the United Kingdom. The British team of seven swimmers and divers brought two coaches, both women, Mme. Jarvis and Mrs. Holmes, to Stockholm,[32] that is if they were not there as chaperons to make sure the British swimmers and divers followed the straight and narrow during the Games.

REACTIONS

Women's participation in aquatics was controversial, not only because women athletes had made their way into a new Olympic arena, but also because they competed with comparatively few clothes on. The very nature of aquatics made it impossible for competitors to hide their bodies under layers of clothes. When the swimming competitions were given attention in the press it was, however, above all the sporting achievements that were the center of focus. Two competitors in particular attracted the interest of the male writers, the Swedish gold medalist in high diving Greta Johanson and the winner of the 100 meters, Sarah "Fanny" Durack, who was said to have swum "100 meters faster than our male champion."[33]

The only special rule for women in the 1912 rules and regulations for the aquatic competitions applied to their swimsuits and it stated that the swimsuit should "be cut straight round the neck, and shall be provided with shaped arms of at least 7½ centimeters length."[34] However, there were also rules to protect the participants' virtue, both men's and women's, amongst other things a rule that said that "cloth drawers, at least 6 centimeters high at the sides, must be worn under the costume."[35]

A strategy that the women swimmers and divers employed so as not to be regarded and condemned as pin-ups or temptresses was to always wear bathrobes when they were not in the water, something that was obligatory in Australia.[36] However, this was not always enough: the swimming association that the Australian 100 meters gold medalist, Fanny Durack, belonged to, the New South Wales Ladies' Swimming Association, had until shortly before the Stockholm Games a clause in its rules and regulations that forbade its members from participating at all in mixed-sex competitions. This applied both in the pool and on the stands. When the rule was changed, several leading people left the association.[37]

In the well-preserved photo archive from the Stockholm Olympic Games there are many photographs of women swimmers, and they were almost entirely photographed in the swimsuits typical of the time. Given the fact that sports officials such as Pierre de Coubertin and James E. Sullivan saw women's sport as something almost immoral, mainly due to the exposure of the human body that it entailed, it was not strange that they opposed women's competitive swimming and diving.

Margareta "Greta" Johanson (photograph by Axel Malmström, SCIF photo collection).

The Tennis Players' Social Composition

The tennis players had two chances to compete in the Stockholm Olympic Games of 1912, as competitions were arranged both indoors and outdoors. In all, players from six nations took part in the two tennis competitions: Denmark, France, Norway, Sweden, UK and Germany.

However, no more than 13 players in all took part in the tennis tournaments, six Swedes and seven from abroad. Of the foreign participants four took part in the indoor tournament and three in the outdoor tournament. Among the Swedish participants four took part both indoors and outdoors. One explanation of the poor participation in the tennis tournament was that the outdoor competition, which had to be seen as the main attraction, coincided with the Wimbledon tournament in which the foremost British players preferred to take part.

Before the Games tennis was regarded as the sport where the Swedes compared worst with the international competition.[38] It was a view that also came to be confirmed, as six out of seven foreign participants were able to travel home as medalists in the women's singles. The only Swedish woman who won medals was Sigrid Fick, who won a silver in mixed doubles outdoors and a bronze indoors together with Gunnar Setterwall despite the fact that they only won one match. Indoors they had a bye in the first round, won by walkover in the quarter final, lost in the semi-final and won by walkover in the match for the third prize. Outdoors they had a walkover in the first round, won the quarter final against another Swedish pair, had a walkover in the semi-final but lost the final.

The tennis players had an average age of 33, a considerably higher age than the swimmers and divers. The women tennis players' average age was also considerably higher than that of the men tennis players, whose average age was 26. However, it should be mentioned here that Ebba Hay, who was born in 1866, brought up the average age quite considerably. The next oldest was Ellen Brusewitz, who was 33 years old. The two eldest participants, unlike the other Swedes, only took part in one event each, mixed doubles indoors and singles outdoors.

The tennis players were not only older than the swimmers and divers, they also had another geographic origin. We do not find any Stockholm domination among them: three were born in Jönköping, two abroad, in Helsinki and Prague, and only one in Stockholm. However, all players represented the prestigious Royal Lawn Tennis Club of Stockholm (KLTK) during the Olympic tournaments.

Another thing that distinguished the different athletes was that the tennis players were not in paid employment, but rather when they had a household of their own they were designated "miss" or in other cases as a housewife. The tennis players thus included married

Lawn-tennis, final mixed-double, to the right the German couple Dorothea Köring and Heinrich Schomburgk, gold medalists (6–4, 6–0), against the Swedish couple Sigrid Fick and Gunnar Setterwall (SCIF photo collection).

Marguerite Broquedis, gold medalist in lawn-tennis singles. Notice the public in the background looking the other way (postcard, National Sports Museum).

women. Two out of six were married at the time of the Stockholm Games, both of them to officers, and a third had already gotten divorced. The three that had not married by 1912 did not do so after the Olympic Games either.

The seven foreign players who took part had an average age of 29.[39] They were also considerably older than their swimming and diving colleagues, but younger than their Swedish rivals.

TRAINING PREPARATIONS

Those responsible for the Olympic tennis also decided to hire a foreign coach, the Englishman Charles Haggett. In the case of tennis, however, it was not direct importation of new coaching competence just for the Olympic Games. Haggett had been active as a professional tennis coach in Sweden since 1899, when he was hired by KLTK's predecessor, Kronprinsens lawntennisklubb (The Crown Prince's Lawn Tennis Club), and must have been one of the first professional coaches in Sweden.[40] As from October 1911 he was in charge of the Swedish tennis players' training. The training squad consisted of eight women and 16 men.[41] Who would then represent Sweden in the Olympic Games was decided by the form that the players displayed in the competitive matches during the spring. No special qualifying competitions were held in tennis, however.[42]

What really distinguished tennis from other sports was, as has already been mentioned, the fact that its special committee, Lawntenniskommittén, included two women among the men in charge, even though the men were in a clear majority, seven out of nine members. The women tennis players were thus not only allowed to take part in the tennis tournament, but they could also be involved in organizing and deciding the design and running of the tournament. In this respect tennis was considerably more equal than aquatics, and was probably the most equal competitive sport in Sweden.

At Jönköping's Lawn-Tennis Club's national competitions in 1907. Ebba Hay (1866–1954) is in the middle of the front row in front of the cup, and to her right is Prince Wilhelm (*Nordiskt Idrottslif,* 1907).

However, it is important to bear in mind that tennis did not challenge the norm for acceptable female behavior in public in the same way as more physical sports. When they began to play tennis, women had increased their opportunities of being physically active in a public setting but at the same time had been careful not to challenge the prevailing social balance between women and men. At the same time as the sexes came closer to one another through the common physical activity, the women confirmed the differences between them through their behavior and their attire. Photographs from tennis tournaments also show women dressed in hardly functional tennis clothes — blouses with long or semi-long sleeves, ankle-length skirts and hats — and when they were photographed after a match they often also wore long coats.

The Gymnasts' Social Composition

In all gymnastic teams from four nations participated in the gymnastics display. In addition to the Swedish team of 48 gymnasts there were also gymnastics teams from Denmark (148 gymnasts), Finland (24 gymnasts) and Norway (22 gymnasts).[43] The Finnish team in particular under the leadership of the ground-breaking gymnastics pedagogue Elli Björkstén made a deep impression on the large public and also came to influence the further development of women's gymnastics in Sweden.[44]

We know that all the gymnasts in the Swedish team were or were going to be gymnastic directors, or possibly physiotherapists. They had been selected from among students and fully trained gymnastic teachers who had been trained at Kungliga gymnastiska centralinstitut (GCI, today GIH), Arvedsons gymnastikinstitut in Stockholm or Sydsvenska gymnastikinstitutet in Lund. This meant that they had, or would soon get, both an academic education and an occupation.[45] The gymnasts should thus be able to be placed tentatively at a social level between the tennis players on the one hand and the swimmers and divers on the other. Other research has shown that several of these gymnastics teachers were strong and independent women with great occupational integrity. As a rule they worked either as gymnastics teachers or as physiotherapists both in Sweden and abroad, where Swedish gymnastics was popular. Gymnastics institutes were common in this time of health concerns and interest in physical activity to promote health.[46]

The 48 women in the Swedish gymnastics team were born all over Sweden. Thus we have here a group whose distribution all over Sweden reflected to a much greater extent than the two competitive sports how the general population was distributed over the country.

The average age of the participants was 22, with a certain spread in age but a clear concentration around the average age. Six of the participants were not even 20 and only one of the participants was over 30. Most gymnasts, 25 in all, were born 1890–1891, and were probably students or had just completed their education at the above-mentioned seats of learning.

It could be argued that all members of the Swedish gymnastics team represented one Stockholm association, Kvinnliga gymnastikföreningen Sveriges uppvisning, which was created in the autumn of 1911 solely for the gymnastics display at the Games. However, the gymnasts were at the same time also members of local gymnastics associations all over Sweden so it is a fairly weak argument. Unfortunately, the gymnasts' home associations are not stated on the registration forms that are preserved in the archive of the Stockholm Games.

TRAINING PREPARATIONS

At the beginning of June the women gymnasts who had been selected after trials during the spring in Stockholm, Lund and Gothenburg, were gathered in Stockholm to prepare together for the display in connection with the opening of the Olympic Games. All the non-Stockholmers, between 30 and 40 gymnasts, were given lodging in a gymnastics institute in the capital, "where they are now sleeping sweetly and soundly among wall bars and ropes, a couple of dozen in each hall."[47] They thus did not need to pay for their own board and lodging. The Organizing Committee contributed to covering the expenses of the Swedish women's gymnastics display team through an allowance of 1,300 kronor.[48]

Training was held at the GCI under the leadership of the gymnastics teacher Marrit Hallström, assisted by Karin Neuendorff, who herself was a member of the display team. The preparations were described in the newspaper *Idun*:

> The spectator for his part admires the beautiful spectacle that these splendid young Swedish women offer, where they practice in the yard of the Central Institute. Our picture gives the illusion of the flight of birds, and can there be any better ideal for young sportswomen than being supple and strong, and fast, silent and exact like migrating birds flying over the countryside?[49]

Scene from display by the Swedish lady gymnasts (*Den femte olympiaden i bild och ord*, p. 123).

And those who went to the Olympic Stadium to see the women's gymnastics display in connection with the opening of the Olympic Games could look forward to "enjoying seeing the Swedish women winning unconditionally and outside the competitions."[50]

Reflections on the Lives of the Women

It would have been interesting to do a deep analysis of one or two of the women in the Swedish Olympic squad and depict their life stories, because several of them had fascinating lives. However, we will have to make do with presenting a few common characteristics of the participants.

Information has been available for all the 23 women who competed for Sweden at the Stockholm Games and this has made it possible to follow the general outline of their lives until they died. The diver Ester Edström can serve as an illustration. We know that she was born in Västerås in 1892, lived in Stockholm from 1912 and worked as a telephonist, a typical female occupation for women from the lower echelons of society on their way to rising a little in the classes up to the lower-middle class. She married in 1926, but had no children. She died after a period of illness, only 53 years old.

A common and slightly surprising feature with regard to the participants who have not been presented previously is that siblings are well represented among the women Olympic participants. Nine out of 23, just over one third, had a sibling who also competed in the Olympic Games. This is true of both of the sports: six in aquatics and three in tennis.[51]

Of the 23 competitors twelve were born in Stockholm. There is a clear difference with regard to geographic origin between aquatics and tennis. Five of the tennis players were born somewhere other than in Stockholm: two abroad and three in Jönköping. Jönköping appears to have been a metropolis of women's tennis at the beginning of the 20th century. We know that Ebba Hay worked for the spreading of the sport in the town and she was a prime mover behind both the formation of the tennis club and the building of a tennis hall in the town.[52]

We can note that the women who participated in the Olympic Games came from established Swedish sports towns. Not even in women's sport, whose development was weak, was there room for athletes from places without an organization and a sports culture.

The vast majority of the women Olympic athletes represented clubs in Stockholm, 21 out of 23. This was due to the fact that the two large clubs from the capital were given the responsibility of training the women Olympic athletes by the Organizing Committee. We can note that the concentration in the capital city of Stockholm also continued after their sporting careers. When the women died, 18 out of 23 lived in Stockholm, one in Nyköping, two tennis players had remained faithful ton Jönköping and two swimmers in the USA, where they had emigrated.

It is also worth noticing that those who competed in Stockholm in 1912 lived relatively long lives. The above-mentioned Edström was an exception. When they died they were almost 79 years old on average, when they participated in the Stockholm Games they were on average 22. In 1910–1919 a 20-year-old woman had an estimated life expectancy of 47 years and a 25-year-old woman 43 years.[53] The women who competed for Sweden in the Olympic competitions in 1912 thus lived just over a decade longer than the Swedish women who did not compete in the Stockholm Games. We do not know if this was due to the fact that they lived physically active lives during the remainder of their lives or whether they had good physical qualities from the very start.

Even if the swimmers and divers were not married at the time of the Games, all except two of them married later. One of the unmarried ones died as early as 1919 as a result of the Spanish flu, which was rampant in Sweden and in other countries at the time. We can also note that aquatics filled a social function for the athletes: they were able to find their other half-to-be within aquatics. For example, the gold medalist Greta Johanson married another Swedish Olympic athlete, the diver Ernst Brandsten who competed for the rival Stockholm club Neptun, while the silver medalist Lisa Regnell married the swimming official Sam Lindh. We do not find this type of marriage pattern within tennis. This can to some extent have been due to the fact that the tennis players were older than the swimmers and divers. Three of them had already married before 1912 while the others remained unmarried for the rest of their lives. Getting married was not an obvious thing to do in Stockholm just over 100 years ago. Many couples, especially those from the working class, decided to live in so-called Stockholm marriages, which meant that they lived together and had children without getting married.[54]

It appears probable that being unmarried was a precondition for being a sportswoman. The swimmers and divers were young and had a short career and got married when their career was over, the first of them only three months after the Stockholm Games. The tennis players had a considerably longer sports career, which was difficult to combine with the demands made of a spouse in those days. Two of the three married tennis players also got divorced, Edith Arnheim Lasch already before the Stockholm Games in 1911 and Sigrid Fick in 1929, whereupon she became a professional tennis coach in 1933.[55] It should also be mentioned that many of the women who competed in Stockholm in 1912 were minors according to Swedish legislation. Unmarried women came of age at the age of 21 but married women were still considered minors, as they were under the guardianship of their husbands. It was not until 1921 that they achieved the status of majority and in this year women also gained the right to vote.[56]

Despite the fact that the population is small and not selected to be representative, the women's Olympic squad can serve as an illustration of the demographic situation in Sweden at the beginning of the twentieth century. Urbanization and moving to built-up areas and towns, primarily Stockholm, was very comprehensive. But in addition, in parallel with this process, there was great emigration on a scale never previously or subsequently seen. It is estimated that over a million Swedes left the country for above all the USA in the decades around 1900, which was an incredible figure for a country with a population of around 5 million and led to concern for the continued existence of the country's population in leading circles.[57]

Summary

The aim of this essay was to analyze the prevailing conditions for women competing in the Stockholm Olympic Games in 1912. As has been clearly seen women were allowed to participate in the Olympic Games in Stockholm in 1912 on sufferance, only to a limited extent and upon the conditions of the men of the IOC and on the Organizing Committee. A total of 53 women from 10 nations participated, compared with 2,327 men from 27 nations, which means that the women representatives constituted 2.2 percent of the participants. Of these almost half, 23, came from Sweden. They competed only in two sports, aquatics and tennis, compared with the men's thirteen. It was thus a small band of women sports pioneers that competed in Stockholm.

The insignificant and conditional female representation in the Stockholm Games can be partly explained by the almost total exclusion of women from the gigantic organizational apparatus that was built up around the Stockholm Olympic Games. The Olympic organization was thus reminiscent of the IOC with regard to its composition, which meant that it was an out and out homosocial environment where men from the same echelons of society made decisions about different questions, amongst other things about women's sport in the Olympic Games. The picture of an exclusive gentlemen's club emerges. Women had no influence over or insight into the almost completely supreme Organizing Committee and its sections. There was female representation in only one of the 22 special committees that were set up for the Games, the committee for tennis. It is beyond all doubt that the organizing of the Olympic Games in Stockholm was a job for men.

Who then were the women who represented Sweden in the Olympic Games in Stockholm in 1912? Regarding their social background it can be seen that there is a clear link between sporting event and social class. There is thus reason to talk about different "tastes," as the cultural sociologist Pierre Bourdieu puts it. The tennis players thus came from the upper echelons of society while the swimmers and divers were primarily of working class origin. The gymnasts, who were or were on the way to becoming gymnastics teachers or physiotherapists, came from the middle class. The women thereby follow approximately the same pattern as the men regarding the link between choice of event and social class.[58] "Taste" was thus related more to class than to gender, at least at the beginning of the previous century. Physical activity for women was thus not just a matter of gender but also of class.

The geographical distribution with regard to place of birth was limited. Of the 23 competing women, just over half came from Stockholm. There was a clear difference between aquatics and tennis with regard to geographic origin. The tennis players were born somewhere other than Stockholm. Olympic women came from established Swedish sports towns. Before the Olympic Games all the women in principle joined the two large special clubs for each event in the capital city; these had been given the main responsibility for preparing prospective Olympic participants. It can also be noted that the women continued to be faithful to Stockholm for the rest of their lives. When they died 18 out of 23 were living in Stockholm.

There were remarkably large differences in age between the competitors in the two sports. In most cases the swimmers and divers were young girls while the tennis players were considerably older. The reason for the difference in age is not obvious but can be partly explained by the fact that it is a question of different sports' cultural environment and different classes' sports preferences. The upper class as a rule engage in sports that they can be active in for a long time (golf, riding, tennis) while the working class is attracted more by physically demanding activities (swimming, sport involving physical strength, football) which can only be engaged in during a short period of one's life.[59]

The Swedish tennis players' high age may have been reinforced by the limited popularity of the sport around 1912. There were quite simply not many other women players than the upper class women, who had time to play often and this was enough for them to be part of the Swedish elite. Moreover, international top level tennis was another sport than it is today and was more reminiscent of a social pastime.

Regarding the decision to include aquatics and tennis in the Olympic program, it can be noted that competitive swimming had its roots in the promotion of good health and being able to swim while tennis had its origins in the upper classes' social life. They thus stemmed from different cultural environments but could both be considered suitable sports for women as well according to the view of women at the time. They developed acceptable female bodily attributes such as suppleness and elasticity.

Regarding tennis, women's participation seems to have been completely uncontroversial, but Sweden had also been represented by women tennis players in London in 1908. Those competing were socially established and the fact that women competed together with men had long been an accepted fact. There were even women in leading positions in the Swedish Tennis Association, and as has been mentioned, on the Olympic tennis committee. The treatment of women's tennis in the Stockholm Games thus does not invalidate the view that engaging in competitive sport was above all the domain of the upper echelons of society. The upper class was perhaps not more equal but women's competitive sport was accepted as long as the sport remained within the class norms. Women's tennis clothes were also hardly aimed at arousing a male observer's lust.

Swimming was definitely more controversial, not only because women were entering a male arena to which they had not had access previously. Swimming was by nature more physical and the swimmers also displayed their bodies in the race arenas in racing swimsuits which, especially when they were wet, revealed bodily details which according to the outlook of the time should remain hidden from men's eyes. However, this could be overlooked as swimming largely took place under the water so that the women's bodies were not within view of men's gaze. Women who wanted to gain access to aquatics arenas had to be careful not to behave in such a way that could be interpreted as provocative by the men around them or seen as a danger to the prevailing gender status quo.

The introduction of aquatics into the Olympic program meant from a Swedish perspective that a new group of women were granted access to the Olympic Games, younger women with their roots in the working class. Previously it had only been women with privileged positions in society who, albeit to a limited extent, had been able to represent Sweden in the Olympic Games, in socially accepted sports such as tennis and figure skating. The Swedish women swimmers had a completely different social background.

The Swedish sports movement and the Organizing Committee gave top priority to the Swedish squad before the Olympic Games. However, it has been seen that it was above all men that were given priority. A strategy that was frequently used was to hire foreign professional coaches, and this was also done to train the Swedish men swimmers. The women swimmers had to make do with a Swedish male trainer. However, the tennis women had the same coach as the men, an Englishman who had already been working in Sweden. The training efforts for both swimming and tennis were based in Stockholm. Unlike what was the case for the male athletes no collective efforts were made to trace and train the sporting talent that was perhaps to be found all over the country.

The term gender contract is used in Swedish gender research to show "the social norm that existed at various points in time with regard to gender: place, work, qualities." This gender contract thus affected when, where and how women could be physically active. According to the Swedish historian Yvonne Hirdman's gender system theory there are two logics driving the balance of power between the sexes. Firstly there is the logic of keeping apart, which means that the sexes are constantly separated into different enclosures, male and female arenas, and secondly male is the norm. Hirdman's contract theory follows the maxim that the more integration there is between the sexes, the greater the problems are. The prevailing genus contract is undermined when the keeping apart of the sexes is weakened.[60] Transferred to this study this would mean that that women's participation in the Olympic Games in Stockholm 1912 would threaten men's sport, at least if the women engaged in sport in the same way as the men.

Did the Olympic Games in Stockholm upset the prevailing gender contract and was the male norm threatened? The answer to these questions is no. Women's participation in the Olympic Games in Stockholm in 1912 never threatened men's sport, despite the fact that some women were allowed to perform in the same arenas as the men. They did not deviate from the given norms for what was perceived as female or male, something which women who wanted to participate in the Olympic Games would not be able to do for at least another half century. When they threatened to deviate from the given norms they continued to be stopped, which is clearly shown by how women's middle distance running was treated after the Olympic Games in Amsterdam in 1928. The introduction of women's athletics in the Olympic program made the Swedish sports official Erik Bergvall, who in 1912 had been in charge of aquatics and was positive to women participating in the modern pentathlon, talk of "a very severe error of judgement."[61]

The subordination and the keeping apart thus continued to prevail. The fears that by including tennis and aquatics for women in the Olympic program Pandora's Box had been opened, fears which Pierre de Coubertin appears to have entertained in his letter to Kristian Hellström concerning the possible participation of women in the modern pentathlon in 1912, proved to be just a concern and nothing else.

However, there were commentators in 1912 who considered that even the minor extent to which women had been allowed to participate in Stockholm was to go too far. These included the influential cultural columnist Carl O. Laurin, who in an article in *Idun* claimed that James E. Sullivan's opinion was correct. The woman's place was in the home where she secured the future of the Swedish people through motherhood and not on the sports tracks:

> In general I feel little attracted by the American view of the position of women, but here I make an exception. I am convinced that public health will benefit from men being more male and women more female. There are many virtues which together constitute womanlihood, but at present I am thinking primarily of what lies deepest in a woman, what Sweden is now in desperate need of, that is that she gladly chooses to be a mother and is happy to take care of her maternal duties.[62]

Notes

1. James E. Sullivan, quoted in *Idun*, no. 31, 1912, p. 520.
2. Lindroth, *Idrott för kung och fosterland* (2007), pp. 163–164, and Suokas, "Klass och kön i svensk simsport kring sekelskiftet 1900" (2000), pp. 115 ff.
3. Mallon and Widlund, *The 1912 Olympic Games* (2009), pp. 29 and 374.
4. Annerstedt, *Kvinnoidrottens utveckling i Sverige* (1984); Hargreaves, *Sporting Females* (1994); Olofsson, *Har kvinnorna en sportslig chans?* (1989).
5. Yttergren, "Questions of Propriety" (2007).
6. Nordlund Edvinsson, *Broderskap i näringslivet* (2010), p. 20 ff.
7. Bolling, *Sin egen hälsas smed* (2005), p. 52 ff.
8. Bergvall (ed.), *V. Olympiaden* (1913), p. 594.
9. Ibid., p. 928 ff.
10. Mallon and Widlund, 2009, p. 29.
11. The modification of sport activities to make them less strenuous and thus suit the prevailing conception of women's physical ability was a common practice during the twentieth century. Bolling, 2005, pp. 52–53.
12. Suokas, 2000, p. 115.
13. Bergvall, 1913, pp. 50 ff.
14. *Nordisk Familjeboks Sportlexikon*, vol. 6 (1946), sp. 1290.
15. Organisationskommittén, 7/5 1912, § 31. Stockholmsolympiadens arkiv, A I:3, National Archives.
16. Ibid., 14/5 1912, § 31.
17. Kommittén för modern femkamp, brev från Pierre de Coubertin till Kristian Hellström, 20/5 1912. Stockholmsolympiadens arkiv, Ö III:1, National Archives.
18. Kommittén för modern femkamp, skriftlig omröstning angående kvinnors rätt att delta i den moderna femkampen vid Stockholmsolympiaden. Stockholmsolympiadens arkiv, Ö III:1, National Archives.

19. Organisationskommittén, 6/6 1910, bilaga 5. Stockholmsolympiadens arkiv, A I:1, National Archives.

20. Bergvall, 1913, pp. 46 ff.

21. The creation of the club was controversial, Suokas, 2000, pp. 120–121.

22. *Svenska Dagbladet*, September 21, 1974; *Dagen Nyheter,* March 22, 1980.

23. Lennartz, *Die Spiele der V. Olympiade 1912 in Stockholm* (Kassel 2009), pp. 43–44 and 280 ff.

24. Bergvall, 1913, pp. 682 ff.

25. Suokas, 2000, p. 101.

26. Lennartz, 2009, p. 290.

27. Sandblad, *Olympia och Valhalla* (Stockholm 1985), p. 241.

28. Bergvall, 1913, p. 276.

29. Suokas, 2000, p. 118.

30. Bergvall, 1913, p. 280.

31. *Idun,* no. 6 (1912), pp. 93–94.

32. Bergvall, 1913, p. 922.

33. Quotation, *Dagens Nyheter,* July 9, 1912. *Stockholmstidningen, Aftontidning, Stockholms Dagblad.*

34. Bergvall, 1913, p. 1014.

35. Ibid.

36. Suokas, 2000, p. 110–111.

37. Lennartz, 2009, p. 282.

38. *Idun,* no. 6 (1912), p. 93.

39. Mallon and Widlund, 2009, p. 52–53.

40. Ivar Lignell, et al. (eds.), *Svensk tennis* (Stockholm, 1938), p. 52.

41. Ibid., p. 64.

42. Bergvall, 1913, p. 273f.

43. Mallon and Widlund, 2009, p. 374.

44. *Nordisk familjeboks sportlexikon,* vol. 1 (Stockholm 1938), sp 837.

45. Bergvall, 1913, p. 273. *Nordisk familjeboks sportlexikon,* vol. 3 (Stockholm 1940), sp 905.

46. Halldén: *Vandringsboken* (Stockholm 1996). Trangbæk, "'Purity of Heart and Strength of Will'" (Copenhagen 1999), p. 48.

47. *Idun,* no. 42 (1911), p. 679, and no. 25 (1912), p. 417, quotation.

48. Organisationskommittén, 2/5 1912, § 6. Stockholmsolympiadens arkiv, AI:3, National Archives.

49. *Idun,* no. 25 (1912), p. 417.

50. Ibid.

51. Wilhelmina and Vera Thulin, diving and swimming; Elsa and Lisa Regnell, swimming; Annie Holmström and Ellen Brusewitz, tennis; Margareta and Hugo Cederschiöld, tennis and shooting; Märta and Erik Adlerz, diving; Selma and Robert Andersson, diving and swimming, diving and water polo.

52. *Jönköpings Posten,* October 29, 1953.

53. SCB: *Befolkningsutvecklingen under 250 år* (Stockholm 1999), p. 118.

54. About the so-called Stockholm marriages, see Matovic: *Stockholmsäktenskap* (Stockholm 1984).

55. Lignell, 1938, p. 341.

56. Clayhills, *Kvinnohistorisk uppslagsbok* (Stockholm 1992), pp. 374, 547.

57. Norberg, *Sveriges historia under 1800- och 1900-talen* (Stockholm 1988), pp. 23 ff.

58. Yttergren, *Täflan är lifvet* (Stockholm 1996), p. 108.

59. Ibid.

60. Overud, *I beredskap med Fru Lojal* (Stockholm 2005), pp. 19–20.

61. Annerstedt, 1983, pp. 116 ff.

62. *Idun,* no. 31 (1912), p. 520.

References

UNPUBLISHED SOURCES

Swedish National Archives: Stockholmsolympiadens arkiv

PERIODICALS AND NEWSPAPERS

Aftontidningen
Dagens Nyheter
Idun
Jönköpings Posten
Stockholms-Tidningen
Stockholms Dagblad.
Svenska Dagbladet

ENCYCLOPEDIAS

Nordisk familjeboks sportlexikon 1–7 (Stockholm 1938–1949).

PRINT SOURCES

Annerstedt, Claes. *Kvinnoidrottens utveckling i Sverige* (Malmö, 1983).
Bergvall, Erik (ed.). *V. Olympiaden. Officiell redogörelse för olympiska spelen i Stockholm 1912* (Stockholm 1913).
Bolling, Hans. *Sin egen hälsas smed: Idéer, initiativ och organisationer inom svensk motionsidrott* (Stockholm, 2005).
Clayhills, Harriet. *Kvinnohistorisk uppslagsbok* (Stockholm, 1992).
Halldén, Olle. *Vandringsboken: En femtioårig brevväxling mellan kvinnor* (Stockholm, 1996).
Hargreaves, Jennifer. *Sporting Females: Critical Issues in the History and Sociology of Women's Sports* (London, 1994).
Lennartz, Karl. *Die Spiele der V. Olympiade 1912 in Stockholm* (Kassel 2009).
Lignell, Ivar et al. (eds.). *Svensk tennis: Historiskt samlingsverk utgivet under samverkan med Svenska Lawntennisförbundet* (Stockholm, 1938).
Lindroth, Jan. *Idrott för kung och fosterland: Viktor Balck den svenska idrottens fader* (Stockholm, 2007).
Mallon, Bill, and Ture Widlund. *The 1912 Olympic Games. Results for All Competitors in All Events, with Commentary* (Jefferson, 2009).
Matovic, Margareta. *Stockholmsäktenskap: Familjebildning och partnerval i Stockholm 1850–1890* (Stockholm, 1984).
Norberg, Lars-Arne. *Sveriges historia under 1800-och 1900-talen: Svensk samhällsutveckling 1809–1986* (Stockholm, 1988).
Nordlund Edvinsson, Therese. *Broderskap i näringslivet: En studie om homosocialitet i Kung Orres Jaktklubb 1890–1960* (Lund, 2010).
Olofsson, Eva. *Har kvinnorna en sportslig chans? Den svenska idrottsrörelsen och kvinnorna under 1900-talet* (Umeå, 1989).
Overud, Johanna. *I beredskap med Fru Lojal: Behovet av kvinnlig arbetskraft i Sverige under andra världskriget* (Stockholm, 2005).
Sandblad, Henrik. *Olympia och Valhalla: Idéhistoriska aspekter av den moderna idrottsrörelsens framväxt* (Stockholm, 1985).
SCB. *Befolkningsutvecklingen under 250 år: Historisk statistik för Sverige* (Stockholm, 1999).
Suokas Paulina. "Klass och kön i svensk simsport kring sekelskiftet 1900," in *Idrott, Historia och Samhälle* (2000), p. 98–127.
Trangbæk, Else. "'Purity of Heart and Strength of Will': The Role of Female Teachers in the Modern Sports Movement" in Else Trangbæk and Arnd Krüger (eds.), *Gender and Sport from European Perspectives* (Copenhagen, 1999), pp. 43–67.
Yttergren, Leif. "Questions of Propriety: J. Sigfrid Edström, Anti-Semitism, and the 1936 Berlin Olympics" in *Olympika XVI* (2007), pp. 77–92.
Yttergren, Leif. *Täflan är lifvet: Idrottens organisering och sportifiering i Stockholm 1860–1898* (Stockholm, 1996).

Art and Sport: Different Worlds?
The Art Competitions
PATRIK STEORN

The Arts have assumed different roles at the Olympic Games over the years — today they are usually to be found in the form of exhibitions, concerts and in cultural programs in connection with the summer Games, but during first half of the twentieth century painting, sculpture, music, literature and architecture were competitive Olympic events. Reviving the antique Games was a strong driving force when Pierre de Coubertin and his circle created the modern Olympic Games. The idea of competing in different art forms was described in the official account after the Games in Stockholm in 1912 as a natural consequence of the Olympic idea.[1] Sports competitions offered historically anchored and peaceful forms for competition between national states. By including art competitions in the Olympic Games, Coubertin's vision was that the very spirit of the antique Games would not only be reconstructed and embraced, but would also be given the chance to flourish again and blow new life into the society of the day. The sports movement and the modern art world are parts of the modernity that emerged in the middle-class urban cultural environment at the turn of the century.

In the light of this it is possible to understand the competing itself as something that was associated with the modern spirit of the time. The modern Olympic Games were perceived as an arena for the fusion of the modern and the antique, something that was very appealing to the intellectuals of the turn of the century. But it was not only a sort of antique fad which made it appear "quite natural" at the turn of the century to combine art competitions and sports competitions within the framework of the Games, but it was at the same time a question of creating a forum where the strengths and competencies of modern nations were pitted against each other in more areas than sport. This essay describes from a cultural history perspective what happened when for the first time in modern Olympic history competitions in painting, sculpture, literature, music and architecture were organized and in particular analyses the winning works of art. The process and the thoughts behind the idea of the art competitions, their practical implementation and their impact on cultural life are also analyzed from the perspective of the prevailing political climate in the Swedish world of art during this period.

Art, Sport and Olympic Fusion

The relationship between art and sport can be studied in different ways. For example, the occurrence of sporting motifs in art and literature can be surveyed to see historical changes and their occurrence in different geographic areas. Another way is to describe the conditions for how the different arts have been used and displayed in the world of sport, for example how music is used in sports displays, or how sports venues have been designed and decorated. In order to define a common arena for these two areas, I suggest a more problematizing approach which consists of investigating the driving forces behind sporting and artistic activities, in order to see what cultural conceptions of creative energy sport and art have in common during a certain period, and how they differ. The Olympic art competitions are an interesting area for this type of investigation.

The art events were given the joint name of Concours d'Art and the idea of combining these competitions with the Olympic Games was primarily driven by Pierre de Coubertin himself. In 1906 he began to work in earnest on including the artistic events in the official competitions.[2] The idea was that competitions in painting, sculpture and architecture would be introduced as early as the Games in London in 1908, but for practical reasons, planning difficulties and lack of time, they were cancelled. A program and regulations for these competitions were formulated by the *Royal Academy of Arts in London* and are very detailed.[3] Victory processions or the struggle between Greeks and Amazons, a football match or a discus thrower are some of the subjects that were stipulated for the participants in the painting and sculpture events, while drawings for swimming baths or a private house with a gym of its own exemplify the tasks in the architecture competition.[4] Coubertin later said that he regretted the program had been drawn up in far too much detail and far too instrumentally and he promised greater freedom in the competitions during the Games in Stockholm. He said that an interpretation of the sporting idea itself or a work inspired by sport should be the only limitation for the works taking part. At the same time he himself mentions in instructions for the 1912 Olympic Games that winter sport, water sport and hunting would be particularly interesting for paintings of all sizes.[5]

Sculptors who often portrayed the naked body should not be deterred by the fact that many athletes are dressed, Coubertin continued, and he said that he could also imagine artists portraying modern athletes, for example golfers, without clothes on so as to allow their muscles to do themselves justice. Architecture did not need to be limited to gymnasiums but should also consider facilities for different modern sports like rowing, sailing and tennis. Novels and poetry were particularly welcomed in the literature class and the Italian author Gabriele d'Annunzio was highlighted as an example. The music event should not be limited to fanfares, marches and victory music; Coubertin also imagined that a Winter Symphony, for example, inspired by Scandinavian fjords would be very fitting. Even if Coubertin himself says in this text that the purpose of the competitions is to restore the Olympic Games' original antique beauty, it is obvious that his ideas about beauty have also been fashioned by his own time.

For Coubertin, an express objective of including the artistic events was to make the Games more harmonious from an aesthetic point of view, or more eurhythmic, to use his own word.[6] This concept was loaded with a desire to make sport an activity where body movement was harmonized with inner, physical energy and aesthetic interpretation. Both the athlete and the observer should be afforded the opportunity to experience aesthetic pleasure during sports competitions, with the aim of including art and sport in a kind of sporting spectacle where bodily strength and classical beauty merged into a whole.

Decorations, processions and music should also contribute to the whole, and Coubertin calls this care about decorative details "Ruskianisme Sportif."[7] The inspiration came from the British art critic John Ruskin, who completely set the tone during the latter part of the nineteenth century. Ruskin's basic idea, as Coubertin formulated it, is that beauty lies in the careful selection and combination of objects and details. Coubertin considered that it is in this work that a eurhythmic judgment can be practiced and formed.[8] The desire to link together body and soul was an overriding goal of this sporting cultural theory and all sorts of aesthetic expression — fireworks, parades and flags as well as marble sculptures and oil paintings — were instruments in this long-term work. It should be pointed out that Coubertin's understanding of his sources within aesthetic theory was not particularly deep. He does not at all touch upon the paradox of transforming the physically powerful, sometimes aggressive energies of competition and rivalry into a spiritual desire for aesthetic harmonization.

The German sports researcher Andrea Petersen considers that Coubertin gave the art competitions a symbolic or ceremonial role, as a way of differentiating the Olympic Games from other international sports competitions that were organized during this period.[9] At the same time, in Petersen's opinion, he truly saw the opportunities afforded by both athletes and spectators at modern sports competitions being inspired in a way that was educational and which could give rise to creative desires. This two-edged way of thinking indicates the obstacles that a planned meeting between art and sport can meet when one party's preconceptions of the other, in this case sport's preconceptions of art, have colored the perception of its role and reduce it to a support so as to achieve one's own purposes.

The idea of antiquity in general and Olympia in particular as a home of ideal beauty often recurs in Coubertin's writings, and according to the historians of ideas Jeffrey O. Segrave and Dikaia Chatziefstathiou this view is characterized by a romantic attitude that was modern at the time.[10] They consider that this attitude upholds a conventionally conservative, middle class and masculinistic view of beauty, which was in fact challenged in Europe at the turn of the century, not least because the concept was perceived as elitist. Segrave and Chatziefstathiou consider that this romanticizing and instrumentalizing view of beauty and its effects was an important reason why the art competitions project was not, at the end of the day, a great success.

The view of art that characterized the organizing of the Concours d'Art contains elements that glorify and idealize aesthetic values and aspirations, in particular those that used antiquity as a model. At the same time, the role of the arts was subordinated to a vision of sport's ability to shape bodies and competition's capacity to instigate peaceful rivalry between nations. Coubertin identified that there were similar driving forces behind artistic creation and the practicing of sport and that the heightened sensory experiences that could be obtained by those looking at art and watching sport had certain similarities. It is true that his visions for the contents of the artistic competitions extended outside the purely instrumental, but the idealistic and romantic view of art and creative inspiration upset the plans he had to realize his vision of sport's role as a source of energy within art and of art's embellishing role within the world of sport.

The Battle Over the Art Competitions

The preparations for the Stockholm Olympics were in full swing in February 1910 when the chairman of the Swedish Organizing Committee, Viktor Balck, took up a letter about the art competitions that the IOC had sent. With Crown Prince Gustaf Adolf taking the lead, the meeting considered that competitions in art were a sensitive question given how many different trends and opinions there were, not least in different countries, and they decided to consult with a number of Swedish artistic associations.[11] They received a letter where the Organizing Committee gave an account of the original proposal from the

IOC. Sculptors and painters were invited to submit works of art representing "sporting pictures and scenes," architects proposals for buildings for physical culture, such as stadiums, gymnasiums, swimming baths etc.[12]

The organizations consulted represented different interests in the Swedish art world. Konstnärsförbundet had been formed in the 1880s in opposition to the Royal Swedish Academy of Fine Arts' traditional teaching methods and exhibition policies, but since the turn of the century they had become an established power in the art world.[13] One association, Svenska konstnärernas förening, was founded as an alternative that would be able to gather all professional Swedish artists irrespective of gender and irrespective of whether they belonged to the Academy or to Konstnärsförbundet.[14] Another association, De frie, represented a younger generation of Swedish artists who were trying to establish a platform of their own in the prevailing divided climate.[15] The choice of organizations can be interpreted as a wish to address all parts of the Swedish art world. The letter displays some enthusiasm for the idea behind the project: "a competition in fine art, in close collaboration with physical exercise and sport, will give our V. Olympiad its true character and restore it to the model provided by antiquity." However, hesitancy is revealed by the Swedish Organizing Committee when it asked the artists whether a competition was the right form for realizing the project. The associations were requested to consider whether an exhibition would not be preferable to a competition.[16]

The thought of reviving the antique Olympic Games attracted the artists. This can be seen in the replies from the different artistic associations. The latter even proposed an increase in the number of events, with reference to the Greeks:

> Antiquity did not divide up people into muscle individuals and brain individuals. For them all human activity not directly linked to the acquisition of their daily bread was sport or, as we call it, culture. Art was one of its highly esteemed expressions. Therefore not only the fine arts but also music and poetry had their due place at the Games in Olympia. Would it not be conceivable to revive these festivities again?[17]

The thought seems to have appealed to Coubertin and the IOC, as literature and music were included as events when the competition was introduced the following year.

Otherwise the replies show that both a competition and an exhibition were acceptable to Svenska konstnärernas förening and they offered to be a part of the jury. De frie replied that the organizing of a competition would be unfortunate, but they considered that an exhibition was a fully acceptable alternative and thought that it should contain a national and an international section.[18] Konstnärsförbundet wanted neither a competition nor an exhibition and said that they did not understand how this would be of benefit to either sport or art.[19] The Academy of Fine Arts also rejected the proposal.[20] There were thus objections from all associations, above all to the fact that the tasks were seen as being far too narrowly formulated. There were fears that painting and sculpture would be seen as illustrations of different sporting events and be judged from the perspective of sporting technique, not artistically. However, they thought that the architectural task was more reasonable. However, the Swedish Association of Engineers, who represented the architects in this matter, considered that it was a very large enterprise, which would be expensive and still not give particularly much in return. Even though the replies were in fact quite varied, the Swedish Organizing Committee followed the Academy of the Fine Arts' and Konstnärsförbundet's line and reported to the IOC that it considered that there were difficulties entailed in the organizing of these competitions. At the same time the proposal concerning an extension of the number of events was forwarded.

The idea of art competitions was, however, a matter of symbolic importance for Coubertin and he informed the Organizing Committee that the requirement of organizing Concours d'Art was "absolute"—they would take place irrespective of what the Organizing Committee thought. The competitions would either be organized from Sweden, or otherwise they could declare that they were unwilling or unable to do so, and pass on the work to the IOC.[21] This led to the Organizing Committee convening a joint meeting together with a large number of artists to discuss the matter again. The invitation to the meeting describes the situation as the honor of the fatherland being at stake, which not only reveals the Organizing Committee's averse attitude to organizing the competitions, but also the nationalistic lens through which the issue was seen.[22] At the meeting that took place in January 1911 opinions had become more sharply defined and on this occasion the whole meeting was against both a competition and an exhibition.[23] Three reasons were given: generally speaking they did not want to have competitions in connection with public art exhibitions and then it was quite unthinkable to make competition the main thing; it was feared that the competing works would not be judged as works of art and finally they thought "that determining the composition of the jury would encounter great, indeed insurmountable, difficulties." The meeting proposed that the Chairman of the IOC should himself organize the competitions.

It can also be seen from some of the comments at this meeting that there was a fear that the Swedish entries would not hold their own against international competition and it was even proposed that only Swedish artists would be allowed to participate if there were an exhibition.[24] It is remarkable that artists from different factions and different generations were united in this question, as they were in opposition to each other in other matters. The artists' discussions in terms of competition between nations show that notions of nation were an actively functioning category on the basis of which they were used to judging art and they were conscious that Swedish artists had found it difficult to hold their own in the established international world of art.

Even though the views of the artists still varied a good deal at this meeting as well, the Organizing Committee chose to refer to the opposition of the artists and sent the question back to the IOC. Coubertin was both disappointed and surprised. He pointed out to the Organizing Committee that the opinions of the Swedish artists were quite irrelevant; the Organizing Committee's primary mission was to implement the decisions of the IOC. However, he took on the task of managing all questions concerning the Concours d'Art.[25] He pointed out in a letter later on that things should not have happened the way they did.[26] One can suspect that it was not only the Swedish artists who were skeptical about arranging art competitions; representatives of Swedish sport also aired their skeptical attitude to these events.

When the competition was announced, Clarence von Rosen wrote somewhat ironically about possible links between artistic creativity and physical sporting activities in *Ny Tidning för Idrott*, the most important publication for sport of the time, which was published by Sweden's Central Association for the Promotion of Sport: "Even though it cannot be claimed that any particular sporting ability is required to paint a picture—yes, it would be when Carl Larsson or Fjaestad 'alfresca' in the National Museum or Olle Hjortzberg take care of a church dome."[27] However, the article concludes with a hopeful challenge to Swedish artists: "how much do the sports, almost all of them, not have to offer as 'motifs' for both the artist's brush and the sculptor's chisel! May the new competition be a source of inspiration to our artists."[28] There were points of contact between the role of the artist and the role of the athlete. Within the world of sport the artist could be seen as a sporting and moral example at the same time as the athlete's masculinity inspired artists during the early twentieth century.[29]

Competitions within the different art forms, where the participants could present proposals for solutions for a pre-formulated program or subject were nothing new for artists at the turn of the century. Ever since the sixteenth century it had been an established form of teaching in literary and artistic academies in Europe to have works compete against each other on the basis of qualitative assessment criteria, and this was also done when scholarships and medals were to be awarded at exhibitions and prize competitions. As the middle-class society of the nineteenth century emerged, prize competitions became a tool that was used by public institutions to get proposals for buildings and town plans and even for how they were to be decorated. The competition format was used to define the best solution for a pre-defined problem. Competing was part of the professional role of artists during the nineteenth century and for a good part of the 20th century, and this is still the case today for the architect profession.

Competitions, at least in architecture, are associated with a certain type of society, according to the architectural historian Rasmus Waern, a society characterized by egalitarian democratic ideals on the one hand, and by market-based competition between different actors in the market on the other.[30] Waern's thesis gives an account of a number of important competitions in architecture during the twentieth century and the architecture historian Stina Hagelqvist has shown in her thesis the importance of competitions in creating a professional field for architects during the first half of the twentieth century.[31]

Examples of much discussed art competitions held in Sweden during the decades around the turn of the century are the decoration of the stair hall of the Swedish National Museum, the second chamber of Sweden's Parliament Building, and the wedding room in the Stockholm City Law Courts, as well as sculpture proposals for the National Monument, the Sten Sture Monument and the Engelbrekt Monument.[32] However, many competitions ended in long drawn out wrangling and the winning proposal was rarely executed.

Competing in artistic creation was thus not something that was foreign to Swedish artists, but this way of proceeding seems to have been primarily associated with public art and public settings, to judge from the competitions that were held. This might explain why the architecture event was more easily accepted by the artist associations asked, while they were opposed to prize competitions in easel art, for example. At the same time, the doing away with art competitions at exhibitions had been a central issue in the criticism of the Academy by Konstnärsförbundet in the Opponent Movement conflict in the 1880s.[33] When all was said and done the competitive element seems to have been a two-edged sword for the artists — on the one hand, they sided with a general perception that competitions were an effective method of obtaining competitive proposals for artistic decoration. On the other hand, they did not want to risk the artist's creativity being reduced to a sporting event.

Concours d'Art 1912: Rules, Participants and Works

It was thus Pierre de Coubertin himself who had the responsibility for the holding of the first Concours d'Art at the Stockholm Olympics in 1912. During the autumn of 1911 *Revue Olympique* published regulations, a short document announcing that competitions in architecture, sculpture, painting, music and literature would be arranged.[34] The artistic content is not specified, other than that the participating works should be directly connected to sport. The competition entries, which were not to have been on previous public display, were to be posted to Coubertin's home address in Paris. On the basis of this it has been put forward that it seems likely that he himself constituted the jury for the art competitions.[35]

It is not possible today to obtain a complete answer to which artists submitted entries to the competitions. A list of names of participants has been found in the IOC's archives in Lausanne.[36] Even if the list is probably not complete — certain of the winning names, for example, are not included in this list — and even if the compiler, date and purpose of the list are not stated, it shows that there were not any particularly well-known artists taking part in the Olympic competitions. They may have reaped some measure of success in their day, but today they are all more or less unknown in an international perspective. The researcher Richard Stanton has tried to identify each of the 35 names found on the list in all five events.[37] Among those who can be considered to be generally known are the Italian author Gabriele D'Annunzio, who as early as in the 1890s had made a breakthrough with his Nietzschian-influenced literature, and the French artist Jean-Francois Raffaelli, who belonged to the circle of impressionist painters in Paris, but was not amongst the most well-known of them. There is no information that any Swedish artist took part in the competitions according to this source material.

During the spring of 1912 Coubertin informed the Swedish Organizing Committee of the result of the competitions: the Italian Carlo Pellegrini won the gold medal in painting for a frieze, *Winter Sports*, the American Walter Winans won the gold medal in sculpture for a statuette called *An American Trotter* and the silver medal was awarded to George Dubois for *Porte du Gymnase Moderne*. The gold medal in architecture was awarded to the Swiss Eugène Monod and Alphonse Laverrière for a building plan for a modern stadium, while the music medal went to the Italian Ricardo Barthelemy for an Olympic march, and Germany and France won the gold in literature through the poem *Ode to Sport* by Georges Hohrod and Martin Eschbach.[38]

Before the Stockholm Games Coubertin had made efforts to get the art competitions accepted in artist circles, but these efforts seem to have been limited above all to the circles he moved in himself. Coubertin had discovered the architects Monod and Laverriere during an international architecture competition in Paris during the spring of 1911, where they were awarded a prize. Enthusiastic reports of their work were published in *Revue Olympique* even before the Olympic competition was officially announced, which gives the impression that Coubertin favored them from the very beginning.[39] The sculptor Georges Dubois was in the society that met in 1906 in Paris when the role of art at the Olympic Games was officially discussed for the first time.[40] He took part both as a speaker and at a fencing display, as he was both a sculptor and an athlete.

An artist who was also an athlete or an athlete who was also an artist was an ideal winner in Coubertin's eyes, and the same can be said of the sculptor Walter Winans. He had won an Olympic gold medal in shooting at running deer in London in 1908 and in Stockholm he was part of the American team that won the silver medal in the same event.[41] All in all it seems as if Coubertin chose winners and maybe also brought in participants from among artists that he already knew of himself and in this way "filled out" the number of entries in certain events. The most flagrant example of this is that it has emerged that Coubertin himself took part in the literature event under the pseudonym Georges Hohrod and Martin Eschbach.[42] Coubertin awarded his own entry first prize in the literature class and this probably shows how far he was prepared to go in his efforts so that the project would not appear to be a failure. Coubertin kept the secret of who was hidden behind the pseudonym all his life.

Medals and diplomas were sent to the winners by post. They did not take part in any formal prize ceremony at the Olympic Stadium, but at Coubertin's request the Swedish Organizing Committee arranged for the winning entries in painting and sculpture to be exhibited in temporary premises during the period that the Games were ongoing.[43] The exhibition was not particularly comprehensive, with just four works taking part — a painted frieze and three sculptures.

The Italian artist Carlo Pellegrini's work, with a winter motif, was executed in a kind of Jugend style, with people doing winter sports dressed in colorful clothes that stand out, sharply outlined against the snow-white landscape. The winning entry is not preserved today, but according to Coubertin's description of all the winning works it depicted skiers on a glacier. To judge by the artist's other remaining works it was a decoratively simple and straight depiction that had great similarities with poster art of the time, not least pictures that would attract travelers to different tourist destinations.

The first prize in sculpture, Winans' *An American Trotter*, is a bronze sculpture representing a trotting driver with his horse, both at rest. The driver is wearing a cap and trousers and has a moustache typical of the time, but neither the man nor the carriage is as painstakingly executed as the proud and powerful animal. With widened nostrils, ears pointing upwards and muscles under the gently portrayed skin, it is the horse that draws the onlooker's

Walter Winans' statuette *An American Trotter*, for which he was awarded a gold medal in Stockholm in 1912 (photograph by Hans Bolling, SCIF).

attention. Winans is also best known as an animal sculptor and worked exclusively in the realistic style that the statuette is also executed in. Every detail contributes to the feeling of a horse and driver prepared for a race — the horse is standing completely still while the driver seems to be ready to take them down to the start. In connection with the Games the artist donated the statuette to a planned Swedish sports museum and Sweden's Central Association for the Promotion of Sport still has it in their possession in their premises in the Olympic Stadium's clock tower.[44]

The plaster sketch that Georges Dubois did for the doors to a modern gymnasium, and which won second prize in the sculpture event, does not exist today. In a text where the reasons for the choice of medalists were given, Coubertin has given this vivid description:

> A plane crowns the whole work with a gracious and original line. On the left the past
> is represented by elderly people who have come to relive their youth by contemplating
> athletes, runners, discus throwers etc. On the right the future is embodied by mothers
> taking their children to the gymnasium. In the background the steps of an
> amphitheatre....[45]

Scenes from modern, popular sporting life seem to have been mixed with elements from antique architecture in this work, which is the one that is most clearly intended as part of a public setting, but which was never executed.

A third work from the sculpture class was exhibited in Stockholm: *Joy of Effort*, a medallion in bronze by the Canadian R. Tait McKenzie. He had in fact not been awarded a medal, but Coubertin still let him take part in the exhibition due to a misunderstanding and the sculptor's high social status.[46] McKenzie was a well known sculptor, gymnast and doctor and he also appears in enthusiastic texts written by Coubertin in *Revue Olympique* even before the art competitions had been announced.[47]

The medal depicts three naked well-trained young men who have been captured just as they are jumping over a hurdle. The tensed muscles of the bodies are reproduced in detail and the faces display the athletes' determination. The joy found in the title of the work and which is also written on a ribbon floating next to the obstacle is in fact not particularly prominent in the motif, to judge from the competitors' facial expressions. On the other hand, sport is depicted as an honorable effort through the fact that the whole medal is bordered by a laurel wreath. Athletes, scouts and soldiers, participants or people posing constitute McKenzie's range of motifs and even if he worked most with freestanding sculptures this medallion belongs to one of several reliefs with a similar motif.[48] The exhibited medallion was donated to the Olympic Stadium in Stockholm

R. Tait McKenzie's medallion *Joy of Effort* (photograph by Hans Bolling).

by the American squad in memory of the Olympic Games in 1912.[49] The medallion is still on the façade of the arena nearby the main entrance.

There were no reviews of either the works or the exhibition as a whole in the Swedish press. A small notice from a British daily newspaper, where the competitions are in spite of everything described as a great success, is the only press cutting to be found among the remaining documents in the Archive of the Stockholm Olympics.[50] In a letter addressed to the Organizing Committee, the winning artist Pelligrini also requests information about his victory.[51]

McKenzie, who was in Stockholm during the Games in 1912, reacted, according to his wife Ethel, to the fact that no one knew that his medallion was on display and was very disappointed by the lack of attention paid to the exhibition.[52] It thus seems that as a whole neither the competitions nor the exhibition had any great impact on either the general public or within the most knowledgeable circles. Coubertin wrote on repeated occasions about his dissatisfaction with the Organizing Committee's lack of commitment to the art events and pointed out that they were not even mentioned in the Games' official propaganda brochure.[53] The unfavorable treatment probably had nothing to do with the individual works, but was rather due to the Swedish Organizing Committee's initial dislike of the project as a whole.

When comparing the selected, prizewinning and exhibited works and the proposals that Coubertin formulated before the announcement of the competitions, there is great agreement with regard to both motif and execution — winter sport and sporting bodies sculpted in detail.[54] Competitive sport and sport as a leisure time activity are both represented and both decorative art in graphic Jugend style and classical realistic sculptures are to be found. The other prizewinning works in architecture, literature and music also seem to comply with the recommendations that Coubertin issued. The plans for the modern sports facility drawn by Monod and Laverriere contain room for both activities on land and on water and it was intended to be located by Lake Geneva.[55] Pictures of preserved source material give the impression of architecture in eclectic classicism in a style typical of the day, but the plans never came to be realized. The poem *Ode to Sport* is a nine-stanza long celebration of sport in an idealizing and highflown style. Sport's different qualities are pointed out and explained one after the other: the pleasure of the Gods and the essence of life, beauty, justice, courage, honor, joy, fertility, progress and peace.[56]

It is remarkable that Coubertin held up the Italian author D'Annunzio as a model for sporting literature before the competition and that later, in spite of the fact that the author had submitted an entry, he only awarded a prize to the text that he himself had written. The winner of the music competition, *Marche olympique*, is difficult to judge today as there is no recording available, even if the score may possibly have been found in the archives in Lausanne.[57] However, a march was not what was at the top of Coubertin's list of favorites — even if it could constitute an artistic element in the eurhythmic staging of sporting competitions, it is not an independent genre inspired on a more creative and esthetic level by the spirit of sport.

The first edition of Concours d'Art may as a whole be seen as an attempt to create a new artistic field where the identity of the art form was in fact to be subordinate to the thematic treatment of sport as a motif. This field, however, was to be situated outside the established arenas of the art forms in the shape of exhibition premises of its own nearby the sporting venues, and with prizewinners with a double background, both within some art form and in the sporting event they had depicted. The works were not paid any attention by cultural correspondents to any notable degree. The Swedish Olympic Committee's reluctant attitude may also be interpreted as there not being a broad consensus around the necessity of opening up sport arenas to art, literature, music and architecture. In the light of this summary, the lack of impact in the cultural sphere is not particularly surprising either.

Konstnärsförbundet's "Olympic exhibition"

It is important to point out that the Swedish art world was not at all so uninterested by the sporting motif or by the Olympic Games as the above account can make it appear.

When Konstnärsförbundet began to plan its next exhibition at the beginning of 1911, it had already expressed itself unfavorably regarding both Concours d'Art and an international exhibition on the subject of art and sport. On the other hand they saw the advantages of arranging an exhibition under their own management in Stockholm during the summer of 1912 in connection with the Olympic Games: "It would most certainly be an advantage for the exhibition that the Olympic Games took place in Stockholm at the same time in 1912."[58] Their actions reveal that there was a certain attraction in the sports competitions both as a public event and as an artistic idea, which Konstnärsförbundet considered they could better make use of to their own advantage rather than taking part in a competition and exhibition under the management of the Olympic Committee. Konstnärsförbundet had acted as a free agent in the Swedish art world since the 1880s and was good at launching its members.

In the summer of 1912 Svenska konstnärernas förening organized a large exhibition of Swedish art at the Royal Academy, where approximately 600 works by about 100 artists were displayed. The Rackstad painter Gustaf Fjaestad had an exhibition of his own of landscape paintings and motifs with naked bodies in the countryside.[59] However, most attention was drawn by Konstnärsförbundet, with a display that was called "The Olympic Exhibition."

Temporary exhibition premises were set up at Konstnärsförbundet's own expense as there were no other premises suitable for the purpose.[60] As the premises were large by exhibition standards, 1,200 m², many members were able to display a large number of works, in all 348 works by 21 artists, all of whom were men.[61] Landscape painting dominated the exhibition according to the catalogue, but many artists also exhibited works with a sporting connection. Carl Eldh exhibited sketches for a sculpture group to decorate the Olympic Stadium, Christian Eriksson displayed a skater and a woman fencer. Eugène Jansson had several of his large paintings on display, with motifs from swimming baths, but also with athletes and acrobats. Johan Axel Gustaf Acke's paintings *Morgonluft* and *Havslyssnaren* do not have a sporting motif, but show naked male bodies in the countryside and may in this way be said to be inspired by the sporting spirit. Realistic depictions of sporting activities were to be found among the works of art, but they differ in style from what Coubertin selected as the winner.

It came to Coubertin's knowledge that Swedish artists had themselves organized an exhibition that they wanted to call Olympic and he reacted immediately. In a letter to the Organizing Committee he asked them to take their responsibility and intervene against the name.[62] I have not found any information that this occurred and it is still this exhibition that in a Swedish context is referred to as "The Olympic Exhibition."[63] The building, the comprehensive exhibition that was launched with a special poster and postcards of works of art that were spread for advertising purposes were used to stage the role in the Swedish art world that Konstnärsförbundet laid claim to. This manifestation was hardly directed at the Olympic organization, but rather at a younger generation of artists headed by Isaac

Attendants carrying King Gustaf V's challenge trophy for the pentathlon, Karl XII bust in bronze, July 15, 1912 (photograph by Axel Malmström, SCIF photo collection).

Grünewald, who through an abstract use of color and form and with mundane motifs heralded a fundamental challenge to the power of Konstförbundet in the Swedish art world.[64] However, it is an interesting reflection that Coubertin's idea of Olympic art competitions probably not only inspired the name of Konstförbundet's exhibition but also the thematic focus and selection of exhibited works. The notion that sporting motifs could act as particularly creatively inspiring was thus something that in fact attracted some of the Swedish artists, but they themselves wanted to keep power over the choice of motifs and any thematic exposition.

Conclusion

This exposition of what happened when competitions in painting, sculpture, literature, music and architecture were organized for the first time in modern Olympic history in connection with the 1912 Olympic Games in Stockholm shows that there were notions of driving forces within the worlds of both art and sport that these activities had in common. Pierre de Coubertin formulated himself on this subject with references to both antiquity and contemporary art theoreticians and some of the Swedish artist associations who were consulted about whether art competitions should be held as part of the Olympic Games in Stockholm were actually positive to the idea as such. But the idea that sports organizers should enter the Swedish art arena and formulate artistic programs and award medals to an international band of artists who preferably were also sportsmen seems to have been completely contradictory to the aspirations of creating a strong national art scene characterized by professionalism and independence.

However, there was a notion that sporting motifs could act as particularly creatively inspiring within both artistic and sporting circles at the turn of the century, not least because sport came to symbolize a kind of modernity. Neither was it inconceivable for Swedish artists to take part in competitions in public decoration, but neither the established institutions, their equally renowned opponents nor the younger generations felt attracted by Concours d'Art as an arena for art. The view of art that characterized the organizing of the art competitions also idealized art in such a way that the arts were given an embellishing role within the world of sport. The skepticism that existed within the Swedish Organizing Committee towards Coubertin's project also contributed to the lack of impact in a broader cultural sphere.

The competitions continued to take place up until 1948. Swedish artists and architects participated and gave Sweden two gold medals and two bronze medals.[65] After that the vision of the Olympic Games as a common arena for art and sport was channeled into cultural peripheral events without any competitive element. From today's perspective, with a hundred years' distance, it can be seen that the chops and changes around Concours d'Art were associated with the constituting of both art's and sport's own individual arenas. Pierre de Coubertin's expansive enthusiasm and the integrity of the Swedish art world therefore seem not only to be mirrors of their own day but were also very much part of the creation of a modern spirit characterized by strategic approaches and dissociation between Olympic visions and an independent world of art.

Notes

1. Bergvall (ed.), *The Fifth Olympiad: The Official Report of the Olympic Games of Stockholm 1912* (1913), p. 806.
2. Müller, *Olympism* (2000), pp. 605 ff.
3. Coubertin, "Art sportif" (1907:11), pp. 355–357.
4. Coubertin, "Olympic Competitions in Painting, Sculpture and Architecture for 1908" (1907:10), pp. 344–346.
5. Coubertin, "Les Concours d'Art de 1912" (1911:3), pp. 35–36.
6. Ibid. p. 35.
7. Coubertin, "Decoration, Pyrothechnie, Harmonies, Cortèges," 1911:4, 1911:5, 1911:7, 1911:8, 1911:10.
8. Coubertin, "Decoration, Pyrothechnie, Harmonies, Cortèges" (1911:4), p. 55.
9. Petersen, "Les concours artistiques aux jeux olympiques de 1912 à 1948" (1986:4–5), p. 249.
10. Segrave and Chatziefstathiou, "Pierre de Coubertin's Ideology of Beauty from the Perspective of the History of Ideas" (2008), p. 32.
11. National Archives, Stockholmsolympiaden 1912: Minutes of the Organizing Committee 1908–1910 A I:1, Minutes of February 28, 1910.
12. National Archives, Stockholmsolympiaden 1912: Minor documents ordered by subject, Concours d'Art F IV: 1, letter of March 16, 1910.
13. Görts, *Det sköna i verklighetens värld* (1999), p. 125.
14. Widman, *Konstnärernas hus* (1999), p. 15.
15. Sandblad, *Anders Trulson* (1944), pp. 11–16.
16. National Archives, Stockholmsolympiaden 1912: Minor documents ordered by subject, Concours d'Art F IV: 1, Letter to the Royal Swedish Academy of Fine Arts, March 16, 1910.
17. National Archives, Stockholmsolympiaden 1912: Minor documents ordered by subject, Concours d'Art F IV: 1, letter from Axel Lindman (Svenska Konstnärernas Förening) to the Organizing Committee, April 15, 1910.
18. National Archives, Stockholmsolympiaden 1912: Minor documents ordered by subject, Concours d'Art F IV: 1, letter from Torgny Dufwa (De Frie) to the Organizing Committee, April 6, 1910.

19. National Archives, Stockholmsolympiaden 1912: Minor documents ordered by subject, Concours d'Art F IV: 1, letter from Karl Nordström (Konstnärsförbundet) to Viktor Balck, April 18, 1910.

20. National Archives, Stockholmsolympiaden 1912: Minor documents ordered by subject, Concours d'Art F IV: 1, letter from the Royal Swedish Academy of Fine Arts to the Organizing Committee, April 23, 1910.

21. National Archives, Stockholmsolympiaden 1912: Minor documents ordered by subject, Concours d'Art F IV: 1, letter from Viktor Balck to Prince Eugen, Nils Anckers, Sam Arsenius, Arthur Bianchini, Ferdinand Boberg, August Brunius, John Böttiger, Gustaf Cederström, Albert Engström, Christian Eriksson, Carl Fagerberg, Gustaf Fjaestad, Gunnar Hellström, Erik Hedberg, Tor Hedberg, Gösta von Hennings, Eugène Jansson, Ernst Küsel, Carl Larsson, Carl G Laurin, Bruno Liljefors, Richard Lindström, Ludvig 250*8 Looström, Carl Milles, Georg Nordensvan, Ernst Norlind, Karl Nordström, Georg von Rosen, Axel Sjöberg, Karl Wåhlin, Anders Zorn and Emil Österman, January 7, 1911.

22. Müller and Wacker (ed.), Pierre de Coubertin et les arts (2008).

23. National Archives, Stockholmsolympiaden 1912: Minor documents ordered by subject, Concours d'Art F IV: 1, Minutes, January 21, 1911. Present: Prince Eugen, Colonel Balck, Georg von Rosen, Gustaf Cederström, Ludwig Looström, Tor Hedberg, Frits af Sandeberg, Torben Grut, 15 or so artists and people interested in art, and the Organizing Committee's secretary Kristian Hellström.

24. National Archives, Stockholmsolympiaden 1912: Minor documents ordered by subject, Concours d'Art F IV: 1, letter from Viktor Balck and Frits af Sandeberg to the Organizing Committee, January 23, 1911, see also letter from Tor Hedberg and Gustaf Cederström to the Organizing Committee, February 3, 1911 and the minutes of January 12, 1911.

25. National Archives, Stockholmsolympiaden 1912: Minor documents ordered by subject, Concours d'Art F IV: 1, letter from Pierre de Coubertin to Balck, January 31, 1911.

26. National Archives: Stockholmsolympiaden 1912: Minor documents ordered by subject, Concours d'Art F IV: 1, letter from Pierre de Coubertin to the Organizing Committee, May 22, 1912.

27. Rosen, "Äfven litterära och artistiska täflingar vid Spelen 1912" (1911), p. 334.

28. Ibid.

29. Steorn, Nakna män, Maskulinitet och kreativitet i svensk bildkultur 1900–1915 (2006), pp. 93–98.

30. Waern, Tävlingarnas tid (1996), pp. 16–21.

31. Hagelqvist, Arkitekttävlingen som föreställning (2010), pp. 75–89.

32. Arvidsson and Lindwall, "Plats för freskomålning" (1969), pp. 7–110; Ellenius, Den offentliga konsten och ideologierna (1971), chap. 3–5; Kjellin, Christian Eriksson 1858–1935 (1953), pp. 181–187; Theorell, Studier kring Axel Törnemans Riksdagshusmålningar (1973), pp. 29–52; and Qvarnström, Vigselrummet i Stockholms rådhus och det tidiga 1900-talets monumentalmåleri (2010), pp. 69–79.

33. Björk, "I skärningspunkten mellan tradition och modernism" (2002), p. 41.

34. "Règlements des Concours littéraires et artistiques de 1912" (1911:9), pp. 131–132.

35. Mallon and Widlund, The 1912 Olympic Games (2009), p. 364.

36. Ibid., pp. 365–366.

37. Stanton, "In Search of the Artists of 1912" (2001:2), pp. 3–13.

38. National Archives, Stockholmsolympiaden 1912: Minor documents ordered by subject, Concours d'Art F IV: 1, letter from Pierre de Coubertin to the Organizing Committee, May 8, 1912, and a letter from Pierre de Coubertin, May 22, 1912.

39. Coubertin, "La fête olympique de Sorbonne" (1911:6), pp. 83–85, and Trelat, "Rapport sur le Concours d'Architecture" (1911:8), pp. 116–120.

40. Coubertin, "Les séances de la conférence consultative" and "Le festival de la Sorbonne" (1906:6), pp. 85 and 94.

41. Search among Olympic medalists, www.olympic.org, December 30, 2010

42. Durry, "Hohrod and Eschbach" (2000:32), pp. 26–28.

43. National Archives, Stockholmsolympiaden 1912: Minor documents ordered by subject, Concours d'Art F IV: 1, letter from Pierre de Coubertin to the Organizing Committee, March 1, 1912, letter from the Organizing Committee to Coubertin, March 27, 1912, letter from Coubertin to the Organizing Committee, May 8, 1912, letter from Coubertin, May 22, 1912, and Bergvall, 1913, p. 809.

44. National Archives, Stockholmsolympiaden 1912: Minor documents ordered by subject, Concours d'Art F IV: 1, letter from Walter Winans, July 11, 1912, letter from the Organizing Committee to Winans, August 7, 1912.

45. Coubertin: "Rapport sur les Concours artistiques et littéraires de la V:me Olympiade" (1912:7),

p. 105: "Un aéroplane couronne l'ensemble d'une ligne gracieuse et originale. A gauche le passé représenté par les vieillards qui viennent revivre leur jeunesse en contemplant les athlètes, coureurs, lançeurs de disques, etc., à droite l'avenir incarné par des mères amenant leurs enfants au gymnase. Au fond les gradins d'un amphithéâtre."

46. National Archives, Stockholmsolympiaden 1912: Minor documents ordered by subject, Concours d'Art F IV: 1, letter from Pierre de Coubertin to the Organizing Committee, May 8, 1912.

47. "The Chronicle of the Amateur Spirit," 1911:9, 1911:10.

48. Kozar, The Sport Sculpture of R. Tait McKenzie (1992).

49. National Archives, Stockholmsolympiaden 1912: Minor documents ordered by subject, Concours d'Art F IV: 1, letter from Pierre de Coubertin to Kristian Hellström, July 22, 1912, and "Några minnestaflor i vårt Stadion" (1912:63), p. 303.

50. National Archives, Stockholmsolympiaden 1912: Minor documents ordered by subject, Concours d'Art F IV: 1, *The Western Daily Press*, Bristol, June 18, 2012.

51. National Archives, Stockholmsolympiaden 1912: Minor documents ordered by subject, Concours d'Art F IV: 1, letter from Carlo Pellegrini to Kristian Hellström, August 9, 1912.

52. Andrew J. Kozar, *The Sport Sculpture of R. Tait McKenzie* (Champaign, 1992), p. 12.

53. National Archives, Stockholmsolympiaden 1912: Minor documents ordered by subject, Concours d'Art F IV: 1, letter from Pierre de Coubertin March 1, 1912, May 22, 1912, June 11, 1912.

54. Coubertin, "Les Concours d'Art de 1912: suggestions aux concurrents" (1911:3), pp. 35–36.

55. "Les archives de CIO s'enrichissent" (1975:95–96), pp. 360–36, and Chappelet, "From the Olympic Institute to the International Academy" (2001:4–5), pp. 52–55.

56. The text is published in German: Bergvall, 1913, pp. 809–811, in French: *Revue Olympique* 1912:12, pp. 179–181 and translated into English: Coubertin, Olympism: Selected Writings (2001), pp. 629–630, and into Swedish: Sandblad, "Kulturen och Stockholms-OS eller Så fick Coubertin sin guldmedalj" (1987), pp. 89–109.

57. Kramer, "Richard Barthélemy: Gold Medallist in the First Olympic Music Competition at Stockholm 1912 — Enrico Caruso's Accompanist" (2003:2), pp. 11–13.

58. Nationalmuseum Archives, Konstnärsförbundet A1 Minutes, March 13, 1911.

59. Bergvall, 1913, p. 829.

60. Nordström, "Berättelse över Konstnärsförbundets utställning vid Karlaplan, Stockholm juni–augusti 1912" (1912).

61. *Konstnärsförbundets Utställning sommaren 1912* (1912).

62. National Archives, Stockholmsolympiaden 1912: Minor documents ordered by subject, Concours d'Art F IV: 1, letter from Coubertin, June 11, 1912.

63. As an example of the confusion that has arisen around the name, the art historian Elisabeth Lidén has stated that Richard Bergh, a central figure on the Board of Konstförbundet, was responsible for "the art exhibition at the Olympic Games" when it is in fact Konstförbundet's own "Olympic exhibition" that is meant. Lidén, "Bildkonsten 1909–1945" (1994), p. 294.

64. Lilja: *Det moderna måleriet i svensk kritik 1905–1914* (1955), p. 85.

65. Jönsson, "Hyllning till Ling gav olympiskt guld" (2003), pp. 160–166, and "Missförstånd bakom svenskt OS-guld i konst" (2002), pp. 150–162, see also Karlsson, "Konsttävlingar i OS" (2002), pp. 148–149.

References

UNPUBLISHED SOURCES

Swedish National Archives: Stockholmsolympiaden 1912
Nationalmuseum Archives: Konstnärsförbundet

ELECTRONIC SOURCES

www.olympic.org

PRINT SOURCES

Arvidsson, Karl Axel, and Bo Lindwall. "Plats för freskomålning" in Lindwall, Bo (ed.), *Carl Larsson och Nationalmuseum* (Stockholm 1969).

Bergvall, Erik (ed.). *The Fifth Olympiad: The Official Report of the Olympic Games of Stockholm 1912* (Stockholm, 1913).

Björk, Tomas. "I skärningspunkten mellan tradition och modernism. Richard Bergh och Konstakademien" in Brummer, Hans Henrik (ed.): *Richard Bergh Ett konstnärskall* (Stockholm 2002).

Chappelet, Jean-Loup. "From the Olympic Institute to the International Academy." *Olympic Review* 2001:4–5.

"The Chronicle of the Amateur Spirit." *Revue Olympique* 1911:9 and 1911:10.

Coubertin, Pierre de. "Art sportif." *Revue Olympique* 1907:11.

Coubertin, Pierre de. "Decoration, Pyrothechnie, Harmonies, Cortèges." *Revue Olympique* 1911:4, 5, 7, 8 and 10.

Coubertin, Pierre de. "La fête olympique de Sorbonne." *Revue Olympique* 1911:6.

Coubertin, Pierre de. "Le festival de la Sorbonne." *Revue Olympique* 1906:6.

Coubertin, Pierre de. "Les Concours d'Art de 1912: suggestions aux concurrents." *Revue Olympique* 1911:3.

Coubertin, Pierre de. "Les séances de la conférence consultative." *Revue Olympique* 1906:6.

Coubertin, Pierre de. "Ode au sport." *Revue Olympique* 1912:12.

Coubertin, Pierre de. "Olympic Competitions in Painting, Sculpture and Architecture for 1908." *Revue Olympique* 1907:10.

Coubertin, Pierre de. *Olympism: Selected Writings* (Lausanne, 2001).

Coubertin, Pierre de. "Rapport sur les Concours artistiques et littéraires de la V:me Olympiade." *Revue Olympique* 1912:7.

Durry, Jean. "Hohrod and Eschbach: A Mystery Finally Solved." *Olympic Review* 2000:32.

Ellenius, Allan. *Den offentliga konsten och ideologierna. Studie över verk från 1800- och 1900-talen* (Stockholm 1971).

Görts, Maria. *Det sköna i verklighetens värld. Akademisk konstsyn i Sverige under senare delen av 1800-talet* (Bjärnum 1999).

Hagelqvist, Stina. *Arkitekttävlingen som föreställning. Den svenska arkitekttävlingens ideologiska, institutionella och professionella villkor under 1900-talets första hälft* (Stockholm 2010).

Jönsson, Åke. "Hyllning till Ling gav olympiskt guld." *Blå boken* 2003.

Jönsson, Åke. "Missförstånd bakom svenskt OS-guld i konst." *Blå boken* 2002.

Karlsson, Ove. "Konsttävlingar i OS." *Blå boken* 2002.

Kjellin, Helge. *Christian Eriksson 1858–1935* (Stockholm 1953).

Konstnärsförbundets Utställning sommaren 1912 (Stockholm 1912).

Kozar, Andrew J. The Sport Sculpture of R. Tait McKenzie (Champaign 1992).

Kramer, Bernhard. "Richard Barthélemy: Gold Medallist in the First Olympic Music Competition at Stockholm 1912 — Enrico Caruso's Accompanist." *Journal of Olympic History* (2003:2).

"Les archives de CIO s'enrichissent." *Revue Olympique* 1975:95–96.

Lidén, Elisabeth. "Bildkonsten 1909–1945" in Sandström, Sten (ed.): *Konsten i Sverige. Del 2 från 1800 till 1970* (Stockholm 1994).

Lilja, Gösta. *Det moderna måleriet i svensk kritik 1905–1914* (Malmö 1955).

Mallon, Bill, and Ture Widlund. *The 1912 Olympic Games: Results for All Competitors in All Events, with Commentary* (Jefferson 2009).

Müller, Norbert. *Olympism: Selected Writings. Pierre de Coubertin 1863–1937* (Lausanne 2000).

Müller, Norbert, and Christian Wacker (eds.). Pierre de Coubertin et les arts (Lausanne 2008).

"Några minnestaflor i vårt Stadion." *Ny Tidning för Idrott* 1912:63.

Nordström, Karl. "Berättelse över Konstnärsförbundets utställning vid Karlaplan, Stockholm juni–augusti 1912," *Konstnärsförbundets årsberättelse 1912* (Stockholm 1912).

Petersen, Andrea. "Les concours artistiques aux jeux olympiques de 1912 á 1948. Eléments d'une étude descriptive." *Revue Olympique* 1986:4–5.

Qvarnström, Ludwig. *Vigselrummet i Stockholms rådhus och det tidiga 1900-talets monumentalmåleri. Historia, reception, historiografi* (Uppsala 2010).

"Règlements des Concours littéraires et artistiques de 1912." *Revue Olympique*, 1911:9.

Rosen, Clarence von. "Äfven litterära och artistiska täflingar vid Spelen 1912," 1911.

Sandblad, Håkan. "Kulturen och Stockholms-OS eller Så fick Coubertin sin guldmedalj." *Idrott, historia och samhälle* (1987).

Sandblad, Nils Gösta. *Anders Trulson. En studie i svenskt sekelskiftesmåleri* (Lund 1944).

Segrave, Jeffrey O., and Dikaia Chatziefstathiou. "Pierre de Coubertin's Ideology of Beauty from the Perspective of the History of Ideas." *Pathways: Critiques and Discourse in Olympic Research. Ninth International Symposium for Olympic Research* (London 2008).

Stanton, Richard. "In Search of the Artists of 1912." *Journal of Olympic History*, 2001: 2.

Steorn, Patrik. *Nakna män. Maskulinitet och kreativitet i svensk bildkultur 1900–1915* (Stockholm 2006).

Theorell, Anita. *Studier kring Axel Törnemans Riksdagshusmålningar* (Stockholm 1973).

Trelat, Gaston. "Rapport sur le Concours d'Architecture." *Revue Olympique* 1911:8.

Waern, Rasmus. *Tävlingarnas tid. Arkitekttävlingarnas betydelse i borgerlighetens Sverige* (Stockholm 1996).

Widman, Dag. *Konstnärernas hus. En mötesplats i svenskt konstliv under 100 år* (Stockholm 1999).

Spectators at the Stockholm Games

Mats Hellspong

It is often said that the Olympic Games in Stockholm in 1912 were a great success for the organizers and for the Olympic idea. After the successful start in Athens in 1896 the Olympic Games had an uncertain journey up to Stockholm. The Games in Paris 1900 and St. Louis 1904 had been overshadowed by contemporaneous World Exhibitions in those cities. Besides, the program was too long and the competitions lasted all summer. Neither had the Games in London 1908 been a clear success. The program was considered too detailed and included too many odd sports. Economic reasons and practical obstacles still prevented sportsmen from foreign continents from taking part in the Games. Sport at the Olympic level was mainly an American and European affair and it was to remain that way for several decades.

Why were the Games in Stockholm a success? They seem to have been quite well organized and the organizational failures seem to have been very few. Stockholm was not a very large city, and the Games were able to dominate the streets and the atmosphere during the Olympic weeks. The weather was marvelous, with exceptionally warm and persistent summer weather, though some days were maybe too hot, for instance during the extremely demanding marathon race. The epithet "The Sunshine Olympic Games" has survived, at least in Sweden.

Oscar Söderlund, at that time a young journalist during the Games, writes in an article that the city of Stockholm "seemed quite fabulous to foreigners, with its brilliant summer weather (one of the most beautiful summers of this century) and its romantic bright nights."[1]

Were the Games also a spectator success? How many spectators actually saw the competitions? I will try to discuss this, but first I have to describe the arenas that were used during the summer Games of 1912 and how many spectators they could hold.

The main arena, the Olympic Stadium (Stadion) was a brick castle in national romantic style, designed by Torben Grut (whose son in 1948 became the Olympic winner in the modern pentathlon in London), in my opinion the most poetic arena for track and field sports in modern Olympic history, after the Marble Stadium of Athens from 1896. Grut's Olympic Stadium replaced the only one decade and a half old *Idrottsparken* at the same place. It could take about 22,000 spectators in 1912, probably more when it was packed in the standing sections. The ring building had room for 15,000 spectators, half of them sitting under a roof in the higher part, the other half sitting without a roof in a temporary wooden stand on the lower part. At the northern end a higher stand was built for about 3,000 people and a lower stand with standing room in the back was constructed for 3,000 people as well. At the very front of the end section there were seats for the active sportsmen. Standing tickets were in other words rather few; originally a much greater number of these had been planned. But the police had, for reasons of order and security, argued against standing room, especially in the higher northern stand.[2] The stands were now dominated by seats, an indication that the organizers were striving to keep the crowd in order. You could say that the development of the theatres in the 19th century was a probable model; there the standing

The grandstand in the Olympic Stadium (*Den femte olympiaden i bild och ord*, p. 368).

room in the deep parterre in front of the stage had disappeared and the entire audience now sat in the auditorium.[3] The transformation of the auditorium had radically changed the behavior of theatre audiences, and the organizers of sports competitions probably wanted to follow this example.

A swimming stadium was built in a sea bay, Djurgårdsbrunnsviken, in the inward bend of the shoreline south of what today is the residence of the American ambassador on Nobelgatan. So the swimming stadium was located close to the boathouse of the Stockholm Rowing Club (Stockholms Roddförening). (This boathouse was demolished after the Games and the rowing club built a new boathouse, designed by the prominent architect Sigurd Lewerentz and located further away alongside Djurgårdsbrunnsviken, close to Lido.) The swimming pool was 100 meters in length and 20 meters in breadth and there were no lane ropes between the swimmers. According to various testimonies the competitors did not find the sea water very appealing. Sven Lindhagen remembers it as "dirty, heavy, yellowish-brown,"[4] and a journalist from Gothenburg describes it as "for a spoiled Gothenburger quite distasteful."[5]

For the football tournament in 1912 three arenas were enough, the new Olympic Stadium and the arenas in Råsunda and Traneberg. The two latter arenas were relatively new, but the organizers still had to improve them, for example by building an extra stand. The most attractive matches were played in Stadion, while the interest in the matches in Råsunda and above all in Traneberg was more modest.

For the rowing competitions a course was arranged in Djurgårdsbrunnsviken. Other locations had been considered, but finally the organizers, for reasons of spectator convenience, had chosen a course in central Stockholm. But this course was not ideal. The start was located in a place close to the Dragoon Regiment (where today the Ethnographic Museum is located) and the boats were rowed towards what today is Nobelparken. But when the boats had passed the towered military bathing-hut, which was then situated off the Nobelparken beach, they had to turn starboard towards Strandvägen and later turn port to be able to pass under the Djurgårdsbron bridge. In other words, the rowing course was not straight. The finish was level with the street Torstenssonsgatan.

There on the quay of Strandvägen a stand for 5,000 spectators had been built. They could follow the end of the race. But public support for the rowing competitions was a disappointment for the organizers. There were not many spectators in the stands. Maybe this showed that the rather monotonous sport of rowing was losing ground as public entertainment compared with new and more spectacular sports. Its days of glory in Sweden at the end of the nineteenth century were now gone. Maybe the lack of interest pointed to the fact that the entertainment value in watching the finish of a rowing competition did not offer enough value for money.

Spectator capacity at the tennis competitions and especially at the fencing tournament was also rather limited. The indoor tennis tournament took place as early as May in a big bright red pavilion on a hill between Stadion and Östermalm Athletic Grounds (the latter were used for the athletes training during the Games). This tennis hall was built in 1900 and was the leading tennis hall in Stockholm until it was destroyed by fire in 1920. During the summer Games it was used as a restaurant. Spectator capacity for the tennis competitions in May was very small, judging from photos of only a few hundred people.

More spectators could see the tennis competitions during the outdoor tournament in the summer. The stands at the outdoor Games quite close to the Östermalm arena had room for about 1,500 spectators and they seemed to have been full during the tournament. This was in spite of the fact that many of the best players of the world were missing as they had chosen to play in the Wimbledon tournament in London, which took place at the same time as the Olympic outdoor competitions. At the indoor tournament in May on the other hand the best players of England and France took part and even the legendary Anthony

Charles Winslow of South Africa, winner of the men's singles lawn tennis competition (postcard, National Sports Museum).

Wilding from New Zealand, who won Wimbledon four consecutive years (1910–1913) and was then killed in the World War in 1915. The outdoor tournament was not in the same class. Englishmen took part only in the indoor tournament, Americans in neither of the tournaments.

Even though they were limited in number, the keen interest of the spectators struck even foreign visitors with surprise. "The Royal Family was daily spectators, the galleries and the columns of the newspapers were filled to overflowing. I cannot recall any contests on which native votaries, from the King downwards, concentrated so much interest or displayed such a feverish anxiety to see every ball served," writes an English journalist.[6] "Thunderous applause has over and over again echoed through the pavilion, the spectators have shouted their bravos hundred times, still as interested although the lines have decreased in numbers towards six o'clock in the evening," a reporter writes after the first day's competitions.[7] Both the quotations concern the indoor tournament in May.

The fencing competitions took place in the old tennis pavilion at Östermalms Athletic Grounds. This pavilion was once built for tennis at Idrottsparken in 1896 and moved to Östermalm when Idrottsparken was demolished in 1911 (to make room for the Olympic Stadion). It is a pavilion still used for tennis in 2012, one of the oldest tennis halls in the world still in use. In this hall the fencers competed on four pistes. Spectator capacity during these competitions was approximately 400 people.

How many spectators were there in all at the Stockholm Olympic Games? In the official report on the Games, edited by Erik Bergvall, there is a statistical presentation of the spectator influx.[8] According to this presentation Stadion had between 6 and 15 July in all roughly 199,000 spectators (track and field sports, wrestling, gymnastics), swimming (in the swimming stadium at Djurgårdsbrunnsviken) 48,000 spectators, football (at three arenas) 33,000, the horse competitions (for the first time on the Olympic program) 27,000, tennis (indoor in May and outdoor in June and July) 13,000, rowing (over three days) 4,000 and fencing 1,000 spectators. For some sports, for example, shooting and sailing, no figures are given. Pistol-shooting and rifle-shooting took place at Kaknäs in northern Djurgården, the big park region in central Stockholm, shooting at running deer and clay-pigeon shooting took place in Råsunda, the sailing regatta off the coastal town of Nynäshamn. The shooting competitions had almost no spectators according to photos from these events. Shooting is not today a spectator sport and was even less so in 1912, when no technical facilities existed that could keep the audience continuously informed about the situation.

The most surprising figure is probably the number of spectators for the entire football tournament: only 33,000. Only 5,000 people saw Sweden's first match at Stadion, which ended in defeat against Holland. It is obvious that in 1912 football still had not become King Football within the family of sports. The football match between Austria and Norway at the Traneberg arena was only seen by 134 paying spectators.[9]

The figures above could in all and superficially be read as if 320,000 people saw the Olympic Games in Stockholm in 1912. But the picture must be balanced a little more. A total of 5,662 multi-event passes were sold to Stadion which entitled their owners admission to the morning competitions as well as to the afternoon competitions every day between 6 and 15 July. But in addition to that daily tickets were sold at the turnstiles at Stadion, always considerably more for the afternoon finals than for the qualification competitions in the morning. The statistical report estimates that 5,662 people were present every day morning and afternoon, but that is not realistic. Many who had bought multi-event passes were certainly not able to use them every day and probably often missed the morning qualification competitions, even if it is very possible that they then transferred the tickets to friends and relatives. The number of 199,000 visitors to Stadion must nevertheless be considered too high: it should be reduced by at least 10,000 to 20,000. If the other figures can be accepted, which seems conceivable, the total number of spectators (and not the number of sold tickets) should be about 300,000.

But to this it should be added that for some sports there are no figures at all for the number of spectators. Many spectators would have seen the cycle race on the public highway (which went around Lake Mälaren and passed the towns of Södertälje, Strängnäs, Eskilstuna, Västerås and Enköping) from the roadside. Many must have seen the marathon race from Stadion to Sollentuna and back again in the same way. The distance riding and the cross-country riding, which took place in the countryside north of Stockholm, also had spectators, how many is difficult to say. Consequently it is impossible to determine figures for the total number of spectators who either paid for tickets or caught glimpses of the competitions. How many could have seen the marathon runners outside Stadion?

How many *different* persons saw at least some of the competitions? That is an even more impossible question. Most spectators saw probably more than one competition, many were maybe present at the arenas every day during the three weeks that the main part of the Games lasted. During the afternoons Stadion was filled by 10,000 to 20,000 people every day from 6 to 15 July. Theoretically it is possible that the same spectators watched all the Stadion competitions and furthermore saw the football and tennis matches before 6 July, and then after 15 July the horse competitions and the rowing races. The swimming races had about 3,500 spectators at the finals, and since these took place in the evenings when the competitions in Stadion were finished, it could theoretically be the same persons. A very cautious and maybe almost meaningless conclusion from this would be that between 30,000 and 350,000 *different* persons watched at least one of the Olympic competitions in Stockholm 1912. The right figure should lie somewhere in between.

For the support and development of sport in Sweden it was important that there were some competitions that "the man in the street" could catch a glimpse of without being very familiar with the rules or competitors and without paying for tickets. And that was possible for some of the most demanding and fascinating contests during the Games, such as the much discussed marathon race north of Stockholm or the cycle race around Lake Mälaren.

The largest arena during the Games was Stadion, which could hold about 22,000 people, but even more when methodically packed. Such a large number of spectators had never been assembled at a sporting event in Sweden before 1912. Abroad, not least in England, arenas had already gathered a considerably larger number of spectators in the nineteenth century. The cities that had arranged Olympic Games before Stockholm had all had access to considerably larger arenas. The Swedish senior sports official Viktor Balck, who watched the Games in Athens in 1896, talked about spectator interest during the marathon race in the leading sport journal *Tidning för Idrott*:

> If you estimate that 60,000 spectators were inside Stadion, that 30–40,000 dressed the hills and that many thousands lined the streets through which the marathon champions should run to the finish, then we arrive with fair probability at a sum of more than 100,000 people, assembled to watch the great competition for the marathon prize; a gathering of people surely greater than any public or sporting event in our modern time up to now had been able to produce.[10]

I shall not here enter deeply into the question of whether Balck was right in his assumption. English football seems to have had crowds of more than 100,000 spectators at the end of the nineteenth century.[11] In Stockholm in 1912 at least the reporter of a newspaper was very impressed by the spectators: "20,000 persons are by the way a very respectable gathering. We have probably seen it before at royal anniversaries and other ceremonies, but there people just form a dead crowd, the silent background to a cruel drama. Yesterday they acted themselves."[12]

This is an important observation. Sport spectators were not passive, they took an active interest in the competitions and could also in some way influence the result. We shall now find out more about how the spectators acted during the Games of Stockholm in 1912.

Spectator Behavior

In the Olympic Games of our time the spectacular opening and closing ceremonies are highlights of the program. They are usually very expensive and artistically well worked-out events, intended to entertain a much greater audience than those just interested in sport. Even at Stockholm in 1912 the solemn opening ceremony attracted great interest from spectators and the media, despite the fact that it did not take place until the track and field competitions at Stadion were about to start, which was a week after the start of many other Olympic competitions (football, shooting, tennis). The reports in the press give the impression that it was mostly the parade of the different nations, where the athletes marched together behind their national flags and name-plates, that fascinated the spectators. The spectators could study how many active sportsmen the different nations would field and how the sportsmen were dressed and performed. Some teams showed elegance and uniformity, e.g. the great American squad with men in dark jackets and white trousers, rhythmically waving their straw hats. In *The New York Times* pride in their own team was expressed: "In the parade of the athletes of all nations the American contingent made a fine showing, looking like a well trained chorus in their navy blue jackets, white trousers, and straw hats."[13]

The spectators' gallery in the Olympic Stadium (*Den femte olympiaden I bild och ord*, p. 64).

Spectators could also notice how the teams of some nations were supported by fellow-countrymen in the stands. The Swedish spectators would meet a new and for many of them provocative way of thinking, a sort of peaceful manifestation of mutually competing teams from different nations, all put together in a framework of national and religious elevation, "a grandiose exposition that late shall be forgotten by those who took part in it and have witnessed it," as a journalist in the Finnish daily *Hufvudstadsbladet* wrote.[14] Once more *The New York Times* may be quoted:

> The picture, when nearly 2,000 bronzed athletes, picked men of the world, with the Scandinavian women gymnasts, the flags of the several nations planted before them, faced the royal box in which were seated the king and most of the royal family, while the bands played and thousands sang the Swedish hymn, was one never to be forgotten.[15]

The newspaper called the opening ceremony "by far the most memorable international event ever."[16] The Olympic Games in 1912 were the last before World War I, the last during la belle époque. Was nationalism then stronger and more unfettered than today? Probably, but the coming World Wars would soon make national orgies somewhat unpleasant. But on the field of sport nationalistic feelings are alive even today and find strong expression. The differences between now and then are probably not very great, but the nationalistic feelings around the competitions in 1912 may seem a little more undisguised and true-hearted than in our time.

The Olympic Games indisputably offered a new arena where nationalistic feelings were allowed to bloom and take their proper space. It was also discovered that the great international sport events offered suitable opportunities for sending out political messages. No foreign guests became more cheered by the spectators than the athletes from Finland. This was noted with satisfaction by the Finnish press. A reporter writes somewhat surprised in *Hufvudstadsbladet*: "When the Finns entered the music band played The March of the Finnish Cavalry and rounds of applause and cheers were heard from stand to stand. It seemed as if the honoring of our team was especially intense and warm."[17] Finland in 1912 was a grand duchy under Russia. Nevertheless Finland was allowed to take part in the Games in its own name and entered with its own team, marching directly after the Russian team, however. The Finns had a national name-plate of their own but not a flag of their own. In Sweden there was naturally strong support for the Finnish separation struggle and a special feeling of kinship with a country that only a century earlier had been the eastern part of Sweden.

The numerous women gymnasts made the female contribution at the opening ceremony quite visible, not least Denmark had a large team of women gymnasts. This made a deep impression on the spectators, who greeted the female athletes warmly: "Whenever the women appeared there was tremendous applause, for the Austrian gymnasts, for the Australian swimmers in their long, green coats, which had a certain similarity to bathrobes, and the Danish female gymnasts."[18]

It seems that the spectators were easily persuaded to show their admiration for women who dared to start in the Olympic Games. Sporting women were not rare in Sweden in 1912; they competed not only in swimming and tennis but also in some other sports, but the average spectator did not expect women to take part in the hard international fight for Olympic medals. The fonder they now became.

If you examine the spectators at the Games in 1912 from preserved photos you may be surprised by the great number of women in the stands. Certainly the men dominate, in the hot weather usually wearing bright straw hats with dark bands, but the women, in bright dresses and wide-brimmed hats, are still numerous. Female hat fashion at that time was remarkable. Oscar Söderlund comments 50 years afterwards:

> Their hats were like round serving trays filled with flower arrangements, small birds and feathers. They were stuck to the head with long hatpins, whose ends were quite dangerous for the surroundings, especially in congestion on trams. In the official report about medical service at Stadion there is an account that a female patient received treatment because she had been injured by one of these dangerous spears.[19]

The female interest in the Games is interesting in a time when sport was so obviously man-defined. The female sports in Stockholm in 1912 can be counted on the fingers of one hand: tennis, swimming, diving and gymnastics. Probably the Stockholm Olympic Games should be considered as much a social event, an exceptional occurrence, as a sports event. The city was permeated by the Games that summer. The foreign tourists were a striking element in the streets, although they were not as many as the organizers, the hotel proprietors and the innkeepers would have wanted. Ships from participating nations with tourists aboard were anchored in the waters off Stockholm; the hotels were decorated with the flags of many countries. A big noticeboard in front of the famous department store Nordiska Kompaniet gave information about the results and attracted many curious strollers.[20] It was very tempting for locals of both sexes to see for themselves what was taking place in the Olympic Stadium. Especially the opening ceremony attracted many female spectators.

Press reports also give the impression that the competitions were by no means an exclusively male interest. The unusually hot day when the marathon race was about to start, one news paper describes the spectators as follows:

> The sun burns with an intensive July glow down at the Olympic Stadium, and the spectators on its uncovered stands suffer as in a sauna. The ladies have dressed in their thinnest and most see-through blouses and keep their fans in constant motion, while the gentlemen ignore Swedish conventions, take off their jackets and sometimes also their waistcoats, and loosen their starched collars a bit.[21]

Fans were sold at a good profit to the female audience during the Games. Parasols and flower-decked hats often stuck up in the stands.

Especially much female elegance was seen in the stands at the tennis tournament. In those cosmopolitan and aristocratic surroundings, full of officers' uniforms and the jingling of spurs, such elegance was probably less conspicuous than it could have been in the Olympic Stadium. Else Kleen (pseudonym Gwen) in daily *Stockholms Dagblad* protested about the female elegance during the competitions. She found the elegance that could be suitable at a horse race or a garden party inappropriate in the Olympic Stadium, even for democratic reasons. "It is alarming to see pearled silk at two o'clock in the afternoon on a sports competition!"[22]

Many women in the upper classes obviously defined a visit to the Olympic Stadium during the Games in the same way as a spring Sunday at the leading racecourses: a society event. The elegance and etiquette of the Olympic Stadium audience this summer came into conflict with the weather. It was 28 degrees Celsius during the marathon race, and this forced many to loosen their starched collars. The practical and the representative were on a collision course. Such things happened rather often in the sport stands at the beginning of the twentieth century.

Some thought they saw on the sport stands marks of a greater openness and more free relations between people of different classes but also of different sexes. Maria Rieck-Müller in the women's magazine *Idun* is surprised at the emotional devotion that she seems to see in women in the stands:

> Who would have imagined thousands of well-mannered Swedish women taking part in ovations with body and soul, the like of which we have hitherto known only through descriptions from exotic gala performances? Not when it has been a matter of deed and action in any case, if even the feeling has often been there. Indeed this feeling has been driven near to boiling point before such irresistible phenomena as an Ödmann, a Forsell and maybe some others. But never has it broken all conventional barriers and so spontaneously found expression as now.[23]

The Swedish woman in the sport stands was, according to Rieck-Müller, cheerful, simple and unaffected. "Only consider this: a gentleman politely addresses a lady, and she does not turn away like an insulted saint, but answers attentively, *although they have not been introduced.* Such things could really happen in these days."[24] It started to show that the sports stands were a form of social free zone, where otherwise rather rigorous social rules could be temporarily eliminated.

A challenge for the organizers was to be able to communicate with the many spectators in an effective way, overcoming the language problems. In the absence of the loudspeakers of our time there were in reality two methods: visual noticeboards and heralds with megaphones. Both were often used in combination. Before every heat the number of the heat and the numbers of the competitors were given on a noticeboard with three sides. The system was thus intended for spectators who had bought the daily program. Immediately after the competition the results were given on another noticeboard: the number of the heat and the numbers of the participants. A herald repeated the results in a megaphone in Swedish and English, walking around the arena from one section to another with his message.

It was hard work for the stewards changing numbers on the noticeboards. Some reporters mention that the work with the noticeboards was done by "small boy scouts."[25] "Sometimes the numbers were mixed up, so that the spectators resentfully shouted 'wrong,' until a correction was made."[26] This, by the way, is a good example of the contributory and controlling role of the crowd at sporting events. The range of the megaphones was limited and the organizers mainly had to rely on optical and visual messages. During the marathon race the situation was continuously reported to the spectators through a signal mast in the Olympic Stadium. The different checkpoints of the race were given letter notations. To announce the situation at, e.g., the checkpoint at Tureberg, the letter for this checkpoint, B, was hoisted. Underneath flags were hoisted that showed the nationality of the leading runners in the order they had passed the checkpoint. For Tureberg a Finnish flag was placed first, then two South African flags, then an English and a Swedish one. The system suggests that for the ordinary spectator the competitions rather seemed to be a struggle between nations than between individuals.

But much was difficult to understand for the spectators and much was misunderstood. A reporter describes how the spectators during the marathon race eagerly waited for news, how the excitement rose whenever a herald put a megaphone to his mouth and how people shouted hush to each other to be able to hear. Still confusion often arose: "Then a man with a megaphone appears and one listens passionately to his partly inaudible sounds. One can catch the words "marathon race" and numbers belonging to a runner. What on earth? Can this already be the results from Stocksund? Oh no! It's just the list of the runners who did not start in the race."[27]

The Finnish runner Hannes Kolehmainen crossing the finish line ahead of France's Jean Bouin and thus winning their highly anticipated duel over 5,000 meters, July 10, 1912 (*Den femte olympiaden i bild och ord,* p. 109).

In the swimming competitions bathing-caps of different colors indicated the swimmers' nationality, and numbers on the caps marked who they were.[28] Now and then bugle calls drew the audience's attention, for example when the spectators were warned about the arrival of the first runners at the Olympic Stadium in the marathon race.

The spectators made their presence known during the competitions by applause, whistles and cheers. Whistles seem to belong to forms of approval that could easily be misunderstood for cultural reasons. One daily magazine talks about the 10,000 meters winner Hannes Kolehmainen from Finland: "'Hej, hej, hej, Suomi, hej,' the Finns are shouting in wild happiness and their Hungarian kinsmen join in with cries and whistles, but the latter are misunderstood as counter-demonstrations. In this country you should not show your delight by whistling."[29]

Enthusiasm should be expressed by clapping and cheers. If you are to believe a report in the news papers, applause represented a higher and warmer sort of enthusiasm than cheers. The report is about the pole vault competition and the Swede Bertil Uggla's struggle for a medal. "Each time he cleared a height — it started with 340 and went well up to 380 — people cheered and there was even applause. When he tried at 385 it was dead silent, and when he missed for the last time came that 'Noo!,' which is so characteristic of national disappointment at Stadion."[30]

The spectators took an active interest in the thrilling drama and that even applied to the seemingly more blasé tennis audience. "The game on the court was followed with intense interest, people stamped, tapped their sticks, feet and umbrellas on the floor when a difficult ball was taken, and sighed worse than the players when a ball was missed or went out."[31]

The quotation can be compared with the English journalist's impression from the indoor tournament, which was reported earlier. The enthusiasm and liveliness of the Swedish spectators were a surprise to many foreigners. A Danish journalist who was at the football match between Sweden and Holland expressed his impressions: "Often during the fight I thought I had come to Spain, so vivacious were the spectators. The large stand at the end of the Olympic Stadium was boiling with life, people were waving their hats and flags, they were waving their sticks, they were shouting and the shouts grew to dreadful roars that shook the earth."[32]

"The large stand at the end of the Olympic Stadium" was the northern stand with its standing spectators. That was the place where passions were fiercest and from there initiatives were taken which spread to other sections of the arena.

Was this really the restrained and correct Stockholmer, the Danish journalist wondered. But the Swedish journalists also expressed their surprise at the Swedish spectators' capacity to show emotions. That they had not quite expected. When there were no Swedish participants the spectators shifted their support to a suitable neighboring country. During the football match between Denmark and England (the final of the football tournament), the Danes had the support of the spectators.

> But then the Danes score, and there's an eruption, people applaud, cheer, stamp, shout, rise up, move their hats, wave small Danish flags — just imagine a shy Stockholmer, who otherwise hardly shows his own country's flag, waving a Danish miniature flagpole. They were not that many up to now, but just wait till next week. The street flag sellers in Sturegatan are already licking their lips.[33]

Manifestations of national delight were obvious elements in the experiences each day during the Olympic Games. One of the leading daily papers, *Dagens Nyheter*, published every day on its front page the current score in the unofficial competition between nations, where Sweden struggled with USA for victory. This certainly contributed to the feeling that success for Sweden at the Games became a concern not only for sports fans but for almost every Swedish man and

Bertil Gustafsson Uggla, who came third in the pole vault with 3.80 meters, in Idrottsparken, Stockholm (postcard, National Sports Museum).

woman. One daily paper, *Aftonbladet,* commented on this rapid extension of sports interest as follows:

> How many human beings in this city have up to now taken an interest in putting the shot? Or in wrestling? This has been roughly on a par with a flea circus in ordinary people's eyes, something extremely vulgar, only adored by "Söderamerikaner" on Sunday afternoons at Novilla, together with deep drags on their cigarettes and swigs of beer. But at this moment director generals and assistant secretaries are on their knees, asking higher powers for victory in wrestling, so as to increase our points score.[34]

Powerful backing from the spectators supported the Swedish athletes: "This throw demonstrated by the way that we are not that bad in the art of cheering, because everything was drowned in the storm wave of acclamation which followed when the javelin, after being seen as a thin streak in the heat haze, elegantly sank down six meters on the other side of the Olympic Record flag." This is how *Dagens Nyheter* wrote about Erik Lemming's winning throw in the javelin competition.[35] When the Swedish policemen had won the gold medals in tug-of-war, the same newspaper noticed that patrolling constables in Sturegatan surprisingly found themselves "surrounded by unknown persons who wanted to shake their hands and congratulate them."[36] When the Swedish triple victory in the modern pentathlon was announced to the spectators and the three Swedish flags were hoisted there came a hurricane of cheering and a voice in the crowd struck up "Du gamla, du fria," which was sung by 20,000 standing and bare-headed people.[37] The same episode was commented on in the American press as follows (with a raising of the number of spectators): "Such a thing had never occurred before, and to celebrate the event 30 000 persons went almost mad for joy. They yelled and laughed and waved thousands of yellow and blue flags, finally sobering down under the strains of the national anthem, most impressively sung."[38]

Songs were also used by foreign supporters in the stands to urge on their fellow countrymen and to create unity. English supporters gave proof of this during the football match between Denmark and England. Suitable songs were put in at strategic moments. When for example Crown Prince Gustaf Adolf entered the ground at the half-time break in order to shake hands with the players, he was greeted by Englishmen in the stands singing "For he's a jolly good fellow," and the Crown Prince expressed his gratitude by waving his hat.[39]

The singing and the national enthusiasm was supported by the presence of bands in the arenas. One daily paper report from the victory ovations after the final in 400 meters breaststroke swimming illustrates what forms spontaneous nationalism could take among the spectators. The race was won by a German swimmer before a Swede and an Englishman:

> The band took the opportunity of striking up "Deutschland, Deutschland über alles." But the Germans had to sing their anthem alone. The rest of the audience remained seated. This was not due to nonchalant impoliteness but to a lack of musical knowledge. The spectators did not know the tune. But then came "Du gamla, du fria." And that one everyone knew, the hats came off and everybody rose, and the song sounded sonorously from the oaks of Djurgården. Flourishes and cheers. And then the audience was ready to sing "God save the King." The same ovation. The same cheers that never wanted to end when the three nations' flags were hoisted.[40]

One might add that the national anthems here were played spontaneously by the band. An official victory ceremony with national anthems did not exist in 1912. It took another 20 years before that ritual was introduced at the Olympic Games. The distribution of prizes in Stockholm took place on a certain day at the end of the Games, and there prizes were given out to medalists in some fifty events. There was simply no time for national anthems for every event. "Du gamla, du fria," which from the beginning of the twentieth century had been regarded as Sweden's national anthem, was, however, spontaneously sung during the Games at especially patriotic moments, as at the triple victory in the modern pentathlon, as was mentioned before.

Live music in the arenas was a natural element in early sport, not only at the Olympic Games. And the role of the music was not only to play national anthems but also to fill up periods of waiting with relaxing light music. The audience knew that and could even abruptly demand it, when it felt a need for it, as while waiting for the arrival of the first runners in the spectacular marathon race:

> It seemed as if the huge Olympic Stadium had gone to sleep. Then some strange rhythmic cries were heard from the northern stand. They were not the usual cries, and the Stadium awoke and listened with surprise. Finally the cries could be decoded. Someone found the situation boring and was shouting for music. It was well-advised, because the music seemed to have gone to sleep too, but was now woken up, and just before the information about the marathon race arrived, a playful waltz was executed, and the northern stand was calm again.[41]

On the whole the 1912 audience must be seen as moderate and disciplined. Sometimes disapproval of a judge could, however, lead to vigorous protests. During the water-polo match between Sweden and England, the spectators became so displeased with the decisions of the referee that someone in the stand loudly suggested that the spectators should protest by leaving the arena and some hundred people seem to have done so.[42] Sometimes situations even came up which are reminiscent of the capricious football crowds of our time, a crowd that easily can pass the limit of senseless destruction when it loses its temper. Immediately

Jósef Sándorm of Hungary and Martin Jonsson of Sweden, lightweight, wrestle without protection from the hot sun in the Olympic Stadium, July 6, 1912 (photograph by Theodor Modin, postcard, National Sports Museum).

after the football final between Denmark and England the following happened according to a newspaper report:

> Not many noticed this event, as attention was drawn to an incident which the Stadion guards had to prevent from being repeated by absolutely any means whatsoever. From the beginning maybe from wild enthusiasm but later from clear mischief, elements among the spectators started to throw seat cushions down on to the inner field, though many landed among the spectators in the lower rows.[43]

This is an embryo of the prohibited and infectious mass behavior that has become much more common in the sports stands in modern times.

The Organized Cheering

The support of the athletes during the Games took forms that must have been strange and unexpected to much of the audience. A journalist noticed with astonishment (but without dislike), that Holland during the football match versus Sweden was "well represented and well placed from the viewpoint of fan club and encouragement" and that a Dutchman was armed with a megaphone through which he supported his fellow-countrymen on the field.[44]

The somewhat clumsy linguistic usage indicates that fan clubs were something new and unexpected in the Swedish stands. American fan clubs with their cheerleaders attracted the greatest attention. They had already left their mark on earlier Olympic Games. "American tourists and sailors also distinguished themselves by their wild college-style cheers," says an American historian about the first Games in Athens 1896.[45] Viktor Balck, who sat in the stands in Athens, seems to have been both surprised and irritated by the organized American cheering. "The victory was as usual greeted by the Americans with enthusiastic cheering, in which a group of American navy sailors high up in the amphitheatre loudly took part," Balck writes.[46] To the reserved sports official and officer Balck the reactions may have seemed childish and uncontrolled. The noisy enthusiasm of the American supporters at the Games in London 1908 had also annoyed both spectators and organizers. A reporter in *The New York Times* observed that the Games in Stockholm were more permissive in this respect and that the difference from London was obvious:

> There yelling and flag waving were frowned upon as bad form, and American spectators were criticised for outbursts of enthusiasm and college yells. Here flags and badges are thicker than leaves on trees. Nearly every nationality breaks into a roar when its men give the smallest excuse. Today's proceedings were as tumultuous as a college football game.[47]

The way of forming organized national support in the stands was in other words spreading in 1912 from the American spectators with their well developed college traditions to the spectators of more and more nations.

The American fan clubs excelled in rhythmic strings of words like "Rah, rah, ra — USA — A-m-e-r-i-c-a!" The names of the American stars were rhythmically chanted. "The 200-meters run was electrified by the American cheering-team. The name 'Craig' was croaked in an absolutely ear-splitting way, but then the name is really suitable for such use," *Dagens Nyheter* commented.[48] The American shouts of encouragement, the yells or the rahs, could, however, out of politeness also be directed towards successful antagonists. "Just to show the good feeling existing, the Americans gave special 'rahs' for the plucky Swede," a reporter in *The New York Times* wrote when an American had defeated a Swede after a hard duel in an 800-meters heat.[49] "After each sprinter ran the American hurrah-leaders shouted their refrain, now known to the entire Stadion, which always ends with the name of the winner," *Aftonbladet* wrote.[50] If a Swede should win, they politely cheered for Sweden.

Canada's supporters also chanted rhythmic strings of words. According to a reporter these could go as follows:

> Hya lacka, hya lacka,
> booma lacka, booma lacka,
> cis boom, bommera, boomera ree,
> Canada, Canada, cross the sea,
> C-a-n-a-d-a
> Canada, Canada, Canada.[51]

These manifestations of American college sports culture or of the world of transatlantic sports seemed naturally both provocative and stimulating to the Stockholm spectators. They tried to give as good as they got.

> It is obvious that the talent among American spectators to manifest themselves at competitions of this sort has inspired our own boys to great efforts, and the Swedish part of the spectators had acquired a battle-cry of their own, which was now tested for the first time. It might have been somewhat more rhythmic and spirited, and we believe that it needs some revision, if it is to be sufficiently effective against the transatlantic guests. It is something about S-w-e-d-e-n, but it needs some sort of rounding in the end.[52]

The appearance of the organized fan clubs ended in them being challenged by other groups of spectators. A journalist, who was reporting on the atmosphere in the stands, described how the standing spectators reacted to the American fan clubs:

> And then they have a special eye on the American hurrah-leaders down in section P.—Watch out, the Americans are starting now! And when the American boys had finished their cheers, the Swedes knock on the railings and shout as much they can:—Four Swedish cheers for the American boys! But their cheers will not be heard at that distance. Nevertheless they cheer.[53]

The cheers can be seen as *collective verbal* reactions to what is happening in the arena. The spectators try to influence their own athletes to perform as well as possible, but sometimes they just want to show their support, or, very rarely, show their appreciation of opponents and guests. This type of collective spectator reaction now had its breakthrough in Sweden at the Olympic Games. *Individual verbal* reactions on the other hand were not unknown or uncommon in arenas before 1912. They found expression in different ways during the Games this summer. Puck in *Hufvudstadsbladet* gives a detailed account of an English supporter's behavior, which should be quoted in its entirety. The scene is the football final between Denmark and England.

> I saw this match, and it was as amusing to watch the spectators as to watch the game. Just below me an English supporter was seated — not a distinguished gentleman but a representative of the less winning loudmouth-type. The proud Albion does not suffer from a lack of them. He followed the game with the utmost eagerness; he was actually working harder than the players on the field. His clean-shaven face with its bulldog-looking touch grew redder and redder as the game went on, his cheeks swelled up and the neck formed over the loose collar in two red folds. He formed a megaphone with his hands and cried and shouted good advice and detailed instructions to his fellow-countrymen: he told them how he would have played if he had been on the field. He mopped the sweat off his forehead, he jumped up and down

on his seat, and when the English team scored, he turned around to the audience with a triumphant gesture that meant: "Look, it will be all right, if they just follow my advice!" If he had been richly paid, he could not have worked harder and shouted more than he did. And when one of his compatriots seemed to make a blunder on the field, he shouted with tears in his eyes: "Charlie, Charlie, think of your old mother!" That could be called patriotism, even if the forms are slightly noisy.[54]

Here we meet the intensely committed supporter and it is hardly a coincidence that he is an Englishman. In England sports had been developed and recognized for a long time, not least the popular game of football, which already at the end of the 19th century attracted large crowds in the English industrial towns. The supporter described by Puck in *Hufvudstadsbladet* lives with his team every minute of the game and does not hesitate to give his pig-headed advice from the stands, completely unconcerned about the fact that the players can't hear him or about what the spectators around him might think about his activity.

Football went England's way in 1912: the team took the gold medal, as expected one may add. But the Olympic Games in Stockholm were not a complete success for England, which four years earlier was the best nation. The English squad came to Stockholm not sufficiently prepared and met with some unexpected setbacks: for instance the tug-of-war team (made up of policemen from London) lost to the Swedish team (also made up of policemen). England finally ended third, far behind Sweden and USA. The reactions from the spectators must be seen in this connection. English spectators preferred that Swedish athletes did not succeed. Swedish spectators preferred that Finnish or German athletes, for example, were victorious at the expense of English and American competitors, the latter being the main opponents in the inter-nations competition at the Games. Only the American fan clubs seemed to be generous enough to cheer their antagonists as well. The Americans nevertheless dominated the competitions, but did not win the inter-nations competition, mostly because they did not start in some sports where the starting expenses were too high (equestrian sports, sailing).

The Swedish spectators also produced some verbal reactions to the events in the arenas. A report may serve as an example: "One individual, who has made himself known, is a middle-aged Swede, who always calls for four cheers for the winning nation. He is doing well in the international market."[55] The sports stands were obviously a place where an individual spectator could take liberties and live out his feelings. Nevertheless few did so without having other spectators behind them.

Puck in *Hufvudstadsbladet* gives an example from the 10,000-meters run, which was won by the Finn Hannes Kolehmainen before an American of Indian origin, Tewanima: "I have my judgement confirmed by real experts, as behind me were seated some hundreds of young Stockholm boys and they understand sport. 'Bloody hot guy. Don't give in, Kolehmainen! Keep a watch out for the redskin!,' those were the encouraging calls."[56] Notice the general sympathy for the Finns but also the antagonism against USA, the main competitor for Sweden in the inter-nations competition.

"Ekenskisen," the quick-witted boy from the Stockholm working-class, appears here and there in the press reports from the 1912 Olympic Games. The stand with standing accommodation only on the north side of Stadion was the place where he was mostly seen. A report gives a vivid and somewhat ironic picture of this part of the arena:

> And as my passe-partout was valid here too, I went along to the standing section, which is despised by the majority of people and, as we all know, is located beneath the large stand. Instead of sitting on benches you have to stand here hanging on a massive square-shaped rail-

ing, indeed reminiscent of a farm show in Skråköping, but nonetheless not unpleasant. You stand in thick soft sand, so you won't get stiff in your legs, and if you insist on sitting you can sit on the railing. But now and then a somewhat officious steward appears and tells you that "you are not allowed to sit here."[57]

Sport as a democratic challenge in class society lies not only in the mixture of competitors from different social strata but also in the fact that the competitions fascinate people from all social classes. The working-class boy with a peaked cap and a cigarette in the corner of his mouth mingles with upper-class ladies in elegant dresses, even though the division into sections in some way managed to keep them apart. Press reports, as the one just quoted from *Hufvudstadsbladet*, show that working-class youth did not hesitate to enter the stands and to express their feelings. This is described by many journalists with an amused curiosity, as a kind of ethnographic reporting.

Naturally the behavior of the spectators was very different in the different sports arenas during the Games. The tennis spectators, always with many members of the royal family present, confined themselves to applause and bravo cheers. But some tennis spectators stamped on the floor or tapped with the metal tips of their sticks.[58] The football crowd was the most expressive one. A reporter describes the spectators during the football match between Sweden and Holland as follows:

> Oh, these spectators under the line of striking Swedish flags high up in the stands. It has no regard for anybody and it firmly declares how it wants the match to be played. It is feverish with enthusiasm and boils with resentment, thousands of clenched fists are raised to the skies, in a death-blow for the defeated, in salute to the favorites. And the throats, where soon no human sound is left, work with hoarse yells under the violent pressure of throbbing pulses and glowing breath.[59]

Conclusion

The Stockholm Olympic Games were a sensational venture by the Swedish sports movement at the beginning of the twentieth century. Today they still stand out as the most spectacular sports event ever in the country. Their capacity to arouse interest in competitive sport among the population can hardly be exaggerated. They demonstrated with great clarity what spectator potential sport had. No sports event in Sweden had up to then been seen by such a large number of people.

The spectators had rich opportunities to rejoice at Swedish success. Sweden was the winner in the unofficial inter-nations competition. As I mentioned before this was partly due to the fact that USA for practical and economic reasons did not start in some sports. Moreover, in 1912 every country had the right to start with quite a number of athletes in each sport, and that certainly favored the organizing nation. In for example the modern pentathlon, where Sweden took all three medals, 12 out of 32 competitors were Swedes. In the triple jump, where Sweden also took all the medals, 8 out of 20 competitors were Swedes. Anyhow, a euphoric feeling of success spread over the country during the Games. In a parliamentary debate in January 1913 the Swedish Conservative leader Ernst Trygger took up the Swedish success in the Games and considered it to be evidence of Sweden being a great power in physical sports. 1912 had been a great year for Swedish national feeling and he regretted that the Olympic Games as well as the very successful fund-raising campaign to be able to build an armored warship were not mentioned either in "the speech from the throne, or in the statement about what had happened in the country."[60] Sport and the euphoria around the Swedish success in the Olympic Games were obviously used as a weapon in the political debate. The political situation at the time was heated, which would soon manifest itself in the "Bondetåg" in 1914.[61]

The Olympic Games in Stockholm played an important role in shaping spectator culture in the sports stands. Sport at an élite level has internationally elaborated rules and it was not evident how these would be understood by inexperienced spectators. Such a large international event as the Olympic Games made a strong contribution to determining the principles for how large sports competitions should be organized. At the same time an etiquette for the behavior of the spectators was developed. There was a contemporary rival to the Olympic Games in the education of the Stockholm sports spectators, namely the Nordic Games, which were arranged every fourth year from the start in 1901 and in practice served as Winter Olympic Games up until the time when these were officially started in the 1920s.[62] The Nordic Games also had significance for the acclimatization of sport spectators in Stockholm. But they were winter Games with a very limited group of sports on the program and the international influx of sportsmen and spectators was modest. The Nordic Games mainly lived up to their name.

The most important contribution of 1912 to Swedish spectator culture in the sports arenas was the transatlantic (American and Canadian) organized cheering in support of their own athletes. As I have tried to show with examples from the Swedish, Nordic and American press this was an obvious feature of the competitions, especially at the track-and-field competitions and at the football matches. Swedish spectators had already come across this phenomenon before 1912, but it had passed almost unnoticed.[63] But the cheering habits of 1912 created a sensation and were soon met by improvised attempts to create strings of words of their own.

In Sweden organized cheering would come to be a lasting heritage from the 1912 Games. It is somewhat ironic that, as time went on, the cheering that took the Swedish spectators by surprise in 1912 and caused many raised eyebrows and critical comments would turn into something of a distinctive feature for Swedish sports events. There is a line of succession from the Olympic Stadium stands in 1912 to the cheerleaders of the 1920s and 1930s, famous leaders like Ernst Rolf and Valdemar Dahlqvist and today forgotten leaders like Erik "Kille" Kihlberg and Thure "Bagarn" Danielsson. Things came to such a pass that Swedish organized cheering became to be considered unsporting by some antagonists, which Torbjörn Andersson has shown with examples from the World Cup in football in Sweden in 1958.[64]

Notes

1. Söderlund, "Stockholm sommaren 1912" (1962), p. 115.
2. Bergvall, *V. Olympiaden* (1913), p. 169.
3. Cf Hellspong, "Att tämja massorna" (1983).
4. Lindhagen, *Mina femton olympiader och några till* (1957), p. 21.
5. *Göteborgs-Posten*, July 7, 1912.
6. Wallis Myers, *Twenty Years of Lawn Tennis* (1920).
7. *Stockholms-Tidningen*, May 6, 1912.
8. Bergvall, 1913, p. 44.
9. Söderlund, 1962, p. 128.
10. *Tidning för Idrott*, May 21, 1896.
11. Baker, *Sports in the Western World* (1988), p. 126.

12. *Aftonbladet,* July 5, 1912.

13. *The New York Times,* July 7, 1912.

14. *Huvudstadsbladet,* July 8, 1912.

15. *The New York Times,* July 7, 1912.

16. Ibid.

17. *Hufvudstadsbladet,* July 8, 1912.

18. *Aftonbladet,* July 6, 1912.

19. Söderlund, 1962, p. 114.

20. See *Dagens Nyheter,* June 30, 1912.

21. *Dagens Nyheter,* July 14, 1912.

22. *Stockholms Dagblad,* July 14, 1912.

23. *Idun* 1912, no. 23, p. 3. Ödmann and Forsell, mentioned by Rieck-Müller, were famous Swedish opera singers.

24. Ibid.

25. *Hufvudstadsbladet,* July 10, 1912.

26. *Aftonbladet,* July 10, 1912.

27. *Nya Dagligt Allehanda,* July 14, 1912.

28. Bergvall, 1913, p. 672.

29. *Dagens Nyheter,* July 9, 1912.

30. *Dagens Nyheter,* July 12, 1912.

31. *Dagens Nyheter,* July 4, 1912.

32. *Stockholms Dagblad,* July 6, 1912.

33. *Aftonbladet,* July 5, 1912.

34. *Aftonbladet,* July 10, 1912. The word "Söderamerikaner" alludes to young men from "Söder," the south part of Stockholm, at that time a working class area, who were said to be Americanized, dressed and behaving in an American way. Novilla was a plain, popular restaurant.

35. *Dagens Nyheter,* July 7, 1912.

36. *Dagens Nyheter,* July 9, 1912.

37. *Dagens Nyheter,* July 13, 1912. "Du gamla, du fria" is the Swedish national anthem.

38. *The New York Times,* July 13, 1912.

39. *Aftonbladet,* July 5, 1912.

40. *Dagens Nyheter,* July 12, 1912.

41. *Stockholms-Tidningen,* July 15, 1912.

42. *Stockholms-Tidningen,* July 12, 1912.

43. *Stockholms-Tidningen,* July 5, 1912.

44. *Dagens Nyheter,* June 30, 1912.

45. Baker, 1988, p. 195.

46. *Tidning för idrott,* May 25, 1896.

47. *The New York Times,* July 7, 1912.

48. *Dagens Nyheter,* July 12, 1912.

49. *The New York Times,* July 7, 1912.

50. *Aftonbladet,* July 10, 1912.

51. *Hufvudstadsbladet,* July 16, 1912.

52. *Dagens Nyheter,* June 30, 1912.

53. *Stockholms Dagblad,* July 11, 1912.

54. *Hufvudstadsbladet,* July 9, 1912.

55. *Göteborgs-Posten,* July 13, 1912.

56. *Hufvudstadsbladet,* July 10, 1912.

57. *Stockholms Dagblad,* July 11, 1912. "Ekenskis" is a slang word for "Stockholm guy." "Eken," actually "the Oak," is an old word for "Stockholm." "Skråköping" is a disparaging word for a backward small town.

58. *Stockholms-Tidningen,* July 1, 1912.

59. *Stockholms-Tidningen,* July 1, 1912.

60. Samuelsson, "Ernst Trygger" (2010), pp. 35–36. The fund-raising to be able to produce a warship was an answer from conservative opinion to the liberal government's refusal to raise defense expenditure.

61. The "Bondetåget," a march of 30,000 farmers in February 1914, was another attack on the liberal

government by conservative opinion in the country. The farmers marched to Stockholm and declared their support for the king and his efforts to strengthen Swedish defense.

62. Jönsson, *Nordiska spelen* (2001).
63. Andersson, *Kung Fotboll* (2002), p. 227.
64. Andersson, 2002, p. 291. Ernst Rolf was a well-known singer and Valdemar Dahlqvist an actor.

References

PERIODICALS AND NEWSPAPERS

Aftonbladet
Dagens Nyheter
Göteborgs-Posten
Hufvudstadsbladet
Idun
The New York Times
Nya Dagligt Allehanda
Stockholms Dagblad
Stockholms-Tidningen
Tidning för Idrott

PRINT SOURCES

Andersson, Torbjörn. *Kung Fotboll. Den svenska fotbollens kulturhistoria från 1800-talets slut till 1950* (Lund 2002).

Baker, William J. *Sports in the Western World* (Urbana and Chicago 1988).

Bergvall, Erik (ed.). *V. Olympiaden. Officiell redogörelse för Olympiska spelen i Stockholm 1912* (Stockholm 1913).

Hellspong, Mats. "Att tämja massorna. Om idrottens publik och teaterns" in Karl-Olov Arnstberg (ed.), *Korallrevet. Om vardagens kulturmönster* (Stockholm 1983), pp. 31–57.

Jönsson, Åke. *Nordiska spelen. Historien om sju vinterspel i Stockholm av olympiskt format 1901 till 1926* (Stockholm 2001).

Lindhagen, Sven. *Mina femton olympiader och några till* (Stockholm 1957).

Samuelsson, MarieLouise. "Ernst Trygger" in Mats Bergstrand and Per T. Ohlsson (eds.), *Sveriges statsministrar under 100 år* (Stockholm 2010).

Söderlund, Oscar. "Stockholm sommaren 1912," *S:t Eriks årsbok 1962* (Stockholm, 1962), pp. 113–132.

Wallis Myers, Arthur. *Twenty Years of Lawn Tennis* (London 1920).

Punch, Splendor and Patriotism
The Olympics Outside the Stadium
HANS BOLLING

In the summer of 1912 the otherwise rather sleepy Swedish capital was bustling with activity. Stockholm was to host the Olympic Games of 1912 and that affected the entire city and the usually strict regulations on the capital's nightlife were made more lenient.

When the sports journalist Sven Lindhagen summarized his experiences from 17 Olympic Games with the book *Mina femton olympiader och några till* [*My Fifteen Olympics and a Few More*] in 1957 the Games of his youth appeared in a rosy light: "I do not believe that any Olympic Summer Game has affected a city as the fifth Olympiad did Stockholm."[1] He went on to write about how the whole city had been decorated with flags, overcrowded hotels, how the Stockholmers had contributed by renting out rooms to tourists, and the unusually beautiful weather.[2] It was, however, not only the 16-year-old Sven Lindhagen who allowed himself to be captivated by the Olympic Games. More experienced men, such as the chairman of the Liberal party's executive committee Ernst Beckman, allowed themselves to be engrossed. In a letter to his colleague, the Prime Minister Karl Staaff, for whom sport, and nationalistic excesses, were of little interest (Staaf holidayed abroad during the Games), Beckman wrote about how he had been swept away and overwhelmed by the event.[3] The Olympic Games of 1912 have been hailed as something more than just another Olympic Games ever since they took place, and have been remembered as the Sunshine Olympics in Sweden.[4]

The Stockholm Olympics were not only a sporting event, for most inhabitants of Stockholm probably not even primarily, but a great party. In addition to the sporting competitions a large number of social activities were arranged for both participants and spectators, and socialites had new events to fit into their gala calendars. The city was tidied up, trees and flowers were planted and there was a more extensive general display of flags than ever before.[5]

How important peripheral activities and social events have been in connection with sporting events and what measures have been taken has varied over time. At the 1958 Football World Cup in Sweden, for example, only scant investments in peripheral activities and social events were made.[6] The historian Jens Ljunggren has, however, shown that major sporting events in Sweden in the early 1900s were closely connected with social gatherings and entertainment, at least for the middle and upper classes.[7]

The fact that sport competitions have been closely connected with social gatherings and extensive festivity programs for dignitaries should, however, not be seen as proof that the competitions have been of secondary importance. The organizing of festivities should rather be seen either as a necessity to draw attention to the sporting event in times with an undeveloped sports press, or as something that courtesy demanded as athletes and officials had sacrificed time and money to attend the event.[8] The concept of offering participants and audiences different kinds of distractions in connection with public events, what we now call offering the visitor a complete or total experience, is thus not a novel one.

The Swedish sportsmen around the dinner table at the sportsmen's home while training for the Olympic Games (*Den femte olympiaden i bild och ord,* p. 21).

The welcoming reception for all participants in the soccer tournament at the Strand Hotel, June 28, 1912 (*Den femte olympiaden i bild och ord,* p. 365).

Sport is not unique in this respect. In his description of the Stockholm Exhibition of 1897 Anders Hasselgren stated that the demands of entertainment at the exhibitions had "grown to the point that if no reaction against them occurs, there is a real danger that exhibitions will soon lose their original character and lapse into a more or less empty pretext for fun at the fair."[9] However, this did not prevent Hasselgren from carefully making clear what amusements the Stockholm Exhibition offered.[10] In the early 1900s organizers of public events were thus well aware of the importance of extracurricular activities in order to make the events successful.[11] Recreation and entertainment had begun to play a more important part in people's lives by the turn of the century than they had before, and sporting events, with their rituals, constituted no exception in this respect.[12] The similarities between the Olympic Games and the great art and industrial exhibitions have also been observed by scholars.[13]

What kind of divertissement was on offer for people who spent time in Stockholm in July 1912 when they were not busy performing, organizing, or witnessing the feats accomplished at the Olympic Stadium and other venues? In what follows that question will be answered with the help of the material preserved by the Reception and the Entertainments Committees formed by the Organizing Committee for the Olympic Games in Stockholm 1912 and comments about the activities made in newspapers and journals. The study has been divided into two sections. First the activities organized for athletes and officials will be examined, after which attention falls on the arrangement made to make life as pleasant as possible for the spectators when they were not in the stands.

Athletes and Dignitaries

Most of the activities connected to the Stockholm Olympics, not only the competitions but also the festivities, were meant to be seen — if not directly then indirectly through the press, which was given access to them — by the public. They were public rituals, intended to be seen by all, that is, to some degree theater. The celebrations were meant to, and had the ability to, create various forms of feeling of solidarity.

The newspapers, not only when they were concerned with the sporting achievements, can be said to have tried to create a sense of community. Sweden as a coherent unit was shaped. Ever since the Stockholm Olympics ended with Prince Wilhelm's garden party on July 27, the Olympic Games of 1912 have been commemorated as a magnificent achievement in the Swedish collective memory, not only among sportspeople. They have been remembered as "a wonderful sporting feast, the like of which the world had previously not seen."[14]

How and to what extent festivities should be arranged in conjunction with the Olympic Games, however, was not entirely clear in the early stages of the preparations. In early February of 1911 Crown Prince Gustaf Adolf, honorary chairman of the Organizing Committee, argued for some restraint when it came to the festivities which were to be held during the Games. He wanted them to be characterized by simplicity and to be few in number, so that the Games should primarily be a sporting event.[15] The crown prince was not the only one of the opinion that festivities sometimes were given too much room when sporting events were organized in Stockholm in the early 1900s. When the City Council had approved grants for the organization of the Nordic Games in 1909, organized largely by the same persons as the Stockholm Olympics, it was with the expressed proviso that the money could not be used for festivities.[16]

In order not to burden the Organizing Committee with issues that did not have anything to do with the Olympic Games as a sporting spectacle it was decided that a reception committee should be set up. Its tasks were: organizing the food service at the stadium and its surroundings, organizing room and board for the Swedish athletes when they were training for the Games, arranging all kinds of celebrations, distributing invitations and placing people with language skills (unpaid sports fans) at the disposal of all the participating nations.[17]

The members of the Reception Committee embraced the crown prince's appeal for restraint when it came to festivities. With the opening of the Games barely a year away a letter proposing the reception arrangements was sent to the Organizing Committee. The letter suggested that two official parties should be held: a welcoming reception for Swedish and foreign dignitaries, senior officials and equals in connection with the opening of the Games and a closing celebration for the above-mentioned and all competitors and officials. In addition, they intended to appeal to private citizens that they should invite "higher dignitaries to private celebrations."[18]

This prudent approach to festivities was not shared by all. Representatives for various sports on the Olympic program complained and argued that they needed to get financial as well as moral support from the Organizing Committee to arrange welcoming receptions and closing celebrations for their respective sports. If they were not given the support and thus would be unable to stage the festivities Swedish sporting honor would be compromised, and Sweden and the Swedes would get a reputation of being a tight-fisted and inhospitable people. The celebrations were thus important to safeguard Sweden's reputation as a good organizer of international sports competitions. And it was not possible to coordinate the festivities for all participating athletes and leaders with the Organizing Committee's celebrations. Many sporting events were organized before and after the so-called Olympic or Stadium week which formed the central part of the Games and was held between July 6 and 15. For these sports its organizers had to be responsible for the "necessary celebrations."[19]

When the Games were held an official program for the festivities had been made up and it turned out that not a day during the Games was without its party.[20] An idea of how extensive the program is given in the official account of the Games where there is a chapter of 14 pages entitled "Official celebrations": even if the Organizing Committee did not stand behind all the festivities mentioned, the mentioning of them gave them an official character. The various sport committees organized receptions and closing ceremonies, the Organizing Committee arranged parties for dignitaries, officials and athletes, royalty organized parties and dinners and so did local and visiting dignitaries (such as Viktor Balck and Pierre de Coubertin).[21]

Crown Prince Gustaf Adolf's call for prudence when it came to festivities during the Games thus had little impact. The German writer and senior sports official, and Olympic ideologist to be, Carl Diem, noted in his book on the Stockholm Olympics that when it came to festivities the Stockholm Games could be said to have had as full and varied a program as it had in sports.[22] It was thus an ample program, a program that placed high demands on those who were called to participate on many occasions: it was an "equal claim on endurance, as a marathon race."[23]

The celebrations were not only rich in number, it was ascertained that they in distinction and elegance were fully comparable to the sporting elite's achievements during the Games.[24] No matter how the Swedish athletes had performed during the Games, the fear expressed by various sports committees' representatives, that Swedish honor would be harmed because they were too niggardly when the foreign guests were received during the Games did not come true. Swedish honor was defended as well in the banquet halls as it was in any stadium.

Festivities

In early May 1912 the Reception Committee presented a study on the costs of festivities paid for by the Organizing Committee during the Games: they amounted to over 45,000

Swedish kronor.[25] In order to contain costs, the Organizing Committee determined, amongst other things, not to invite ladies to its welcoming reception, not to invite representatives of different communities and corporate bodies to the closing celebrations, not to allocate any money for separate welcoming receptions to the committees for rowing and cycling, and not to allow the special committees' closing festivities to cost more than five kronor per person.[26] According to the official accounts of the Games, the final costs for representation during the Games came to 43,474.09 Swedish kronor.[27]

The press paid attention to the festivities and reported on them in extensive articles in which the public could read about who had been there and what they had had to eat and drink. Accounts were also given of several of the speeches held, and, especially when ladies were present, descriptions of how the guests had been dressed.[28] The articles written from the festivities given for dignitaries can be compared with high society and fashion reports. The festivities also seem to have been part of Stockholm socialites' festival calendar, as were visiting the tennis tournament and the horse riding competitions and attending the inauguration of the Games.

When the king hosted a garden party in one of the courtyards of the royal palace, Logården, much was written about ladies "in airy dresses, meter wide hats, gorgeously loaded with roses and other heavy flowers" and men "in frock-coats or the ever more popular tail-coat" and "adorable uniforms."[29] The royal event also attracted attention as a high society event outside the country.[30]

It was not necessary to arrange festivities in order to get the press to write about women's attire. When members of high society, especially royals and their coterie, visited the competitions their clothes and elegance were a theme that was given as much space in the newspapers as any sporting performance.[31] Parts of the female tennis audience were described as follows:

> Of course there are many women among the spectators, elegant, beautiful ladies of different nations. And they develop a very likable luxury in their clothing. The prettiest, most delicate, are French, the most slender and lively English, the most perspiring and chubby Germans. They are enthusiastic these young ladies, and have their favorites whom they give loud applause.[32]

The party given for Olympic officials by the Organizing Committee at the Grand Hotel Royal was, according to newspaper reports, the most elegant of all the festivities given during the Olympic Games. It was seen as a party that thus well defended Sweden's reputation as a gracious host. The correspondent of the leading daily newspaper was enthusiastic when he described the event:

> That Swedes are able to arrange parties is an old truth. The brilliant and pompous in life are as created for our poor country, and as long as Sweden is the host nothing will be lacking when it comes to lights and crystal, wine, fruit and southern splendor, when the tables are laid for joy and merriment. Yesterday it was once again one of those not too rare occasions when it came to making a tremendous feast to commemorate and celebrate a great national event.[33]

The author then continued in the same tone. He presented the menu and wines, speeches held and concluded by noting that a similar feast had probably never before been held in Stockholm.[34] The party ended with a social gathering on the terrace of the Opera in order to give the visitors a chance to enjoy Stockholm in the Nordic summer light.[35]

Two festivities were held in honor of the majority of the athletes. On July 9 they, but

N   *Program*

VID

SKANSENS OLYMPISKA FEST

Tisdagen den 9 juli 1912 kl. 8—11 e. m.

◉

Nordiska gruppen.

1. Spårvagnar (N:r 7) afgå från Norrmalmstorg hvar tredje minut kl. 6.30—7.15 e. m. (Därefter hvar femte minut i vanlig ordning.)
2. Afstigning vid Carl XV:s staty. (Hållplatsen Skansen.)
3. Samling vid »Hufvudingång» närmast Djurgårdsteatern kl. 7.30 e. m.
4. Marsch till Orsakullen, där välkomsttal hålles kl. 8 e. m. af chefredaktör H. SOHLMAN.
5. Förevisning af Skansen.
6. Smörgåsservering vid Solliden kl. 9.30—10.30 e. m. Sång och militärmusik. Illumination med tjärtunnor.

◉ ◉

Admission ticket to the Olympic festivities at the open-air museum Skansen, July 9, 1912 (National Sports Museum).

also all the dignitaries, Swedish and foreign, and officials with ladies, were invited to Skansen (an open-air museum in Stockholm). Altogether there were about 4,000 people who responded to the invitation and in addition to a simple meal were offered songs and music, and speeches in Swedish, English, French and German. In order to make all the participating athletes feel welcome the Navy's band played the national anthems of all participating nations. According to one newspaper report the event had been a "rare, striking celebration for the Olympic participants." Athletes from the participating nations had responded with a heartfelt tribute for Sweden and the Swedes.[36]

The second general party was the closing ceremony. With the large number of participants at the Games it could not, as first scheduled, be held indoors; the organizers calculated that it would bring more than 4,000 people together. It was therefore held at the Olympic Stadium and that meant that it could be affected by the weather. In the event of rain the festivities would be forced indoors and divided among different locations: the Royal tennis pavilion and the indoor equestrian arena north of the Stadium, and tents. The weather in Stockholm, however, was excellent throughout the Olympic week. The increased number of participants also meant an increase in costs, but the move outdoors had reduced the cost per person from seven to five Swedish kronor. As seen above, that amount was also the maximum amount of money the special committees could spend per person on their closing celebrations.

After the marathon race 43 long tables were set up in the infield of the Stadium to make room for all the participants. In order to make it possible for all guests to eat at the same time the menu consisted of nothing but cold food and beer, followed by alcohol-free punch. The dinner was served by 250 waiters under the supervision of 12 head waiters.[37]

After the meal the guests were entertained with songs by a three thousand head strong choir singing from the western stand of the Stadium, speeches were held, music played and it all ended with a fireworks display. The general public was given access to the latter part of the festivities. The price for a "dinner-ticket" was between one and two Swedish kronor and all available tickets were sold.[38]

The change of location had also led to a change of day. The closing ceremony was moved from Monday to Sunday due to the fact that the equestrian events would commence at the Stadium and it was thus busy after the award ceremony had been held there on Monday. This meant that some of the athletes competed after the closing ceremony for their sport had taken place, including the decathletes led by the outstanding Jim Thorpe and the

INBJUDNINGSKORT
till
Stadionfästen

söndagen den 14 juli för funktionärer och deltagare i Olympiska Spelens täflingar i *Allmän idrott, Brottning, Fäktning, Gymnastik, Simning* och *Modern femkamp.* Klädsel: uniform eller hvardagsdräkt. *Samling kl. 8.55 e. m. precis* enligt omstående skiss. Inmarschen i Stadion sker på trumpetsignal från tornen precis kl. 9 e. m.

CARTE D'INVITATION
pour
la fête du Stade,

le dimanche 14 Juillet pour fonctionnaires et participants, des concours des Jeux Olympiques *des Sports Athlétiques, de la Lutte, d'Escrime, de Gymnastique, de la Natation* et *du Pentathlon moderne.* Habit: uniforme ou toilette de jour. *Réunion à 8 h. 55 du soir precise* suivant le plan au verso. L'entrée dans le Stade sera signalée du sommet des tours par des fanfares de trompetes á 9 h. du soir précise.

Invitation card to the closing ceremony at the Olympic Stadium, July 14, 1912 (National Sports Museum).

wrestlers Anders Ahlgren and Ivar Böling, who after nine hours of final wrestling were both disqualified for passivity, declared losers, and, exhausted, had to settle for silver medals.[39]

It may well be that the numerous parties affected some Swedish athletes' performance during the Games. The Swedish American track and field coach Ernie Hjertberg at least made a statement suggesting this after the Games, when he in an interview made it clear that the Swedish athletes had not behaved as one might have expected — they had in many cases not even reached the level of perform- ance they had shown during training, and despite that not hesitated to go out partying at night.[40] A short article in connection with the U.S. Olympic team's departure suggests that the American athletes also had had time to enjoy themselves in Stockholm. Among the few Swedish words they had learned were "svenska punschen" (Swedish punch).[41]

The extensive range of festivities during the Olympic Games in Stock-

Anders Ahlgren with the Finish wrestling instructor Ivar Tuomisti (postcard, National Sports Museum).

holm perhaps meant that some Swedish athletes did not perform at their peak, but on the other hand it gave the organizers and Sweden as a nation the reputation of being good hosts. This is an opinion of the Games that has survived at least as much as the memory of Swedish athletic success.

> In addition to staging the athletic events, the Swedes showed that they understood how to celebrate festivals and entertain guests by an attractive cultural program and by receptions and celebrations that demonstrated Swedish hospitality. There were receptions organized by representatives of all sports. Among the most elegant were the festival honoring the IOC, the garden festival hosted by the king in the courtyard of the royal palace, and two dinners given by the crown prince.[42]

Olympic Visitors

One reason for cities taking on the hosting of major international sporting events is that they are expected to generate revenue. The Olympic Games in Stockholm in 1912 was no exception in this regard.[43] Expectations of the Olympics were great. There was talk of over 100,000 visitors for the Olympics, of whom 30,000 were Swedish Americans.[44] The newspapers speculated about what the coming onslaught of both foreign and Swedish visitors would mean. Among the issues highlighted were: How would the visitors be entertained when they were not sitting in the stands? Would it be possible to feed all the visitors? How should public order be maintained with so many people in the streets? There were commentators who saw coming chaos and turmoil in the wake of the Games, disorder comparable with the chaos that prevailed in Reno, USA, in connection with "the fight of the century" between Jack Johnson and Jim Jeffries on July 4, 1910. Tens of thousands of boxing fans "like grasshoppers flooded the small town.... Food prices rose enormously in the beginning, the price of housing as well. Later on you could not get a roof over your head, regardless of what you were willing to pay."[45]

Entertainment activities were thus organized not only for those who were involved in the Games (athletes and organizers), but also for the spectators. There were a number of arrangements designed to make life as pleasant as possible for the Olympic spectators (locals as well as guests) when they were not following the exploits of the athletes at the stadiums.

Before the Olympic Games there was almost complete consensus among people that the regulation of Stockholm's nightlife should be liberalized during the Games. This was because those involved in the Games feared that the rather strict regulations that existed would make the Olympic visitors disappointed with what the host city had to offer outside the stadiums. According to one newspaper, not known for its frivolity, Stockholm was a dull city — it could even be seen as a maxim proclaimed to axiom.[46] The number of temporary liquor licenses was also increased during 1912.[47]

There is no expression of opinions opposed to a more generous licensing policy during the Olympics in surviving sources. The Swedish Women's National Association, however, expressed concern about the dangers that the holding of public dances could mean for young people's morality in a letter to the Olympic organizers in April 1912:

> Though well aware that there are grounds to suppose that the Entertainments Committee will try to prevent this by adequate means, we would, however, be extremely grateful if you would tell us what provisions will be taken at the dance pavilions, especially regarding closing hours and the retailing of liquor. A late closing time as well as the sale of alcohol has at other dance pavilions been known to have deleterious consequences.[48]

The anxious women were given a calming response. They were told that the dance pavilion was not directly integrated with the restaurant setting, that it was open and in full view of the public, and that the members of the committee had full confidence in the man they had entrusted the operation of the public dance to. In addition, the closing time of the dance pavilion was to coincide with that of the whole establishment.[49]

The Entertainments Committee

The question of how to amuse the locals and the tourists who came to visit the city during the Olympic Games, when they were not being thrilled by the achievements of the athletes had been discussed within the Organizing Committee one year before the opening ceremony. Different opinions had been expressed within the committee. Bernhard Burman, banker and chairman of the Finance Section, thought it was important to be involved with recreational activities in addition to the sporting events and stressed the need to effectively organize all the visitors' recreational needs. He recommended that a special Entertainments Committee should be set up and referred to how successful such an approach had been during the 1906 intercalary Games in Athens, where concerts, illuminated processions and other arrangements had been organized in an extremely attractive way. Burman's position was supported by Astley Levin and Sven Hermelin, amongst others.

Crown Prince Gustaf Adolf, however, recommended that they should not get involved in the actual implementation of such activities but get in touch with individuals who might be interested in organizing recreational activities for the public and be content with a certain percentage of the income they generated. Sigfrid Edström, Vice President of the Organizing Committee and future IOC president, also argued against direct involvement in recreational activities and pointed out that several of the entertainment activities which had been discussed in the committee would clash with the essence of the Games, the competitions.

An even more critical stance to entertainment activities was taken by the President of the Organizing Committee Viktor Balck, who was completely opposed to making any effort to entertain the populace during the Games. He pointed out that the Organizing Committee should focus on its "serious, sporting task, the execution of the Olympic Games, from which the public's interest should not be diverted."[50]

Balck's position corresponded with the entertainment-critical view that used to be put forward when popular entertainment was discussed in connection with exhibitions at the turn of the twentieth century: "that there was a conflict between popular entertainment and the 'higher' purpose of the exhibitions."[51] On the other hand, Burman and his supporters represented the opposite view, that saw entertainment activities as a way of attracting visitors to the event.

In order to determine the issue it was decided to refer the matter to the Finance Section, which had to find the answer to the questions: Should an Entertainments Committee be set up? What powers should it be given if it was set up? How would such a committee affect the economy of the Games?[52]

The result of investigations and probes was that an Entertainments Committee was appointed, which was to be responsible for the preparation of suitable entertainment for the tourist arriving in Stockholm. The committee should, however, work in the manner advocated by the crown prince and not organize any activities, but leave the implementation and the financial risk to individual entrepreneurs in exchange for a certain percentage of turnover and profit. In addition, the committee should seek to safeguard the Organizing Committee's interests and seek to increase its revenues through the organization of entertainment evenings at the Olympic Stadium. Among the activities which were discussed at an early stage were theater performances, cinemas, popular festivals, different amusement park rides, regattas, pleasure trips to the archipelago, exhibitions of various kinds, aeronautic and other demonstrations, tours and lectures, pantomimes and carnival processions.[53]

The members of the Entertainments Committee also managed to persuade several of the city's theaters to continue to play during the summer: the Royal Swedish Opera, the Oscar Theater, the Intimate Theater and Djurgården's Theater, which together could accommodate approximately 4,500 visitors.[54] However, the theaters were not very successful and went on to play in front of sparsely filled houses.[55] The members of the committee had hoped to be able to bring the theater tycoon Albert Ranft, who controlled a large part of Stockholm's private theaters in the early 1900s, on to the committee. He was, however, a tough-skinned businessman and found to be totally uninterested and announced that he was not even willing to discuss the opening up of his theaters during the Olympic Games with the committee.[56]

Among the activities organized to entertain locals and tourists during the Olympic Games we find: a concert by a big military band, concerts and a general song festival, displays of Gotlandic sports, Glima (Icelandic wrestling) and boy scouts, fireworks and an illumination celebration at the Olympic Stadium, gala and festive performances at the Opera, illumination celebrations in Djurgårdsbrunnsviken and pleasure trips in the archipelago on steamships.

The gala performance at the Opera, which was held on the same night that the Organizing Committee held its celebration, without any ladies present, at the Grand Hotel, was one of the few really successful indoor activities and also a black tie event. While the princes dined with sports dignitaries the king and the crown princess visited the Opera which was "filled from floor to ceiling by a formally dressed and very cosmopolitan crowed; the foreign elements were heavily represented, especially in the parquet, and you could see there a variety of charming garments." Among the participants were Signe Rappe, court singer by special appointment to the king, Lisa and Sven Scholander, and a corps of student singers.[57]

An account of entertainments on offer in Stockholm during the Olympic Games cannot ignore the general song festival which was held while the Games were going on. With its public concerts it contributed greatly to the entertainment on offer during the Olympics. It was arranged by the Swedish Song League (Svenska sångarförbundet) and attracted 4,000 male singers. A provisional singing hall with seating for an audience of 8,000 persons was built at Engelbrekt School, north of the Olympic Stadium. On the Saturday during the Olympic week, a national singing pageant, culminating in a concert at the Olympic Stadium with 6,000 participants, was held.[58]

Among the entertainment activities that the committee supported so that the public would be able to enjoy themselves during the Olympic Games, people preferred the lighter forms of entertainment to those infused with high art, especially open-air entertainment. The fairground, cafés and restaurants were well attended, while the theaters lured into playing during the summer had to be satisfied if they played before half-full houses. However, it is possible that "the Olympics were to blame" for some of the bad outcome for some vendors of entertainment as the competitions did not "end in time."[59] There was thus no doubt about what the essence of the Games was. Nor is it possible to overlook the beautiful weather that must have contributed to Stockholmers and tourists choosing to spend their evenings outdoors.

The Entertainments Committee was nevertheless successful, although some of the initiatives it induced the capital's entertainment entrepreneurs to undertake failed. After the Games, the committee was able to make a contribution of 36,664.83 Swedish kronor to the Olympic budget. The principal part was the close to 29,000 Swedish kronor generated by the Olympic fairground Olympia.[60] This amount almost exactly corresponded with the surplus its entrepreneur Hjalmar Tornblad budgeted with when the Entertainments Committee accepted his offer to run the fairground in February 1912.[61]

The Fairground

In accordance with the convention for exhibitions, shooting parties and other similar events a fairground was built near the main Olympic Stadium. Thanks to the close relations between the men behind the Games and the military authorities, the fairground could be built on a meadow normally used by the armed forces between the Olympic Stadium and Lake Värtan.[62]

The construction and operation of the venue was entrusted to Hjalmar Tornblad, direc-

**The official Olympic fairground Olympia, situated north of the Olympic Stadium along Sturevä-
gen (today Lidingövägen) at Storängsbotten (*Den femte olympiaden I bild och ord*, p. 363).**

tor of Hotel Continental, who in turn promised to pay the Entertainments Committee 25
percent of the admission revenues and ten percent of "all other gross income."[63]

The fairground, which was named Olympia, was open every day between midday and
midnight from June 14 to August 18. The entrance fee was set at 25 öre and well inside the
area the visitors had a large number of activities to chose from: four dance floors, a fully
licensed restaurant with outdoor dining facilities, a variety of simple entertainment attractions, throwing and shooting ranges, fortune tellers, cinema and circus, waffles and refresh-
ment, and, of course, vendor stalls of various kinds. The musical entertainment was provided
by the Band of the Royal Scanian Infantry Regiment.

According to comments in the press after the opening ceremony, there was no reason
for "the Stockholmer or his guests to hesitate about where to spend a cheerful evening
during the Olympic summer."[64] The fairground was considered to be a place where you
could have fun in a good atmosphere during summer evenings in Stockholm.[65]

Olympia became the focal point for evening entertainment for tourists as well as the
inhabitants of Stockholm during the summer. On average 10,000 people gathered there
every night. When the festival area closed down in the middle of August 350,000 people
had paid 25 öre to get in, more people than had bought tickets to the sporting contests
during the Olympic Games, 320,000 tickets were sold to the Olympic arenas.[66]

In an interview in connection with the closing down of the fairground, Tornblad commented on how it had been to operate Olympia. He was, even though the project had given
him only a small profit, by and large satisfied, everything had been calm and quiet, both
young and old had understood how to entertain themselves and keep their joy within reasonable limits. It was above all the dance pavilion that had attracted visitors, and it led him
to conclude "that public dances under public control should be made permanent." The
notion that public dances were degenerating should be seen as nonsense, and according to
Tornblad's experiences as manager of the Olympic fairground, the same could also be said

about the notion that public dances contributed to excesses in alcohol consumption. The consumption of alcohol at Olympia had not exceeded one centiliter per day and visitor.[67] Whatever Tornblad thought, the opinion that public dances were degenerating and closely connected to excessive alcohol consumption lived on.[68]

The centiliter of alcohol that was consumed by every visitor must nevertheless have been important for Tornblad because in the contract that was established when he took on the running of the fairground there was a clause which stipulated that the contract was not valid if Tornblad did not get "full liquor licensing rights for the premises."[69] If 3,500 liters should be seen as a small amount of alcohol is of course an entirely different issue.

Food and Drink

The question of how to go about feeding all the visitors expected in the city during the Olympic Games had been discussed and caused some concern during the preparations for the Games. The number of restaurants in the city would simply not be enough if the organizers' optimistic predictions regarding the number of visitors to the Games came true. According to one count, purporting to be liberal, Stockholm's restaurants and vending machines could serve 18,000 guests in 1912, a number that would not suffice if a six-digit number of people wanted to eat dinner at roughly the same time.[70]

Besides restaurants, Stockholm was thus equipped with vending machines from which customers could buy prepared meals for between 25 and 30 öre, and a sandwich or something to drink, but not alcohol, for 10 öre. These vending machines can be compared to modern fast-food restaurants. Diners had no problems with different cultural codes, they served themselves and sat down to eat; the prices were specified on the machines.[71]

Although the Olympic Stadium was rarely crowded, it was only in connection with

Diners at the Tennis Restaurant's terrace watch the crowd at the entrances to the Olympic Stadium (*Den femte olympiaden i bild och ord*, p. 354).

the opening of the Games and on the day of the marathon race that the stands were congested. Stockholm's restaurants were, if not constantly crowded, quite full. It happened more than once that popular restaurants were forced to close down for a few hours at midday because they had run out of food, even though they had hoped and prepared for a far larger number of guests than ever before. Several of them had expanded their "dining rooms" to double their usual size.[72]

In order to accommodate more dinner guests the Olympic organizers decided to rent the tennis hall usually used by the Royal Lawn Tennis Club of Stockholm, on the hill just north of the Olympic Stadium (where the School of Sport and Health Sciences is now located) and set up a restaurant in it. The plan was to rent the building and then enter into an agreement with a willing and appropriate contractor who was able to run the restaurant business.[73]

In early 1912 an agreement was reached between the organizers and the restaurateur Carl Löfvander on the lease of the tennis hall during the period June 7 to July 21. Under the agreement the Organizing Committee was promised 2,000 Swedish kronor, and five percent of the gross income. The contract was conditional and would only enter into force if a liquor license was granted to "the Tennis Restaurant."[74]

The relationship between Löfvander and the men on the Entertainments Committee, however, was strained. When the committee signed the agreement to create the Olympic fairground Löfvander reacted with dismay. He considered that the establishment of a fairground in close vicinity to his restaurant would interfere with his ability to make a profit from his restaurant project. He therefore wanted compensation for the increased competition, to pass up on certain costs and to get exclusive rights for the catering at Östermalm Athletic Grounds (the training ground for the Olympic athletes, situated between the Olympic Stadium and the fairground Olympia).[75]

When the Entertainments Committee advertised the measures taken in order to amuse the Olympic spectators outside of the Stadium during the Games, but refrained from mentioning Löfvander's establishment, he made his feelings clear in a pungently worded letter to the committee dated May 22, a letter that summarized what the Tennis Restaurant had to offer its customers:

> But I cannot help that I was astonished when I read about what has been done to entertain the public at the Olympics. Everything is mentioned at some length, while not one word is spent on the Stadium Restaurant. It seems almost as if its existence was unknown to the Committee. In such circumstances I take the liberty of disclosing that the Stadium Restaurant, the Olympic Games official restaurant, far from being a mere trifle is a very substantial business. It is my intention to serve no less than 10,000 persons satisfactorily each day. It is my intention to be able to serve food to 3,000 persons at the same time. The Stadium Restaurant will house a complete first class restaurant operating indoors, several open-air cafés, a special pastry cafeteria, waffle-making, a soda fountain bar, which will be managed by an expert from New York (something new for Sweden), a large terrace-restaurant built in ten terraces and holding 1,000 persons, a large beer garden, confectionery and candy stands, private rooms for celebrations of all kinds, etc. If I also mention that the Band of the Crown Prince's Hussar Regiment will be playing every day — there will perhaps also be singing — it should be clear to everyone that people will be able to amuse themselves within the Stadium Restaurant, where so much of varied interest is on offer. It certainly does not deserve to be forgotten when we talk about what our Olympic Games have to offer when it comes to entertainment activities. If the honored commissioners want more information about the restaurant it is always my pleasure to be of service.[76]

Spectators at the Stockholm Olympics refresh themselves in the park outside the Olympic Stadium. (*Den femte olympiaden i bild och ord*, p. 366).

It was thus a grand establishment, even if Löfvander exaggerated a little. According to an article in *Dagens Nyheter* in late June 1,500 guests could be served at the same time in the restaurant and in one day it could serve 6,000 dinners, which in any case made it Stockholm's biggest restaurant. The restaurant also had extended opening hours; the doors opened at nine in the morning and closed half an hour after midnight.[77]

On the whole the Tennis Restaurant did well despite being ignored by and forced to compete with the Entertainments Committee's fairground at Storängsbotten. All was not peace and joy, however; according to reports in the press well-inflated prices were charged.[78]

The Tennis Restaurant also provided food and drink inside the Olympic Stadium. However, the prices there could be said to be effrontery. According to reports in the press a glass of juice would cost "50 öre!," while a cup of tea with bread commanded a price of "not less than 1.50 kronor!!"[79] In comparison with the data available about the average salary for male workers in 1912, 42 öre an hour, the newspaper's upset punctuation when mentioning the prices at the Stadium is easily understood.[80]

When the newspaper *Hvad Nytt* summarized how it had been to dine during the summer it was, however, on the whole in positive terms. Even if one had been "eating one's meals in crowded restaurants with increased Olympic prices" one had nonetheless felt "that everyone was nice and friendly, happy and satisfied with everything."[81]

The Well-Mannered Games

One thing is missing when one reads about the festivities during the Olympic Games in the summer of 1912 — there are no reports of fights and rowdiness. Just as the sporting part of the Games, thanks to the generally good arrangements, has been called the Swedish masterpiece, the Stockholmers' big party summer appears in a rosy glow. Was it really like that, or was it just the way media chose to recount the course of events? It could be that the lack of scandalous reports and no mention of drinking, adultery and theft in connection with the Stockholm Olympics were due to the fact that the reporting of such events would have damaged the established order that the Games were meant to protect. And that the press, as it had done with the raids and looting on the last day of the Stockholm Exhibition in 1897, had chosen not to write about such occurrences.[82]

The details of unfavorable behavior available, however, support the thesis that it was a festive summer without much disturbing behavior. The number of drunkenness offenses amounted to 1,177 in July 1912 compared with 1,216 in 1911 and 1,427 in 1910, the figures for June and August 1912 were 1,364 and 1,640 respectively. July was normally the year's quietest month when it came to the selling of alcohol, but not so in 1912 when it was the year's best month in terms of sales. Year high sales were recorded for brandy, whisky and punch.[83]

Neither did the number of reported crimes increase during July 1912. 616 were reported for the Olympic month compared to 633 in July 1911, but only 453 in 1910. The only increase that can be seen in the crime statistics was for the number of complaints concerning fraud, which showed a clear peak in July 1912, accounting for nearly 40 percent of the year's filings.[84]

There were only a few records in the press about brawls and crimes and the seriousness of them does not indicate any imposed media silence. A week before the official opening of the Games at the Stadium it was announced that the Criminal Investigation Department had made its first Olympic arrest, a gang of foreign pickpockets who were suspected of five thefts in Gothenburg and Stockholm. That this was no ordinary gang of petty criminals was corroborated by the fact that the leader of the gang had been "punished 12 times for pickpocketing and was equipped with eight different sets of identification cards."[85]

When the activities of the police during the Stockholm Olympics were summarized, it was found that the above-mentioned pickpocketing was crime epidemic of the Games. According to a police superintendent the public order during the Games had been unusually good and everything had, from the police's point of view, been brilliant. With the exception of the pickpocketing, no crimes had been reported that could be solely linked to the Games. A remarkable calm had prevailed and the public had been sober![86]

The cause of the police's success when it came to overcoming pickpocket gangs and other threats to property and public safety could have been that the police had been given access to an extra "wallet guard" of 25 detectives. In all, the police force was reinforced with 55 extra police officers from June 26 until the Games ended, while all holidays for police staff were cancelled during the Games.[87]

Was there then nothing that disrupted the image of an epic sporting event where people enjoyed themselves at the Stadium and in the city in a lavish, hot and sunny Stockholm? Not really, the closest we come to seriously rowdy crowd behavior, where such behavior was even hinted at, was when a gang of youths threw "road dirt, burdocks, turfs of grass and sand" at passing cars during the bicycle race, which resulted in some minor scuffles. But according to the police the youths' behavior was probably due to them being young sports fans that had been outraged by the fact that cars were allowed to drive on the road where the cyclists were competing. This could prevent the competitors from cycling and the dust the cars stirred up could also obscure the spectators' view.[88]

This assumption, made by a local police officer, cannot be seen only as an attempt to cover up a stain on the Olympic shield because when the bicycle race was summarized it could be established that one competitor, the Swede Karl Josef Landsborg, had been rammed by a motorist nearby where the incident occurred, a motorist who was driving on the wrong side of the road.

The Number of Visitors

A contributing factor to the Stockholm Olympics on the whole passing so quietly was that the Games did not attract the number of tourists the organizers had hoped for. Prior to the Games it had been said that a six-digit number of tourists would travel to Stockholm in connection with the Olympics. The number of foreign visitors in Stockholm during the Olympics was not even close to those figures. According to the available statistics on visitors to Stockholm, there were 4,431 strangers in Stockholm during the Olympic week compared to 3,479 the same week the year before.[89] The number of visitors was thus only marginally higher during the second week of July in 1912 than the year before.

Table 1. The Number of Foreigners and Reported Visitors in Stockholm in July 1910 to 1914

Year	1910	1911	1912	1913	1914
Foreigners	5,163	5,469	7,052	5,639	5,512
Reported visitor	15,282	15,086	16,945	14,020	12,620

Source: *Statistisk årsbok för Stockholms stad 1915* (1916), p. 317.

If we compare the number of foreigners in Stockholm during July between 1910 and 1914, see Table 1, we see an increase during July 1912. The same tendency cannot be seen

The procession of the choir passing Norrbro bridge and Gustav Adolf's square on their way to the stadium and the national singing pageant, July 13, 1912 (*Den femte olympiaden i bild och ord*, p. 184).

for June and August. The statistics for visitors show a similar peak in July 1912. But given the number of foreign athletes and officials who participated at the Olympic Games during the summer of 1912, it seems as if the number of actual tourists in Stockholm during the Olympics was slightly lower during 1912 compared to the other years. The total number of foreign athletes competing in Stockholm was 1,935, and to that number 550 display gymnasts must be added.[90]

Despite the fact that Stockholm appeared at its best it was only a trickle of the expected tourist flood that emerged. In one of the first compilations of the Stockholm Olympics it was correctly noted: "What the Olympic Games would bring to the city itself was, as usual in the capitals of small countries, overestimated."[91]

The reasons behind the non-show by the tourists were said to be several. By far the most important reason, however, was that the press, both foreign and domestic, long before the start of the Games had made potential visitors aware of the problems they were likely to meet if they traveled to Stockholm during the Olympic Games, first and foremost with regard to accommodation, and that prices were likely to be unwarrantedly high during the Games.[92]

Conclusion

What then should be the verdict on Stockholm as host and tourist city for the fifth Olympiad? Can Sven Lindhagen's memories from his youth be accepted as being consistent with *wie es eigentlich gewesen?* Sven Hermelin and Erik Peterson, who were closely associated with the Organizing Committee of the Games and published a book about the Games directly after the Stockholm Olympics also painted a colorful picture of Stockholm during the Olympic summer. Stockholm had been shown from its best side, and had not, as usually was the case during the summer, remained silent and deserted.[93] It is a verdict that has not been contradicted in any significant way by other statements. The Sunshine Olympics are, after all, a designation that has stood the test of time. The German writer and senior sports official Carl Diem, after Pierre de Coubertin the greatest Olympic ideologue of the twentieth century, even claimed that an Olympic spirit had characterized Stockholm during the Games.[94]

That the 1912 Olympic Games made their mark on Stockholm seems evident, but Lindhagen's statement about overcrowded hotels appears to be not an ex-post-, but possibly a pre-, construction. Whatever the Olympic Games were, they were no tourist magnet. If those who were directly involved in the Games are disregarded fewer people visited Stockholm than usual during the summer of 1912. The huge apparatus that was launched in order to ensure that no visitor of the Games should be without a room to sleep in, which got the locals offering rooms and apartments for rental to such an extent that 25,000 "new" rooms were created, turned out to be largely redundant.[95] But by any other measure the Stockholm Olympics must be regarded as a success.

The people who, in spite of the alleged difficulties, made their way to Stockholm in the summer of 1912 were welcomed with open arms. It is plausible that the non-tourist invasion was instrumental in making it possible for tourists and locals alike to fully enjoy the sporting competitions and everything that had been done to revitalize the normally so gloomy entertainment life in the Swedish capital, as the city was not congested with people. Festivals and sport created, along with the sunny weather and the spectators' good behavior, the Sunshine Olympics.

Interior of the large dining room in the Tennis Restaurant (*Den femte olympiaden i ord och bild*, p. 357).

It was the rich supply of peripheral activities that made the Stockholm Olympics something more than just a sports competition. The newspapers reported from the festivities for dignitaries and commoners, athletes and spectators. They concerned themselves with everything, from the royal garden party at Logården and dinner parties at the Royal Palace to dances in the oak groves at the fairground Olympia. Nevertheless, it was sport that symbolized the modern, and that which was continuous. Many of the celebrations held in conjunction with the Olympics rather represented a dated bourgeois punch patriotism which, together with the long nineteenth century, was on its way into the history books. The Stockholm Olympics would never have become the Sunshine Olympics without the many festivities in connection with the Games, but would only have been the greatest sporting event ever held in Sweden.[96]

The accounts of the Stockholm Olympics also provide an image of a nation in social harmony and with national unity, something that was seen as desirable in an age where society for many seemed to be characterized by increasing fragmentation. One could argue that the Olympic celebration helped to heal the social wounds caused by the great labor conflicts of 1909. It is during such times that national traditions tend to be created; feasts and celebrations are used to create a sense of community.[97]

Several of the symbols used in connection with the Games were relatively new and their status as national unifying symbols came to be strengthened by their use in connection with the Games. The use of the Swedish flag as a national symbol, for example, was still regarded as a sign of upper class snobbery at the turn of the century.[98] And the anthem "Du gamla, du fria" had not yet acquired the status of a unifying Swedish national anthem. The great composer and choirmaster Hugo Alvén, for example, refused to include it in his repertoire; he found it absurd that it could even be thought of as a national anthem: "It is simply so that I find 'Du gamla, du fria,' text as well as music, to be an insipid flabby song, which lacks spirit and verve, and I should regard it as an accident if that song were to become our national anthem."[99]

It might, after all, prove that the song had every chance of establishing itself as a popular national anthem; it was according to Alvén "a Swedish punch song, composed by a particular composer in a moment of intoxication."[100]

The plethora of festivities during the Stockholm Olympics were important not only because they offered entertainment to the people who were in Stockholm during the Games, but also because the organizers managed to make sure that no subversive interpretations of their message of national unity and loyalty to the prevailing system were expressed. That was important since more people visited and were affected by the festivities than by the sporting competitions. We have to remember that Olympia alone had more visitors than all the sporting competitions put together. The Games thus played a part in the transformation of the Swedish population into Swedes.

Notes

1. Lindhagen, *Mina femton olympiader och några till* (1957), p. 21. "Jag tror inte att några sommarolympiader så präglat en stad som de femte Olympiska Spelen gjorde Stockholm."
2. Ibid., pp. 21–22.
3. Lindroth, *Idrottens väg till folkrörelsen* (1974), pp. 302–303.
4. Ringius, *Vägvisare genom olympiaderna* (1913); Balck, *Minnen* (1931); *V. olympiadens minnesutställning* (1937), and Ueberhorst, "Stockholm 1912" (1996).
5. *Dagens Nyheter,* May 12, 1912. *Stockholms-Tidningen,* May 10, 1912.
6. Norlin, *1958* (2008).
7. Ljunggren, "Tradition eller tävling?" (1997), p. 373.
8. The press in Stockholm, for example, did not pay real attention to soccer before Count Clarence von Rosen started to promote the game with the competition for von Rosen's cup and got high society interested in matches by staging them at the local racetrack (Lindarängen). Bolling and Johrén, *De första 116 åren* (2012).
9. Hasselgren, *Utställningen i Stockholm 1897* (1897), p. 552, "vuxit till den grad, att, om icke en reaktion däremot inträder, det är fara värt att utställningarna snart skola helt och hållet förlora sin ursprungliga karaktär och nedsjunka till en mer eller mindre tom förevändning för ett mer eller mindre ovärdigt marknadsgyckel."
10. Ibid., pp. 552–592.
11. *Socialdemokraten,* June 13, 1912, and *Stockholms-Dagblad,* April 14, 1912. During the preparations for the Olympic Games in Stockholm it was above all the fairground that had been erected in connection with the Arts and Crafts Exhibition of 1909 which set the example. To read about the exhibition, its fairground and public, see Ekström, *Viljan att synas, viljan att se* (2010), part two.
12. Myerly and Hunt, "Holidays and Public Rituals" (2001), pp. 185 ff, and Hellspong and Löfgren, "Umgängesformer" (1994), pp. 322 ff.
13. Ekström, *Den utställda världen* (1994), p. 60.
14. *V. olympiadens minnesutställning* (1937), p. 5, "en underbar idrottsfest, vars make världen dessförinnan icke skådat." For a discussion about sport competitions' function as reference points and time markers for the human memory, see Hellspong, "Idrottens årsrytm och fester" (1994), pp. 246 ff.
15. National Archives, Stockholmsolympiaden 1912: The Minutes of the Organizing Committee A I:2, Organizing Committee February 6, 1911, § 11.
16. Jönsson, *Nordiska spelen* (2001), p. 97.
17. National Archives, Stockholmsolympiaden 1912: The Minutes of the Organizing Committee A I:4, the Reception Committee September 29, 1911, § 2. The responsibility for room and board for the visiting nations' athletes fell primarily on the participating nations themselves at this time, although they could expect assistance from the organizers. The Olympic Village, where athletes were housed together, was not introduced until the 1932 Olympic Games at Los Angeles.
18. National Archives, Stockholmsolympiaden 1912: The Reception Committee's documents Ö Ig:1, August 18, 1911.

19. National Archives, Stockholmsolympiaden 1912: The Minutes of the Organizing Committee A I:3, October 16, 1911, § 3.

20. National Archives, Stockholmsolympiaden 1912: The Reception Committee's documents Ö Ig:1, Festivities etc.

21. Bergvall (ed.), *The Fifth Olympiad* (1913), pp. 786–799.

22. Diem, *Die Olympischens Spiele 1912* (1912), pp. 32 ff.

23. Hermelin and Peterson (eds.), *Den femte olympiaden* (1912), p. 357, "lika stora anspråk på uthållighet, som någon maratonlöpning."

24. *Nordland,* 14:1912.

25. According to the official report 1 krona equaled 27 cents. Bergvall, 1913, p. 43.

26. National Archives, Stockholmsolympiaden 1912: The Minutes of the Organizing Committee A I;3, May 21, 1912, § 13.

27. Bergvall, 1913, p. 45.

28. *Dagens Nyheter,* July 6, July 9, and July 10, 1912. Several of the speeches held were also printed in the official account of the Olympic Games. Bergvall, 1913, pp. 787–798.

29. *Dagens Nyheter,* July 7, 1912.

30. *Nordland,* 14:1912, and *The Times,* July 8, 1912.

31. *Dagens Nyheter,* July 4, 1912, and *Svenska Dagbladet,* July 7, 1912.

32. *Aftontidningen,* July 2, 1912. "Naturligtvis finns det många damer bland åskådarna, eleganta, vackra damer av olika nationer. Och de utveckla en högst sympatisk lyx i klädedräkten. De vackraste, ömtåligaste, äro fransyskor, de slankaste, hurtigaste engelskor, de svettigaste, tjockaste tyskor. De äro entusiastiska, dessa unga damer, och ha sina favoriteter, som de bestå kraftiga applåder."

33. *Dagens Nyheter,* July 8, 1912. "Att svenskarna förstå sig på att göra fest är en gammal erfarenhet. Det glansfulla i livet och pompösa är som skapat för vårt fattiga land, och så länge Sverige sitter med fötterna under eget bord skall det inte saknas ljus och kristall, vin, frukter och all sydländsk härlighet på det bordet, när det dukas för glädje och glam. I går var det åter ett sådant där icke alltför sällsynt tillfälle då det gällde att göra ett hejdundrande gästabud för att hugfästa och avfesta en stor nationell tilldragelse."

34. Ibid.

35. *Idun,* nr 28, 1912, p. 458. "Operaterrassen för att främlingarne skulle få njuta av Stockholm i nordisk sommarbelysning."

36. *Dagens Nyheter,* July 10, 1912.

37. National Archives, Stockholmsolympiaden 1912: The Minutes of the Organizing Committee A I:3, May 21, 1912, § 12.

38. Royal Library, Vardagstryck: Olympiska spelens i Stockholm — samling av trycksaker, Dagsprogram July 11, p. 25; Ringius: *Vägvisare genom olympiaderna* (1913), p. 50, and *Aftonbladet,* July 15, 1912.

39. Uggla, *Olympiska spelen i Stockholm 1912* (1912), p. 8.

40. *Arbetet,* July 16, 1912,

41. *Aftontidningen,* July 18, 1912.

42. Ueberhorst, "1912," p. 45

43. However, there is no evidence the representatives of the City were involved, or even consulted, when Stockholm was awarded the 1912 Olympic Games by the IOC in 1909.

44. *Aftonbladet,* April 4, 1912.

45. National Archives, Sveriges Olympiska Kommitté: Tryck och pressklipp L I:1, undated newspaper cutting, November, 1911. "gräshoppor översvämmade den lilla och oansenliga staden.... Livsmedelspriserna stego oerhört till en början, prisen på rum likaså. Sedermera kunde man ej uppbringa tak över huvudet ens för pengar."

46. National Archives, Stockholmsolympiaden 1912: The Entertainments Committee's documents Ö Id:1, November 15, 1911, and *Socialdemokraten,* November 14, 1911.

47. *Statistisk årsbok för Stockholms stad 1915* (Stockholm, 1916), p. 336.

48. National Archives, Stockholmsolympiaden 1912: The Entertainments Committee's documents Ö Id:2, letter from the Swedish Women's National Association, April 24, 1912. "Ehuru väl att anledning finnes att antaga, att Nöjeskommittén genom betryggande anordningar vill söka avvärja detta, skulle vi dock vara synnerligen tacksamma, om Ni ville meddela oss, vilka bestämmelser, som kommer att bli gällande vid dansbanorna särskilt rörande stängningstider och spritutskänkning. En sen stängningstid liksom tillhandahållandet av sprituosa ha ju vid andra dansbanor visat sig ha fördärvliga följder."

49. Ibid., letter to the Swedish Women's National Association, April 30, 1912.

50. National Archives, Stockholmsolympiaden 1912: The Minutes of the Organizing Committee A I:3, September 18, 1911, § 5, and October 2, 1911, § 5. Quote from October 2, 1911.

51. Ekström, 2010, p. 150.

52. National Archives, Stockholmsolympiaden 1912: The Minutes of the Organizing Committee A I:3, October 2, 1911, § 5.

53. Ibid., October 6, 1911, Appendix 2.

54. Åsbrink, 1912, p. 52.

55. Hermelin and Peterson, 1912, p. 357.

56. National Archives, Stockholmsolympiaden 1912: Entertainments Committee's documents Ö Id:1, November 6, 1911.

57. *Dagens Nyheter,* July 8, 1912.

58. Royal Library, Vardagstryck: Olympiska spelen i Stockholm — samling av trycksaker, *Olympiska spelen Stockholm 1912*, p. 12, and Åsbrink, 1912, p. 317.

59. *Socialdemokraten,* July 9, 1912.

60. Bergvall, 1913, p. 44.

61. National Archives, Stockholmsolympiaden 1912: The Entertainment's Committee's documents Ö Id:2, financial estimates done by Hjalmar Törnblad on the basis of 200,000 visitors, February 22, 1912.

62. National Archives, Stockholmsolympiaden 1912: The Entertainments Committee's documents Ö Id:1, November 6, and November 15, 1911.

63. Ibid., Ö Id:2, contract, February 19, 1912.

64. *Svensk Dagbladet,* July 15, 1912.

65. *Idun,* no. 27, 1912; *Socialdemokraten,* June 13, 1912; *Svenska Dagbladet,* June 14; June 15 and July 16, 1912, and Åsbrink (ed.), *Stockholm* (1912), p. 320.

66. Hermelin and Peterson, 1912, p. 357. The fact that so many people chose to amuse themselves at Olympia during the summer of 1912 did, however, mean that the number of visitors at Gröna Lund (Stockholm's leading amusement park) went down significantly during the summer. Stockholm's leading amusement park was simply located too far from the Olympic core area to be able to take advantage of the Games. Ekström, 2010, p. 159.

67. *Aftontidningen,* August 19, 1912.

68. Frykman, *Dansbaneeländet* (1988).

69. National Archives, Stockholmsolympiaden 1912: The Entertainments Committee's documents Ö Id:2, contract, February 19, 1912.

70. *Hvad Nytt,* February 3, 1912.

71. Åsbrink, 1912, p. 48 f.

72. Hermelin and Peterson, 1912, pp. 356–357.

73. National Archives, Stockholmsolympiaden 1912: The Minutes of the Organizing Committee A I:3, July 20, 1911, § 4, and August 21, 1911, § 5,

74. Ibid., January 16, 1912, § 25, and February 6, 1912 § 6.

75. Ibid., March 26, 1912, § 27; April 16, 1912, § 26, and April 30, 1912, § 22.

76. National Archives, Stockholmsolympiaden 1912: The Entertainments Committee's documents, Ö Id:2, letter from Carl Löfvander to the Entertainments Committee, May 22, 1912. "Men jag kan icke hjälpa att mitt intresse blandats med förvåning, då jag ser huru allting omtalas ganska utförligt, under det att icke ett enda ord spilles å Stadionrestauranten. Det synes nästan som om dennas tillvaro vore Kommittén obekant. Under sådana omständigheter tar jag mig friheten upplysa om att Stadionrestauranten, de Olympiska Spelens <u>officiella</u> restaurant, ingalunda blir någon obetydlighet, snarare skulle man kunna kalla den ett högst betydande företag. Det är min avsikt att där på en gång tillfredsställande kunna servera icke mindre än omkring 10.000 personer. Mat är det min mening att kunna samtidigt servera åt 3000 personer. Den stora Stadionrestauranten kommer att inrymma fullstädig första klass restaurantrörelse inomhus, flera friluftsserveringar, särskild konditoriservering, våffelbruk, Soda fountain Bar, vilken skall skötas av en expert från Newyork (något nytt för Sverige), en större Terrass-servering, uppbyggd i 10 terrasser och rymmande 1000 personer, storartad Biergarten, konfekt- och candieskiosker, enskilda rum för festligheter av alla slag m.m. om vidare nämnes att Kronprinsens Husarregementes musikkår spelar varje dag, möjligtvis blir det också sång, så bör det vara klart, att man skall kunna <u>förströ</u> sig även inom Stadionrestauranten, där så mycket av skiftande intresse bjudes. För visso är den

icke förtjänt att glömmas bort, då det talas om vad våra Olympiska Spel ha att prestera i förströelseväg. Om herrar kommitterade önska närmare kännedom härom, så står jag städse med nöje till tjänst."

77. Ibid., June 27, 1912.
78. *Aftontidningen,* July 1, 1912.
79. Ibid., July 6, 1912.
80. Prado, "Nominal and Real Wages of Manufacturing Workers, 1860–2007" (2010), p. 511.
81. *Hvad Nytt,* September 4, 1912.
82. Ekström, 1994, pp. 200 and 244.
83. *Statistisk årsbok för Stockholms stad 1915* (1916), p. 335.
84. *Statistisk årsbok för Stockholm stad 1914* (1915) p. 201.
85. *Dagen Nyheter,* July 2, 1912.
86. *Svenska Dagbladet,* July 18, 1912, and *Dagen,* July 18, 1912.
87. *Dagen Nyheter,* July 2, 1912.
88. *Aftontidningen,* July 8, 1912.
89. Hermelin and Peterson, 1912, p. 355
90. Mallon and Widlund, *The 1912 Olympic Games* (2009), pp. 29 ff.
91. Hermelin and Peterson, 1912, p. 355.
92. National Archives, Stockholms Olympiaden 1912: The Minutes of the Organizing Committee A I:3, Organizing Committee February 20, 1912, § 5.
93. Hermelin and Peterson, 1912, p. 355.
94. *Nordland,* 14:1912.
95. National Archives, Stockholmsolympiaden 1912: The Press Committee's documents Ö Ii:3, official notification through the Swedish News Agency, May 7, 1912.
96. Hobsbawm, *Age of Extremes* (1995), pp. 6, 22 ff. Roshwald and Stites (eds.), *European Culture in the Great War* (2002).
97. Hobsbawm, *Massproducerade traditioner* (2002), p. 51; Hunt and Myerly: "Memory and the Invention of Tradition" (2001), p. 115; Löfgren: "Nationella arenor" (1993), pp. 22 ff, and Unowsky: *The Pomp and Politics of Patriotism* (2005).
98. Löfgren, 1993, pp. 74–75.
99. *Dagens Nyheter,* July 4, 1912. "Det är nu en gång så att jag finner Du gamla, du fria, såväl texten som musiken, vara en fadd, blekfet sång, vilken saknar allt det som tänder och värmer; och jag betraktar det som en olycka om denna sång bleve vår nationalsång."
100. Ibid., June 22, 1912.

References

UNPUBLISHED SOURCES

Swedish National Archives: Stockholmsolympiaden 1912, Sveriges Olympiska Kommitté
Royal Library: Vardagstryck: Olympiska spelen i Stockholm

PERIODICALS AND NEWSPAPERS

Aftonbladet
Aftontidningen
Arbetet
Brand
Dagen
Dagens Nyheter
Hvad Nytt
Idun
Nordland
Socialdemokraten
Stockholms-Dagblad
Stockholms-Tidningen
Sundbybergs och Solna Tidning

Svenska Dagbladet
The Times

ENCYCLOPEDIAS

Nordisk familjeboks sportlexikon 1–7 (Stockholm 1938–1949).

PRINT SOURCES

Åsbrink, Gunnar (ed.). *Stockholm. Olympiska Spelens officiella vägvisare* (Stockholm 1912).

Balck, Viktor. *Minnen. II Mannaåren* (Stockholm 1931).

Bergvall, Erik (ed.). *The Fifth Olympiad: The Official Report of the Olympic Games of Stockholm 1912* (Stockholm 1913).

Bolling, Hans, and Anders Johrén. *De första 115 åren. Boken om AIK-fotboll* (Solna, 2012).

Diem, Carl. *Die Olympischens Spiele 1912* (Neukölln 1912).

Ekström, Anders. *Den utställda världen. Stockholmsutställningen 1897 och 1800-talets världsutställningar* (Stockholm 1994).

Ekström, Anders. *Viljan att synas, viljan att se. Medieumgänge och publik kultur kring 1900* (Stockholm 2010).

Frykman, Jonas. *Dansbaneeländet. Ungdomen, populärkulturen och opinionen* (Stockholm, 1988).

Hasselgren, Andreas. *Utställningen i Stockholm 1897. Beskrivning i ord och bild övfer Allmänna konst- & industriutställningen* (Stockholm 1897).

Hellspong, Mats. "Idrottens årsrytm och fester," in Schön, Ebbe (ed.), *I glädje och sorg* (Stockholm, 1994).

Hellspong, Mats, and Orvar Löfgren. "Umgängesformer," in Mats Hellspong and Orvar Löfgren (eds.), *Land och Stad. Svenska samhällen och livsformer från medeltid till nutid* (Malmö 1994), pp. 319–339.

Hermelin, Sven, and Erik Peterson (eds.). *Den femte olympiaden: Olympiska spelen i Stockholm i bild och ord* (Stockholm 1912).

Hobsbawm, Eric. *Age of Extremes: The Short Twentieth Century, 1914–1991* (London, 1995).

Hobsbawm, Eric J. *Massproducerade traditioner* (Lund 2002).

Holt, Mack P. "Festivals," in Peter N. Stearns (ed.), *Encyclopedia of European Social History: From 1350 to 2000* (New York 2001), pp. 41–51.

Hunt, Tamara L., and Scott Hughes Myerly. "Memory and the Invention of Tradition," in Peter N. Stearns (ed.), *Encyclopedia of European Social History: From 1350 to 2000*, vol. 5 (New York 2001), 115–129.

Jönsson, Åke. *Nordiska spelen. Historien om sju vinterspel i Stockholm av olympiskt format 1901 till 1926* (Stockholm 2001).

Lindhagen, Sven. *Mina femton olympiader och några till* (Stockholm 1957).

Lindroth, Jan. *Idrottens väg till folkrörelse. Studier i svensk idrottsrörelse till 1915* (Uppsala 1974).

Ljunggren, Jens. "Tradition eller tävling? Nordiska spelen och kampen om vad idrott är." *Historisk tidskrift* (1997:3), pp. 351–374.

Löfgren, Orvar. "Nationella arenor" in Billy Ehn, et al. (ed.): *Försvenskningen av Sverige. Det nationellas förvandling* (Stockholm 1993), pp. 22–117.

Löfgren, Orvar. "Vardagsliv, söndagstankar," in David Gaunt and Orvar Löfgren (eds.), *Myter om svensken* (Stockholm 1985).

Mallon, Bill, and Ture Widlund. *The 1912 Olympic Games. Results for All Competitors in All Events with Commentary* (Jefferson 2009).

Myerly, Scott Hughes, and Tamara L. Hunt. "Holidays and Public Rituals," in Peter N. Stearns (ed.): *Encyclopedia of European Social History: From 1350 to 2000*, vol. 5 (New York 2001), pp. 183–200.

Norlin, Arne. *1958. När folkhemmet fick fotbolls-VM* (Malmö 2008).

Prado, Svante. "Nominal and Real Wages of Manufacturing Workers, 1860–2007" in Edvinsson, Rodney, et al. (eds.): *Historical Monetary and Financial Statistics for Sweden: Exchange Rates, Prices, and Wages, 1277–2008* (Stockholm 2010).

Ringius, Albert. *Vägvisare genom olympiaderna, med förord af hertigen af Vestergötland H.K.H: prins Carl* (Göteborg 1913).

Roshwald, Aviel, and Richard Stites (eds.), *European Culture in the Great War: The Arts, Entertainment, and Propaganda, 1914–1918* (Cambridge, 2002).

Statistisk årsbok för Stockholm stad 1914. (Stockholm 1915).

Statistisk årsbok för Stockholms stad 1915. (Stockholm 1916).

Ueberhorst, Horst. "Stockholm 1912" in Jon E. Findling and Kimberley D. Pelle (eds.), *Historical Dictionary of the Modern Olympic Movement* (Westport 1996), pp. 41–46.

Unowsky, Daniel L. *The Pomp and Politics of Patriotism: Imperial Celebrations in Habsburg Austria 1848–1916* (West Lafayette, 2005).

V. olympiadens minnesutställning. Liljevalchs konsthall 10–25 juli 1937 (Stockholm 1937).

"A New Experience in Life"

The Olympics and the General Debate in the Swedish Daily Press

Jan Lindroth

The setting up of the Olympic movement in the 1890s and the first Olympic Games in 1896 changed the conditions for international competitive sport radically.[1] It should be borne in mind that the network of international championships at the turn of the century only consisted of weak attempts; nothing was particularly advanced as far as Sweden was concerned. Inter-nation sporting events were also in their infancy. The notion of the individual sporting hero had not come far. The Olympic phenomenon should be seen in this light. It was something fundamentally new.

Now as is well known the Olympic Games did not become an immediate success around the civilized world. Each country followed its own development curve with regard to participation, successes and public support. The Swedish sports movement's breakthrough undoubtedly came through the intercalary Olympic Games in Athens in 1906. On the running track this was expressed by several excellent results and a seventh place in the total inter-nations points. At the same time this was paid considerable attention by the Swedish daily press. The contours of national sporting heroes began to be seen. These developments were consolidated through the 1908 London Olympic Games. A large number of clubs were formed in the period 1906–08.[2] The magnificent Nordic Games had been arranged in Stockholm in 1901, 1905 and 1909.[3] The ground was well prepared for an Olympic event in this city. The above is the historical sporting background. The question can be asked how the daily press viewed Olympic competitive sport as a form of physical exercise.

In addition to this the general political situation must be considered. It was characterized by growing nationalism, a nationalism with aggressive elements. The question of defense, or if you like, militarism escalated. In concrete terms this was expressed by two voluntary appeals to raise funds for a battleship which were initiated in 1912, to secure through private initiative the building of a large and effective warship that contributed to Swedish naval defense. In party political terms the liberal minister Karl Staaff (1911–14) was trapped between a defense-friendly, nationalistic right and a strongly advancing social democracy with a pacifist and international orientation. The Stockholm Olympic Games were held in this political environment. The question may be asked how it affected the daily press's view of the Olympic Games as a social phenomenon.[4]

It turned out that the daily press paid the 1912 Olympic Games a great deal of attention, with few exceptions. Most space was of course given to the many concrete features of the event, the competitions as such and the surrounding events. What is more surprising is that the Games were found so interesting and important at an editorial level, among leader writers and the like, that they could receive at least ten articles of an editorial nature discussing general principles.[5] Even small provincial newspapers felt themselves called upon to record their opinions in at least one editorial article. In the summer of 1912 it was thus

Swedish diver Lisa Regnell during an exhibition in Malmoe 1912 in a promotional postcard (National Sports Museum).

possible to get a general picture of what the Swedish daily press thought about the Olympic event as such, and of Olympic sport and modern competitive sport in general. Neither before nor afterwards has competitive sport been so comprehensively discussed editorially. The editorial sporting comments of 1912 are quite unique with regard to breadth and depth, the abundance of views, willingness to debate and the freshness of opinion. Individual themes may have been discussed in more detail at some later occasion but not the total picture. It is reasonable to talk about a general debate. And just less than a year later the Swedish Parliament had its equivalent.[6]

To be able to understand the press interest that the Stockholm Olympic Games gave rise to, it is necessary to consider the conditions at the time. As has been pointed out the ground was well-prepared through previous good Swedish Olympic performances in Europe. Now it was harvest time in the form of appearances on home ground, which furthermore led to incredibly great competitive successes. It helped that the weather was sunny and that the organization of the games ran smoothly. But it was the concrete events that played out inside the walls of the impressive Olympic Stadium and in other arenas that were crucial for the reactions. For the first time the Swedish general public could with its own eyes experience international competitive sporting drama with national identity as an important feature. Location-competition-patriotism formed a strong triad that obviously surprised many a representative of public opinion. There is also a fourth factor: the general public. It is clear that the members of the press took great note of the general public's spontaneous reactions. At the same time they themselves were a part of this. Together all of this was perceived as something strong and significant, as a "new experience in life."[7]

The editorial material in the daily press regarding the 1912 Stockholm Olympic Games has been used in research in astounding moderation. My own thesis from 1974 contains to my knowledge the only attempt to capture the debate as a whole. It is based on a comprehensive review of all Swedish daily newspapers in the Olympic summer of 1912, but is limited to most of one chapter in the thesis. It has a party political perspective and the main result, with one exception, is unambiguous: the further you go to the left on the political scale, the greater the opposition to the competitive sport of the day. The exception is to be found on the extreme right, in clerical-country opinion (the parish priest right) that could not reconcile itself with the new, half-naked, muscle-bursting phenomenon. This means that the extremes united. But the opposite standpoint was prevalent close at hand, on the conservative right, where the most wholehearted support was to be found.[8]

The following presentation of the editorially representative press debate in 1912 is organized by theme, not by party political views. Several lines can thus be followed, and the perspective becomes clearer. First of all the hottest subject of debate is brought up: nationalism. There then follows the closely related military theme. The two following themes are both related to culture, each in its own way. Firstly, competitive sport is combined with "culture" and the spiritual aspect in different ways. And secondly, it is seen in the light of the culture of physical exercise as a whole. The two following themes are also closely related. The fifth is about opinions on the road that competitive sport was taking (professionalization, specialization, the focus on records, Americanization etc.). Finally, it is complemented by the (different) value of sporting events, a theme that also has a bearing on the area of politics.

Nationalism

This theme follows three lines: the results of the competitions, the reactions of the general public (mainly from the Olympic Stadium) and how the Games were organized. The last of these three had least significance. The results and the general public were both surprising. Together they gave food for thought both for and against sporting nationalism.[9]

Two social democratic politicians and opinion leaders, August Nilsson ("Nilsson i Kabbarp") and Ture Nerman, brought the debate to a head. They put forward their opinions in their respective party newspapers *Arbetet* (Malmoe) and *Nya Samhället* (Sundsvall), and these were the most sensational in the whole Olympic debate. From the left, surprise combined with condemnation dominated. From the right there was an equal amount of surprise combined with applause. What the two Social Democrats did was to unreservedly acknowledge nationalism as a strong force in society which was fully justifiable.

The socialistic newspaper, *Arbetet,* was obviously divided with regard to Olympic sport. It expressed itself skeptically against it and its nationalistic elements.[10] Nilsson radically dissented from this attitude, which was the norm in the social democratic press. In an irreverent article he wanted social democracy to acknowledge nationalism and loosen its one-sided internationalism. It should reject "all the old words about silly sport and patented patriotism." Nilsson expressed his admiration for the strength and beauty that were manifested during the Games and his dislike of the working class press's perception of sport.[11]

Nerman formulated his ideas in two consecutive articles in a more nuanced, less provocative fashion. But his message in the main question was along the same lines. He relativized the criticism of nationalism — even the beggar has a home country — and expressly agreed with Nilsson's opinion. Even social democrats should be able to acknowledge the importance of nationalism. He found a good "forum for Swedishness" in the Olympic Games. Nerman was de facto preaching the solemn song of love of one's native country, with only a few reservations.[12]

How should this two-man opinion be explained? It is reasonable to assume that it must have originated in a personal disposition for free thinking, for challenging dogma. But this time there was probably another crucial factor: they had both been eyewitnesses at the Olympic Stadium. And what is more, when they were there they had let themselves be carried away by the competitions and the nationalistic enthusiasm of the general public. This "new experience" had affected their view of nationalism in an unorthodox direction from the socialist point of view. Here we have an early sign of competitive sport's potential to carry people away, of its mass psychological effect.

These signs of social democratic nationalism were greeted with open arms by the right,

A promotional postcard of the U.S. discus thrower Martin Sheridan, who won Olympic gold medals in 1904, 1906 and 1908. He did not compete in Stockholm (National Sports Museum).

who also took advantage of the theme for their own purposes. One example is to be found in *Göteborgs Aftonblad*. It was observed after the overall Swedish victory that "we are a robust nation that is to be reckoned with." Self-deprecation was a thing of the past. The more or less explicit allusions to Sweden's period as a great power were evident in the view that this national support had not been equaled for centuries. The newspaper's praise of the organizational success was more original. This success is illustrated, for example, by the efforts of the secretary of the Organizing Committee Kristian Hellström and the Crown Prince (active honorary chairman of the Organizing Committee). The nationalistic rhetoric was taken to great lengths. The Olympic effect was believed to reach the simplest shack and it was considered that the present generation had never before felt such pride in being Swedish. The young socialist became a patriot, the defense nihilist pro-defense. This mixture of wishful thinking and reality expresses a high point in nationalistic interpretation.[13]

A right-wing local colleague, *Göteborgs Morgonpost*, adopts the same pattern by talking of increased respect "among the peoples of the world" and expressly drew parallels with Sweden's period as a great power.[14] The leading right-wing newspaper in Malmoe, *Sydsvenska Dagbladet Snellposten*, which had kept a distance to competitive sport itself for a long time, spoke of public scenes that were like a stormy sea and of "national fervor." In the light of this it found the notion of sport's ability to bring different nations together illusional.[15]

Lunds Dagblad represents the one-sided political interest in the Olympic Games. They found proof of "national unity of feeling," saw that class prejudices and party differences had been defeated, and that national confidence had increased.[16]

It can be seen as self-evident that the right-wing press in Stockholm, primarily represented by *Stockholms Dagblad* and *Svenska Dagbladet*, followed along the same lines. The former's arguments for sport's socially unifying qualities are original and are to be found under the headline of "the democratic significance of sport." This could be seen in both the participants and the general public. Here the poor, the rich, races, ethnic groups and nationalities were mixed together in a melting pot. Of course it was admitted that certain events were more adapted to the rich, whereas football for example was more generally accessible. But the point was the opposite, that the interest in sport was spreading, was increasingly becoming a common factor, a nationally unifying element. Here there was a common platform for mutual understanding, something beneficial to society according to the newspaper. But, it added, for extreme socialists the opposite conclusion was to be drawn. It is not surprising that the same newspaper would also make use of the two social democratic "defectors."[17]

Svenska Dagbladet briefly tried to harmonize the national and international perspective. They found on the one hand that nations came closer to each other, with friendship and solidarity as a consequence, and on the other that a nationally unifying process came about at the same time. This combination was rare in the debate and appears to conflict with the talk about national fervor. One of the leading cultural personalities of the time, Gustaf Stridsberg, was impressed by the public reactions, by the fact that the national anthem was sung spontaneously after the triple Swedish victory in the modern pentathlon. Later the Stockholm Olympic Games were linked to both the battleship fund raising and the dissolution of the Union with Norway.[18]

Those who were skeptical found it difficult to stand up to this nationalistic offensive. The theme was touched on far less by liberal and social democratic newspapers. *Dagens Nyheter* was one of those who were skeptical, and they warned about too far-reaching Swedish "chauvinism." A similar restrained view of sport's national and international implications is evident in three liberal newspapers based in Gothenburg.[19] In the liberal provincial press the warnings about "sports chauvinism" were nuanced somewhat more. It was acknowledged that the successes in shooting and riding gave Sweden increased respect. But a Swedish renaissance required broad-ranging work on a daily basis, education for all and the like, not primarily Olympic victories.[20]

Even less could the majority of the social democratic press make room for nationalistic interpretations. The views stated by Nilsson and Nerman fell by the wayside. This took on several indirect expressions, which were well represented by *Social-Demokraten*, the leading party newspaper. One could be seen in the irreverent attitude which led to the whole Olympic event being made fun of, for example. At the same time it was discussed and followed factually. In this way both negative and positive readers could be satisfied. Such a double attitude did not leave room for nationalistic ecstasy. The working class press as a whole was divided. Half of the fourteen acknowledged party newspapers were quite positive to and/or in any case interested in the Olympic sport, and the other half was negative.[21]

Another indirect expression of anti-nationalism in this connection is the tendency to relativize the Swedish successes in the competitions. When *Social-Demokraten* under the heading "Summary of the results in the Olympic Games" drew its conclusions, there was no lack of realistic factors of a restraining nature: the home advantage and having been able to affect the composition of the program. The day after it was stated that the results did not constitute a "reliable measure of the nations' standings vis-à-vis each other" with regard to sport.[22] They differ greatly here from the right-wing press's far-reaching interpretation of the significance of the results as a measure of both the status of Swedish sport and that of the whole country. This brings to the surface a large and interesting complex of questions.

A third indirect expression can be seen in the working class press's emphasis on the physical side of sport. *Social-Demokraten* is a good representative here as well. In its Olympic article it stressed the importance of physical culture and working class health in the light of the development of industrial society. Sport, it was pointed out, was edifying for the working class as well. Many of the competing Swedish athletes were workers. Their greatest role was to strengthen the workers in their struggle for their existence. Nerman argued along the same lines when he urged to "fight for the body" as a reaction to the physically destructive forces of Christianity and industrial society.[23] Such a body and class focused ideology was in opposition to the notion of a unified nation joined in jubilation over Swedish successes.

Corresponding class thinking can be found in a fourth, indirectly anti-nationalistic expression: the proposal to set up separately organized working class sport. This rare idea in the debate was clearly proposed by *Ny Tid* from Gothenburg. They doubted the suitability of the "bourgeois" sports associations and found it unlikely that these would be reformed. There thus remained internal social democratic sport, preferably within the framework of the youth association. Well-planned sport would give an attractive complement to other activities. This exhortation was not heard in the pre-war years. Between the wars it had, as is known, just a parenthetic follow-up to no great extent compared with other countries.[24] Of course, separate working class sport was in total opposition to both the nationalism of right-wing opinion and the claim of the established sporting world to full hegemony.

The Officers and Militarism

The Swedish sporting movement was strongly linked to the military sector from the very beginning. In terms of organization this found expression in sports associations in military units. In the capital city *Styrelsen i Stockholm för militär idrott* (the Stockholm Board for Military Sport) was formed in 1893.[25] In 1909 the time was ripe for a national organization, Sweden's Military Sports Association. Competitions in the armed forces were arranged with events on the program that had a place in both civil sport and that of a military nature. Here can be seen the growth of a separate military sporting movement, but with links with the civil sporting movement.

Of greater relevance for the Olympic debate is military involvement in the civil sporting movement. This involvement was very strong, in particular in the national organizations. The officer corps can be described as the most driven occupational group in the pre-war years. Officers were a large and active group on the Boards of the two leading national organizations — Sweden's Central Association for the Promotion of Sport (1897) and The Swedish Sports Confederation (1903).[26] Not only did they work with organizational matters, but they also took part in competitions. This was most likely to be in events such as shooting, equestrianism and gymnastics. At the Stockholm Olympic Games the newly introduced modern pentathlon event was particularly suitable. It was not a coincidence that the triple Swedish victory was achieved by officers. It is also significant that Victor Balck was an officer, and as far as we can judge he was a prerequisite for the choice of Stockholm as the organizer of the Olympic Games.

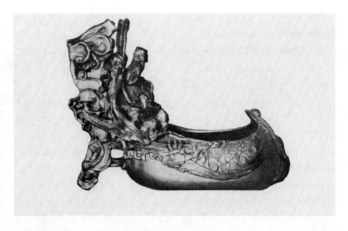

The emperor of Russia's challenge cup to the winner of the decathlon (postcard, National Sports Museum).

The other background factor is political, the critical situation in the years leading up to the outbreak of war in 1914. In particular the fund raising for a battleship became a reference point. Together the sporting and political situation invited a wide variety of comments. Such comments can indeed be traced in the Olympic debate but not as frequently as with regard to the nationalistic theme. As can be expected, however, they are closely related.

For right-wing opinion the military theme was solely positive. *Göteborgs Aftonblad* saw in the Swedish successes in the competitions a sign of an ability to defend the country if it was attacked by a foreign power. This was the most positive thing to come out of the Games, in the opinion of the newspaper. For *Lunds Dagblad* the will to win and training were important factors. They found here a common denominator between competitive sport and military defense.[27]

The theme was commented on in more detail in the right-wing press of the capital city. *Stockholms Dagblad* went furthest. Under the headline "The Swedish officer as a sportsman" they reminded readers of and praised the officer corps' historical feats in sport. Its successes in competitions had allowed the corps to concretize its central position in the sporting movement for a broader general public. In another article, with the equally telling headline "Discipline and organization," the arguments were filled out. Here the focus was on the demands of effective, organized cooperation that successful participation in competitions required. It was considered that these demands would be able to increase sympathies for the armed forces. The officer had thereby been praised both as a competitor and as an organizer. At the same time reference was made, as so often in the right-wing press, to statements in the liberal and social democratic press that were in agreement with this basic view.[28]

In *Svenska Dagbladet*, Stridsberg, who always had a lot of opinions, shared his colleagues' view of sport as a favorable forum for the officer corps' public appearances. It was more difficult to win appreciation for the real work of the armed forces than for their sporting efforts. Their performances in the Olympic Games had gained the corps the attention and sympathies of the general public. Stridsberg linked to this the winning Swedish tug-of-war team, seven-eighths of which consisted of policemen, which beat the English police team in the final. This was interpreted as yet another contribution to the increase in respect for "the Swedish uniform."[29]

The military theme was solely a worry for liberals and social democrats concerned with molding public opinion. They solved this largely through evasive maneuvers or by keeping quiet. The liberal press took a relatively restrained line in the question of military defense, and thus enthusiasm for defense questions and praise of officers were difficult topics. For the social democrats resources for military defense were in principle dubious or reprehensible.

The liberal dilemma can be clearly seen in an editorial article by the editor-in-chief of *Dagens Nyheter,* Otto von Zweigbergk. He formulated two positions in dialogue form. The one that was negative to the armed forces stated that "the 133 Olympic points are just as much a triumph for militarism." The opposite position was just as clear: it would be shameful not to acknowledge military competence "when it is genuine and consists of a test in a democratic competition."[30] The conclusion of this expression of opinions was that the armed forces' sporting successes were acknowledged — but not without a lot of willpower.

An interesting point of view was given by *Eskilstuna-Kuriren.* The liberal newspaper disapproved of the politicization of the Olympic debate with the phrase "fishing in the close season." They pointed out what a modest role the militarily strong Germany played during the competitions.[31] The point was of course to question a positive connection between the armed forces and the development of sport.

The social democrats also disapproved of this combination of course, though it did not lead to much discussion of the topic. An example of a reaction can be found in *Örebro-Kuriren.* The headline of the leader is telling enough: "Militaristic speculation in sporting interest." They objected to *Stockholms Dagblad's* nationalism and praising of officers, declaring their opposition to drill and Prussianism in general.[32]

Sport as Spiritual Culture

Anyone opening a leading daily newspaper in the 1890s could with a little luck be met with headings such as "Sports Section" or "Sport." Permanent, though not daily, headings for current events in sport had been introduced. This indicates that people had begun to see sport as having come to stay. Previously there were corresponding headlines for (other) cultural features such as art, the theatre, music and literature.[33] But was sport seen as a parallel phenomenon? Was it even culture?

The theme of sport as culture has fuzzy edges. In general two opposite standpoints can be discerned. First, that sport, in line with the inclusive view of Greek antiquity, was regarded as an excellent cultural element in living interaction with others. Second, it was the antithesis of spiritual culture. The former standpoint was represented at the 1912 Olympic Games by the art competitions that the antique freak Pierre de Coubertin tried to force upon reluctant organizers. The latter was represented during the inter-war years by Ivar Lo-Johansson and several other left-wing radical authors and by post-war doubt that sport should be included in the concept of culture.

The question is now whether the Olympic debate encompassed this theme and in that case in what way. It is clear that the art competitions did not bring about editorial comments in connection with the Summer Games. This did not mean that comments were not made about competitive sport as a cultural expression. But did this happen? The answer is that interesting comments in that direction occurred but only sporadically. The right-wing press generally seems to have refrained from entering this area, fully occupied by a more applause eliciting perspective.

The biggest salvo was fired by socialistic *Arbetarbladet* in Gävle. The editor-in-chief N. Norling saw competitive sport as a sign of the superficiality of cultural people. Books were not read. "The average person did not know the leading figures of culture and science, but knew very well who the goalkeeper in the Serbian football team is." The art of running was held in higher regard than thinking. This expressly conservative cultural lamentation even comprised a desire to return to the old games of billiards and skittles.[34]

A more politicizing approach to the subject was taken in an editorially approved letter to the editor of *Ny Tid*. Here sport was seen as a means for capitalism to hold down the working class spiritually and culturally. A higher spiritual level would constitute a danger for capitalistic society. By extension the view of sport as opium for the people can be found here, a notion that was clearly put forward by the extreme left.[35]

A circular article in the liberal provincial press joined the ranks of the sport skeptics. It played off an expanding education for everyone against Olympic victories. The soul was more important than the body. It warned about exaggerated interest in sport, about believing that "Sweden's honor and welfare are to be found in the legs."[36] It can be added that the Workers' Educational Association was founded in 1912.

There is not an abundance of relevant comments on the positive side either. The opposite pole to Norling can be found in his party colleague Harald Åkerberg in *Örebro-Kuriren*. In his opinion "a soul without a body is not as ready for existence as a body without a soul." "The ideal is neither cultural waffle nor sporting silliness." It is interesting that he, possibly as the only example in the whole Olympic debate, stressed the cultural status of sport through the rhetorical question "What is all of sport, if not part of the work on culture?"[37]

A few liberal newspapers also approached the theme, which tended, however, to be more about the body–soul dichotomy than cultural status. *Handelstidningen* in Gothenburg saw the Olympic Games as a combination of muscles and brain. For example, a football match required both: "We mustn't separate the brain from the rest of the body as we have done before." *Göteborgs-Posten* discussed the relationship between physical and spiritual culture. In an attempt to mediate, the former was seen as a prerequisite for the latter. Somewhat contradictorily the spiritual was described as being more valuable at the same time as they were "on a par with" each other. And then the party colleague in Västerås was of the opinion that the over-refined cultural person needed sport as a counterbalance to intellectualism. England was named as a leading country.[38]

There are not many comments and they do not go very deep. It is still a sign of the many facets of the Olympic debate that this theme that was touched on so seldom in later years was brought up in several articles. The opinions offered are disparate, most clearly personified by the social democratic pair of opposites Norling–Åkerberg. It is striking that the Christian dichotomy body–soul has almost completely disappeared. In *Svenska Morgonbladet*, an important Free Church magazine of the time which has been specially studied in another connection, there was a lively discussion about sport during the Olympic summer. Widely differing opinions were put forward. Amongst other things there was a sport–(higher) spiritual-religious interests contrast.[39] It seems natural that this contrast primarily concerned Christian opinion, but they have distanced themselves from the concept of culture in a wider sense. It has become body–soul instead of sport–culture. Furthermore one can wonder how the highly frequent expression physical culture fits in this complex picture.

Sport as Physical Culture

The modern competitive sport that was on display in Stockholm during the Olympic summer of 1912 was only one form of several within physical exercise culture. Other times could display other forms. There were also contemporary alternatives. Relating to these could appear to be a reasonable task for a daily press opinion that wanted to give perspective. The question is therefore which alternative forms they could reasonably connect with, and what they actually chose — if anything.

Antique Greece offered a first natural connection. Neo-classicism was a living force a century ago. Irrespective of social area there was a tendency to return there: "The ancient Greeks had already...." The strong position of sport in classical Greece could make such retrospection natural. All the more so as it was in fact the foremost of the four Pan-Hellenic Games that had its modern renaissance. By extension, as a second alternative, there was this renaissance, that is the coming into being of the Olympic movement, including the new Games. A detailed presentation of the pioneer Coubertin and the steps from thought to deed appears to be a natural theme.[40]

Outside the Olympic sphere lies the development of English sport, which from the second half of the nineteenth century spread over the civilized world. Its links with school, associations, the armed forces, the upper class and the working class were the background to the modern competitive sport that was being held at Stockholm's Olympic Stadium. Furthermore, anyone looking for older predecessors could find, although it was perhaps a little far-fetched, models in the increasingly sophisticated jousting tournaments in the Age of Chivalry or in the Vikings' crude single combat duels and other tests of strength.

It turns out that none of all this attracted any particular interest. The focus was entirely on another alternative: gymnastics. But not any old kind of gymnastics. There were several schools within this ideologically charged area. But press opinion concentrated entirely on Swedish gymnastics, also called Ling gymnastics. How is this limited perspective to be explained?

One explanation of course lies in nationalistic thinking, in the opportunity to cling to a Swedish identity through Ling gymnastics. Patriotism could be shown by giving exposure to both Swedish Olympic successes and Ling gymnastics. But it was also possible to choose one of the two, to play them off against each other. A second explanation lies in the fact that commentators had their own experience of Ling gymnastics from their school days, where this form of physical exercise greatly dominated. A third may have to do with Ling gymnastics' objectives: moderation, a scientific base, harmonious physical development for everyone, skepticism with regard to individuals competing and elitism.[41] To put it briefly, there was a domestic pedagogic alternative here.

One newspaper that championed Ling gymnastics was *Smålands Folkblad*. They had doubts about the popular breadth of the sports movement, which was not seen as living up to external claims. Ling gymnastics was not widespread enough in Sweden, even in Småland (P.H. Ling's home province). The public health value of the Olympic Games was questioned. But it was regrettably observed that "people are more interested in English football than in Swedish gymnastics."[42]

Otherwise, there is no evidence of strong ties between social democratic press opinion and Ling gymnastics. Positive factors should have been found in this form of gymnastics' focus on the population as a whole, the collective physical movements, the all-round bodily ideal and rationalism. But these were counteracted by negative features: the influence of the officers among teachers and instructors, the pedagogics of command and the formalism, and the impression of something old-fashioned (the opposite of modernity).

Otherwise it was the bourgeois newspapers that referred to Ling gymnastics, always as a positive alternative. Sometimes it was used as a stick to beat competitive sport with, and sometimes it was a harmonious, cooperative factor. In some quarters it was regretted that it was little widespread in the country. In other quarters it was merited with having constituted a springboard for the Swedish successes in the competitions. These claimed effects were thus disparate in nature. A few examples are warranted.

Göteborgs Aftonblad regretted that Ling gymnastics was limited to civil and military education. A picture was conjured up of expanding sport, and stationary or retreating gymnastics. *Göteborgs Morgonpost*, on the other hand, thought that Ling gymnastics underlay the Swedish victories. In *Sydsvenska Dagbladet* a picture emerged of an aesthetic state of opposition between aesthetically pleasing gymnastics and "quite vulgar" sport. Gymnastics should be the basis of "all modern physical culture."[43]

Some newspapers proved to be well acquainted with Swedish gymnastics' situation. *Handelstidningen* in Gothenburg recommended a strong connection between gymnastics and sport. The newspaper thought, as did several others, that competitive sport must be based on the all-round physical training that Ling gymnastics gave those practicing it. But regrettably the country's voluntary gymnastics was at a standstill, unlike the situation in Denmark. Hopes were tied to the coming reform of schoolteaching. *Norrköpings Tidningar* also saw Ling gymnastics as the explanation of the Swedish victories. The common denominator was "a physical culture that had been implemented." Swedish gymnastic pedagogues from the first father Per Henrik Ling to those still alive were praised and the whole gymnastic teaching profession was included. The aim should be for sport to develop according to the principles of Ling gymnastics and for this to be an international guiding principle.[44]

A liberal provincial newspaper plays off Ling gymnastics against "glossy competitive victories in sport specialities" and the need for gymnastic halls in public schools against sports trainers with a salary of 18,000 Swedish kronor a year. It noted that school gymnastics was still neglected. Similar thoughts were presented after the Olympic Games in other parts of the liberal press. This includes the proposal to create special gymnastic halls or to house gymnastic facilities in non-conformist and Good Templar buildings. An effort to broaden gymnastics was the recurring theme in this attempt to mould public opinion. Consciously or unconsciously, this was in opposition to competitive sport, though normally in a restrained tone.[45]

It is easy to point out contradictions and inconsistencies in opinion favoring Ling gymnastics. It is not made clear how Ling gymnastics formed the basis of the Swedish victories. The opinion that it was neglected in Sweden could be interpreted in the opposite way. It can be considered unlikely that something that was neglected had had such positive effects. Danish voluntary gymnastics was clearly much stronger than its Swedish counterpart, which was not noticeable in the results of the competitions.[46] Furthermore, no mention was made of the unfathomable rift between orthodox Ling gymnasts and the Olympic sports officials.[47] In the light of this, the editorial press's treatment of the gymnastic theme can be seen as little more than pious wishful thinking. It is obvious that many different people preferred physical training for the whole nation rather than one-sidedly concentrating on the elite. Ling gymnastics was to be the means. The opinion that Ling gymnastics had also laid the foundation for the sporting victories can be seen as a factually dubious attempt to combine broad objectives and elite objectives.

Competitive Sport as Such

Political and cultural opinions came naturally to the newspapers' editorial staff. "The new experience in life" was put in a known framework. It was more difficult to have a point of view on this experience, that is to say competitive sport itself, its characteristics and future development.

Svenska Dagbladet most clearly expressed a positive view of the fundamental features of competitive sport. The element of competition and records was seen as something universal and developing. The individual's competing was included in that of the nation and could in this way contribute to a strong national feeling. Too high ideals would go over the heads of the broad masses. People needed more concrete sources of inspiration. The newspaper even dared to describe Ling gymnastics, the national jewel of physical culture, as somewhat insipid. It accepted American techniques/training and warned about an aristocratization of the Olympic Games: "Gloss on the surface and excitement deeper down, extreme competitiveness and new world records. We cannot see the purpose of all this sporting flashiness, so to speak, but the working man must have this foothold and point of aim."[48]

An original, and equally sympathetic view was expressed by the liberal *Stockholms-Tidningen* when it brought equality into the debate. In its opinion, "unrealizable ideas of equality" had no place in competitive sport, which was obviously accepted. The winners were appreciated so much more as it was in the nature of things that they changed all the time. More defensive but still accepting was *Dagens Nyheter*. The newspaper considered elite athletes as something inspirational, "the sacrificial creatures of culture" with the task of spreading interest. The marathon runner aspired to develop naturally given capacities. But the results of the race only had value if they were echoed by the level of the whole population. Specialist performances in individual events should not be the main thing.[49]

Promotional postcard for the marathon race (National Sports Museum).

The last opinion is a natural transition to doubts and lack of acceptance. One-sided specialization was one of the features that was focused on. An otherwise serious debate article in the social democrat *Ny Tid* pushed its criticism of specialization to absurd extremes by proposing animal competitions: hares in running events, fleas in the high jump, kangaroos in the long jump, while people were recommended the harmonious physical training of Ling gymnastics. A party colleague acknowledged the occurrence of competitive and record-breaking mania and one-sided specialization. However, he saw such elements as natural developments in a powerful popular movement with elements of almost religious fervor.[50]

These "developments" were also criticized in a number of bourgeois newspapers. It can be said that this was part of the conventional view of sport at the time. All-round ability and a focus on the whole population were named as an opposing ideal. The view that it was a question of maintaining the link between the elite level and sport as a whole also points in the same direction. "Specialist performances" recorded in centimeters and seconds were disapproved of.[51] The orthodox supporters of Ling gymnastics had put forward such views for decades both internally and publicly. The question was one of whether the "developments" were accepted or led to the conclusion that the whole movement had to be rejected.

Two special phenomena, partly linked, were criticized by some: professionalization and Americanization.[52] For example, the liberal *Aftonbladet* wanted to have Swedish sporting ideals rather than one-sided American specialization.[53] Two circular articles in the liberal provincial press went furthest in their criticism. Under the headline "Schoolchildren's Olympification" they warned about developing along American lines. The Swedish American trainer Ernie Hjertberg, employed to give Swedes victories, represented such a development.[54] He was, it was claimed, not at all the right man to take care of public physical education in Sweden. Americanized specialist sport and "professional circus competition" on the one hand were set against "gentlemen's sport" and gymnastics for the whole population on the other. Participation in the 1916 Olympic Games was not at all the most important thing. Furthermore, it was claimed that specialized competitive athletes did not reach the best possible physical status for themselves.[55]

The view of competitive sport included both approval and disapproval. There were "developments" that were generally acknowledged. Most of press opinion could understand and accept them, but in a minority of newspapers they led to more or less outright rejection. In the background was Ling gymnastics, which for many was the far superior alternative. It can be hypothetically asked how things would have been judged if the Stockholm Olympic Games had turned out to be a fiasco instead of a success.

The Events

Sport consists of different "sports." This is not easy to handle or logical from a terminological point of view. Here "events" is preferred to "sports," even if objections can be made regarding the term "event."

Olympic commentators were faced with the difficulty of expressing themselves in general terms about an abundance of events, each with its own special features. It was not easy to capture in the same phrase both shooting, a calm event with its roots in a popular movement of its own from the 1860s, and athletics, an event dominated by the Anglo-Saxons, with its strong physical expression. The differences between the events gave room for different priorities. According to press opinion there were more or less valuable events. The values were based on political, cultural and sporting aspects that have been touched on above. The question is whether any pattern can be traced.

It is immediately clear that the right-wing press was most interested in valuing the events. On repeated occasions *Göteborgs Morgonpost* drummed into its readers the importance of shooting and the Swedish victories there. They talked about "gentlemen sports" and "more noble sports events" characterized by all-round ability. This particularly applied to shooting and gymnastics, followed by riding and sailing. Less "noble" were football, wrestling, running "and such events that required professional training." In another connection shooting and gymnastics were again praised, with the addition of multi-event competitions and in opposition to "specialist performances" judged in centimeters and seconds.[56]

This valuation was by and large a feature of all the opinions put forward on the subject. The reasons and occasionally the events could vary. Wittiest were *Handelstidningen's* words about the fact that hopefully "our men are better at shooting than running." This formulation was gratefully received by the right wing as a sign of liberal willingness to defend the country.[57] It was particularly stressed in some quarters that shooting was based on a large national movement. Another voice dedicated itself to out-and-out shooting romanticism: here there was an Olympic activity on the Kaknäs shooting range that managed without thunderous applause, with officers and civilians competing side by side. In other quarters football, wrestling and the marathon were rejected from a principal point of view.[58] Surprisingly enough the Olympic marathon performance was not criticized, although the heat sapped the strength of many, and took the life of the Portuguese Lazaro.

The *Stockholms Dagblad* and *Svenska Dagbladet* stable were loathe to downgrade any events. On the other hand they were happy to point out the most valuable, which indirectly

Crown Prince Gustaf Adolf conversing with the Games' oldest participant, Oscar Swahn, at the shooting range at Råsunda (postcard, National Sports Museum).

could have the same significance. They particularly appreciated "events of benefit to the country" such as shooting, gymnastics and the modern pentathlon.[59] They had in common, together with riding, that officers played a large part, both as officials and as active participants. All-round physical ability and military defense lay behind such a valuation. Conversely, football, wrestling and athletics were less appreciated events, and these were also less military in nature.

It is clear that the value of the events for military defense was a leading factor in the right-wing press. A corresponding prioritization of events that were civil or popular in nature has not been found among editorial comments in the working class press. This may be due to the fact that it was difficult to take in all the details of modern competitive sport and therefore they were content to judge it as a whole. With regard to the physical education criterion, all-round ability was preferred, and one-sidedness was rejected. However, the judgments are only partly convincing here, for example with regard to gymnastics and the multi-event competitions. Shooting, which received so much praise, cannot readily be seen as all-round, rather the opposite. What made sailing and riding more all-round than running, football and wrestling is not clear. In actual fact a collision can be seen here between politically and physically steered values, to the former's advantage. Neither was it noted that the officers' performances were largely in events that were a part of or close to their duties. They could be regarded as at least semi-professional. But professionalism was rejected in the debate. Here we have yet another example of contradiction and inconsistency in a sporting debate that all in all displays greater multi-facetedness than any other in the history of the Swedish press.

Summary

The underlying thesis has been that the 1912 Stockholm Olympic Games gave rise to the general debate in the Swedish daily press concerning modern competitive sport. Neither before nor later has anything equivalent to this been acted out in the newspaper columns. Its exceptional nature was expressed both quantitatively and qualitatively: a combination of the number of editorial articles and the variety of subjects and of angles taken. It is justified to talk about a unique mobilization of views by the mass media on the phenomenon of sport, in particular from a qualitative point of view.

Sport was judged from both socio-political and physical culture standpoints. It cannot be denied that in one case positive conclusions were reached, and in the other negative conclusions. Social democratic opinion was the most negative. Here nationalistic and militaristic elements were rejected, with very few exceptions. At the same time several elements of how the sports competitions were run were criticized. The bourgeois right had only good things to say about the social and political function of the sport on display at the Olympic Games. An interesting grading can be observed inasmuch as sports closely related to the armed forces were ostentatiously prioritized. How the events were run also met understanding in the main, which did not rule out the "obligatory" criticism of professionalism, one-sided specialization and so on. In liberal quarters they were less positive and more divided.

In the field of physical exercise there was a narrow perspective regarding objects of comparison, which in fact was limited to Swedish (Ling) gymnastics. Its strong position as the only notable point of reference can be clearly seen. Opinion critical of sport had here an alternative respected by everyone to play off against the new, at the same time fascinating and frightening competitive sport. No one claimed that the latter was superior to Ling gymnastics. Other reasonable associations were absent: antiquity, the culture of the Age of Chivalry, the Old Norse theme (Sweden's period as a great power was remembered, however), the Olympic movement and the Coubertin gestalt, Anglo-Saxon sport (though there were warnings about Americanization).

One of the most contradictory debate subjects was about gymnastics. It was considered to have contributed to the Swedish successes in the competitions (an unproved claim) but at the same time it was regretted that it was neglected in Sweden (especially compared with Denmark, who performed modestly in the sporting competitions). Another contradiction that has not been paid any attention lay in the officers' duties of a partly sporting nature, which remarkably enough did not lead to their amateur status being questioned. The absence of critical articles vis-à-vis how the Olympics were organized is also striking, for while it is true the Games went smoothly, they did not contain only sunshine.

Notes

1. MacAloon, *This Great Symbol* (1981).
2. Lindroth, *Idrottens väg till folkrörelse* (1974) and Lindroth, "Sports in the Daily Press" (1977).
3. Jönsson, *Nordiska spelen* (2001).
4. For the daily press and the society at the time of the 1912 Olympic Games, see Widholm, *Iscensättandet av solskensolympiaden* (2008), for example pp. 53 ff. This thesis does not focus on the editorial molding of public opinion. Neither does Ulf Wallin's standard work, *Sporten i spalterna* (1998).
5. At least this number reached *Stockholms Dagblad*: June 1, 2 and 30, July 7, 14 (2), 16, 18, 24, 28 and 30, August 7 and 8, 1912.
6. Lindroth (1974), pp. 296 ff. Norberg, *Idrottens väg till folkhemmet* (2004), pp. 72 ff.
7. *Stockholms Dagblad* July 24, 1912 (1912; this year will not be henceforth given in connection with references to daily newspapers).
8. Lindroth (1974), chap. 12. cf. chap. 13:2.
9. For nationalism and closely related concepts and their relation to sport, see most recently Stark, *Folkhemmet på is* (2010), especially pp. 48 ff.
10. *Arbetet*, July 2, 12 and 29.
11. *Arbetet*, July 17 (headline "Bits").
12. *Nya Samhället*, July 23 and 24.
13. *Göteborgs Aftonblad*, July 20 (quot.) and July 31.
14. *Göteborgs Morgonpost*, July 26.
15. *Sydsvenska Dagbladet Snellposten*, July 24, signed "T.B." For the newspaper's general opinion on sport, see Lindroth 1977 pp. 130, 145.
16. *Lunds Dagblad*, July 17 (quot.) and July 25.
17. *Stockholms Dagblad* July 14 (quot.) and July 24.
18. *Svenska Dagbladet*, June 28, July 14 (Stridsberg), July 29 and August 16.
19. *Dagens Nyheter*, July 17 and Lindroth (1974), p. 321.
20. *Sundsvalls Tidning*, July 6, 11 and 25 (quot.).
21. Lindroth (1974), pp. 324 ff.
22. *Social-Demokraten*, July 24 and 25 (quot.).
23. *Social-Demokraten*, June 29, and Nerman in *Nya Samhället*, July 23.
24. *Ny Tid*, July 8 and 12. For working class sport, see Pålbrant, *Arbetarrörelsen och idrotten 1919–1939* (1977).
25. Yttergren, *Täflan är lifvet* (1996), pp. 65 f.
26. Lindroth (1974), chap. 5.
27. *Göteborgs Aftonblad*, July 31, and *Lunds Dagblad*, July 25.
28. *Stockholms Dagblad*, July 14, 28, and Lindroth (1974), p. 311.
29. *Svenska Dagbladet*, July 14.

30. *Dagens Nyheter*, July 24.

31. *Eskilstuna-Kuriren*, July 17.

32. *Örebro-Kuriren*, July 29.

33. Lindroth (1977), p. 127.

34. *Arbetarbladet*, July 1 (cf. July 24).

35. *Ny Tid*, August 15. The extreme left, Lindroth 1974 chap. 13:2.

36. *Sundsvalls Tidning*, July 25.

37. *Örebro-Kuriren*, June 28.

38. *Göteborgs Handels- och Sjöfartstidning*, July 11; *Göteborgs-Posten*, July 13; and *Västmanlands Läns Tidning*, June 29.

39. Lindroth, "Kors eller boll?" (1986) pp. 117 ff.

40. Neo-Classicism, the culture of physical exercise, the Olympic movement, see Sandblad, *Olympia och Valhalla* (1985).

41. Holmberg, *Den svenska gymnastikens utveckling* (1939).

42. *Smålands Folkblad*, June 29.

43. *Göteborgs Aftonblad*, July 31; *Göteborgs Morgonpost*, July 12; and *Sydsvenska Dagbladet Snellposten*, July 24 ("T.B.").

44. *Göteborgs Handels- och Sjöfartstidning*, July 16 and 23, August 14, and *Norrköpings Tidningar*, August 29.

45. *Sundsvalls Tidning*, July 11 (quot.) and July 25. Lindroth 1974 p. 322.

46. *Olympiska spelen i Stockholm 1912* (1913), p. 816. For Danish gymnastics, see, for example, Korsgaard, *Kampen om kroppen* (1982).

47. Lindroth 1974:III.

48. *Svenska Dagbladet*, June 28 and July 24 (quot.).

49. *Stockholms-Tidningen*, July 6, and *Dagens Nyheter*, June 30.

50. *Ny Tid*, August 15 (letter to the editor), and *Örebro-Kuriren*, June 28.

51. *Göteborgs Handels- och Sjöfartstidning*, July 16, and *Göteborgs Morgonpost*, July 24 (quot.).

52. Wikberg, *Amatör eller professionist?* (2005), pp. 125 ff.

53. *Aftonbladet*, July 21.

54. See Leif Yttergren's "The Jewel in the Olympic Crown."

55. *Sundsvalls Tidning*, July 17 and August 2.

56. *Göteborgs Morgonpost*, July 10; July 23 and 24.

57. *Göteborgs Handels- och Sjöfartstidning*, July 11 and *Nya Dagligt Allehanda*, July 12.

58. *Sydsvenska Dagbladet Snellposten*, July 24 ("T.B."); *Nya Dagligt Allehanda*, July 6 (two articles); and *Östergötlands Dagblad*, July 23.

59. *Stockholms Dagblad*, July 14, 24 and 28, and *Svenska Dagbladet*, July 16 (quot.) and July 24.

References

PERIODICALS AND NEWSPAPERS

Aftonbladet
Arbetarbladet
Arbetet
Dagens Nyheter
Eskilstuna-Kuriren
Göteborgs Aftonblad
Göteborgs Handels- och Sjöfartstidning
Göteborgs Morgonpost
Göteborgs-Posten
Lunds Dagblad
Norrköpings Tidningar
Ny Tid
Nya Dagligt Allehanda
Nya Samhället

Örebro-Kuriren
Östergötlands Dagblad
Smålands Folkblad
Social-Demokraten
Stockholms Dagblad
Stockholms-Tidningen
Sundsvalls Tidning
Svenska Dagbladet
Sydsvenska Dagbladet Snellposten
Västmanlands Läns Tidning

ENCYCLOPEDIAS

Nordisk familjeboks sportlexikon 1–7 (Stockholm 1938–1949).

PRINT SOURCES

Bergvall, Erik (ed.). *V. Olympiaden. Officiell redogörelse för olympiska spelen i Stockholm 1912* (Stockholm 1913).

Holmberg, Oswald. *Den svenska gymnastikens utveckling. Per Henrik Ling och hans verk* (Stockholm 1939).

Jönsson, Åke. *Nordiska spelen. Historien om sju vinterspel i Stockholm av olympiskt format 1901 till 1926* (Stockholm 2001).

Korsgaard, Ove. *Kampen om kroppen. Dansk idraets historie gennem 200 år* (Copenhagen 1982).

Lindroth, Jan. *Idrottens väg till folkrörelse. Studier i svensk idrottsrörelse till 1915* (Uppsala 1974).

Lindroth, Jan. "Kors eller boll? Kyrkan och idrotten i Sverige 1900–1914" in *Idrott, historia och samhälle 1986.*

Lindroth, Jan. "Sports in the Daily Press: Case Studies of Some Swedish Newspapers, 1850–1915." *Zeitschrift für Geschichte des Sports und der Körperkultur*, III, Köln/Leiden 1977.

MacAloon, John J. *This Great Symbol: Pierre de Coubertin and the Origins of the Modern Olympic Games* (Chicago 1981).

Norberg, Johan R. *Idrottens väg till folkhemmet. Studier i statlig idrottspolitik 1913–1970* (Stockholm 2004).

Pålbrant, Rolf. *Arbetarrörelsen och idrotten 1919–1939* (Uppsala 1977).

Sandblad, Henrik. *Olympia och Valhalla* (Stockholm 1985).

Stark, Tobias. *Folkhemmet på is. Ishockey, modernisering och nationell identitet 1920–1972* (Malmö 2010).

Wallin, Ulf. *Sporten i spalterna. Sportjournalistikens utveckling i svensk dagspress under 100 år* (Gothenburg 1998).

Widholm, Christian. *Iscensättandet av solskensolympiaden. Dagspressens konstruktion av föreställda gemenskaper vid Stockholmsolympiaden 1912* (Umeå 2008).

Wikberg, Karin. *Amatör eller professionist? Studier rörande amatörfrågan inom svensk tävlingsidrott 1903–1967* (Stockholm 2005).

Yttergren, Leif. *Täflan är lifvet. Idrottens organisering och sportifiering i Stockholm 1860–1898* (Stockholm 1996).

Patriotic Games as a Breakthrough for the Olympic Movement

ANSGAR MOLZBERGER

Of all countries in the world, Sweden, at the present moment, possesses the best conditions necessary for organizing the Olympic Games in a way that will perfectly satisfy all the claims that athletics and our expectations can demand. The Olympic Games of Stockholm are, even now, assured of perfect success.[1]

With these words, Pierre de Coubertin persuaded the members of the International Olympic Committee (IOC) at the 1909 Session in Berlin to award the Games celebrating the fifth Olympiad to Stockholm. The IOC President's statement should, however, also be viewed as a reaction to the withdrawal of Berlin, which, as a long-favored host city, had, as is well known, to withdraw its candidacy in 1909 because of financial problems. At the same time, de Coubertin's plea demonstrates that the Swedes, and IOC founder member Viktor Balck[2] in particular, had established a very good reputation in the Olympic Movement during previous years. This was also affirmed by the unanimous selection of Stockholm at the Berlin Session.

The available reports on the 1912 Olympic Games to be found in the literature about the history of the Olympic Movement confirm, in retrospect, that de Coubertin was right. Since, in general, the organizational apparatus and the layout of the competition venues were described as exemplary,[3] thus confirming that the Stockholm Olympic planners had done an excellent job. Moreover, thanks to the beautiful summer weather in Sweden, the 1912 festival went down in history as the — incorrectly termed —"Solskensolympiaden" (The Sunshine Olympiad).

However, in Olympic history, the Stockholm Games generally receive even higher "plaudits," as they are usually regarded as a breakthrough for the then almost twenty-year-old Olympic Movement. On the one hand, unlike the 1900, 1904 and 1908 Games, which were merely staged as adjuncts to (World) Exhibitions, they were a stand-alone, self-contained, festive event during the "Stadium Week" from 6 to 15 July 1912. On the other hand, they introduced a number of innovations, which were to become integral parts of future Olympic Games. Some major examples were the official poster advertising the Games, the Olympic art competitions, the equestrian competitions, the modern pentathlon and the decathlon. Moreover, unprecedented in Olympic history, in 1912, athletes from countries on five continents participated and, for the first time, women were allowed to take part in the swimming competitions and diving events. Although, in the early phase of the immature and not yet ritualized Olympic Games before the First World War, innovations were rather the rule than the exception, not least due to its durability the premiere character of the Stockholm event seems to justify the term "breakthrough."

And that is not all that can be said about the significance often ascribed to the festival: Had the 1912 Olympic Games not been staged as such a festive "Complete Work of Art," the subsequent forced interruption caused by the First World War could have spelled the

217

demise of the Olympic Games, according to an often expressed, though, due to its hypothetical character, difficult to verify statement.

It is not without a certain irony, that the 1912 Olympic Games of all games are frequently regarded as the "savior" of the Movement founded by de Coubertin: In fact, this excellent global sporting event was the result of outstanding commitment. However, it was not the main objective of the Organizing Committee (OC) under Balck's chairmanship to use these Stockholm Games to make a lasting contribution to the existence and further development of the international Olympic Movement. Rather, his main concern was "patriotism":

> The importance of the transfer of the Olympic Games to Sweden cannot be rated highly enough. [...] Sweden has completed a responsible task with panache. In 1912, the entire world press published articles full of sympathy and deep respect for Sweden, to an extent never before seen. Our reputation among other nations has grown. The most valuable success for us, however, is not just the results gained in the arena but rather the awakening of Swedishness and the communal spirit they have engendered.[4]

In his *Minnen* (memoirs) published posthumously, long after the Stockholm event, Balck clearly stated once again that he regarded the 1912 Olympic Games primarily as part of a patriotic mission. With his extreme patriotic ideals, of course, he did not represent the views of all the members of the 1912 Organizing Committee. However, being acknowledged internationally as the most influential Scandinavian sports official of the day, for most representatives in the world of sports Balck represented the true face of the Games.

Thus, most of the reasons for the sporting diplomatic crises and disputes with the IOC can be traced back to the patriotic stance taken by the Stockholm Organizing Committee, primarily influenced by Balck, which in the course of the planning and the staging of the festival had to be frequently reined in: To put it in "sporting" terms; the patriotic Stockholm Organizing Committee versus the Cosmopolitan International Olympic Committee.

The participants in the shooting competition having lunch at the shooting range at Kaknäs (postcard, National Sports Museum).

However, a more precise description of the controversies at this point would take too long. As examples we may cite here just the discussions about the content of the Olympic competition program, on which Pierre de Coubertin alone exerted a strong personal influence, and about the "Sporting Geography" favored by the IOC. This embraced the right of athletes from, at that time, non-sovereign but IOC represented states, such as Bohemia, Hungary and Finland to participate in the Olympics.[5] This requirement, which did not reflect state-political reality, meant that controversial issues had not only to be resolved with different Olympic committees, but also with the political and diplomatic bodies.[6]

Despite all the differences of opinion, time after time the Swedes co-operated successfully with the IOC, resulting in these impressive Olympic Games. The objective of this article is to illustrate how the Stockholm event was received internationally and what effect the 1912 festival had on the Olympic Movement.

Reactions to the 1912 Olympic Games

Although, thanks to the requirements laid down by the IOC, with 13 sports disciplines and the Olympic art competitions the Stockholm Olympic Games program turned out to be more extensive than the Swedish side had originally planned, the organizing committee managed to stage a relatively compact event. The Games arranged around the central "Stadium Week" from 6 to 15 July, and in particular their festive presentation with a comprehensive supporting program, made a very positive impression on the sporting world, since they demonstrated the great potential of the Olympic Movement. Athletes, sports officials and visitors had become accustomed to the format of previous Games staged in Paris, St. Louis and London, in which the individual events didn't really stand out from the International Exhibitions and the great metropolitan offerings. However, in Stockholm they witnessed an autonomous, dedicated and well-organized international sporting event, which held virtually the entire Swedish capital under its spell.

The words of thanks from the international sport community published in the official report on the 1912 Olympic Games were couched in extremely friendly terms indeed; they gave polite thanks for the Swedish hospitality and confirmed that the Stockholm Organizing Committee had done a great job. Pierre de Coubertin also shared the international opinion and described the Stockholm Games as an absolutely "brilliant" event.[7]

But apart from the official sports diplomatic response, the public at large was quite impressed; the staging of the Games in particular had made a big impact. The Swedes were highly praised for their organizational talents by representatives of such major sporting nations as Great Britain and USA. The British IOC members Cook and Courcy Laffan wrote for example: "The arrangements for the Press, for telegraphs and telephones, ambulance, competitors' dressing-room, committee rooms [...] were admirable, and a large contingent of Boy Scouts performed innumerable useful services throughout."[8]

The U.S. track and field athletics official James Sullivan was so enthusiastic, that he even used the superlative term "Greatest" in his review: "The Fifth Olympiad [sic!], held under the auspices of the Swedish Olympic Committee at Stockholm, will unquestionably go down in history as the greatest of all international contests, as well as the premier gathering of the world's most competent athletes."[9]

The IOC published its appreciation of what had been achieved in Stockholm via its house magazine *Revue Olympique*:

The perfection of the organizers deserves the highest praise. Almost all possible problems had been anticipated and dealt with in the simplest and most practical way. The work of the administration was characterized by an extraordinary wealth of ideas, remarkable order and modus operandi in every respect. A minimum number of workers carried out a maximum amount of work such that many a government and public administration could learn a lesson here. A great wave of patriotism animated everyone. "For the honor of Sweden" was the motto.[10]

It is remarkable that the strong patriotic character bestowed on the festival by the Swedes wasn't criticized in the *Revue Olympique* in any way. On the contrary, it was explicitly praised as "stimulating." Freely translated: The Olympic Movement experienced a revival in Stockholm.

Nevertheless, the sporting world did not view the 1912 Olympics as a perfectly organized event. Details of the organizational work and especially the planning and staging of the individual competitions were evaluated very critically indeed by the sports officials of various countries. Such feedback was initially sent to the IOC and thence passed on to the Stockholm Organizing Committee.[11]

Often, the reason for the criticism was the strong influence of the Swedish organizers and the resulting country-specific character of the competition program — a well-known problem in the early days of the Olympic Movement.[12] However, to the credit of the organizers, the critics had to admit that in various sport disciplines, especially wrestling and track and field athletics, the rules had not yet been standardized internationally at the time the Games were held, which made the staging of the competitions extremely difficult. The fact that remedial action was required in this respect was the prime lesson learned from the 1912 Olympics.

Thus, the IOC was prepared to deal seriously with the Stockholm Games. Following a suggestion by the Dutch IOC member van Tuyll, it had been decided at the final meeting of the Stockholm Session on 17 July 1912, to set up a three-man commission, to which, apart from the initiator, Viktor Balck and the German IOC member von Venningen were appointed.[13] It was the commission's task to critically assess the 1912 Olympic Games — in the context of the Stockholm Session "problem cases" of the current Games played hardly any part — and to present its findings at the next IOC Session in 1913 in Lausanne.

The Stockholm Organizing Committee had big problems dealing with the negative criticisms of the 1912 Olympic Games stemming from foreign countries. In fact, thanks to the sometimes strongly controversial discussions with the world of sports during the planning and preparation of the Games, the committee members had already become inured to criticism. Both during and immediately after the event, they had to tolerate critical opinions, particularly with respect to the sometimes dubious decisions taken by the Swedish referees and judges.[14] These objections and complaints may have been dismissed by the Swedes as personal opinions and, to some extent, as emotional reactions to the disappointing outcome of a competition.

By the end of 1912, several IOC members, in consultation with the National Olympic Committees (NOC) of their home countries, had completed detailed assessments of the Stockholm Games, which, despite the general praise for the organizational work, listed in detail all the failures and shortcomings. First, these "Deficiency Lists" were sent to Coubertin, who passed them on to the internal commission appointed at the 1912 IOC Session.

The contents of the assembled reviews can be subdivided into two main themes: On the one hand, the exposure of problems of a purely "sporting" nature, such as the inclusion of internationally unrecognized disciplines, and on the other hand the specific competition conditions resulting from the sporting venues and equipment. However, criticisms of this type hardly affected the Stockholm planners, since, although the 1912 competition program clearly had a Swedish "bias," it had finally been accepted by the IOC on the occasion of its 1910 and 1911 sessions. The Stockholm Organizing Committee could not even be blamed for the fact that many athletes were not familiar with the conditions as a consequence of the lack of international standard competition (venue) rules.

Of more concern to the Stockholm planners, however, was the second category of international criticism, i.e. the organizational deficiencies, particularly the controversial decisions made by the Swedish referees and judges. Although authors always pointed out in their reviews, that in no way did they want to impute partiality to the Swedish officials,[15] the cumulative result of the individual cases gave precisely this impression.

Balck was accordingly offended (although officially one of the three-member IOC Commission, von Venningen as author of the review had probably not or perhaps inadequately informed him in advance of the results of the investigations) when the assembled

The International Olympic Committee with ladies and their Hungarian hosts in Budapest, May 1911. Top row from left: J. Sigfrid Edström (representing the Stockholm Organizing Committee), Selim Sirri Bey (Turkey), Johan Sverre (Norway), Maurice Pescatore (Luxemburg), Count Clarence von Rosen (Sweden), Kristian Hellström (representing the Stockholm Organizing Committee) and two unidentified men. Second row: R. S. de Courcy Laffan (England), Angelo C. Bolanschi (Egypt), Attilo Brunialti (Italy), Jiri Guth (Bohemia), Albert Gautier-Vignal (Monaco), Count von Wartensleben (Germany), W. M. Sloane (USA), Lord Desborough of Taplow (England) and Allison v. Armour (USA); the four men standing at right are unidentified. Seated in front row: Count Geza Andrassy (Hungary), Count Eugène Brunetta d'Usseaux (Italy), Viktor Balck (Sweden), Count Pierre de Coubertin (France), Madame Maurice Pescatore (Luxemburg), Anna Balck (Sweden), Károly Khuen-Héderváry and his wife Margit Teleki (Hungary), Countess Clarence von Rosen (Sweden), Miss Balck (Sweden), and Baron von Venningen (Germany). Sitting on floor: Jules de Muzsa (Hungary) (*Den femte olympiaden i bild och ord*, p. 370).

critical feedback arrived in the Swedish capital in March 1913 and immediately "alerted" his Organizing Committee's secretary:

> My dear Hellström,
>   Enclosed are difficult to swallow comments about our Olympic Games, which are unlikely to meet with the approval of our strict referees. However, each individual point must be answered in the most accurate and objective terms. This should be done at the congress in Lausanne. Therefore, all leaders of each sport discipline [i.e. the responsible officials of each OC Subcommittee, ed.] should be given the relevant extracts from these letters immediately[...], so that they can personally respond as soon as possible. Their replies must be translated into three languages [i.e. French, English and German, ed.] and sent to me.[16]

As the letter shows, Balck was seriously concerned about the reputation of the 1912 Olympic Games and feared damage to the Swedish (and his own) reputation in the IOC. Against the background that the next IOC Session was to be held as early as May 1913 in Lausanne, Balck needed his colleagues' responses urgently to avert long-term image damage from the Stockholm event. In addition, the international criticism entailed the danger of a negative domestic knock-on effect in Sweden, as, when the commission's report arrived, in the Swedish Parliament, they were in the act of debating the pros and cons of governmental support ("Statsanslag") for the domestic sports movement. In order to deprive the opponents of this sports promotion, which was within reach for the first time, of ammunition, the assembled criticisms should not be published under any circumstances, wrote Balck in his instructions to Hellström.[17]

The reason for Balck's concern is understandable. In the eyes of the various authors, these often very specific points of criticism in individual cases probably did not detract from the overall praise bestowed on the 1912 Olympic Games. However, added together, one might get the impression that, behind the glittering façade, the Stockholm Games were heavily pervaded with organizational failures and, most important, by the bias of the Swedish referees and judges. Von Venningen's listing of the individual criticisms affected virtually all the Stockholm Games' sporting disciplines. For example, in the case of the fencing discipline, juries were appointed contrary to the rules, track violations by Swedish runners in the track and field athletics were "disregarded" as were forbidden pacemakers for the Swedish cyclists in road racing, referees' decisions were overturned without reason by jury members in the swimming events, the judges lacked objectivity in the dressage; the list of complaints was extensive.[18] However, the most severe criticism that the Swedes had to face was with respect to the staging of the Olympic wrestling competitions. In this case, von Venningen also wrote a personal review in the IOC commission's report:

> I received the most complaints about this sport discipline. The Swedish committee is certainly aware that the wrestling competitions could not be conducted in a satisfactory manner thanks to the complaints and severe discontent of the participants. I am an expert in this discipline, since I was a wrestler for many years. In Stockholm, I spent many hours at the three wrestling mats, and I can tell you quite frankly, that I found the manner of refereeing and many decisions totally incomprehensible. I couldn't detect any strictly observed rules; most decisions were left to the sole disposal of the referee.[19]

In view of such feedback from the IOC members, it could only be scant consolation for the Swedish planners, that von Venningen in the introduction to his report had repeatedly emphasized that in no way did he just want to criticize the Stockholm colleagues, but that it was his sole intention, based on the comments he received, to make suggestions for the improvement of future Olympic Games.[20]

However, the Stockholm Organizing Committee representatives had a different interpretation of the feedback, which is perfectly understandable if one bears in mind the term "disposal": Therefore, Balck, who was by no means prepared to accept the criticisms, required his colleagues to provide strong counter-arguments. To some extent, it was not difficult to find reasons for such responses. Many a detailed criticism could be invalidated quite easily by the Swedish side, since it was obvious that they were simply reflections of the disappointment felt about the poor performance of a compatriot or simply made in a non-objective, reproachful tone.

An interesting source of the latter type is the eight-page analysis by the Hungarian IOC member de Muzsa,[21] who had sent this assessment first to Coubertin before it was passed on to Stockholm in March 1913. In this analysis, covering all the sporting disciplines, Muzsa lists all the points in which, from his point of view, the 1912 Olympic Games exhibited shortcomings. The sometimes brusque formulation of his sentences, perhaps due to the fact that Muzsa had written his review in German which was not his mother tongue, was rather unacceptable in IOC diplomatic circles: Muzsa was voicing criticisms such as "The decathlon [...] was completely superfluous" or "The declaration of results should be better organized" with respect to the track and field athletics competitions and "The composition is simply absurd" with respect to the modern pentathlon.[22] However, he gave no in-depth explanations for his assessment, not to mention constructive proposals for improvement. Thus, Muzsa's analysis lacked gravity and, with his derogatory comments about the modern pentathlon, he would hardly have endeared himself to Coubertin, the founder of this discipline.[23]

However, the response from the criticized Swedish officials was not long in coming; by the end of March, the first counter-claims arrived in the Organizing Committee office. This was hardly surprising, since Muzsa's expressions in particular had met with a violent reaction. On behalf of the track and field official Låftman, a member of the responsible Organizing Committee subcommittee and a referee at the 1912 Games, the Swedish officials, feeling attacked, now turned the tables and the critic became the criticized: "After reading this [Letter, ed.] my general impression is [...] that it is of very little value: [...] The criticism is almost exclusively <u>negative</u> and the comments raised lack both reason and evidence. In view of these circumstances, it should be superfluous to offer any response whatsoever."[24]

When replying the letter, the Stockholm Organizing Committee representatives did not mince their words: "It [i.e. Muzsa's letter, ed.] hardly contains anything, which one might expect, i.e. informed, judicious criticism and constructive suggestions, but just a lot of idle talk. This might be forgiven, since this letter proves the Hungarian committee's own inability, to address the questions raised."[25]

However, those criticized, and in particular Helgesson as president of the much-maligned Organizing Committee Subcommittee for wrestling, also defended themselves against the points raised by von Venningen:

My final statement is that the rules applied in Stockholm were the most detailed and best prepared rules that have ever been laid down for a wrestling competition. Furthermore, these rules were strictly and impartially applied without fear or favor at each and every wrestling match, irrespective of personality or nationality.[26]

Thus, in the discussion about the organizational shortcomings and dubious decisions taken by the referees and judges at the Stockholm Games, a stalemate was reached in the spring 1913: On the one hand, was the international gaggle of critics with their detailed lists of alleged shortcomings aimed at the Swedish officials, and on the other hand, these self-same officials with their rejection of all criticisms as pure invention or at least over-exaggeration. The claims of which side would gain acceptance in the long run were resolved at the IOC Session in Lausanne in May 1913. Surprisingly enough, the minutes of this meeting published in the June edition of the *Revue Olympique* contained no relevant information about the consequences of the commission's report submitted by von Venningen, nor is there a single word about the heated discussions between the Swedish and the other IOC members. It just says in a nutshell:

> The Committee: After reviewing the documents submitted to the appointed commission about the comments and the criticisms of the Vth Olympiad it has been decided to drop all those criticisms, which cannot be used in future. The remaining comments will be passed on to the organizing committee of the VIth Olympiad which should take account of them as far as possible.[27]

Since the second Swedish IOC member, Clarence von Rosen,[28] was hardly involved in the Organizing Committee correspondence about the negative feedback on the Stockholm Games, it can be said that, in Lausanne, Balck was able to successfully prevent an IOC-internal escalation of the criticism of "his" Games, although von Venningen and Muzsa, the two major protagonists of the international group of critics were present.[29] This interpretation of the session report published in the *Revue Olympique,* is also supported by the minutes of the Stockholm Organizing Committee's Session of 20 June 1913. Therein, it states that Balck had succeeded at the IOC Session to "soften" the tones of both the international criticism and the sharp Swedish counter-claims.[30] Thus, after the critics and criticized in previous weeks had given vent to their anger in, at times, robust words, in Lausanne the IOC took a diplomatic line and decided to handle von Venningen's commission report discreetly: The Berlin Organizing Committee was secretly given some good advice from the Stockholm Olympics as pointers for the organization of the 1916 Olympic Games. A potential escalation of the criticism, and consequent damage to the reputation of the Olympic Movement, which had just been substantially enhanced in Stockholm, was thus averted.

Despite the detailed criticism, the 1912 Olympic Games could go down in history as a particularly excellent example of the organization and staging of this global sports festival. If one studies the development of the IOC over the following years it becomes clear what a strong influence the Stockholm Games exerted on the Olympic Movement.

The Effect of the Stockholm Games on the Olympic Movement

Some foreign protagonists were certainly surprised, that of all cities, in internationally obscure Stockholm the Olympic Movement's potential had emerged so strongly. However, disciplined organizational efforts over the years and a strong will to achieve great things, although primarily patriotically motivated, had yielded success. But, at the same time, it had been shown that with the available rules the IOC was hardly able to stage the Olympic Games as a global multi-sport event.

With this knowledge and the determination to change things, the scene was set during the Stockholm Games for the development of the Olympic Movement. Thus, within the framework of the IOC Session, the meetings of which were held in the Swedish House of Parliament on 4 July, from 8 to 10 July and on 17 July 1912, it was agreed to lay down certain basic rules for the competition program of future Olympic Games by categorizing the various sport disciplines and creating three groups: First the "Indispensables," i.e. track and field athletics, gymnastics, fencing, boxing, wrestling, rowing, swimming, shooting, equestrian events, road cycling, modern pentathlon and art competitions; second, the "Desirables," i.e. football, rugby, hockey, lawn tennis, sailing, skating, and track racing; and third the "Admissibles," to which category admission would only be granted to a specific sport discipline, which was practiced in at least six IOC member home countries.[31]

It was by no means intended to scrap the IOC principle of "All Games, All Nations" with the introduction of these rules[32] nor should the sphere of influence of the respective organizing committees be completely restricted in the future. Still mindful of the tough negotiations with the extremely idiosyncratic Stockholm Organizing Committee officials, one nevertheless could see the need for creating a stable foundation for the selection of the Olympic program, on which one could rely during future discussions.

Also within the context of the Stockholm Games, but on the Swedish initiative, came the decisive impetus for the further development of the central Olympic discipline, the track and field athletics, the internationally as yet non-standardized rules of which had significantly hampered the work of the organizers of the 1912 Games. Although, just over a year ago, an attempt by the Swedish track and field athletics official Englund to found a world association had been regarded by de Coubertin as an attack on IOC sovereignty and was therefore rejected,[33] now the Stockholm Organizing Committee Vice President J. Sigfrid Edström[34] seized his opportunity:

> We were particularly concerned, that at that time internationally standardized competition rules for several Olympic disciplines were non-existent, in particular for track and field athletics. Thus, the question was soon raised as to whether an international association of athletics should be founded. Following the motto, "Strike while the iron's hot," one of my life's principles had always been to act immediately. Therefore I sought an audience with Crown Prince Gustaf Adolf [...] and asked him, whether he wanted to attend a meeting of the athletics officials [at present in

King Gustaf V arrives at the tennis tournament (postcard, National Sports Museum).

Stockholm, ed.]. He agreed, whereupon the meeting took place in the parliament building on 17th July, 1912: Representatives from 17 nations attended the meeting, which I chaired since Crown Prince Gustaf Adolf did not want to lead the negotiations himself.[35]

Although the official foundation of the International Amateur Athletic Federation (IAAF) did not take place until August 1913 in Berlin, which according to Edström the US official Sullivan had demanded postponement, as the latter first wanted to consult his domestic association, the Amateur Athletic Union (AAU),[36] the meeting in Stockholm can nevertheless be regarded as a milestone in the development of track and field athletics and thus of the Olympic Games.

Edström has to be accorded the major credit for the IAAF foundation, although Englund and his Swedish Athletics Confederation were involved in setting up the Stockholm meeting. Edström, who became the first IAAF President in 1913, saw in the international plethora of officials on site an opportunity for change and displayed sport-diplomatic skills by initiating the federation's foundation in the presence of de Coubertin and the IOC members. In this way, he could convince the IOC President, that the foundation of the IAAF was in the interest of the development of the Olympic Movement. Particularly, since the discussions about the rules in athletics, which had once again cropped up at the Stockholm Games, had made all participants acutely aware of the need for internationally standardized rules.[37] Moreover, de Coubertin had got to know and appreciate Edström at the previous IOC sessions, so that in 1912 he did not argue against his initiative to found the IAAF.

However, de Coubertin must have been aware from the outset that the IAAF would be an influential partner sitting at the negotiating table in future. This turned out to be the case at the 1914 Olympic Congress in Paris, when Edström, aware of his position as a top official, decisively supported the interests of the IAAF.[38] Although his appearance was characterized by self-confidence, Edström, nevertheless, always strove to present a balanced picture to avoid a snub to the international sport community. The "reward" for his negotiating style followed in 1920, when Edström became a member of the IOC and also in this position rapidly climbed the ladder: Only a year after his appointment, Edström was already acting president at the Olympic Congress sessions on the subject of the "Modification of the Olympic Programme and Conditions of Participation" in 1921 in Lausanne. He did the job so well, that Coubertin appointed him in the same year to the first IOC Executive Committee.[39] In 1931, Edström became IOC vice president and in 1942/1946 reached the pinnacle of his international career as an official when he was elected IOC president, a position he occupied until 1952.[40] Unlike Balck, who was of a different generation and went down in sporting history as the "Father" of the Stockholm Games, reaching his peak as a sports official in 1912, Edstrom's career was sparked off during the 1912 Olympic Games. In allegorical terms: Balck contributed to the birth of the Olympic Movement in 1894 and gave advice and support particularly during its infancy and adolescence. His successor Edström nurtured the adult movement, initially as IAAF president, and played a major role in its further development and survival through two world wars. Both were supported by their compatriot Clarence von Rosen, who was for almost half a century a permanent member of the IOC.

Whereas the long-term Swedish influence on the development of the Olympic Movement, resulting from the successful Stockholm Games, was based personnel-wise on the ambitious Edström and the IOC veterans Balck and von Rosen, institutionally, the foundation in 1913 of the Swedish Olympic Committee (SOC) also had a positive impact on the international "influence" of the Swedes. They now had a stable base in their home coun-

Scene from the Royal Stand during the Crown Prince's speech during the solemn opening of the Olympic Games (*Den femte olympiaden i bild och ord,* p. 84).

try, from which they could actively participate in the Olympic Movement.[41] For example, the Swedish sport officials submitted several drafts for the 1914 Olympic Congress in Paris to be held on the occasion of the 20th anniversary of the Olympic Movement, the subject of which was the "Standardisation of the Olympic program and conditions of participation": Thanks to their expertise with respect to international potential for conflict in the planning and staging of the competition program, acquired unintentionally when organizing the Stockholm Games, the SOC members presented recommendations for both a standard program and a standard set of the basic rules of participation. The first pleaded in favor of restricting future Olympic Games to the staging of the sporting disciplines of fencing, football, lawn tennis, and track and field athletics without the two-handed classified throwing events, modern pentathlon, cycling, equestrian events, wrestling, rowing, swimming, sport shooting and gymnastics.[42] The second draft contained suggestions on uniform Olympic tournament rules in various sporting disciplines such as fencing, football, wrestling and water polo.[43]

Together with Edström and his work on track and field athletics, the Swedish protagonists of the Olympic Movement concentrated precisely on those areas, which had led to the biggest problems and disputes at the Stockholm Games due to the unsatisfactory initial situation: i.e. the drawing up of the competition program and rules.[44]

Thus, the direct effect of the 1912 Olympic Games on the Olympic Movement also contains a category of "negative examples"[45] for which the Swedes can hardly be blamed. As was demonstrated both by the frequent disputes between the Stockholm Organizing Committee and the IOC in the planning phase of the Games and by the unclear rules, which again became evident in the competitions, it was no longer possible to satisfactorily stage an event, in which outstanding sporting performances should be demonstrated, as long as the lack of international rules, which conflicted with this demand, was the status quo.

Both the practice applied hitherto of granting the respective organizing committee a free hand in planning and implementing the program when awarding the right to host the Olympic Games to a city, and the staging of international competitive sport in the arena were no longer in keeping with the times.

With respect to the "Effect of the Stockholm Games," this knowledge and the resulting introduction of reforms in the Olympic Movement are to be regarded as just as important as the example set by the staging of the event for future Olympic Games. The IOC and the international sport community are to be applauded for their will to change and the determination to implement the necessary (rule) changes. The fact that the 1912 Games were regarded as a classic example of an Olympic global multi-sports event by many contemporary pundits should be attributed primarily to the Swedish officials. Of all people, the patriotically motivated Stockholm organizers had shown the sporting world how impressive an international event could develop from de Coubertin's Initiative.[46]

The characterization of the Stockholm Games as a breakthrough for the Olympic Movement is therefore not just based on their role as an example. Rather, they must be viewed as the result of a complex interaction between aspects that can be described as both retrospective and future-oriented: The international sport community would always have pleasant memories of the successful 1912 Olympic Games.[47] Moreover, this event had an extremely powerful impact on the world of sports, i.e. in having to react to the demands of modern competitive sport and, as already dealt with at the 1914 Olympic Congress in Paris, to reorganize.

The complexity of these effects is a crucial factor in the Olympic Movement's survival of the life-threatening interruption by the First World War, to the extent that in 1920, less than two years after the end of the war, the Olympic Games were again up and running in Antwerp.

Notes

1. Coubertin's speech at the 1909 IOC Session in Berlin, published in Bergvall (ed.), *The Fifth Olympiad* (1913), p. 9 as well as Balck, "Olympic Congress in Berlin," *Ny Tidning för Idrott*, July 22, 1909.

2. Viktor Balck (1844–1928), IOC member from 1894 to 1920, president of the Stockholm Organizing Committee for the 1912 Olympic Games. The Officer Balck — characterized by the Swedish gymnastics system rejecting competitive sport and, apart from his military career, professionally employed at the Stockholm "Gymnastiska Centralinstitutet" (Central Gymnastic Institute) — progressed to become in the nineteenth century the most outstanding figure in the Swedish sports movement. Without denying his gymnastic roots, he had become increasingly dedicated to sport, to which as an ardent patriot and supporter of the Swedish national movement he attributed "patriotic" significance: Swedish gymnastics should continue to serve the maintenance of the health of mankind. The training of fearless energetic men for the good of the fatherland, however, should be part of the sporting "School of Life." Balck also regarded the participation of local athletes on the international competitive stage as patriotic; as the athletes should show Sweden to its best advantage by their success. Balck tirelessly promoted "his" sport movement for decades. With his fundamental patriotic conservative conviction, he gained the support of the Swedish upper class and the sport-loving royal family, thus contributing decisively to sport establishing an early foothold in Sweden.

3. Daniels, *The V & VI Olympiad — Stockholm 1912* (2000), p. 10.

4. Balck, *Viktor Balcks minnen II* (1931), pp. 156f.

5. Coubertin's idea that the IOC should be a self-constituted association whose members should represent the interests of the IOC in their home countries was not very popular at the beginning of the twentieth century. Contemporary sources indicate that the IOC members regarded themselves almost

exclusively as representatives of their home country within the IOC. Especially where the subject of "Sporting Geography" was concerned, this attitude became obvious.

6. With regard to the discussions and disputes about the content of the Olympic program and the conflicts resulting from the "Sporting Geography" at the Stockholm Games see also Molzberger, *Die Olympischen Spiele 1912 in Stockholm* (2010).

7. Letter from Coubertin to the Stockholm OC of 22 July 1912. Bergvall, 1913, p. 1104.

8. British Olympic Council (ed.), *Official Report of the Olympic Games of 1912 in Stockholm* (1912), p. 12.

9. Sullivan (ed.), *The Olympic Games Stockholm 1912* (1912), p. 9.

10. Anon., "Une Olympiade à vol d'oiseau," *Revue Olympique* (1912:8), pp. 115–119, here p. 116. 'La perfection des rouages organisateurs fut au-dessus de toute louange. Presque tous led détails avaient été prévus et toujours de la façon la plus simple et la plus pratique. Une extréme ingéniosité, un ordre et une méthode admirables présidaient au fonctionnement des bureaux. Un minimum de travailleurs donnant un maximum de travail, c'est un résultat que bien des gouvernements et des administrations publiques auraient pu venir étudier sur place. Un grand souffle de patriotisme animait chacun. 'Faire honneur à la Suède' était le mot d'ordre des consciences."

11. In the National Archives, where the records of the 1912 Olympic Games are kept, the correspondence concerning the international criticism of the Games and the Swedish reaction thereto runs to ca. 300 pages. National Archives, "Stockholmsolympiaden 1912," A I / A I:4.

12. The inclusion of unusual disciplines, such as the two-handed throwing events in athletics enforced vigorously by the Swedes was not a specific feature of the Stockholm Games. At the 1908 Olympics, less internationally practiced sports such as motorboat racing, jeu de paume and polo were included in the Olympic competition program thanks to the influence of the London OC.

13. Minutes of the 1912 IOC Session, pp. 43f. IOC Archive: "Sessions 1894–1985."

14. Within the framework of the Stockholm IOC session, at the meeting on 10 July 1912, protests by the IOC members Muzsa and von Venningen were lodged demanding the withdrawal of the disqualifications issued imposed in the Games on a Hungarian swimmer and the German 4 × 100m relay team. The IOC, however, regarded the disqualifications by the Swedish referees as decisions based on facts, and therefore they saw no reason to intervene. Minutes of the 1912 IOC Session, pp. 34ff. IOC Archive: "Sessions 1894–1985." Moreover, at the meeting of the Stockholm OC on 29th July 1912, Balck also reported a Russian criticism of points decisions in wrestling and equestrian events. The Stockholm OC decided not to react to the Russian criticisms as they were only submitted verbally. Minutes of the OC meeting of 29 July 1912, p. 2. National Archives, "Stockholmsolympiaden 1912," A I / A I:3.

15. The British NOC representatives, for example, looking back on their own experience made in 1908 in their own country, wrote full of understanding, "No question is more difficult than that of fair judging." British Olympic Council, 1912, p. 13.

16. Letter from Balck to Hellström of 19 March 1913. National Archives, "Stockholmsolympiaden 1912," A I / A I:4.

17. Ibid. Balck's fear of a negative impact on state sports promotion due to the international criticism proved to be groundless. The Swedish parliament voted in 1913 for the first time in favor of annual funding.

18. IOC Commission's report on the 1912 Olympics, pp. 11ff. National Archives, "Stockholmsolympiaden 1912," A I / A I:4.

19. Ibid., p. 17.

20. Von Venningen had introduced his report with the following words: "It is not my intention, neither is it the intention of the Commission, to cast a critical light on the Stockholm Games; I only wish to propose improvements for future events. [...] I express the hope and sincere wish that our Swedish friends will not feel embarrassed by my work. I consider it absolutely impossible to organize, manage and stage an Olympiad, in which many thousands of athletes of almost all nations compete, in such a way that no one would submit more or less justified complaints and criticism." Ibid., p. 1. Von Venningen also wrote that he was aware that, with the Berlin hosting of the 1916 Olympics in his native Germany, in the next IOC report of this kind he himself would be the focus of international criticism. This too might have been a motive for his carefully chosen introductory words.

21. Letter from Muzsa to Coubertin of 7 December 1912. IOC Archive: "Jeux Olympiques de Stockholm 1912," Box 2: "JO-1912S-CORR-PROGR," File 6: "JO-1912S-CORR, Corresp. génér. des JO de Stockholm 1912 (adressée à Coubertin), 1909–1924" / SD 5: "Corresp. génér. à Coubertin, Sept.–Déc. 1912."

22. Ibid.

23. Muzsa's criticism of the modern pentathlon also shows that even the IOC internally were lagging behind in terms of acceptance of the Coubertin's most favored discipline—although Muzsa had participated in the IOC sessions of 1910 and 1911, when the individual events for the modern pentathlon were discussed in detail and finally approved.

24. Letter from Låftman to the Stockholm OC of 15 April 1913. National Archives, "Stockholmsolympiaden 1912," A I / A I:4.

25. Addendum to the letter from Taube (President of the OC Sports Shooting subcommittee) to the Stockholm OC of 11 April 1913, p. 8. Ibid.

26. Letter from Helgesson to the Stockholm OC. Undated copy. Ibid. However, although the Swedish officials vehemently rejected the criticism of their handling of the competitions, they admitted in the official report on the 1912 Olympic Games published at the end of 1913 that the wrestling competitions were sometimes chaotic. At the same time, they expressed the hope that, as a result of the work done by the International Wrestling Federation founded in Stockholm in 1912, the wrestling would, in future, be subject to standard international rules. Bergvall, 1913, pp. 764f.

27. Anon., "La XVme Session du Comité International," *Revue Olympique* (1913:6), pp. 97–100, here p. 99. "Le Comité: ayant pris connaissance des documents émanant de la Commission désignée pour recueillir les observations et critiques formulées à l'occasion de la Vme Olympiade décide de laisser tomber toutes celles qui ne peuvent être utilisées pour l'avenir et de transmettre les autres au Comité de la VIme Olympiade afin qu'il en tienne compte dans la mesure du possible."

28. Count Clarence von Rosen (1867–1955), IOC member from 1900 to 1948, was one of the most outstanding personalities during the pioneering phase of sport in Sweden. Apart from tennis, rowing and various winter sport disciplines, Rosen was primarily concerned with equestrian sports. In this discipline, he celebrated his greatest successes and became a Swedish equestrian sport idol during the 1890s. As an official, however, von Rosen also made a name for himself in motorsport, bandy and football. As the first president of the *Svenska Fotbollförbundet* (Swedish Football Association) founded in 1904, von Rosen donated the trophy which was awarded as a challenge cup to the current football league winners until the year 2000. Research in recent years into the von Rosen family involvement in Swedish Nazi Organizations during the 1930s and '40s resulted in the *Svenska Fotbollförbundet* withdrawing the Cup donated by von Rosen. Both Clarence von Rosen himself and his brother Eric von Rosen (1879–1948) in particular, were declared by the latest research to be active supporters of Swedish National Socialism. See also Lööw, *Nazismen i Sverige 1924–1979* (2004), p. 18.

29. Anon., "La XVme Session du Comité International," *Revue Olympique* (1913:6), pp. 97–100, here p. 97.

30. Minutes of the OC meeting of 20 June 1913, p. 5. National Archives, "Stockholmsolympiaden 1912," A I / A I:3.

31. Minutes of the 1912 IOC Session, pp. 18ff. IOC Archive, "Sessions 1894–1985."

32. Ibid., p. 18.

33. Molzberger, 2010, pp. 104ff.

34. Johan Sigfrid Edström (1870–1964, usually called J. Sigfrid Edström or just Sigfrid Edström), IOC member from 1920 to 1952 and (commissary) IOC president from 1942/46 to 1952. Edström, who had studied and worked as an engineer at the end of the nineteenth century in Gothenburg, Zurich and Pittsburgh, made an early career in Sweden in the energy industry. As early as 1903, he became managing director of ASEA *(Allmänna Svenska Elektriska AB,* a company founded in 1883 in Västerås which merged in 1987 with the Swiss company *Brown Boveri* to form *ABB—Asea Brown Boveri Ltd.).* As a student, Edström had been a very fine track and field athlete and had set many national sprint records.

35. Edström, *Minnen ur mitt liv* (1959), p. 196.

36. Ibid., p. 197.

37. The internationally unclear rules for the handover in relay races, for example, had led to controversies at the 1912 Olympics; several disqualifications imposed on individual teams by the Swedish judges for alleged faulty baton changes met with disbelief by athletes and officials and had given rise to protests. Bergvall, 1913, pp. 374 f. Although critical of the first Swedish initiative, the U.S. official Sullivan welcomed the founding of the IAAF enthusiastically: "The delegates attending the conference represented sixteen nations, and their deliberations and suggestions form the basis of what will be eventually a universal code of laws to govern all athletic contests — not only Olympic Games, but also the smallest events

at the most remote points of the world." Minutes of the meeting of the IAAF 1913 foundation congress, p. 3. Private archive Karl Lennartz, "IAAF-Kongresse 1913–1952."

38. The German ambitions to introduce at the 1916 Olympics the *German Hexathlon*—a multi-discipline event consisting of three gymnastic and three track and field disciplines — to be performed within the framework of the Olympic gymnastics program, met in Paris with fierce opposition from Edström, who claimed the sole responsibility of the IAAF for the entire track and field athletic disciplines performed at the 1916 Olympics. However, out of consideration for the Berlin hosts, Edström ultimately gave in and the German special wish was granted. Müller, *Von Paris bis Baden-Baden* (1981), p. 81, as well as the minutes of the meeting of the 1914 IOC Congress, 21 June 1914, pp. 2 f., Private archive Karl Lennartz: "Olymp. Kongress Paris 1914."

39. In his memoirs, Coubertin wrote approvingly: "Edström demonstrated his usual dedication, his intelligent skill ... and a rock-hard authority." Coubertin: *Mémoires olympiques* (1931), p. 170.

40. After the death of Count Henri de Baillet Latour (1876–1942), Edström took over the management of the IOC and in 1946 he was elected president.

41. This doesn't apply to the Olympic Congress on "Psychology and Physiology of Sport," that took place from 7 to 11 May 1913 directly after the IOC Session in Lausanne, and which dealt, inter alia, with the question of the extent to which the increasingly occurring quest for records in sport posed a threat (in this respect the 1912 Olympics had also set new standards). Although they had attended the previous IOC session, like most IOC members, Balck and von Rosen had left the congress after the opening ceremony. Müller, 1981, pp. 65 ff. as well as Anon., "La XVme Session du Comité International," *Revue Olympique* (1913:6), pp. 97–100, here p. 97.

42. At the same time, the Swedish side again spoke out explicitly against the inclusion of boxing, all-in wrestling, skiing, ice skating, archery, golf and hockey in the Olympic program. The SOC proposal also advised against the admission of women in the fencing competition and a ladies doubles in lawn tennis. Swedish Olympic Committee (ed.), *Sveriges Olympiska Kommittés förslag till standardprogram för kommande Olympiska spel — utarbetadt af arbetsutskottet*, Stockholm 1914, pp. 1ff. National Archives: "Sveriges olympiska kommittés arkiv," F I / F I:2.

43. Sveriges Olympiska Kommitté (ed.), *Sveriges Olympiska Kommittés förslag till ny utslagsmetod vid täflingar i fotboll, vattenpolo, brottning, fäktning, Lawn Tennis o.d.*, Stockholm 1914. Ibid.

44. There were also protests in Paris against the negative consequences that came to light during the planning and staging of the 1912 Olympics of the allocating the right to participate, which on de Coubertin's insistence, was based on the "Sporting Geography": The German officials, already sharp critics of the rules in 1912, insisted on the withdrawal of the right of Bohemia and Finland to participate in the Olympics. Due to the sovereignty of Finland in 1917 and the dismantling of the Habsburg Dual Monarchy in the following year, the decision made at the 1914 Olympic Congress was invalidated after the end of World War II. Diem, *Die Olympischen Spiele 1912* (1990), pp. 8 ff, as well as Lennartz: *Der Einmarsch der Nationen — ein Symbol politischer Legitimation* (2002), p. 27.

45. The "Thorpe Affair" exposed in 1913, which had led to the subsequent disqualification of this outstanding athlete, also belongs to this category. In order to prevent future violations of the amateur paragraphs, at the 1914 Paris Olympic Congress the athletes' Olympic Oath was introduced, as an appeal to their sense of honor. Due to cancellation on account of the war of the 1916 Olympics, the oath celebrated its Olympic debut in 1920, when the Belgian fencer Victor Boin swore the oath on behalf of the participating field. Lyberg, *The IOC Sessions* (1989), p. 85.

46. Coubertin was deeply impressed by the staging of the 1912 Olympics. In his memoirs, he emphasized once again with respect to the 1920 Olympics, how important, in his opinion, the Stockholm Games had been for the development of the Olympic Movement. Coubertin, 1931, p. 159.

47. The good reputation that the Swedish officials had acquired with the 1912 Olympics led also to Stockholm's inclusion in discussions about the possible change of venue for the 1916 Olympics as a result of the First World War, probably proposed by the English. An SOC correspondent, for example, quotes Carl Diem, general secretary of the Organizing Committee for the (planned) Berlin Games, on the subject of the 1916 Olympics with the words: "From the press, we learned that the Swedish Olympic Committee has rejected England's request to move the 1916 Games from Berlin to Sweden. Although we cannot imagine in which form the English committee, if this report is true, intends to move the Games, we wish in any case to say thank you to our Swedish sporting friends for their sportsmanlike behavior." Correspondence between the SOC Executive Committee and the SOC, December 1914, National Archives, "Stockholmsolympiaden 1912," Ö I a / Ö I a: 2.

References

UNPUBLISHED SOURCES

Swedish National Archives: Stockholmsolympiaden 1912, Svenska Olympiska Kommittén 1905–2001
IOC-Archive (Lausanne, Switzerland): Jeux Olympiques de Stockholm 1912, Sessions 1894–1985
Private archive Karl Lennartz (St. Augustin, Germany): IAAF-Kongresse 1913–1952, Olymp. Kongress Paris 1914

PERIODICALS AND NEWSPAPERS

Revue Olympique
Ny Tidning för Idrott

PRINT SOURCES

Balck, Viktor. *Viktor Balcks minnen II — Mannaåren* (Stockholm 1931).
Bergvall, Erik (ed.). *The Fifth Olympiad: The Official Report of the Olympic Games of Stockholm 1912* (Stockholm 1913).
British Olympic Council (ed.): *Official Report of the Olympic Games of 1912 in Stockholm* (London 1912).
Coubertin, Pierre de. *Mémoires olympiques* (Lausanne 1931).
Daniels, George G. *The V & VI Olympiad — Stockholm 1912, Inter-Allied Games 1919* (Los Angeles 2000).
Diem, Carl. *Die Olympischen Spiele 1912*, reprint of the 1912 Berlin edition (Kassel 1990).
Edström, J. Sigfrid. *Minnen ur mitt liv* (Ystad 1959).
Lennartz, Karl. *Der Einmarsch der Nationen — ein Symbol politischer Legitimation,* Herausgegeben vom Carl und Liselott Diem-Archiv, Olympische Forschungsstätte der Deutschen Sporthochschule Köln (Cologne 2002).
Lööw, Helene. *Nazismen i Sverige 1924–1979: pionjärerna, partierna, propagandan* (Stockholm 2004).
Lyberg, Wolf. *The IOC Sessions, I: 1894–1955*, Typoscript (Lausanne 1989).
Molzberger, Ansgar. *Die Olympischen Spiele 1912 in Stockholm — "Vaterländische" Spiele als Durchbruch für die Olympische Bewegung*, Dissertation DSHS Köln (Cologne 2010).
Müller, Norbert. *Von Paris bis Baden-Baden, Die Olympischen Kongresse 1894–1981* (Niedernhausen 1981).
Sullivan, James E. (ed.). *The Olympic Games Stockholm 1912* (New York 1912).

The Results of the Competitions
The 1912 Olympic Games in Numbers
INGEMAR EKHOLM

Olympic Games are very much about results and records, and these interest many people. There are several different compilations of results from the Stockholm Olympics. The presentation below is an attempt to make a compilation of the results from the Stockholm Olympics based on two central sources: *The Fifth Olympiad. The Official Report of the Olympic Games of Stockholm 1912* (1913), with Erik Bergvall as the editor, referred to as OR, and Bill Mallon's and Ture Widlund's *The 1912 Olympic Games* (2009), called MW below. These sources are not in total agreement. When they report different results or a different order in the list of results, the information in OR has been used. The difference is reported in a comment after each event. In the individual events, the top six finishers have in most cases been included in the list of results as well as the best Swede/Swedes when they were not in the top six. In some events the best Swedes have been given after the table for reasons of space. Participants' first names have been taken from MW, as OR has only noted the first name initial in many events. The Swedish names are spelt in accordance with the signatures on the entry forms that have been found in the National Archives. Sven Lindhagen's *Olympiaboken*, Sven Hermelin's and Erik Peterson's *Den femte olympiaden 1912* and Sune Sylvén's and Ove Karlsson's *OS, Historia & statistik* have been used as supplementary sources.

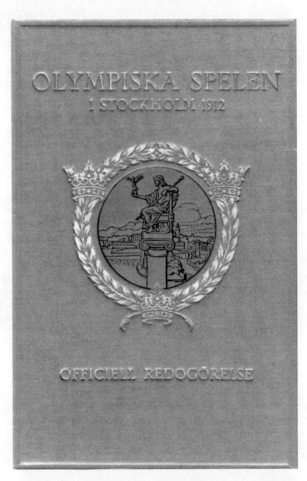

The Swedish edition of the official report of the Olympic Games in Stockholm 1912: *V. Olympiaden. Officiell redogörelse för olympiska spelen i Stockholm 1912.* It is 1,068 pages of facts about the Olympic organization, venues, rules and results (National Sports Museum).

Nations and Participants by Nation

The squads of the participating countries marched into Stadion, the Olympic Stadium, through Sofia Gate in alphabetical order (Swedish denominations) at the opening ceremony on July 6. The official account states that "the Olympic Stadium was full to the last place," but photos from the ceremony suggest that the Olympic Stadium was well-filled, but definitely not full.

Belgium (34 men, 1 woman)
Chile (14 men)
Denmark (151 men, 1 woman)
France (108 men, 1 woman)
USA (174 men)[1]
Greece (21 men)
Holland (33 men)
Italy (62 men)
Japan (2 men)
Luxembourg (21 men)
Norway (188 men, 2 women)
Portugal (6 men)
Russia (159 men)
Finland (162 men, 2 women)[2]
Switzerland (1 man)
Serbia (2 men)
Great Britain (261 men, 10 women)
Canada (36 men)[3]
Australia (22 men, 2 women)
New Zealand (3 men)
South Africa (21 men)
Germany (178 men, 5 women)
Austria (80 men, 6 women)
Bohemia (42 men)[4]
Hungary (123 men)
Sweden (421 men, 23 women)
Iceland (2 men)[5]
Turkey (2 men)[6]
Egypt[7]

1. USA marched in under the Swedish name, Förenta Staterna.
2. In 1912 Finland was a Grand Duchy under Russia. Finland came in under its own name at the same time as the Russian squad, but without a flag.
3. Canada, Australia, New Zealand and South Africa were a part of the British Empire in 1912 and marched in at the same time as Great Britain. Australia and New Zealand competed at the Olympics under the joint name of Australasia.
4. In 1912 Bohemia was a kingdom in name but part of the double monarchy of Austria-Hungary. The squad marched in under its own name and behind its own flag after the Austrian squad.
5. According to OR, Iceland did not have any participants while MW says two participants, but that they did not take part in the Parade of Nations.
6. OR says that Turkey had two participants taking part in the Parade of Nations. MW says that Turkey probably took part in the Parade of Nations, but without a flag bearer.
7. MW says that Egypt had one participant/flag bearer in the Parade, but he probably did not start in the competitions.

Number of Paying Spectators During the Olympic Games

The Olympic Stadium	226,636[1]
Rowing competitions	4,218
Football tournament	33,864
Fencing competitions	1,010
Swimming competitions	48,560
Tennis indoors	3,000
Tennis outdoors	10,000
Total	327,288[2]

1. The figure for the number of spectators at the Olympic Stadium includes multi-event passes, 106,818. There is no information about how many of these were used. The highest number of spectators at the Olympic Stadium was 18,713 on the afternoon of July 14 when the marathon was held. At the Olympic opening ceremony on July 6 there were 13,653 spectators. The Olympic Stadium could hold approximately 22,000 spectators.
2. Only multi-event passes were sold up until each day of competition. After that day tickets were also sold. The multi-event passes to the Olympic Stadium cost 50, 75, 100 and 200 Swedish kronor, to the Swimming Stadium 20, 30 and 50 kronor, to the fencing com-

petitions 10 kronor, to tennis and football 25 kronor. For the equestrian events at the Olympic Stadium the tickets cost 5, 10 and 20 kronor per day. The day tickets for the different arenas varied in price from 1 to 25 kronor.

1. Lists of Results

ATHLETICS

The rules for qualifying for the finals in athletics in 1912 and the number of finalists were different from today's rules. In some events only three men went to the final, for example. In those cases the lists of results in OR put the fourth best qualifying result in fourth place and so on. For the events below the 1912 rules have been given in brief. The competitions in athletics were held at the Olympic Stadium during the so-called Olympic week or Stadion week.

RUNNING

In the 100 meters, 200 meters and 110 meters hurdles six semi-final heats were held where only the winner in each heat went to the final. In the 400 meters there were five semi-finals and finalists.

100 Meters

1	Ralph Craig	USA	10.8
2	Alvah Meyer	USA	10.9[1]
3	Donald Lippincott	USA	10.9
4	Georg Patching	South Africa	11.0
5	Frank Belote	USA	11.0
	Howard Drew	USA	Did not start in the final

1. The times for the second to fifth places are estimates. The final was preceded by seven false starts. There was no rule for disqualification because of a false start.
Note: The Swedes Karl August "Charles" Luther, Knut "Knatten" Lindberg and Ivan Möller were knocked out in the semi-final while Rudolf Smedmark slowed down in his semi-final as he wrongly thought that it was a false start.

200 Meters

1	Ralph Craig	USA	21.7
2	Donald Lippincott	USA	21.8
3	William Applegarth	Great Britain	21.9[1]
4	Richard Rau	Germany	22.2
5	Charles Reidpath	USA	22.3
6	Donnell Young	USA	22.3

1. The times for the third to sixth places are estimates.
Note: The Swedes Ture Person, Skotte Jacobsson, Ivan Möller, Karl August "Charles" Luther and Knut "Knatten" Lindberg were all knocked out in the semi-final.

110 Meters Hurdles

1	Frederick Kelly	USA	15.1
2	James Wendell	USA	15.2
3	Martin Hawkins	USA	15.3
4	John Case	USA	15.3[1]
5	Kenneth Powell	Great Britain	15.5
6	John Nicholson	USA	Fell in the final

1. The times for the fourth and fifth places are estimates.
Note: Eleven Swedes were entered according to entry forms at the NA, but none started.

400 Meters

1	Charles Reidpath	USA	48.2[1]
2	Hanns Braun	Germany	48.3[2]
3	Edward Lindberg	USA	48.4
4	James Meredith	USA	49.2
5	Carroll Haff	USA	49.5

1. Olympic record.
2. In the heats and semi-finals the 400 meters was run without separate lanes. After an incident in one of the semi-finals separate lanes were introduced for the final. Braun came second in his semi-final heat but went to the final when the American, Young, was disqualified for pushing.
    Note: The Swedes Eric Lindholm, Knut Stenborg and Paul Zerling were knocked out in the semi-final.

In the middle distance events different ways of qualifying for the final were used. In the 800 meters two semi-finals were held where the best four in each race went to the final, while in the 1,500 meters seven heats were held, where the best two in each race went to the final.

800 Meters

1	James Meredith	USA	1:51.9[1]
2	Melvin Sheppard	USA	1:52.0[2]
3	Ira Davenport	USA	1:52.0
4	Hanns Braun	Germany	1:52.2[3]
5	David Caldwell	USA	1:52.3
6	Clarence Edmundson	USA	
7	Melville Brock	Canada	
	Evert Björn	Sweden	Knocked out in semi-final

1. World record.
2. Sheppard was a hand's breadth ahead of Davenport at the finish.
3. The order at the finish for places 4–7 has been later questioned by several sources. Possible order is Caldwell, Brock, Braun and Edmundson.

1,500 Meters

1	Arnold Jackson	Great Britain	3:56.8[1]
2	Abel Kiviat	USA	3:56.9[2]
3	Norman Taber	USA	3:56.9
4	John Paul Jones	USA	3:57.2
5	Ernst Wide	Sweden	3:57.6
6	Philip Baker	Great Britain	4:01.0[3]

1. Olympic record.
2. The order between Kiviat and Taber was decided by means of a photo finish camera. This was the only race in the Olympic Games to be decided in this manner.
3. The time is an estimate.

In the longer distances heats were used: five for the 5,000 meters, where the best three in each race went to the final, and three for the 10,000 meters, with the best five to the final.

5,000 Meters

1	Hannes Kolehmainen	Finland	14:36.6[1]
2	Jean Bouin	France	14:36.7
3	George Hutson	Great Britain	15:07.6
4	George Bonhag	USA	15:09.8[2]
5	Tell Berna	USA	15:10.0
6	Mauritz "Sörle" Carlsson	Sweden	15:18.6[3]

1. World record and the first 5,000 meters race ever under 15 minutes.

2. The times for places 4–6 are estimates.

3. Some sources give Alex Decoteau, Canada, in sixth place and Mauritz Carlsson in seventh place.

10,000 Meters

1	Hannes Kolehmainen	Finland	31:20.8[1]
2	Lewis Tewanima	USA	32:06.6
3	Albin Stenroos	Finland	32:21.8
4	Joseph Keeper	Canada	32:36.2
5	Alfonso Orlando	Italy	33:31.2
	Mauritz "Sörle" Carlsson	Sweden	Did not finish

1. Olympic record. Noted by the IAAF as the first world record time for the 10,000 meters in 1913. The Frenchman Bouin had already recorded 30:58.8 in 1911 but the time was not approved as a world record until 1926 by the IAAF.

Note: Eleven of fifteen qualified runners started in the final, but only five finished.

The marathon, which was 40,200 meters long, started and finished at the Olympic Stadium, turned back in Sollentuna, north of Stockholm, nearby Sollentuna church and had checkpoints at Stocksund, 5 km from the Olympic Stadium and Tureberg, 15 km from the Olympic Stadium. Today there is a monument set up in memory of the race near the turning point in Sollentuna. The marathon was run in sunshine and great heat (approx. 30 degrees Celsius). Only 34 out of 69 starters finished. The Portuguese Francisco Lazaro collapsed after approximately 30 km and died the morning after the race. "The Japanese who disappeared"—Shizo Kanakuri—dropped out after approximately 20 kilometers. Despite his "disappearance" he took part in the marathon races in the Games in both 1920 and 1924.

Program for July 14 at the Olympic Stadium, the day of the marathon race (National Sports Museum).

Spectators tensely follow how the results from the marathon race are put up outside the NK department store at Stureplan in central Stockholm, July 14, 1912 (photograph by Axel Malmström, SCIF photo collection).

Marathon

1	Kennedy McArthur	South Africa	2:36:54.8
2	Christopher Gitsham	South Africa	2:37:52.0
3	Gaston Strobino	USA	2:38:42.4
4	Andrew Sockalexis	USA	2:42:07.9
5	James Duffy	Canada	2:42:18.8
6	Sigfrid "Sigge" Jacobsson	Sweden	2:43:24.9

The 8,000 meters cross country race had a very hilly course, was unknown to the runners and was marked by red tape just before the start. Start, one lap and finish at the Olympic Stadium. The course went north of the Olympic Stadium by road and cross country. The runners' times imply that the race was considerably longer than 8,000 meters, probably closer to 12,000 meters.

Cross Country Race 8,000 Meters

1	Hannes Kolehmainen	Finland	45:11.6
2	Hjalmar Andersson	Sweden	45:44.8
3	John Eke	Sweden	46:37.6
4	Jalmari Eskola	Finland	46:54.8
5	Josef Ternström	Sweden	47:07.1[1]
6	Albin Stenroos	Finland	47:23.4

1. The time 47:07.6 is also given.
Note: Only 28 out of 45 starters finished.

There were two types of team competitions in the running events, relays over 400 (4 × 100) meters and 1,600 (4 × 400) meters, and a team race over 3,000 meters where there were five men in the team and the placing of the first three gave team points. All the teams in the team race started at the same time. There were three heats in all three events and only the winner went to the final. There was also a team competition in the 8,000 meters cross country, where the total figure for the placings of the first three from each nation in the individual race gave the team points.

Relay, 400 Meters

1	Great Britain	42.4[1]
2	Sweden	42.6[2]
	Germany	Disqualified[3]

1. David Jacobs, Henry Macintosh, Victor d'Arcy and William Applegarth ran in Great Britain's team.
2. Sweden finished third but Germany was disqualified due to an illegal baton change. Ivan Möller, Karl August "Charles" Luther, Ture Person and Knut "Knatten" Lindberg ran for Sweden.
3. Germany set a world record in the semi-final of 42.3.

Relay, 1,600 Meters

1	USA	3:16.6[1]
2	France	3:20.7
3	Great Britain	3:23.2

1. Melvin Sheppard, Edward Lindberg, James Meredith and Charles Reidpath were in the USA team. The time was a world record.
Note: Sweden (Paul Zerling, John Dahlin, Eric Lindholm and Knut Stenborg) knocked out as second in their semi-final heat.

Team Race, 3,000 Meters

1	USA	9 points[1]
2	Sweden	13 points[2]
3	Great Britain	23 points[3]

1. The three Americans who took points were Tell Berna (1st), Norman Taber (3rd) and Georg Bonhag (5th).
2. Thorild Olsson (2nd), Ernst Wide (4th), Bror Fock (7th), John Zander (10th) and Nils Frykberg (11th) ran for Sweden.
3. Great Britain was the only team in its heat, finished and went to the final.
Note: Finland knocked out in the semi-final but the individual time of 8:36.9 for Hannes Kolehmainen was a new world record.

Cross Country Race, 8,000 Meters — Team Competition

1	Sweden	10 points[1]
2	Finland	11 points[2]
3	Great Britain	49 points
4	Norway	61 points
5	Denmark	63 points
6	USA	Did not finish[3]

1. Sweden's team points were taken by Hjalmar Andersson (2nd), John Eke (3rd) and Josef Ternström (5th).
2. Finland's points were taken by Hannes Kolehmainen (1st), Jalmari Eskola (4th) and Albin Stenroos (6th).
3. Only two of the five American runners finished. Only 28 out of a total of 45 starters finished the 8,000 meters cross country.

10,000 Meters Walk (Two Heats, with the Best Five from Each Heat to the Final)

1	George Goulding	Canada	46:28.4[1]
2	Ernest Webb	Great Britain	46:50.4
3	Fernando Altimani	Italy	47:37.6
4	Aage Rasmussen	Denmark	48:00.0[2]

1. Olympic record.
2. Four competitors finished. Of the others in the final, three dropped out and three were disqualified.
Note: First time the event was in the Olympic program. The whole race was held in the Olympic Stadium. No Swedes participated.

JUMPING

High Jump (Qualifying Height 183 cm, Three Qualifying Groups)

1	Alma Richards	USA	1.93[1]
2	Hans Liesche	Germany	1.91
3	George Horine	USA	1.89
4	Egon Erickson	USA	1.87[2]
4	James "Jim" Thorpe	USA	1.87[3]
6	Harry Grumpelt	USA	1.85
6	John Johnstone	USA	1.85
8	Karl-Axel Kullerstrand	Sweden	1.83

1. Olympic record.
2. For jumpers with the same height the rules prescribed a jump-off only to decide medals.
3. Disqualified for a breach of the amateur rules in 1913. The IOC restored Thorpe's amateur status in 1982. The official account was published in 1913 and, contrary to the pentathlon and decathlon, Thorpe is still in the results list for the high jump.

Standing High Jump (Qualifying Height 150 cm, One Qualifying Group)

1	Platt Adams	USA	1.63
2	Ben Adams	USA	1.60
3	Konstantinos Tsiclitiras	Greece	1.55
4	Edvin Möller	Sweden	1.50[1]
4	Leslie Byrd	USA	1.50
4	Leo Goehring	USA	1.50

1. For jumpers with the same height the rules prescribed a jump-off only to decide medals.
Note: Last time the event was in the Olympic program. Platt and Ben Adams were brothers.

In the long jump, standing long jump and triple jump, only the three best jumpers, irrespective of which qualifying group they had jumped in, went to the final. The finalists took their qualifying results to the final.

Long Jump (Three Qualifying Groups)

1	Albert Gutterson	USA	7.60[1]
2	Calvin Bricker	Canada	7.21
3	Georg Åberg	Sweden	7.18[2]
4	Harry Worthington	USA	7.03
5	Eugene Mercer	USA	6.97
6	Fred Allen	USA	6.94

1. Olympic record, set in the qualifying round.
2. In the final only Åberg improved his result from the qualifying round.

Standing Long Jump (Four Qualifying Groups)

1	Konstantinos Tsiclitiras	Greece	3.37
2	Platt Adams	USA	3.36
3	Ben Adams	USA	3.28
4	Gustaf Malmsten	Sweden	3.20
5	Edvin Möller	Sweden	3.14
5	Leo Goehring	USA	3.14

Note: The last time the event was in the Olympic program.

Pole Vault (Qualifying Height 365 cm, Two Qualifying Groups)

1	Harold Babcock	USA	3.95[1]
2	Frank Nelson	USA	3.85[2]
2	Marc Wright	USA	3.85
3	Bertil Uggla	Sweden	3.80
3	William Happenny	Canada	3.80[3]
3	Frank Murphy	USA	3.80

1. Olympic record.
2. There was a jump-off rule if two people had the same height but it does not seem to have been used. In the results list two competitors are recorded as second and three as third.
3. Dropped out after having broken two ribs when landing after having cleared 3.80.

Triple Jump (Three Qualifying Groups)

1	Gustav "Topsy" Linblom	Sweden	14.76[1]
2	Georg Åberg	Sweden	14.51
3	Erik Almlöf	Sweden	14.17
4	Erling Vinne	Norway	14.14
5	Platt Adams	USA	14.09
6	Edvard Larsen	Norway	14.06

1. The three finalists/medalists all did their best jump in the qualifying round.

THROWING

In the throwing events of discus, shot put and javelin in the 1912 Stockholm Olympics there were best-hand competitions and competitions with both the right and left hand, combined. In the two-hand events the competitors first threw several rounds with their right hand and then several rounds with their left hand. The longest right-hand and left-hand throws combined, irrespective of which round they were achieved in, constituted the total result. The three best throwers overall, irrespective of which qualifying group they had thrown in, went to the final. The finalists took their qualifying results to the final and this also applied to the hammer.

Discus Throw, Best Hand (Five Qualifying Groups)

1	Armas Taipale	Finland	45.21[1]
2	Leslie Byrd	USA	42.32
3	James Duncan	USA	42.28
4	Elmer Niklander	Finland	42.09
5	Hans Tronner	Austria	41.24
6	Arlie Mucks	USA	40.93
8	Emil Magnusson	Sweden	39.91

1. Olympic record.

Discus Throw, Both Hands (Three Qualifying Groups)

1	Armas Taipale	Finland	82.86 (44.68 + 38.18)[1]
2	Elmer Niklander	Finland	77.96 (40.28 + 37.68)
3	Emil Magnusson	Sweden	77.37 (40.58 + 36.79)
4	Einar Nilsson	Sweden	71.40 (40.99 + 30.41)
5	James Duncan	USA	71.13 (39.78 + 31.35)
6	Emil Muller	USA	69.56 (39.83 + 29.73)

1. Olympic record.
Note: The only time the event has been in the Olympic program.

Shot Put, Best Hand (Three Qualifying Groups)

1	Patrick McDonald	USA	15.34[1]
2	Ralph Rose	USA	15.25
3	Lawrence Whitney	USA	13.93
4	Elmer Niklander	Finland	13.65
5	George Philbrook	USA	13.13
6	Imre Mudin	Hungary	12.81
7	Einar Nilsson	Sweden	12.62

1. Olympic record.

Shot Put, Both Hands (Two Qualifying Groups)

1	Ralph Rose	USA	27.70 (15.23 + 12.47)[1]
2	Patrick McDonald	USA	27.53 (15.08 + 12.45)
3	Elmer Niklander	Finland	27.14 (14.71 + 12.43)
4	Lawrence Whitney	USA	24.09 (13.48 + 10.61)
5	Einar Nilsson	Sweden	23.37 (12.52 + 10.85)
6	Paavo Aho	Finland	23.30 (12.72 + 10.58)

1. Olympic record.
Note: The only time the event has been in the Olympic program.

Hammer Throw (Two Qualifying Groups)

1	Matthew McGrath	USA	54.74[1]
2	Duncan Gillis	Canada	48.39
3	Clarence Childs	USA	48.17[2]
4	Robert Olsson	Sweden	46.50[3]
5	Carl Johan Lind	Sweden	45.61
6	Denis Carey	Great Britain	43.78

1. Olympic record.
2. Childs overstepped the mark in all his throws in the final.
3. Robert Olsson was the Swedish flag bearer at the Olympic opening ceremony.

Javelin Throw, Best Hand (Four Qualifying Groups)

1	Eric Lemming	Sweden	60.64[1]
2	Juho Saaristo	Finland	58.66
3	Móric Kóczán-Kovács	Hungary	55.50
4	Juho Halme	Finland	54.65
5	Väinö Siikaniemi	Finland	52.43
6	Rickard Åbrink	Sweden	52.20

1. Olympic record.

Javelin Throw, Both Hands (Three Qualifying Groups)

1	Juho Saaristo	Finland	109.42 (61.00 + 48.42)[1]
2	Väinö Siikaniemi	Finland	101.13 (54.09 + 47.04)
3	Urho Peltonen	Finland	100.24 (53.58 + 46.66)
4	Eric Lemming	Sweden	98.59 (58.33 + 40.26)
5	Arne Halse	Norway	96.92 (55.05 + 41.87)
6	Rickard Åbrink	Sweden	93.12 (50.04 + 43.08)

1. Olympic record combined, but Saaristo's best right-hand throw was also an Olympic record.
Note: Only time the event has been in the Olympic program. When the Finns discovered that only their countrymen had gone to the final, they requested that they refrain from further throwing and that the qualifying results should be counted as the final results. This request was approved by the organizers.

MULTI-EVENTS

In the pentathlon, which was a one-day competition, the events were the long jump, javelin, 200 meters, discus and 1,500 meters. One point to the winner in each event, two points to the person who came second, and so on. The best twelve after the 200 meters went on to the fourth event, discus, and the best six (in fact, seven) after the discus went on to the final event, 1,500 meters.

The decathlon, which was in the Olympic program for the first time in 1912, was decided over three days and the order of events was: 100 meters, long jump, shot put (day 1); high jump, 400 meters, discus, 110 meters hurdles (day 2); pole vault, javelin, 1,500 meters (day 3). A special points table for the decathlon had been worked out before the Games.

Pentathlon

1	James "Jim" Thorpe	USA	7 points[1]
2	Ferdinand Bie	Norway	21 points
3	James Donahue	USA	29 points[2]
4	Frank Lukeman	Canada	29 points
5	Austin Menaul	USA	30 points
6	Avery Brundage	USA	31 points[3]
7	Hugo Wieslander	Sweden	32 points

1. James Thorpe, who won both the pentathlon and the decathlon at the 1912 Olympic Games, was disqualified in 1913 for breaching the amateur rules. He had played professional baseball. Thorpe had to return his medals and Olympic challenge trophies, which went to those finishing second, Bie and Wieslander. In 1982 he was posthumously restored as an amateur by the IOC and he regained his placings, but only as joint winner with Bie and Wieslander! The above is the results list current at the closing of the Olympic Games in 1912. In OR, which was published in 1913, Thorpe is not included in the results list.

2. Donahue and Lukeman were separated in the results list by recalculating their results according to the decathlon table.

3. Later President of the IOC 1952–1972 and an uncompromising advocate of keeping the concept of amateur in the Olympic Games.

Decathlon

1	James "Jim" Thorpe	USA	8,412 points[1]
2	Hugo Wieslander	Sweden	7,724 points
3	Charles Lomberg	Sweden	7,413 points
4	Gustaf "Gösse" Holmér	Sweden	7,347 points
5	James Donahue	USA	7,083 points
6	Eugene Mercer	USA	7,074 points

1. World record. Regarding Thorpe's disqualification and later restored amateur status, see the pentathlon. The above is the results list current at the closing of the Olympic Games in 1912.

CYCLING

The cycle road race was decided around Lake Mälaren, starting just south of Liljeholm Bridge in Stockholm, and with checkpoints at Södertälje, Läggesta, Strängnäs, Eskilstuna, Kungsör, Köping, Kolbäck, Västerås, Enköping, Bålsta and Järva, and finishing at Valhallavägen just before the Olympic Stadium's marathon entrance. The course was approximately 315.3 km. "Reserve machines" could be deposited at the checkpoints, where the "competitors could receive free food and refreshments" as well. In all 123 cyclists started at intervals of two minutes from two o' clock in the morning, the earliest starting time ever in an Olympic Games. In the team competition the times for the four best cyclists per nation in the individual race were counted.

Road Race — Individual

1	Rudolph Lewis	South Africa	10:42:39.0
2	Frederick Grubb	England	10:51:24.2[1]
3	Carl Schutte	USA	10:52:38.8
4	Leon Meredith	England	11:00:02.6
5	Frank Brown	Canada	11:01:00.0
6	Antti Raita	Finland	11:02:20.3
7	Erik Friborg	Sweden	11:04:17.0
	Karl Landsberg	Sweden	Did not finish[2]

1. In cycling, unlike other sports in the 1912 Olympics, competitors from England, Scotland and Ireland were allowed to start for these nations instead of for Great Britain. This was due to a misunderstanding in the cycling committee. Nevertheless, OR lists Great Britain as a nation in the individual race.

2. Landsberg collided a few hundred meters after the start with a "taxi cab, thus wrecking his machine." The taxi cab took him back to the start for further transportation to a hospital, from which he was discharged a few days later.

Road Race — Team Competition

1	Sweden	44:35:33.6[1]
2	England	44:44:39.2[2]
3	USA	44:47:55.5
4	Scotland	46:29:55.6
5	Finland	46:34:03.5
6	Germany	46:35:16.1

1. Sweden's team: Erik Friborg (7th), Ragnar Malm (8th), Axel "A.W" Persson (9th) and Algot Lönn (10th).

2. MW gives England's time as 44:44:39.6 as there is varying information about one of the Englishman's times. Regarding participating nations, see the individual competition.

EQUESTRIAN EVENTS

The 1912 Stockholm Olympic Games were the first time that equestrian events were in the Olympic program. Initially the Committee wanted to give money prizes to the participants because of the heavy expenses involved. As money prizes were not allowed to be awarded and to get nations interested in taking part despite this, the organizers managed to get a number of emperors and monarchs to give challenge trophies to the Games. There were money prizes, given by the Nobel brothers, at the Swedish qualifying competitions, but these were not paid until the Games were over. The rules stated that "only gentlemen riders may take part in the competitions; professionals are not allowed," which in practice meant that only officers took part in the equestrian events.

The Military riding event consisted of five disciplines in the following order: an endurance phase consisting of 50 km on the roads and 5 km cross country, in all 55 km. Start and finish at Fältrittklubben (Stockholm Cross Country Riding Club), just north-east of the Olympic Stadium, and the course went via Stocksund, Danderyd, Täby, Vallentuna, Sollentuna, Solna and Haga. Then a 3,500 meters steeplechase at Lindarängen racecourse, 3 km east of the Olympic Stadium, a jumping test over 15 jumps and a double bridle dressage test at the Olympic Stadium. Maximum of four participants per nation. The competition lasted four days.

The dressage competition consisted of a fixed dressage program, jumping over five fences and a test of obedience where a colored cylinder was rolled towards the horse. Maximum of six participants per nation. Seven judges, where the sum of their placing figures for each rider gave the number of points. The competition took place at Fälrittklubben's course near the Olympic Stadium.

The show jumping competition was held at the Olympic Stadium. Maximum of six participants per nation, 15 jumps, where four jumps were done twice and the length of the course was 1,533 meters.

Military Riding Event — Individual

1	Axel Nordlander	Sweden	46.59 points. Lady Artist
2	Friedrich von Rochow	Germany	46.42 points. Idealist
3	Jean Cariou	France	46.32 points. Cocotte
4	Nils Adlercreutz	Sweden	46.31 points. Atout
5	Ernst Casparsson	Sweden	46.16 points. Irmelin
5	Rudolf von Schaesberg-Tannheim	Germany	46.16 points. Grundsee

Note: Max. points 50. There was no challenge trophy awarded in the individual military riding event.

Military Riding Event — Team Competition

1	Sweden	139.06 points[1]
2	Germany	138.48 points
3	USA	137.33 points
4	France	136.77 points

1. Four-man teams and the total points for the best three in the individual competition were counted as the team result. The Swedish team comprised Axel Nordlander, Nils Adlercreutz, Ernst Casparsson and Henric Horn af Åminne, who came ninth in the individual competition with the horse Omen, with 45.85 points. The Swedish team was awarded the Emperor of Germany's challenge trophy.

Note: Only four out of seven teams starting had three riders who completed all five disciplines in the competition.

Dressage

1	Carl Bonde	Sweden	15 points. Emperor[1]
2	Gustaf Adolf Boltenstern Sr.	Sweden	21 points. Neptun
3	Hans von Blixen-Finecke Sr.	Sweden	32 points. Maggie
4	Friedrich von Osterley	Germany	36 points. Condor
5	Carl Rosenblad	Sweden	43 points. Miss Hastings
6	Oscar af Ström	Sweden	47 points. Irish Lass

1. Bonde was awarded the Emperor of Austria's challenge trophy.

Show Jumping — Individual

1	Jean Cariou	France	186 points. Mignon[1]
2	Rabod Wilhelm von Kröcher	Germany	186 points. Dohna
3	Emanuel de Blommaert de Soye	Belgium	185 points. Clonmore
4	Herbert Scott	Great Britain	184 points. Shamrock
5	Sigismund Freyer	Germany	183 points. Ultimus
6	Vilhelm von Hohenau	Germany	181 points. Pretty Girl[2]
6	Ernst Casparsson	Sweden	181 points. Kiriki
6	Nils Adlercreutz	Sweden	181 points. Ilex

1. Max. points 190 and time limit 3 min 50 sec. In the jump-off over six jumps between Cariou and von Kröcher for the gold medal the former had five faults and the latter seven. Cariou was awarded the Hungarian Count Andrassy's challenge trophy.

2. According to the rules there should be a jump-off in the event of equal points. There was no jump-off and the results list gives three riders in sixth place. The rules probably only required a jump-off to decide medals.

Show Jumping — Team Competition

1	Sweden	545 points[1]
2	France	538 points
3	Germany	530 points
4	USA	527 points
5	Russia	520 points
6	Belgium	510 points

1. The team competition was held as a competition of its own. It was held at the Olympic Stadium the day after the individual jumping. Four-man teams where the points for the best three gave team points. Same course and time limit as in the individual competition. The team max. points were 570. The Swedish team comprised Carl Gustaf Lewenhaupt 188 p Medusa, Gustaf Kilman 180 p Gåtan, Hans von Rosen 177 p Lord Iron and Fredrik Rosencrantz 171 p Drabant. The Swedish team was awarded the King of Italy's challenge trophy.

FENCING

The rules for fencing at the Stockholm Olympic Games were comprehensive. Before the Games the fencing committee had intensive correspondence with the competing nations about the rules. Finally there remained discussions with Italy, who wanted to lengthen the blade of the epée from 90 to 94 cm, and France, who wanted the upper arms to be part of the target area in foil. The rejection of these wishes in both cases led to the two countries not taking part in the respective fencing event. France announced two days before the start of the competitions that they would not take part in fencing at the Games at all. The fencing competitions took place on four pistes in the Tennis Pavilion at Östermalms IP (Östermalm Athletic Grounds) and there was room for 400 spectators.

In the individual competitions eight fencers went on to the final round. In the team competitions four teams went on to the final. In each team match, which consisted of 16 matches, four fencers from each nation took part. Each individual match in the team competition was decided by the first to score three hits.

Foil — Individual

1	Nedo Nadi	Italy	7 wins 0 defeats
2	Pietro Speciale	Italy	5–2
3	Richard Verderber	Austria	4–3[1]
4	Lázló Berti	Hungary	4–3
5	Edoardo Alajmo	Italy	4–3
6	Edgar Seligman	Great Britain	3–4

1. If the number of wins was the same, the placing was decided by the number of hits received. Verdeber and Berti had both received 25 hits and fenced again, where the first hit decided. Alajmo had received 26 hits.

Note: The best Swedes were Axel Jöhncke and Carl Hjorth, who were both knocked out in round two of the three before the final round.

Epée — Team Competition

1	Belgium	3 wins 0 defeats[1]
2	Great Britain	1–2[2]
3	Holland	1–2
4	Sweden	1–2[3]

1. Belgium's team was made up of Gaston Salmon, Henri Anspach, Jacques Ochs, Paul Anspach, Robert Henner and Victor Willems.
2. According to the rules there would be a new deciding match if two teams had the same number of wins, but because of lack of time it was agreed before the start of the competition that the least number of hits received during the final would decide the order and here the number of hits was 28, 30 and 32.
3. Einar Sörensen, Eric Carlberg, Georg Branting, Gustaf Lindblom, Louise Sparre and Pontus von Rosen fenced in the Swedish team. Carl-Gustaf Krokstedt, Erik de Laval and Henry Peyron were also entered but did not take part in any team match.

Epée — Individual

1	Paul Anspach	Belgium	6 wins 1 defeat
2	Ivan Osiier	Denmark	5–2
3	Philippe Le Hardy de Beaulieu	Belgium	4–2[1]
4	Victor Boin	Belgium	4–2
5	Einar Sörensen	Sweden	3–4
6	Edgar Seligman	Great Britain	2–4

1. If the number of wins was the same, the order was decided by the least number of hits received. There is no information about this number in OR.

Sabre — Team Competition

1	Hungary	3 wins 0 defeats[1]
2	Austria	2–1
3	Holland	1–2
4	Bohemia	0–3

1. Hungary's team: Jenö Fuchs, Zoltán Schenker, Lázló Berti, Ervin Mészáros, Péter Tóth, Lajos Werkner, Oszkár Gerde and Dezsö Földes.
Note: Sweden's team withdrew from the competition after a 9–1 defeat against Great Britain in the first round and never fenced against the third team in the group, Germany. The team consisted of Axel Jöhncke, Helge Werner, Birger Personne and Carl-Gustaf Klerck. Gustaf Armgarth, Nils Brambeck and Martin Nordenström were also entered for the team but did not take part.

Sabre — Individual

1	Jenö Fuchs	Hungary	6 wins 1 defeat
2	Béla Békessy	Hungary	5–2[1]
3	Ervin Mészáros	Hungary	5–2
4	Zoltán Schenker	Hungary	4–3
5	Nedo Nadi	Italy	4–3
6	Péter Tóth	Hungary	2–5
	Birger Personne	Sweden	Knocked out in semi-final

1. If the number of wins was the same, the order was decided by the least number of hits received. For places 2–5 the number of hits received was 11, 12, 13 and 17 respectively.

FOOTBALL

The Organizing Committee was hesitant about including football in the Olympic program, but because of the popularity of the sport and inquiries from abroad it was decided in October 1910 to include football. FIFA's (Fédération Internationale de Football Association) rules applied. Great Britain was entitled to take part with four national teams but at FIFA's request only one was entered — England. Bohemia, who took part in the Olympic Games but was not a member of FIFA, was not allowed to take part in football. The venues were the Olympic Stadium, Råsunda IP (where the national stadium for Swedish football was built in 1937) and Tranebergs IP. The dimensions of the football pitches were to be 65 × 108.5 meters according to the invitation, but as the Olympic Stadium's pitch was only 105 meters long, all the countries had to undertake in writing not to protest about this afterwards. Each country was to have entered 11 men in the team plus 22 reserves by the end of the entry period on May 29.

Eleven nations in all took part in the tournament, which was decided as a cup. The seven teams who were knocked out in the first two rounds of the main tournament were given the opportunity of going on to play in a consolation competition.

Football — The Main Tournament

1	England[1]
2	Denmark
3	Holland[2]
4	Finland

1. England won the final at the Olympic Stadium 4–2. The gold medalists were Ronald Brebner, Thomas Burn, Arthur Knight, Douglas McWhirter, Henry Littlewort, Joseph Dines, Arthur Berry, Vivian Woodward (captain), Harold Walden, Gordon Hoare, Ivor Sharpe, Edward Hanney, Edward Wright and Harold Stamper. The last three did not take part in the final.
2. Holland beat Finland in the bronze medal match 9–0 at Råsunda IP.

Football — The Consolation Competition

1	Hungary[1]
2	Austria
3	Germany[2]
3	Italy
5	Russia
5	Norway
5	Sweden[3]

1. Hungary won the final against Austria 3–0 at Råsunda IP.
2. There was no match for third prize in the consolation competition.
3. Sweden was knocked out at the Olympic Stadium in the first round of the main tournament by Holland, 4–3 after extra time and lost in the consolation competition's first round 1–0 against Italy at Råsunda IP. Sweden was represented in the two Olympic football matches by Karl Ansén AIK, Helge "Ekis" Ekroth AIK (against Holland), Erik Börjesson IFK Göteborg, Ivar Svensson IFK Norrköping, Herman Myrberg Örgryte IS (captain), Karl "Köping" Gustafsson Köpings IS, Gustaf Sandberg Örgryte IS (Holland), Ragnar Wicksell Djurgårdens IF, Jacob Lewin Örgryte IS (Holland), Erik Bergström Örgryte IS, Josef Börjesson Göteborgs FF (goalkeeper), Erik Dahlström IFK Eskilstuna (Italy), Götrik Frykman Djurgårdens IF (Italy) and Konrad Törnqvist IFK Göteborg (Italy).

GYMNASTICS

At the time of the Stockholm Olympic Games in 1912 there were different schools in Europe with regard to gymnastics, for example Ling gymnastics in Sweden and Turnen gymnastics in Germany. At the IOC session in 1910 in Luxembourg the Swedish Organizing Committee put forward the proposal that only displays should be held. The IOC, however, spoke out in favor of competitions, and the Committee took note of this. Team competitions were therefore organized in three different kinds of gymnastics as well as an individual competition and displays. The competitions and the displays were held on the Olympic Stadium's infield, where a lot of gymnastic apparatus was set up. Teams could be between 16 and 40 strong in the team competitions and the maximum time was 1 hour including entry and departure.

Team Competition 1 — Swedish System

1	Sweden	937.46 points
2	Denmark	898.84 points
3	Norway	857.21 points

Note: Five judges and maximum points per nation 1,035 points. Only three nations took part. Four judges had Sweden as first but the Danish judge gave his vote to Denmark. The Swedish team consisted of 24 men and the flag bearer Karl Erik Ekblad. The team leader was Ebbe Lieberath. Denmark had 28 men in its team while Norway's team consisted of 22 men.

Team Competition 2 — According to Special Rules

1	Italy	53.15 points
2	Hungary	45.45 points
3	Great Britain	36.90 points
4	Luxembourg	35.95 points
5	Germany	32.40 points

Note: Five judges and maximum points per nation 58 points. Five nations took part. Details of the number of participants in the teams vary, but the numbers per nation were probably as follows: Italy 18, Hungary 16, Great Britain 23, Luxembourg 16 and Germany 19. Sweden did not take part.

Team Competition 3 — Free Choice of Movements and Equipment

1	Norway	22.85 points
2	Finland	21.85 points
3	Denmark	21.25 points
4	Germany	16.85 points
5	Luxembourg	16.30 points

Note: Five judges and maximum points per nation 25 points. Five nations took part. Details of the number of participants in the teams vary, but the numbers per nation were probably as follows: Norway 24, Finland 20, Denmark 21, Germany 18, Luxembourg 19. Sweden did not take part.

Individual Event

1	Alberto Braglia	Italy	135.00 points
2	Louis Ségura	France	132.50 points
3	Adolfo Tunesi	Italy	131.50 points
4	Giorgio Zampori	Italy	128.00 points
4	Guido Boni	Italy	128.00 points
6	Pietro Bianchi	Italy	127.75 points

Note: The disciplines were horizontal bar, parallel bars, rings and pommelled horse. Each nation could have six participants and the maximum time for the competitors was two minutes per apparatus. Three judges per apparatus, 36 points per apparatus and 144 points in all. Nine nations took part, but not Sweden, as in their opinion at the time gymnastics (Ling gymnastics) should be done as a group and in a display format.

MODERN PENTATHLON

Upon the initiative of Pierre de Coubertin it was decided at the IOC session in Budapest in 1911 that the modern pentathlon would be introduced into the Olympic program. As it was a completely new sport, the Swedish Organizing Committee had to draw up a proposal for events and rules. The events and their order and venues were: duel shooting, 25 meters, 20 shots at the Kaknäs shooting range, a 300 meter swimming race at the Swimming Stadium at Djurgårdsbrunnsviken, epée fencing on the outdoor courts at the Tennis Pavilion at Östermalms IP, a 5,000 meter cross-country steeplechase equestrian event in the Barkarby–Spånga–Hjulsta area north of Stockholm and a 4,000 meter cross-country run starting and finishing at the Olympic Stadium. The competition lasted six days, with two days for fencing, where 351 matches were decided by the first to score three hits. The competitors could bring their own horse to the riding discipline.

1	Gustaf "Gösta" Lilliehöök	Sweden	27 points[1]
2	Gösta Åsbrink	Sweden	28 points
3	Georg de Laval	Sweden	30 points
4	Åke Grönhagen	Sweden	35 points
5	George Patton	USA	41 points[2]
6	Sidney Stranne	Sweden	42 points

1. The sum of the placing figures in the five events made up the total points. Lilliehöök's placing figures were 3, 10, 5, 4 and 5.
2. Later a well-known tank general during the Second World War.

ROWING

The rowing course started at Lido in Djurgårdsbrunnsviken, went under the arches of the bridge at Djurgårdsbron and had its finish at Nybroviken level with Torstenssonsgatan, where a stand for 5,500 spectators had been built. However, the rowing competitions attracted few spectators. The course was 2,000 meters but not completely straight, so just before Djurgårdsbron the boats first veered to starboard and then immediately afterwards to port. Two boats per heat and finally two boats went to the final. No race for third prize and the losing semi-finalists only received a so-called diploma of merit. Each nation could enter two boats per event and in all 45 boats took part. Sailors and fishermen were considered to be professionals and were not allowed to participate.

Coxed Eights, Outriggers

1	Great Britain	6:15.7[1]
2	Great Britain	6:19.2[2]
3	Germany	

1. Great Britain's winning team (Leander Rowing Club) comprised Edgar Burgess, Sidney Swann, Leslie Wormwald, Ewart Horsfall, James Gillan, Arthur Garton, Alister Kirby, Philip Fleming (stroke) and Henry Wells (cox).
2. As a result of the number of boats and heats three boats went to the semi-final. Great

Britain (New College) rowed alone in its semi-final in the time 7:47.0 but the time 7:22.4 can also be found. Germany (Berliner Ruderverein von 1876) lost the other semi-final against Great Britain (Leander Rowing Club).

Note: The Swedish team (Roddklubben af 1912), which was knocked out in the quarter final against Great Britain (New Collage), comprised the following oarsmen: Gustaf Brunkman, Per Mattson, Sebastian Tamm, Schering Wachtmeister, Conrad Brunkman, William Bruhn-Möller, Ture Rosvall, Herman Dahlbäck (stroke) and Wilhelm Wilkens (cox). Roddklubben af 1912 was a combination of rowers from Malmö and Hälsingborg's rowing clubs.

Leander Rowing Club's team from Great Britain on its way down in its outrigged eight at the start of the rowing competitions. After the competitions the boat was given to the Organizing Committee. Today "The Eight" is kept at the Swedish National Sports Museum, which is close to where the rowing competitions started in 1912 (photograph by Axel Malmström, SCIF photo collection).

Coxed Fours, Outriggers

1   Germany   6:59.4[1]
2   Great Britain 2 lengths after[2]
3   Denmark[3]
3   Norway

1. Albert Arnheiter, Herman Wilker, Rudolf Fickeisen and Otto Fickeisen (stroke) rowed for Germany (Ludwigshafener Ruderverein). OR gives Karl Leister as the cox and MW Otto Maier.

2. Great Britain was represented by Thames Rowing Club.

3. Denmark (Polyteknic Roklub) lost in the semi-final against Germany and Norway (Kristiania Roklub) against Great Britain.

Note: Sweden (Vaxholms Roddklubb) was knocked out by the gold medalists Germany in the first round. John Lager, Axel Eriksson, Ernst Wetterstrand, Gunnar Lager (stroke) and Karl Sundholm (cox) rowed in the team.

Coxed Fours, Inriggers

1	Denmark	7:47.0[1]
2	Sweden	7:56.9[2]
3	Norway	

1. Ejler Allert, Jörgen Hansen, Carl Möller, Carl Pedersen (stroke) and Poul Hartman (cox) rowed in Denmark's boat (Nykjöbings paa Falster Roklub). The time 7:44.6 can also be found. Inrigged fours was an event popular in the Nordic countries and 1912 is the only time it has been in the Olympic program. An inrigged four was the only boat clearly defined in the rules; the others were more optional. Besides three Nordic countries only France took part. Six boats took part, of which three went to the semi-final. Denmark rowed alone in its semi-final and Norway (Ormsund Roklub) was ¾ length behind Sweden in its semi-final.

2. Ture Rosvall, William Bruhn-Möller, Conrad Brunkman, Herman Dahlbäck (stroke) and Wilhelm Wilkens (cox) participated for Sweden (Roddklubben af 1912, see outrigged eights).

Single Sculls

1	William Kinnear	Great Britain	7:47.6[1]
2	Polydore Veirman	Belgium	7:56.0
3	Everard Butler	Canada[2]	
3	Hugo Maksimilian Kusick	Russia	

1. The time 7:47.3 can also be found.

2. Butler just lost in the semi-final to Kinnear, where both passed Djurgårdsbron at the same time. Kusick lost to Veirman by 1.5 lengths.

Note: No Swedes took part in single sculls.

SAILING

The Organizing Committee for the Stockholm Olympiad gave the Royal Swedish Yacht Club the task of organizing the Olympic sailing competitions. The Royal Swedish Yacht Club proposed that they should be held in conjunction with the Club's annual regatta. The water off Nynäshamn, south of Stockholm, was chosen as the venue for the Olympic sailing competitions and the regatta as a whole was held at Nynäshamn and Sandhamn. Spectators could easily get to Nynäshamn by train and the competitions could be seen from land. Each nation could enter a maximum of two boats per class. In each class there were two races, where the points were 7, 3 and 1 for the three best boats in each race. If points were equal after two races, one further race was held to decide the medals. The sailing races were the final competitions in the Stockholm Olympic Games. A total of 24 boats from six nations were entered for the Olympic sailing competitions, and of these 20 actually started. The Royal Swedish Yacht Club regatta as a whole attracted 144 boats in all. The Olympic sailing races thus only constituted a limited part of the competitions.

12 Meter Class

1	Norway, Magda IX	14 points (7 + 7)[1]	
2	Sweden, Erna Signe	6 points (3 + 3)[2]	
3	Finland, Heatherbell	2 points (1 + 1)	

1. The following sailed for Norway: Alfred Larsen (helmsman), Johan Anker, Nils Berthelsen, Halfdan Hansen, Magnus Konow, Petter Andreas Larsen, Eilert Falch-Lund, Fritz Staib, Arnfinn Heje and Gustaf Thaulow. Maximum 10-man crew. Distance 36.2 nautical miles.

2. Sweden's crew: Hugo Clason (helmsman), Nils Persson, Richard Sällström, Nils Lamby, Kurt Bergström, Dick Bergström, Erik Lindqvist, Per Bergman, Sigurd Kander and Folke Johnson. The owners were Nils Persson and Nils Asp.

10 Meter Class

1	Sweden, Kitty	14 points (7 + 7)[1]
2	Finland, Nina	4 points (3 + 1)[2]
3	Russia, Gallia II	4 points (1 + 3)
4	Sweden, Marga	0 points

1. Sweden's crew on Kitty: Carl Hellström (helmsman), Erik Wallerius, Harald Wallerius, Humbert Lundén, Herman Nyberg, Harry Rosenswärd, Paul Isberg and Filip Ericsson. The owner was Nils Asp. Maximum 8-man crew. Distance 36.2 nautical miles.

2. In the extra race for the silver medals Nina beat Gallia II by 1 min 36 sec.

8 Meter Class

1	Norway, Taifun	14 points (7 + 7)[1]
2	Sweden, Sans Atout	3 points (3 + 0)[2]
3	Finland, Lucky Girl	3 points (0 + 3)
4	Finland, Örn	2 points (1 + 1)
5	Russia, Norman	0 points
5	Sweden, KSSS 1912	0 points[3]
5	Russia, Bylina	0 points

1. The crew of the Norwegian boat: Thoralf Glad (helmsman), Thomas Valentin Aas, Andreas Brecke, Torleiv Corneliussen and Christian Jebe. Maximum 5-man crew. Distance 21.3 nautical miles.

2. The Swedish crew on Sans Atout: Bengt Heyman (helmsman), Emil Henriques, Herbert Westermark, Nils Westermark and Alvar Tiel. The owner was Bengt Heyman. In the extra race for the silver medals Sans Atout beat Lucky Girl by 57 sec.

3. The boat was owned by The Royal Swedish Yacht Club (Kungliga Svenska Segel Sällskapet), thereby the name. The rules stipulated a five-man crew but six men are named in the result lists.

6 Meter Class

1	France, Mac Miche	10 points (3 + 7)[1]
2	Denmark, Nurdung II	10 points (7 + 3)
3	Sweden, Kerstin	1 points (0 + 1)[2]
4	Sweden, Sass	1 points (1 + 0)
5	Finland, Finn II	0 points
5	Norway, Sonja III	0 points

1. The following sailed in the French boat: Gaston Thubé (helmsman), Amédée Thubé and Jacques Thubé. In the extra race for the gold medals Mac Miche beat Nurdung II by 2 min 52 sec. Maximum 3-man crew. The distance was 21.3 nautical miles.

2. The Swedish crew on Kerstin: Harald Sandberg (helmsman), Eric Sandberg and Otto Aust. Owner Dan Broström. In the extra race for the bronze medals Kerstin beat Sass by 1 min 39 sec.

SHOOTING

According to the competition program for the Olympic Games, shooting was divided into six categories: (1) Military rifle (2) Free rifle (3) Small-bore rifle (4) Revolver and Pistol (5) Clay Trap shooting (6) Running Deer shooting. In all there were 18 shooting events. The rifle, small-bore rifle and revolver/pistol competitions were held at Kaknäs in northern Djurgården, close to the present Kaknäs tower. The clay trap shooting and shooting at running deer competitions were held near Råsta Lake in Råsunda (Solna) north of Stockholm. The range for small-bore rifle and pistol shooting at Kaknäs and the range at Råsunda were newly built before the Olympic Games.

MILITARY RIFLE

Each country's military rifle in accordance with a fixed model. Free position. Five-ring target 140 × 170 cm from 200 meters and a five-ring target 180 × 170 cm from 400, 500 and 600 meters. "Number five" 20 and 40 cm in diameter, respectively.

Military Rifle, 200, 400, 500 and 600 Meters, Team Competition

1	USA	1,687 points[1]
2	Great Britain	1,602 points
3	Sweden	1,570 points[2]
4	South Africa	1,531 points
5	France	1,515 points
6	Norway	1,473 points

1. Six men in the team who all fired 15 shots from each distance. Max. points per marksman 300 and per team 1,800. Cornelius Burdette 288 p, Allan Briggs 283 p, Harry Adams 283 p, John Jackson 279 p, Carl Osburn 278 p and Warren Sprout 276 p were in USA's team.

2. Mauritz Eriksson 266 p, Verner Jernström 262 p, Carl Björkman 261 p, Tönnes Björkman 261 p, Bernhard Larsson 261 p and Hugo Johansson 259 p shot for Sweden.

Military Rifle, 600 Meters

1	Paul Colas	France	94 points[1]
2	Carl Osburn	USA	94 points
3	John Jackson	USA	93 points[2]
4	Allan Briggs	USA	93 points
5	Philip Plater	Great Britain	90 points
6	Verner Jernström	Sweden	88 points

1. 20 shots and max. points 100 per marksman. Colas won the 20 shot shoot-off against Osburn by 91 points against 90.

2. Jackson won the shoot-off against Briggs for the bronze medal by 90 points against 89.

Military Rifle, 300 Meters

1	Sándor Prokopp	Hungary	97 points (47 + 50)[1]
2	Carl Osburn	USA	95 points (45 + 50)[2]
3	Embret Skogen	Norway	95 points (45 + 50)
4	Nikolaos Levidis	Greece	95 points (45 + 50)
5	Nils Romander	Sweden	94 points (49 + 45)[3]
6	Arthur Fulton	Great Britain	92 points (42 + 50)

1. 20 shots in two series. First series of ten shots in 3 min, with four in the prone position, four kneeling and two standing. Five-ring precision target 170 × 140 cm with a 50 cm wide half figure as "number five." Second series of ten shots in 3 min with five shots in prone position and five kneeling. The target was a half figure of 50 × 90 cm where hitting the figure gave 5 points. Max. points 100 per marksman.

2. In the shoot-off for the silver and bronze medals Osburn had 99 points, Skogen 91 points and Levidis 70 points.

3. Romander led the competition before his final shot. Spectators then gathered around him, he was disturbed and completely missed the figure.

FREE RIFLE

Rifle and ammunition of any kind at all, bead and sight open. International target, white, ten rings, 100 cm in diameter with a black circular dot 60 cm in diameter.

Feverish activity in the shooting stand at Kaknäs shooting range (postcard, National Sports Museum).

Free Rifle, 300 Meters, Team Competition

1	Sweden	5,655 points[1]
2	Norway	5,605 points
3	Denmark	5,529 points
4	France	5,471 points
5	Finland	5,323 points
6	South Africa	4,897 points

1. Six men in the team, each firing 120 shots, 40 in standing position, 40 kneeling and 40 in prone position. Max. points per marksman, 1,200 points and per team 7,200 points. Mauritz Eriksson 976 p, Hugo Johansson 975 p, Erik Blomqvist 962 p, Carl Björkman 954 p, Bernhard Larsson 914 p and Gustaf Adolf Jonsson 874 p shot for Sweden.

Free Rifle, 300 Meters

1	Paul Colas	France	987 points (283, 342, 362)[1]
2	Lars Jørgen Madsen	Denmark	981 points (318, 333, 330)
3	Niels Larsen	Denmark	962 points (273, 334, 355)
4	Hugo Johansson	Sweden	959 points (292, 326, 341)
5	Gudbrand Gudbrandsen Skatteboe	Norway	956 points (305, 308, 343)
6	Bernhard Larsson	Sweden	954 points (274, 339, 341)

1. Same rules as in the team competition. Points making up total score given in the order standing, kneeling and prone position.

SMALL-BORE RIFLE

Any breech loading rifle at all with a caliber no greater than 6 mm. Weight of the bullet no more than ten grams and departure speed no more than 450 m. Free position, where probably prone was chosen.

Small-Bore Rifle, 50 Meters, Team Competition

1	Great Britain	762 points[1]
2	Sweden	748 points[2]
3	USA	744 points
4	France	714 points
5	Denmark	708 points
5	Greece	708 points

1. Five-ring target 40 × 40 cm. Black centre 6 cm in diameter where "number five" was 4 cm in diameter. Four men in the team who each fired 40 shots in four series of ten shots. Max. points per marksman 200 points and for the team 800 points. Edward Lessimore 192 p, William Pimm 193 p, Joseph Pepé 189 p and Robert Murray 188 p shot for Great Britain. It has later been shown that Lessimore's result was 195 p and Murray's 185 p, which also means team points of 762.

2. Sweden's team consisted of Arthur Nordenswan 190 p, Eric Carlberg 189 p, Ruben Örtegren 185 p and Wilhelm Carlberg 184 p. Eric and Wilhelm were twin brothers.

Small-Bore Rifle, 50 Meters

1	Frederick Hird	USA	194 points
2	William Milne	Great Britain	193 points
3	Harold Burt	Great Britain	192 points[1]
4	Edward Lessimore	Great Britain	192 points
5	Francis Kemp	Great Britain	190 points
6	Robert Murray	Great Britain	190 points
8	Erik Boström	Sweden	189 points

1. In the event of equal points the following decided: (1) number of fives, (2) hits in the black centre (3) number of fours etc.

Note: Same rules as in the team competition.

Small-Bore Rifle, Disappearing Target, 25 Meters, Team Competition

1	Sweden	925 points[1]
2	Great Britain	917 points
3	USA	881 points
4	Greece	716 points

1. Reduced whole figure, ten rings. The figure, which was 12 cm high and 3.5 cm at its broadest point, was shown 25 times, three sec per time and with an interval of five sec between. After each series of five shots the figure was changed. Four men in the team and max. points per marksman 250 points and for the team 1,000 points. Johan Hübner von Holst 238 p, Eric Carlberg 238 p, Wilhelm Carlberg 229 p and Gustaf Boivie 220 p were in the Swedish team. Both Sweden and Great Britain had 99 hits in the figure, which was the main deciding factor for the team's placing. If the number of hits was the same, the points were counted. Only four teams started.

Small-Bore Rifle, Disappearing Target, 25 Meters

1	Wilhelm Carlberg	Sweden	242 points[1]
2	Johan Hübner von Holst	Sweden	233 points
3	Gideon Ericsson	Sweden	231 points[2]
4	Joseph Pepé	Great Britain	231 points
5	Robert Murray	Great Britain	228 points
6	Axel Gyllenkrok	Sweden	227 points

1. Same rules as in the team competition. The individual competition was held in the morning on the same day as the team competition was held. Placings were decided primarily

by the number of hits in the figure. Then the total points in the ten-ring target were counted, then the number of tens, and so on. The first six marksmen all had 25 hits in the figure.

2. Ericsson and Pepé both had 25 hits in the figure and the same total points but Ericsson had twelve hits in "number ten" against Pepé's nine.

REVOLVER AND PISTOL

Any revolver or pistol at all with an open sight and bead. "Hair trigger" not allowed. Standing shooting position with outstretched arm.

Free Pistol, 50 Meters, Team Competition

1	USA	1,916 points[1]
2	Sweden	1,849 points[2]
3	Great Britain	1,804 points
4	Russia	1,801 points
5	Greece	1,731 points

1. Ten-ring target 50 cm in diameter with black centre circle 20 cm in diameter (points 7–10). Four men in the team who each fired 60 shots in ten series of six shots. Max. shooting time four min per series. Max. points per marksman 600 points and for the team 2,400 points. Five teams took part. Alfred Lane 509 p, Henry Seas 474 p, Peter Dolfen 467 p and John Dietz 466 p were in USA's team.

2. Georg de Laval 475 p, Eric Carlberg 472 p, Wilhelm Carlberg 459 p and Erik Boström 443 p shot for Sweden.

Free Pistol, 50 Meters

1	Alfred Lane	USA	499 points
2	Peter Dolfen	USA	474 points
3	Charles Stewart	Great Britain	470 points[1]
4	Georg de Laval	Sweden	470 points
5	Erik Boström	Sweden	468 points
6	Horatio Poulter	Great Britain	461 points

USA's winning team in the 50-meter free pistol team competition, July 2, 1912 (postcard, National Sports Museum).

1. Same rules as in the team competition. If the total points were the same, the placing was decided by the greatest number of "tens" etc. Stewart won the bronze as he had more "tens" than de Laval. There is no information about how many tens they had.

Dueling Pistol, 30 Meters, Team Competition

1	Sweden	120 hits, 1,145 points[1]
2	Russia	118 hits, 1,091 points[2]
3	Great Britain	117 hits, 1,107 points
4	USA	117 hits, 1,097 points
5	Greece	115 hits, 1,057 points
6	France	113 hits, 1,041 points

1. Full figure, ten rings, 1.7 meters high. Four men in the team who each fired 30 shots in six series of five shots. Initial position fully lowered arm with muzzle facing ground. Firing upon command, the figure was shown for three sec, ten sec interval between the shots in the series. Max. points per marksman 300 points and for the team 1,200 points. The competition was held over two days on June 29 when France, Russia, Sweden and the USA shot and on July 3 when the other competing nations shot. Wilhelm Carlberg 290 p, Eric Carlberg 287 p, Johan Hübner von Holst 284 p and Paul Palén 284 p represented Sweden. 120 hits means that all the team's shots hit the target.

2. The total number of hits in the figure decided the team's placing. Then the team points were counted. Russia therefore came second even though both Great Britain and the USA had more points.

Dueling Pistol, 30 Meters

1	Alfred Lane	USA	30 hits, 287 points[1]
2	Paul Palén	Sweden	30 hits, 286 points
3	Johan Hübner von Holst	Sweden	30 hits, 283 points[2]
4	John Dietz	USA	30 hits, 283 points
5	Ivan Törnmarck	Sweden	30 hits, 280 points
6	Eric Carlberg	Sweden	30 hits, 278 points

1. Same rules as in the team competition. The total number of hits in the figure decided the placing, then the total points.

2. Hübner von Holst won the shoot-off for the bronze medal against Dietz by 284 points against 282.

CLAY TRAP SHOOTING

Gun no more than 12 caliber. Free choice of cartridge with no more than 35.5 gram loads and shot size no bigger than 2.5 mm.

In the team competition, there were six men in the team, 100 clay birds per marksman in total in three rounds with 20, 30 and 50 birds, respectively. Sustained fire, unknown trajectories from known traps except for the last ten shots in the third round with unknown trajectories from unknown traps and with single fire. Two shots at each bird allowed. A certain number of teams knocked out each round. "Max. points" per marksman and round 20 + 30 + 50 = 100 and for the team 600.

Same rules in the individual competition, with the difference that the last ten shots in the third round were with sustained fire. A certain number of marksmen knocked out each round. The individual competition was held on July 2–4 and the team competition on June 29 and July 1.

Clay Trap Shooting, Team Competition

1	USA	532 (108 + 161 + 263)[1]
2	Great Britain	511 (104 + 160 + 247)
3	Germany	510 (107 + 156 + 247)
4	Sweden	243 (95 + 148)[2]
5	Finland	233 (95 + 138)
6	France	90

1. James Graham 94 birds, Charles Billings 93, Ralph Spotts 90, John Hendrickson 89, Frank Hall 86 and Edward Gleason 80 were in the American team. In brackets in the results list, the number of birds hit per round.

2. Sweden and Finland knocked out after the second round and France after the first round. Åke Lundeberg 48 birds, Alfred Swahn 45, Johan Ekman 41, Victor Wallenberg 40, Hjalmar Frisell 38 and Carl Wollert 31 birds for Sweden.

Clay Trap Shooting

1	James Graham	USA	96 (19 + 28 + 49)
2	Alfred Goeldel-Bronikoven	Germany	94 (18 + 28 + 48)
3	Harry Blau	Russia	91 (15 + 27 + 49)
4	Harold Humby	Great Britain	88 (18 + 24 + 46)[1]
4	Albert Preuss	Germany	88 (17 + 25 + 46)
4	Anastasios Metaxas	Greece	88 (18 + 26 + 44)
4	Franz von Zedlitz und Leipe	Germany	88 (19 + 23 + 46)
4	Gustaf Adolf Schnitt	Finland	88 (18 + 26 + 44)
17	Åke Lundeberg	Sweden	84 (17 + 24 + 43)

1. There was a rule that there would be a 10-bird shoot-off if scores were tied, but this probably only applied to the medal places. OR gives the marksmen in the above order without giving their placings while MW states that everyone with 88 birds hit came in fourth place.

RUNNING DEER SHOOTING

Rifle of any construction and caliber at all with an open sight and bead. Free choice of ammunition. 100 meters to the target (deer of a natural size) with an open stretch of 23 meters in the terrain where the deer was seen for 4 seconds. Free shooting position but the rifle against the shoulder only when the target was visible. The deer was marked from 0–5. Circular dot on the shoulder 30 cm in diameter (4–5 points) with the "five" 15 cm in diameter. 0 points for a hit on the head, the rear and legs. The markings on the deer were so discreet that they could not be seen from where they were shooting.

In the team competition there were four men in the team who each fired ten shots in a row, one shot per run. Maximum points per marksman 50 points and for the team 200 points. Same rules in the individual competition, single shot, where the competition was spread out over June 29–July 1. In the individual competition, double shot, the marksmen had 20 shots and could shoot two shots per run, maximum points per marksmen 100 points.

Running Deer, 100 Meters, Single Shot, Team Competition

1	Sweden	151 points[1]
2	USA	132 points
3	Finland	123 points
4	Austria	115 points
5	Russia	108 points[2]

1. Oscar Swahn 43 p, Åke Lundeberg 39 p, Alfred Swahn 37 p and Per-Olof Arvidsson 32 p were in the Swedish team. Oscar Swahn was 64 years and 257 days old on the day of the competition, which makes him the oldest gold medalist ever in Olympic history.
2. Five nations took part.

Running Deer, 100 Meters, Single Shot

1	Alfred Swahn	Sweden	41 points[1]
2	Åke Lundeberg	Sweden	41 points
3	Nestor Toivonen	Finland	41 points
4	Karl Larsson	Sweden	39 points[2]
4	Oscar Swahn	Sweden	39 points
4	Sven August Lindskog	Sweden	39 points

1. The rules stipulated a shoot-off if scores were equal after five shots. In the shoot-off for the medals Swahn shot 20 p, Lundeberg 17 p and Toivonen 11 p, but Toivonen dropped out of the shoot-off after three shots.
2. There is no mention of a shoot-off for places 4–6.

Running Deer, 100 Meters, Double Shot

1	Åke Lundeberg	Sweden	79 points
2	Edvard Benedicks	Sweden	74 points
3	Oscar Swahn	Sweden	72 points
4	Alfred Swahn	Sweden	68 points
4	Per-Olof Arvidsson	Sweden	68 points
6	Sven August Lindskog	Sweden	67 points

SWIMMING (AQUATICS)

The Swimming Stadium was at Djurgårdsbrunnsviken in a bay at Laboratoriebacken (more or less at the present Nobelparken). The dimensions of the pool were 100 × 20 meters and there were no lines separating the lanes. The pool was surrounded by floating rafts. There was a diving tower on the far side of the pool and on the land side there was a stand for 4,000 spectators. The Swimming Stadium was demolished as soon as the competitions were over.

In swimming the first two in each heat and the best person finishing third went on to the next round, and finally a maximum of five swimmers went to the final. In diving the best diver in each of three qualifying groups (for women two groups) went to the final and then the divers with the highest points irrespective of group, so that the final consisted of eight divers. There were five judges in the diving and the points were 0–10.

The size and appearance of the swimsuits were carefully defined in the rules and the swimmers wore numbered swimming caps in different colors. It was the first time that women took part in aquatics in the Olympic Games.

Water polo was also played at the Swimming Stadium. The water polo goals were hauled out on steel wires stretched over the middle part of the pool. There were seven players in each team and the match time was 2 × 7 minutes effective time. Six nations took part and the draw up until the final was decided in advance (using a knockout method and without seeding). In the final Great Britain beat Austria 8–0. Austria did not then become the silver medalist but had to continue to play for second place with the teams that had previously been knocked out by the winner in the final. Third place was also played for at the same time. The order of play was constructed by Erik Bergvall, the Chairman of the

Swimming Committee (and later the head of the Olympic Stadium), and the idea was, because of the first not seeded draw, to give strong nations that had been knocked out a new chance to win medals.

100 Meters Freestyle — Men

1	Duke Paoa Kahanamoku	USA	1:03.4[1]
2	Cecil Healy	Australasia	1:04.6
3	Kenneth Huszagh	USA	1:05.6
4	Kurt Bretting	Germany	1:05.8
5	Walter Ramme	Germany	1:06.4
	William Longworth	Australasia	Did not start in the final[2]
	Robert "Robban" Andersson	Sweden[3]	

1. Three Americans, including Kahanamoku and Huszagh, and an Italian did not start in the semi-final two due to a misunderstanding and the German Bretting swam alone. The jury then allowed these four to start in an extra semi-final where the winner would go to the final provided that he had a better time than the person finishing third in semi-final one. Kahanamoku set a new world record of 1:02.4 in the extra semi-final. Huszagh finished second and equaled the time of the person who finished third in semi-final one and was the sixth person to go to the final.
2. Longworth underwent surgery on the day of the final for an abscess on his head.
3. Robert Andersson was knocked out in the second qualifying round.

400 Meters Freestyle — Men

1	George Ritchie Hodgson	Canada	5:24.4[1]
2	John Gatenby Hatfield	Great Britain	5:25.8
3	Harold Hardwick	Australasia	5:31.2
4	Cecil Healy	Australasia	5:37.8
5	Béla von Las-Torres	Hungary	5:42.0

1. Olympic record.
Note: The Swedes Nils Erik Haglund, Johan Eskil Wedholm and David Theander were knocked out in the qualifying round.

1,500 Meters Freestyle — Men

1	George Ritchie Hodgson	Canada	22:00.0[1]
2	John Gatenby Hatfield	Great Britain	22:39.0
3	Harold Hardwick	Australasia	23:15.4
4	Malcolm Champion	Australasia	Did not finish in the final
4	Béla von Las-Torres	Hungary	Did not finish in the final
	Wilhelm Andersson	Sweden	Knocked out in semi-final

1. Hodgson's time was a world record. His intermediate time at 1,000 meters was a new world record of 14:37.0. After the finish at 1,500 meters he continued and also set a world record for the English mile (1,609 meters) of 23:34.5.

100 Meters Backstroke — Men

1	Harry Hebner	USA	1:21.2[1]
2	Otto Fahr	Germany	1:22.4
3	Paul Kellner	Germany	1:24.0
4	András Baronyi	Hungary	1:25.2
5	Otto Gross	Germany	1:25.8
	Gunnar Sundman	Sweden	Knocked out in semi-final

1. Hebner set an Olympic record of 1:20.8 in the semi-final.

200 Meters Breaststroke — Men

1	Walter Bathe	Germany	3:01.8[1]
2	Wilhelm Lützow	Germany	3:05.0
3	Paul Malisch	Germany	3:08.0
4	Percy Courtman	Great Britain	3:08.8
5	Thor Henning	Sweden	Did not finish in final

1. Olympic record.

400 Meters Breaststroke — Men

1	Walter Bathe	Germany	6:29.6
2	Thor Henning	Sweden	6:35.6
3	Percy Courtman	Great Britain	6:36.4
4	Paul Malisch	Germany	6:37.0
5	Wilhelm Lützow	Germany	Did not finish in the final

Team Relay, 800 Meters — Men (4 × 200 M Freestyle)

1	Australasia	10:11.6[1]
2	USA	10:20.2
3	Great Britain	10:28.2[2]
4	Germany	10:37.0
	Hungary	Did not start in the final[3]

1. World record. OR gives 10:11.6 in the results list but in the list of Olympic records 10:11.2. MW gives a time of 10:11.2. Cecil Healy, Malcolm Champion, Leslie Boardman and Harold Hardwick swam in Australasia's team.

2. MW gives the time as 10:28.6.

3. Hungary came second in its qualifying heat but did not start in the final.

Note: Qualifying heats were organized, even though only five nations started. All the nations were in practice qualified for the final before the heats. Sweden was entered (according to the NA) but did not start. This may be the reason for the two heats being planned and then held.

100 Meters Freestyle — Women

1	Sarah "Fanny" Durack	Australasia	1:22.2[1]
2	Wilhelmina Wylie	Australasia	1:25.4
3	Jennie Fletcher	Great Britain	1:27.0
4	Margareta "Grete" Rosenberg	Germany	1:27.2[2]
5	Annie Speirs	Great Britain	1:27.4

1. Durack set a world record of 1:19.8 in the qualifying heat.

2. Rosenberg swam in the final as the next best third in the semi-finals instead of Daisy Curwen, Great Britain, who was operated on for appendicitis after the semi-final.

Note: The Swedes Margareta "Greta" Johanson, Karin Lundgren, Sonja Jonsson, Elsa Björklund, Greta Carlsson and Vera Thulin were all knocked out in the qualifying round.

Team Relay 400 Meters — Women (4 × 100 Meters Freestyle)

1	Great Britain	5:52.8[1]
2	Germany	6:04.6
3	Austria	6:17.0
4	Sweden	No time given

1. Olympic record. Isabella Moore, Jennie Fletcher, Annie Speirs and Irene Steer swam for Great Britain. As only four teams were entered the final was swum straight away. Australasia had two women swimmers in their squad (first and second in the 100 meters freestyle) and requested that they be allowed to start, with the two women swimming two alternate legs each. This was rejected.

Note: Sweden's team: Greta Carlsson, Margareta Johanson, Sonja Jonsson and Vera Thulin.

Start of the 400 meters team relay for women, July 15, 1912 (SCIF photo collection).

Plain High Diving — Men

1	Eric "Loppan" Adlerz	Sweden	Placing fig. 7 — 40.0 points[1]
2	Hjalmar Johansson	Sweden	Placing fig. 12 — 39.3 points[2]
3	Johan "John" Jansson	Sweden	Placing fig. 12 — 39.1 points
4	Victor Gustaf Crondahl	Sweden	Placing fig. 22 — 37.1 points
5	Toivo Aro	Finland	Placing fig. 26 — 36.5 points
6	Axel Runström	Sweden	Placing fig. 26 — 36.0 points

1. Five dives in all (from a selection of thirteen) from 5 and 10 m diving platforms. One dive without and one with a run-up from 5 m and one dive without and two with a run-up from 10 m.

2. The sum of the judges' placing figures decided the divers' placing first, then the total number of points.

Plain and Fancy High Diving — Men

1	Eric "Loppan" Adlerz	Sweden	Placing fig. 7 — 73.94 points[1]
2	Albert Zürner	Germany	Placing fig. 10 — 72.60 points
3	Gustaf Blomgren	Sweden	Placing fig. 16 — 69.56 points
4	Hjalmar Johansson	Sweden	Placing fig. 22 — 67.80 points[2]
5	George Yvon	Great Britain	Placing fig. 22 — 67.66 points
6	Harald Arbin	Sweden	Placing fig. 31 — 62.62 points

1. A total of seven compulsory and varying dives from 5 and 10 m diving platforms. The compulsory dives were a plain dive with a run-up and a backward somersault dive from 5 m and a plain dive without and a plain dive with a run-up from 10 m. The varying dives were three from 10 m and freely chosen from a selection of thirteen. The rules stated that seven dives must be performed and that the highest points per dive were 10. Therefore it is somewhat surprising that the divers finishing first and second have more than 70 points. Probably eight or more dives were performed.

2. The sum of the judges' placing figures decided the divers' placing first, then the total number of points.

Springboard Diving — Men

1	Paul Günther	Germany	Placing fig. 6 — 79.23 points[1]
2	Hans Luber	Germany	Placing fig. 9 — 76.78 points
3	Kurt Behrens	Germany	Placing fig. 22 — 73.73 points
4	Albert Zürner	Germany	Placing fig. 23 — 73.33 points
5	Robert Zimmerman	Canada	Placing fig. 24 — 72.54 points
6	Herbert Pott	Great Britain	Placing fig. 28 — 71.45 points
7	Johan "John" Jansson	Sweden	Placing fig. 32 — 69.64 points

1. A total of seven compulsory and varying dives from 1 and 3 m springboards. The compulsory dives were a plain dive with a run-up and a forward somersault dive with a run-up from 1 m and a plain dive without and a plain dive with a run-up from 3 m. The varying dives were three from 3 m and freely chosen from a selection of eighteen. For the divers' total points, see under plain and fancy diving.

Plain High Diving — Women

1	Margareta "Greta" Johanson	Sweden	Placing fig. 5 — 39.9 points[1]
2	Lisa Regnell	Sweden	Placing fig. 11 — 36.0 points
3	Isabelle White	Great Britain	Placing fig. 17 — 34.0 points
4	Elsa Regnell	Sweden	Placing fig. 20 — 33.2 points
5	Ella Eklund	Sweden	Placing fig. 22 — 31.9 points
6	Elsa Anderson	Sweden	Placing fig. 25 — 31.3 points

1. Free choice of five dives (chosen from a selection of thirteen) from 5 and 10 m platform. One dive without and one with a run-up from 5 m and one dive without and two with a run-up from 10 m, that is the same as for the men. Twelve out of fourteen competitors in the event were Swedish.

Water Polo

1	Great Britain	3 wins 0 losses[1]
2	Sweden	3 wins 1 loss[2]
3	Belgium	3 wins 2 losses
4	Austria	1 win 3 losses
5	Hungary	2 losses
5	France	2 losses

1. Charles Smith, Georg Corner, Charles Bugbee, Arthur Hill, George Wilkinson, Paul Radmilovic and Isaac Bentham played for Great Britain.

2. Sweden's matches: France 7–2, Great Britain 3–6, Austria 8–1 and in the match for the silver Belgium 4–2. The Swedish team was the same in all matches and consisted of: Torsten Kumfeldt (goalkeeper and also one of the three building committee members who were responsible for the construction of the Swimming Stadium), Harald Julin, Pontus Hanson, Robert "Robban" Andersson, Max Gumpel, Wilhelm Andersson and Eric "Berka" Bergqvist.

TENNIS

There were both indoor and outdoor tennis competitions at the Stockholm Olympic Games. The very first competition in the Games was the indoor competition. The venue was the Royal Tennis Pavilion outside the Olympic Stadium where the present Swedish School of Sport and Health Sciences is situated. The pavilion burnt down in 1920. At 1.15 pm precisely on May 5, 1912, the referee made signal to the umpires for the game to start. Carl Kempe (1884–1967) gave the first serve, thereby beginning the Games of the Fifth Olympiad; a very simple ceremony, in all truth (Carl Kempe was the uncle of Matts Carlgren, member of the IOC 1976–92). The covered court tennis tournament was played two months prior to the official opening of the Olympic Games in Stockholm.

The outdoor tournament was played on four newly laid courts next to the Tennis Pavilion at Östermalms IP and here there was room for 1,500 spectators. The Tennis Pavilion, built in Idrottsparken in 1897 and moved in 1911, is still left and is still used to play tennis. Players from Great Britain did not take part in the outdoor competition as it was held at the same time as the Wimbledon tournament. The maximum number of players per nation was eight in singles and four pairs in the doubles and mixed doubles. The men's matches were decided in the best of five sets while the women's matches and the mixed doubles were decided in the best of three sets. The umpires scored in English and according to the rules Slazenger balls were to be used. During the outdoor tournament it was 26–28 degrees in the shade every day except for one day when it rained, and then play was cancelled between ten and five.

Men's Singles — Indoors

1	André Gobert	France[1]
2	Charles Dixon	Great Britain
3	Anthony Wilding	Australasia[2]
4	Gordon Lowe	Great Britain
	Gunnar Setterwall	Sweden[3]

1. Gobert won the final 8–6, 6–4, 6–4.
2. Wilding won the match for third prize 4–6, 6–2, 7–5, 6–0.
3. Setterwall was knocked out in the quarter final.

Ladies' Singles — Indoors

1	Edith Hannam	Great Britain[1]
2	Sofie Castenschiold	Denmark
3	Mabel Parton	Great Britain[2]
4	Sigrid Fick	Sweden

1. Hannam won the final 6–4, 6–3.
2. Parton won the match for third prize against Fick 6–3, 6–3.

Men's Doubles — Indoors

1	André Gobert/Maurice Germot	France[1]
2	Gunnar Setterwall/Carl Kempe	Sweden
3	Charles Dixon/Alfred Beamish	Great Britain[2]
4	Arthur Gore/Herbert Roper-Barrett	Great Britain

1. Gobert/Germot won the final 6–4, 12–14, 6–2, 6–4.
2. Dixon/ Beamish won the match for third prize 6–2, 0–6, 10–8, 2–6, 6–3.

Mixed Doubles — Indoors

1	Edith Hannam/Charles Dixon	Great Britain[1]
2	Helen Aitchison/H Roper-Barrett	Great Britain
3	Sigrid Fick/Gunnar Setterwall	Sweden[2]
4	Margareta Cederschiöld/Carl Kempe	Sweden

1. Hannam/Dixon won the final 4–6, 6–3, 6–2.
2. Fick/Setterwall won the match for third prize by a walkover.
Note: The tactics in mixed doubles in 1912 were the men at the net and the women at the baseline.

Men's Singles — Outdoors

1	Charles Winslow	South Africa[1]
2	Harry Kitson	South Africa
3	Oscar Kreuzer	Germany[2]
4	Ladislav Zemla	Bohemia
	Charles Wennergren	Sweden[3]

1. Winslow, who was fourteen years younger than his opponent, won the final 7–5, 4–6, 10–8, 8–6.
2. Kreuzer won the match for third prize 6–2, 3–6, 6–3, 6–1.
3. Wennergren was knocked out in the round of the last sixteen.

Ladies' Singles — Outdoors

1	Marguerite Broquedis	France[1]
2	Dorothea Köring	Germany
3	Anna Bjurstedt	Norway[2]
4	Edith Arnheim Lasch	Sweden

1. Broquedis won the final 4–6, 6–3, 6–4.
2. Bjurstedt won the match for third prize 6–2, 6–2.

Men's Doubles — Outdoors

1	Harry Kitson/Charles Winslow	South Africa[1]
2	Felix Piepes/Arthur Zborzil	Austria
3	Albert Canet/Edouard Marc Mény	France[2]
4	Ladislav Zemla/Jaroslav Just	Bohemia
	Wollmar Boström/Curt Benckert	Sweden[3]
	Charles Wennergren/Carl Olof Nylén	Sweden

1. Kitson/Winslow won the final 4–6, 6–1, 6–2, 6–2.
2. Canet/Mény won the match for the third prize 13–11, 6–3, 8–6. Mény's full name was Mény de Marangue.
3. The two Swedish pairs were knocked out in the quarter final.

Mixed Doubles — Outdoors

1	Dorothea Köring/Heinrich Schomburgk	Germany[1]
2	Sigrid Fick/Gunnar Setterwall	Sweden
3	Marguerite Broquedis/Albert Canet	France[2]
4	M Rieck/Oscar Kreuzer	Germany
5	Annie Holmström/Thorsten Grönfors	Sweden

1. Köring/Schomburgk won the final 6–4, 6–0.
2. The French pair won the match for third prize by walkover against the German pair Rieck/Kreuzer. The German pair did not play any matches, but were given a bye, won by a walkover or themselves left a walkover. MW also records this but has placed Holmström/Grönfors in fourth place. They lost in the quarter final against Fick/Setterwall but took part in the tournament, unlike the German pair.

Note: Of thirteen scheduled matches, only five were played due to the many walkovers.

TUG-OF-WAR

The tug-of-war was the responsibility of the Athletics Committee at first, but in 1911 it gained its own committee. The competition was held at the infield of the Olympic Stadium. Teams from Bohemia, Luxembourg, Great Britain, Sweden and Austria were entered.

All the teams were to meet each other over a five-day period. On the first day Sweden and Great Britain turned up, but not their opponents Austria and Bohemia. They won by a walkover. On the second day Luxembourg did not turn up either. On the same day Sweden and Great Britain thus met in a final consisting of the best of three pulls and Sweden won 2–0.

Tug-of-War

1   Sweden[1]
2   Great Britain[2]

1. Sweden's team consisted of Arvid Andersson (team captain), Adolf Bergman, Johan Edman, Erik Fredriksson, August Gustafsson, Carl Jonsson (anchor), Erik Larsson and Herbert Lindström.
2. Great Britain's team consisted of Alexander Munro, James Shepherd, John Sewell, Joseph Dowler, Edwin Mills, Frederick Humphreys, Mathias Hynes and Walter Chaffe.

WRESTLING

The competitions were decided at the Olympic Stadium. The wrestling was in Greco-Roman style. The maximum time per match was 60 minutes in principle. But after 30 minutes a decision could be taken regarding an extension of 30 minutes at a time, if the judges assessed that the match was still a tie, and so on. Some matches went on for hours. The wrestling was held in rounds and a wrestler was knocked out after two defeats. There were three wrestlers left for the final round in each weight class, and they all met each other. The competition was mainly held in strong sunshine without any overhead shelter over the wrestling mats. There were 303 wrestling matches in all.

Featherweight — 60 kg

1   Kaarlo Koskelo   Finland[1]
2   Georg Gerstacker   Germany
3   Otto Lasanen   Finland
     Erik Öberg   Sweden[2]

1. Won both final matches.
2. Knocked out by Lasanen in the seventh round, the last one before the final round.

Lightweight — 67.5 kg

1   Emil Wäre   Finland[1]
2   Gustaf Malmström   Sweden
3   Edvin Mattiasson   Sweden

1. Won both final matches. Had a total of six wins by fall during the tournament.

Middleweight A — 75 kg

1   Claes Johansson   Sweden[1]
2   Martin Klein   Russia
3   Alfred Asikainen   Finland

1. The final round was begun with Klein against Asikainen, and Klein was judged to be the winner after the match had gone on for 11 hours and 40 minutes, with short breaks every half hour. Both of them were to meet Johansson later the same day but both understandably left a walkover.

Middleweight B — 82,5 kg

2	Anders Ahlgren	Sweden[1]
2	Ivar Böling	Finland
3	Béla Varga	Hungary

1. Ahlgren and Böling wrestled for an effective time of nine hours. The judges then declared "both defeated" and the rules prescribed that no winner was to be designated in the class, but the two of them were judged to be joint second and received silver medals.

Note: The class corresponds to the light heavyweight class of later times.

Heavyweight — Over 82.5 kg

1	Yrjö Saarela	Finland
2	Johan Olin	Finland
3	Søren Marinus Jensen	Denmark[1]
	Frans Gustaf Lindstrand	Sweden[2]

1. Jensen dropped out after just over three hours in his match against Saarela as he was suffering from sunburn. He later left a walkover against Olin.
2. Was knocked out by Saarela in the third of the six rounds preceding the final round.

Concours d'Art (The Art Competition)

There was great opposition to an art competition within Sweden's artistic circles. After the Organizing Committee had consulted with art associations and the like the Organizing Committee decided on February 6, 1911, that an art competition would not be included in the Olympic program. But it set aside 5,000 francs in case the IOC wanted to run the competition itself, which the IOC later decided to do, and the competition was divided into five categories. Applications to take part were to be made by January 15 and the competition entries were to have reached the jury by March 1, 1912. The entries were to be sent direct to Pierre de Coubertin's home in Paris. The composition of the jury is still not clear today. Gold, silver and bronze medals could be awarded in each category. A total of five gold medals and one silver medal were awarded. The prizewinning entries were transported after the decision of the jury to Stockholm and exhibited in premises on Karlavägen, near the Olympic Stadium.

Literature (A Total of Seven Entries Came in)

1	Georges Hohrod/Martin Eschbach	Germany	Ode to Sport[1]

1. Far later the winner proved to be Pierre de Coubertin.

Sculpture (A Total of Eight Entries Came in)

1	Walter Winans	USA	An American Trotter[1]
2	Georges Dubois	France	Model of an entrance to a modern Stadium

1. The gold medalist and the unplaced Canadian Tait McKenzie gave away their entries to the Swedish Olympic Committee. In the case of the latter, it was a cast copy of a large medallion, "The Joy of Effort," which is today to be found in the southern arcade in Stockholm's Olympic Stadium. In an inscription by the medal it says instead that it was given by the American Olympic Committee. Winans' sculpture was given away for incorporation in a newly set up sports museum in the Olympic Stadium, but is today to be found in the premises of the Central Association for the Promotion of Sport in the Olympic Stadium. Walter Winans also took part in the shooting at the 1912 Olympic Games and won a silver medal in the team competition in shooting at a running deer.

Painting (A Total of Four Entries Came in)

1   Carlo Pellegrini   Italy   Winter Sports (three friezes)

Architecture (A Total of Nine Entries Came in)

1   Eugène Monod/Alphonse Laverrière   Switzerland   Construction drawings for a modern Stadium

Music (A Total of Six Entries Came in)

1   Riccardo Barthelemy   Italy   Olympic festival march

THE PRIZES IN MOUNTAIN CLIMBING AND HUNTING

In the 1912 Olympic program there was a prize in mountain climbing "for the person or persons who during the years 1908–1911 have carried out the best achievement in the area of mountain climbing" and a prize in hunting "for the best achievement in the area of hunting during the time span of 1908–1911." The latter prize was the result of an initiative by Pierre de Coubertin. Both prizes were gold medals. In 1911 the Organizing Committee sent out an invitation to a number of alpine clubs and hunting clubs within and outside Europe requesting the entry of candidates, and some entries came in.

Each jury realized the difficulty of declaring a winner in these competitions and therefore proposed that no prize should be awarded and that the Organizing Committee should make a proposal that the competitions should not be included in the Olympic program in the future. The Organizing Committee decided on July 2, 1912, that the prizes would not be awarded. The prizes have not been competed for in the Olympic Games since then.

2. Displays

In the 1912 Olympic Games there were official displays in troupe gymnastics, baseball, games from Gotland and *glima* (Icelandic wrestling).

GYMNASTICS

The display gymnasts performed on the infield of the Olympic Stadium, just like the competitive gymnasts. They had approximately 45 minutes at their disposal including their marching in and out and like other participants in the Olympic Games they had to fill in an entry form where they gave assurances about their amateur status.

1	Sweden — male troupe	192 gymnasts	Saturday July 6[1]
2	Sweden — female troupe	48 gymnasts	Saturday July 6[2]
3	Denmark — female troupe	148 gymnasts	Monday July 8[3]
4	Denmark — male troupe	320 gymnasts	Monday July 8
5	Norway — female troupe	22 gymnasts	Monday July 8
6	Finland — female troupe	18 gymnasts	Monday July 8[4]
7	Hungary — male troupe	16 gymnasts	Wednesday July 10
8	Russia — male troupe	18 gymnasts	Thursday July 11

1. The Swedish troupe was led by Ebbe Lieberath. It can be seen in the entry forms at the NA that many male gymnasts took part in both the team competition and the display. The Swedish male and female troupes performed their displays immediately after the Olympic opening ceremony and after the competing nations had paraded out from the Olympic Stadium.

2. The leader of the Swedish troupe was Marrit Hallström and the flag was carried by Franziska Grob. In the NA there are 57 entry forms and a list of the 48 gymnasts + the flag bearer who finally took part in the display.
3. MW gives 150 gymnasts.
4. MW gives 24 gymnasts, which is confirmed by the photo.

BASEBALL

On Monday July 15 a baseball display match was played at Östermalms IP between the USA and Sweden. The American team consisted of athletes from their Olympic squad while Sweden was represented by Västerås Bäsboll Klubb. To make the match more even Sweden were allowed to "borrow" a catcher and three pitchers from the Americans. The match was won by the USA 13–3. According to the program the match should have been played at the Olympic Stadium on July 10, but the American Olympic Committee did not allow its athletes to take part before they had finished competing in their own events in the Olympic Games. On July 15 the Olympic Stadium was being used for the equestrian competitions, so the match was moved to Östermalms IP. On July 16 a display match was played between two American teams with Olympic athletes from the "East" and the "West" and the former won 6–3.

GAMES FROM GOTLAND

The Organizing Committee considered *pärk*, tossing the caber and *varpa* to be suitable sports from Gotland to put on display, and this happened at the Olympic Stadium on July 7. *Pärk* is a ball game where an out-team and an in-team kick and hit with an open hand a ball covered in lambskin. The object of the game is to win ground from the opposing team and to score points. Two teams of seven men competed — one from Visby and one from Gotland's rural districts, and the latter won. In tossing the caber an approximately five-meter long pole with a small end and a big end is used. The pole should be lifted up from the ground, held at the small end, thrown so that the big end lands on the ground and then the pole must fall over so that the small end is pointing in the direction of the throw. In 1912 there was only *stone varpa* and points were played for. The *varpa* is an oval stone approximately 15 cm in diameter (nowadays made of metal) where the throwers are to try to come the closest to a stick knocked into the ground 20 meters away. The person coming closest gets one point and the first thrower to 12 points wins "the ball." Usually the best of three balls is played.

GLIMA

Glima is a form of wrestling exclusive to Iceland with roots in the Viking Age. A display between two wrestlers was held on July 7 at the Olympic Stadium at the same time as the games from Gotland were ongoing. The wrestlers wore leather girdles, with "handles" sewn on, fastened around their waist and thighs. The wrestlers had to hold their opponent's "handles" all through the match and through feints, lifts, pulls and jerks try to make his opponent fall to the ground. On July 15 a formal *glima* competition was held at the Olympic Stadium between six Icelandic wrestlers. They competed for a trophy that was donated by "Icelanders in Denmark."

3. The Inter-Nations Competition

At the 1912 Olympic Games the following points system was used: first prize = 3 points, second prize = 2 points and third prize = 1 point. The standings in the inter-nations competition was something that greatly engaged people at the time and the newspapers adorned their front pages with the current standings. The points system has varied in later Olympic Games. Below is the table published in the "Official Report" published in 1913.

Nation	Number of Points	Number of 1st Prizes	Number of 2nd Prizes	Number of 3rd Prizes	Number of Prizes
Sweden[1]	136	24	24	16	64
USA	124	23	18	19	60
Great Britain	76	10	15	16	41
Finland	52	9	8	9	26
Germany	47	5	13	6	24
France	32	7	4	3	14
Denmark	19	1	6	4	11
Norway	17	4	1	3	8
South Africa	16	4	2	-	6
Hungary	16	3	2	3	8
Canada	14	3	2	1	6
Italy	13	3	1	2	6
Australasia	13	2	2	3	7
Belgium	11	2	1	3	6
Russia	6	-	2	2	4
Austria	6	-	2	2	4
Greece	4	1	-	1	2
Holland	3	-	-	3	3

1. The winner of the pentathlon and decathlon, James Thorpe, was disqualified after the Games for a breach of the amateur rules. When he was restored in 1982 he regained his victories. The USA should therefore have +6 and -1 = +5 points compared with the above table while there is a 3 point deduction for Sweden and -1 point for both Norway and Canada. Compare the result lists for the pentathlon and decathlon. Despite the change Sweden wins the inter-nations competition with 133 points ahead of the USA with 129 points.

4. The Olympic Games Challenge Trophies

A number of challenge trophies were donated to the Olympic Games in London in 1908 and a few more were donated to the Olympic Games in Stockholm. A total of 20 challenge trophies were awarded in 1912. The winners had to sign a guarantee

The Challenge Trophy to the winner of the women's diving, donated by the Countess de Casa Miranda (the famous Swedish opera singer Kristina Nilsson) and won by Margareta Johanson (postcard, National Sports Museum).

that they would return the trophies by January 1, 1916, to the Organizing Committee for the next Olympic Games, which were due to be held in Berlin, but which were cancelled due to the World War. The trophies were then taken away before the 1920 Olympic Games in Antwerp. The Countess de Casa Miranda's trophy is the only one that was awarded to a woman participant—Greta Johanson, the Swedish diver. The Countess is identical with the well-known Swedish opera singer Kristina Nilsson, whose married name was de Casa Miranda.

Donor of the Prize	Event	Won in 1912 by
King of Greece	Marathon	Kennedy McArthur, South Africa
Mme G de Montgomery	Discus	Armas Taipale, Finland
The Gold & Silversmiths	Heavyweight wrestling	Yrjö Saarela, Finland
Football Association (FA)	Football	England
English Fencers	Team fencing, epée	Belgium
City of Prague	Gymnastics, individual	Alberto Braglia, Italy
Count Brunetta d'Usseaux	Rowing, eights	Great Britain
Count Brunetta d'Usseaux	Swimming, 1,500 m freestyle	George Hodgson, Canada
Lord Westbury	Clay trap shooting	James Graham, USA
French government	Sailing, 6 m class	G Tubé/G Fitau, France[1]
Count Geza Andrassy	Show jumping, individual	Jean Cariou, France
King of Sweden	Pentathlon	James Thorpe, USA[2]
Emperor of Russia	Decathlon	James Thorpe, USA[2]
City of Budapest	Team fencing, sabre	Hungary
Emperor of Germany	Team military riding event	Sweden
Emperor of Austria	Dressage	Carl Bonde, Sweden
King of Italy	Team show jumping	Sweden
Swedish Cavalry	Best nation, equestrian events	Sweden
Baron Pierre de Coubertin	Modern pentathlon	Gustaf Lilliehöök, Sweden
Countess de Casa Miranda	Plain high diving, women	Greta Johanson, Sweden

1. Tubé and Fitau were the owners of the boat and Tubé was also the helmsman. The prize was evidently awarded to the owners as the other crew members of the boat are not mentioned.

2. The challenge trophies for the pentathlon and decathlon were awarded at the prize ceremony in 1912 to James "Jim" Thorpe. As he was later disqualified for a breach of the amateur rules, the prize went instead to the person finishing second in each event, Ferdinand Bie, Norway and Hugo Wieslander, Sweden.

About the Contributors

Per **Andersson** is a professor of marketing at the Stockholm School of Economics and is director of the Center for Information and Communication Research at the school. His research includes a focus on industrial marketing and distribution and service innovation and value creation in networks.

Hans **Bolling** graduated from Stockholm University in 2005, and his dissertation was "The Maker of His Own Health: Ideas, Initiatives, and Organizations within Swedish Sports for All Between 1945 and 1981." His previous work has addressed football, Paralympics, and sports clubs and associations, and he is researching sport for the disabled.

Ingemar **Ekholm** is a certified gymnastics teacher and graduate of the Swedish School of Sport and Health Science. He has also worked in various administrative staff functions at the Social Insurance Office in Stockholm.

Mats **Hellspong** is a professor emeritus of ethnology at Stockholm University. His writing includes *The Sport of Boxing in Sweden: A Study of the Cultural Environment of the Sport* and *Traditional Sports: Studies in the Sport and Physical Games of the 18th and 19th Century Swedish Peasant Society*. His new manuscript is on the sports audience in Stockholm in the 1800s and the 1900s.

Hans **Kjellberg** is an assistant professor at the Stockholm School of Economics. His research is primarily on the organization of markets and of marketing's role in such processes. He has previously studied the ICA movement's role in the modernization of the grocery distribution in postwar Sweden. His latest book is the anthology *Reconnecting Marketing to Markets*.

Jan **Lindroth** is a professor emeritus of history at Stockholm University. His primary research is on the early development of the Swedish sports movement. Among his publications are *Athletics Becomes a Popular Movement*, *Sports Between the Wars*, *Gymnastics with Play and Sport*, *Ling: From Greatness to Dissolution* and *Sport for King and Country*.

Ansgar **Molzberger** is an associate professor at the German Sports University, Cologne. His thesis was "Die Olympischen Spiele 1912 in Stockholm — 'Vaterländische Spiele' als Durchbruch für die Olympische Bewegung." He works as curator at the German Sports and Olympic Museum in Cologne.

Therese **Nordlund Edvinsson** is an assistant professor of economic history and researcher at the Department of Economic History, Stockholm University. Her research is primarily on gender and leadership in business, and her latest publication is *The Brotherhood of the Economy: A Study of Homo-Sociality in King Orre's Hunting Club, 1890–1960*.

Patrik **Steorn** is working at the Centre for Fashion Studies at Stockholm University on the project "Fashioning the Early Modern: Creativity and Innovation in Europe 1500–1800," researching fashion caricatures in Sweden during the 1700s. His dissertation was

"Naked Men: Masculinity and Creativity in Swedish Image Culture, 1900–1915," from Stockholm University.

Leif **Yttergren** is an associate professor at the Swedish School of Sport and Health Sciences, Stockholm. His dissertation was on sports in Stockholm in the latter half of the 1800s. His research has primarily dealt with traditional sports on the island of Gotland, the sports leader Sigfrid Edström, and the history of training in sport.

Index

Page numbers in *bold italics* indicate illustrations.

Aas, Thomas Valentin 254
AAU *see* Amateur Athletic Union
ABB *see* Asea Brown Boveri Ltd.
Åberg, Georg 241–2
Accommodation Committee 9, 30, 58, 67
accommodation problems 48, 52, 191
account of the games, official 31, 37, 43, 46, 87, 90, 101–2, 137, 177–8, 234, 241
Acke, Johan Axel Gustaf 147
Adams, Ben 241
Adams, Harry 255
Adams, Platt 241–2
Adams Ray, Evert 2, 115, 233
Adlercreutz, Nils 246
Adlerz, Erik "Loppan" 135*n*51, 264
Adlerz, Märta 109, 120, 135*n*51
Advertising and Information Committee 28, 30, 35, 38
Advertising and Reception Section 30
advertising brochure: Finnish 37–8; official 28–9, 31, 35, 37–43, 45–7, 52, 146
Advertising Committee 9, 27–8, 31, 33, 37–43, 46, 48, 50–1, 67
advertising materials 30–1, 38, 40–3, 46
advertising stamps 31, 35, *36*, 37–8, 42, 46
Aeronautiska Sällskapet 50
Africa 82, 111
African American 68
af Sandeberg, Fritz 33, *59*, 62–3
af Ström, Oscar 246
Aftonbladet 90, 165, 168, 211
age of chivalry 214
Åhlén & Åkerlund 49
Ahlgren, Alexis 82
Ahlgren, Anders *181*, 269
Aho, Paavo 243
AIK 249
Aitchison, Helen 266
Åke Wiberg's Foundation 1
Åkerberg, Harald 207
Aktiebolaget Lux 41
alcohol 89, 182, 186, 189
Allen, Fred 241
Allert, Ejler 253
Allmänna Svenska Elektriska AB (ASEA) 59
Almlöf, Erik 83, 242
Almqvist, Arno 96
Altimani, Fernando 240
Alvén, Hugo 192–3
Amateur Athletic Union (AAU) 47, 226

American & Dominion Lines 40
American General Consulate 42
American Olympic Committee 269, 271
An American Trotter 143, *144*
Amsterdam 42
Amsterdam, 1928 Olympic Games 79, 134
Anderson, Elsa 265
Andersson, Arvid 268
Andersson, Carl Nicanor 108
Andersson, Hjalmar 239–40
Andersson, Per 23, 275
Andersson, Robert "Robban" 135*n*51, 262, 265
Andersson, Selma 135*n*51
Andersson, Torbjörn 171
Andersson, Wilhelm 262, 265
Andrassy, Geza *221*, 246, 273
Anglo-Saxons 211; Anglo-Saxon sport 214
Anker, Johan 253
Annunzio, Gabriele de *see* d'Annunzio, Gabriele
Ansén, Karl 249
Anspach, Henri 248
Anspach, Paul 248
Antwerp, 1920 Olympic Games 85, 228, 273
Applegarth, William 235, 239
aquatics 100, 109–10, 112–3, 115, 117–20, 122–3, 126, 130–4, 261
Arbetarbladet 207
Arbetet 201
Arbin, Harald 264
Archive of the Stockholm Olympic Games 2, 27, 95–6, 128, 146
Argentinean Consulate 41
armed forces 59, 71, 101, 110, 184, 204–6, 208, 213
Armgarth, Gustaf 248
Armour, Allison *221*
Arnheim Lasch, Edith 131, 267
Arnheiter, Albert 252
Aro, Toivo 264
Art Competition *see* Concours d'Art
Arts and Craft Exhibition of 1909 193*n*11
Arvedsons Gymnastikinstitut, Stockholm 128
Arvidsson, Per-Olof 261
Åsbrink, Gösta 251
Åsbrink, Gustaf 30
Åsbrink, Rickard 243
ASEA *see* Allmänna Svenska Elektriska AB
Asea Brown Boveri Ltd. (ABB) 59
Asia 111
Asikainen, Alfred 268

Asp, Nils 253–4
Association for the Promotion of the Art of Fencing 104
Athens, 1896 Olympic Games 16–8, 50, 77, 91, 154, 158, 167, 199
Athens, 1906 intercalary Olympic Games 21–2, 60–1, 77, 108, 113*n*18, 182–3, 199
athletics 10, 12, 14, 22–3, 24*n*26, 67, 97, 100, 102–3, 108, 110–1, 117, 113*n*11, 116, 117, 122, 134, 211, 213, 217, 219–20, 222–3, 225–7, 229*n*12, 235–44
Athletics Committee 9, 62, 75, 82–3, 85, 92, 267
Atout (horse) 246
Aust, Otto 254
Australasia 111, 234, 262–3, 266, 272
Australia 82, 93*n*22, 111, 118, 120, 124, 160, 234
Austria *18*, 82, 118, 120, 122, 157, 234, 248–9, 260–1, 263, 265, 267–8, 272

Babcock, Harold 241
Baker, Philip 236
Balck, Anna *221*
Balck, Viktor 2, 4–5, 9, 12, *14*, 17, 23, 30, 32–3, 37, 44, 57–9, *59*, 61–5, 67–8, 70, 72*n*22, 72*n*25, 72*n*43, 72*n*55, 73*n*64, 75, 104, 115–6, 119, 122, 139, 158, 167, 177, 183, 205, 217–8, 220–4, *221*, 226, 228*n*1, 228*n*2, 228*n*4, 229*n*14, 229*n*16, 229*n*17, 231*n*41
Bålsta 244
Band of the Crown Prince's Hussar Regiment 187
Band of the Royal Scanian Infantry Regiment 185
Barkarby 251
Baronyi, András 262
Barthelemy, Ricardo 143, 270
baseball 244, 270–1
Bathe, Walter 263
Beamish, Alfred 266
Beamon, Bob 75
Beckman, Ernst 174
Behrens, Kurt 265
Békessy, Béla 248
Belgium 43, 82, 118, 120, 234, 246–8, 253, 265, 272–3
La Belle Époque 3, 160
Belote, Frank 235
Benckert, Curt 267
Benedicks, Edvard 261
Bentham, Isaac 265
Berg, Gustaf 41
Bergman, Adolf 268

Bergman, Åke 109
Bergman, Per 253
Bergqvist, Erik "Berka" 265
Bergström, Dick 253
Bergström, Erik 249
Bergström, Kurt 253
Bergvall, Erik 2, 67, 69–70, 115, 119, 134, 157, 233, 261
Berlin 4–5, 43–4, 58, 91, 217, 273
Berlin, IAAF Congress 1913 226
Berlin, IOC session 1909 2, 4–5, 9–10, 23n1, 97, 217
Berlin, local advertising committee 30, 42
Berlin, 1916 Olympic Games 5, 12, 91–2, 211, 224, 229n20, 231n38, 231n47, 273
Berliner Ruderverein von 1876 252
Berna, Tell 237, 240
Berry, Arthur 249
Berthelsen, Nils 253
Berti, Lázló 248
Bianchi, Pietro 250
Bie, Ferdinand 79, 244, 273
Bikila, Abele 75
Billings, Charles 260
Björklund, Elsa 263
Björkman, Carl 255–6
Björkman, Tönnes 255
Björkstén, Elli 127
Björn, Evert 236
Bjurstedt, Anna 267
black market 8
Blau, Harry 260
Blixen-Finecke, Hans von Sr. see von Blixen-Finecke, Hans Sr.
Blomgren, Gustaf 264
Blommaert de Soye, Emanuel de see de Blommaert de Soye, Emanuel
Blomqvist, Erik 256
Boardman, Leslie 263
Boathouse of the Stockholm Rowing Club 16, 155
Boberg, Ferdinand 31
Bohemia 82, 219, 234, 248–9, 267–8
Boin, Victor 231n45, 248
Boivie, Gustaf 257
Bolanschi, Angelo C. 221
Böling, Ivar 181, 269
Bolling, Hans 23, 275
Boltenstern, Gustaf Adolf Sr. 246
Bonde, Carl 246, 273
Bondetåget 171
Bonhag, Georg 237, 240
Boni, Guido 250
Boon, Thérèse 42, 44, 47
Borgström, William 106
Börjesson, Erik 249
Börjesson, Josef 249
Boston 41
Boström, Erik 107, 257–8
Boström, Wollmar 267
Botkyrka 85
Bouin, Jean 163, 237
Bourdieu, Pierre 132
boxing 22, 100, 182, 225, 231n42

Braglia, Alberto 250, 273
Brambeck, Nils 248
brand infringements 49
Brandsten, Ernst 130
brandy 189
Branting, Georg 248
Braun, Hanns 236
Brebner, Ronald 249
Brecke, Andreas 254
Bretting, Kurt 262
Bricker, Calvin 241
Briggs, Allan 255
British Amateur Swimming Association 118
British Olympic Association 118
Brock, Melville 236
Broquedis, Marguerite 126, 267
Broström, Dan 254
Brown, Frank 245
Bruhn-Möller, William 252–3
Brundage, Avery 58, 60, 116, 224, 244
Brunetta d'Usseaux, Eugène 221, 273
Brunialti, Attilo 221
Brunkman, Conrad 252–3
Brunkman, Gustaf 252
Brusewitz, Ellen 109, 125, 135n51
Budapest 273
Budapest, IOC session 1911 62, 64, 72n33, 221, 251
Bugbee, Charles 265
Building Committee 9, 72
Building Committee, swimming 20, 205
Burdette, Cornelius 255
Burgess, Edgar 251
Burman, Bernhard 31, 44, 59, 71n17, 182–3
Burn, Thomas 249
Burt, Harold 257
Butler, Everard 253
Buzzadors 52
Bylina (yacht) 254
Byrd, Leslie 80, 241–2

Caldwell, David 236
Canada 40, 42, 82, 89, 103, 117, 168, 234, 236–7, 239–41, 243–5, 253, 262, 265, 272–3
Canet, Albert 267
Carey, Denis 243
Cariou, Jean 246, 273
Carlberg, Eric 106, 107, 248, 257–9
Carlberg, Wilhelm 107, 257–9
Carlgren, Matts 265
Carlsson, Greta 109, 120, 263
Carlsson, Mauritz "Sörle" 237
Carlstedt, Ragnar 75
Case, John 235
Casparsson, Ernst 246
Castenschiold, Sofie 266
Cederschiöld, Hugo 135n51
Cederschiöld, Margareta 135n51, 266
celebrations, official 177
Central Association for the Promotion of Sports 57–8, 75, 141, 145, 204, 269

Centraltryckeriet 35
Chaffe, Walter 268
Challenge Trophies 244, 272
Champion, Malcolm 262–3
Chatziefstathiou, Dikaia 139
Chicago 5, 21
Childs, Clarence 243
Chile 82, 111, 234
China 44
Chipping Campden 17
cinematography 49
Clason, Hugo 253
Clonmore (horse) 246
closing celebrations 177–8, 180
closing ceremonies 18, 159, 177, 179–80
Club Alpin 45
Co-branding 27, 38, 52
Cocotte (horse) 246
Colas, Paul 255–6
commemorative books 38, 49
commemorative medals 31, 46
Committee for Stockholm Research 1
company sports association 106
complete experience 174
Concours d'Art 64, 138–9, 141, 146–7, 149, 269
Condor (horse) 246
Connell, Raewyn 68
Cook, Theodore 64, 219
Cook's Travel Agency 44
Corneliussen, Torleiv 254
Corner, Georg 265
Coubertin, Pierre de see de Coubertin, Pierre
Countess de Casa Miranda 272–2
Courcy Laffan, Robert Stuart de see de Courcy Laffan, Robert Stuart
Courtman, Percy 263
Craig, Ralph 235
crime 189
Criminal Investigation Department 189
Crondahl, Victor Gustaf 264
Crown Prince see Gustaf Adolf
Crown Prince's Golf Club 17
Cunard and Allen Line 40–1
customs and stamp duties 38
Customs department 49
cycle race 10, 158, 189
cycling 12, 21, 24n26, 83, 100–1, 110–1, 113n22, 117, 178, 189, 225, 227, 244–5
Cycling Committee 9, 245
cycling track 12, 22

Dagens Nyheter 8, 48, 164–5, 167, 188, 203, 206, 210
Dahlbäck, Herman 252–3
Dahlin, John 239
Dahlqvist, Valdemar 171
Dahlström, Erik 249
Daily Mail 45
dance pavilions 182, 185
Danderyd 245
Danielsson, Daniel 48

Danielsson, Ture "Bagarn" 171
d'Annunzio, Gabriele 138, 143, 146
d'Arcy, Victor 239
Davenport, Ira 236
de Blommaert de Soye, Emanuel 246
decathlon 50, 58, 64, 79, 80, 91,
    102, 180, 205, 217, 233, 241,
    244, 272–3
de Coubertin, Pierre 2, 4–5, 9–10,
    17–8, 20, 23n1, 57–8, 64–70,
    100, 115, 118, 124, 134, 137–49,
    177, 191, 206, 208, 214, 217–20,
    221, 223, 225–6, 228, 230n23,
    231n39, 231n44, 231n46, 251,
    269–70, 273
de Courcy Laffan, Robert Stuart
    219, 221
Deficiency Lists 220
De frie (art association) 140
de Laval, Erik 248
de Laval, Georg 107, 119, 251,
    258–9
de Mas Latrie, Jean 97
de Muzsa, Jules 221, 223–4
Denmark 47–8, 82, 102, 115, 118,
    124, 127, 160, 164–5, 167–8, 209,
    214, 234, 240, 248–50, 252–4,
    256–7, 266, 269–70, 272
Desborough of Taplow, Lord 221
Dickson, Charles 59
Diem, Carl 116, 177, 191
Dietz, John 258–9
Dines, Joseph 249
displays: Baseball 271; Games from
    Gotland 271; Glima 271; Gym-
    nastics 270–1
Dixon, Charles 266
Djurgården 3, 17, 157, 165, 254
Djurgårdens IF 249
Djurgården's Theater 183
Djurgårdsbron Bridge 156, 251, 253
Djurgårdsbrunnsviken 16, 20, 155,
    157, 184, 251, 261
Dohna (horse) 246
Dolfen, Peter 258
Donahue, James "Jim" 79, 244
Dowler, Joseph 268
Drabant (horse) 247
Dragoon Regiment 155
Drew, Howard 235
drunkenness 189
Dubois, Georges 143, 145, 269
Duffy, James 239
Duncan, James 80, 242
Durack, Sarah "Fanny" 123–4, 263
Dutch 44, 47, 167, 220
Dutch state railways 43

Edman, Johan 268
Edmundson, Clarence 236
Edström, Ester 130
Edström, Sigfrid 35, 37, 59, 60–7,
    70, 72n20, 72n53, 77, 103–4,
    106, 116, 183, 221, 225–7,
    230n34, 230n35, 231n38,
    231n39, 231n40, 276
Edvinsson, Therese Nordlund 5,
    23, 275

Egypt 234
Ekblad, Karl-Erik 250
Eke, John 82–3, 113n24, 239–40
Ekholm, Ingemar 23, 275
Eklund, Ella 265
Ekman, Johan 260
Ekroth, Helge "Ekis" 249
Eldh, Carl 147
Emperor (horse) 246
Emperor of Austria 246, 273
Emperor of Germany 246, 273
Emperor of Russia 273
Emperor of Russia's Challenge
    Trophy 205
Engelbrekt Monument 142
Engelbrekt School 184
England 30, 41, 43, 62, 96, 156,
    158, 164–9, 207, 231n47, 245,
    249, 273
English Fencers 273
English-French Exhibition, 1908 22
Englund, Leopold 75, 225–6
Enköping 158, 244
entertainment program, official 177
Entertainments Committee 9, 49,
    176, 182–5, 187–8
Equestrian Committee 9, 11
equestrian competitions 100
equestrian events 9–10, 14, 24n12,
    72n33, 96, 100–2, 104–5, 109,
    111–2, 113n22, 117, 169, 180, 205,
    217, 225, 227, 229n14, 230n28,
    235, 245–7
Erickson, Egon 240
Ericsson, Filip 254
Ericsson, Gideon 257–8
Eriksson, Axel 252
Eriksson, Christian 147
Eriksson, Mauritz 255–6
Erna Signe (yacht) 253
Eschbach, Martin 143, 269
Eskilstuna 120, 158, 244
Eskilstuna-Kuriren 206
Eskilstuna simsällskap 120
Eskola, Jalmari 239–40
Ethnographic Museum 155
ethnographic reporting 170
Europe 22, 37, 43–4, 48, 68, 82,
    85, 95, 101, 111, 139, 142, 154,
    200, 250, 270
event marketing 27, 51–2
Executive Committee 9, 37, 44, 58
Executive Committee, liberal party
    174
expatriate Swedes 30, 42, 52
experience marketing 52

Fahr, Otto 262
Falch-Lund, Eilert 253
Fältrittklubben *see* Stockholm
    Cross Country Riding Club
Falun 1
Fast, Ernst 20–1
Fédération Internationale de Fot-
    ball Association (FIFA) 249
Den femte olympiaden 80, 233
fencing 8, 10, 15, 24n26, 83, 96–7,
    100, 105–6, 110–2, 113n22, 117,

143, 156–7, 222, 225, 227,
    231n42, 234, 247–8, 251, 273
Fencing Committee 9, 62
festivities 23, 140, 174, 176–81,
    188, 192–3
Fick, Sigrid 108, 125, 131, 266–7
Fickeisen, Otto 252
Fickeisen, Rudolf 252
*The Fifth Olympiad: The Official
    Report of the Olympic Games of
    Stockholm 1912* 2, 115, 233
Finance Section 9, 29, 31, 35, 38,
    43, 49, 58, 182–3
Finland 37–8, 46, 48, 80, 82, 89,
    96, 102, 115, 118, 120, 127, 160,
    162–3, 169, 219, 231, 234, 237,
    239–40, 242–3, 245, 249–50,
    253–4, 256, 260–1, 264, 268–
    70, 272–3
S.S. *Finland* 63
Finn II (yacht) 254
First World War 5, 104, 157, 160,
    217, 226, 228, 231, 273
Fitau, G 273
Fjaestad, Gustaf 141, 147
Flanagan, John 81
Fleming, Philip 251
Fletcher, Jennie 122, 263
Fock, Bror 240
Földes, Dezsö 248
football 16, 62, 83, 100–1, 108,
    110–1, 113n22, 117, 132, 138, 155,
    157–9, 164–71, 174, 203, 207–8,
    212–3, 225, 227, 230n28, 234–
    5, 249, 273, 275; *see also* soccer
Football Association (FA) 273
Football Committee 84; *see also*
    Soccer Committee
Football World Cup in 1958 171, 174
foreigners 39, 43, 45, 154, 157,
    160–1, 164–5, 177, 179, 181, 184,
    189–91
Förenta Staterna *see* USA
France 18, 40, 43–6, 52, 54n27,
    62, 65–6, 70, 82, 96, 102, 117–8,
    124, 143, 156, 178–9, 234, 237,
    239, 246–7, 250, 253–7, 259–
    60, 265–7, 269, 272–3
fraud 189
Fredriksson, Erik 268
French government 273
Frestadius, Eric 33, 59
Freyer, Sigismund 246
Friborg, Erik 245
Frisell, Hjalmar 260
Frykberg, Nils 240
Frykman, Götrik 249
Fuchs, Jenö 248
Fulton, Arthur 255

Gäfvert, Björn 59
Gallia II (yacht) 254
game shooting 17, 64
Games from Gotland 271; *see also*
    Gotlandic Sports
garden party 161, 176, 178, 192
Garton, Arthur 251
Gåtan (horse) 247

Gautier.Vignal, Albert *221*
Gävle 207
Genberg, A. 96
gender contract 133
gender system 133
General Program of the Games 31, 35, 46, 70
General Secretariat 38
General Secretary of the Stockholm Olympic Games 65–7
General Song Festival 184
George I, King of Greece 17, 273
Gerde, Oszkár 248
German Adverting Committee 38
German Olympic Committee 5, 48
German Team 48
Germany 4–5, 18, 41, 43, 45, 65, 70, 82, 95–6, 102, 111, 118, 120, 124, 143, 165, 169, 178–9, 206, 229n20, 234–6, 239–40, 245–52, 260–9, 272
Germot, Maurice 266
Gerstacker, Georg 268
Gillan, James 251
Gillis Duncan 243
Gitsham, Christopher "Chris" 90, 239
Glad, Thoralf 254
Gleason, Edward 260
Glima, Icelandic wrestling 100, 184, 270–1
Gobert, André 266
Goehring, Leo 241
Goeldel-Bronikoven, Alfred 260
The Gold & Silversmiths 273
Gore, Arthur 266
Göteborgs Aftonblad 202, 205, 209
Göteborgs damers simklubb 120
Göteborgs FF 249
Göteborgs Morgonpost 202, 209, 212
Göteborgs-Posten 207
Gothenburg 19, 40, 75, 80, 104–5, 113n27, 120, 128, 155, 189, 203–4, 207, 209
Gothenburg's Yacht Club 104
Gotland 271
Gotlandic Sports 184; *see also* Games from Gotland
Goulding, Georg *103*, 240
government 4–5, 7, 29, 61, 172n60, 173n61; grants for sport 4, 50; *see also* State
graded voting rights 3
Graham, James 260, 273
Granbergs Konstindustri AB 49
Grand Hotel Royal 178, 184
Great Britain 82, 89, 102, 111, 219, 234–7, 239–40, 243, 246, 248–53, 255, 257–68, 272–3
Great Labor Conflict, 1909 2, 192
Greco-Roman style 268
Greece 18, 21, 70, 82, 138, 140, 206, 208, 234, 241, 255, 257–60, 272
Griffith-Joyner, Florence 75
Grist, David 1
Grob, Franziska 271
Grönberg, Åke *119*

Grönfors, Thorsten 267
Grönhagen Åke 251
Gross, Otto 262
Grubb, Frederick 245
Grumpelt, Harry 240
Grundsee (horse) 246
Grünewald, Isaac 147
Grut, Torben *14*, 75, 154
Gullberg, Anders 1
Gumpel, Max 265
Günther, Paul 265
Gustaf Adolf, Crown Prince of Sweden 11, 33, *59–60*, 64, 70, 116, 139, 165, 176–7, 181, 183, 202, *212*, 225–7
Gustaf V, King of Sweden 1, 10–1, 50, 70, 148, 178, 181, 184, *225*, 273
Gustafsson, August 268
Gustafsson, Karl "Köping" 249
Gustav Adolf's square *190*
Guth, Jiri *221*
Gutterson, Albert 241
Gyllenkrook, Axel 257
gymnastics 10, 14, 24n26, 68, 79, 97, 100, 102, 104, 106, 111, 113n22, 115–7, 119–20, 127–9, 157, 161, 205, 208–9, 211–4, 225, 227, 231n38, 250; Ling 77–8, 102, 208–11, 213–4, 250–1; Swedish 21, 80, 102, 106, 128, 208–9, 213, 228n2
Gymnastics Committee 9, 107
gymnastics teachers 128, 132

Haff, Carroll 236
Haga 245
Hagelqvist, Stina 142
Haggett, Charles 126
Haglund, Nils Erik 262
Halifax 41
Hall, Frank 260
Halldin, Oscar 46
Hallström, Marrit 128, 271
Halme, Juho 243
Halse, Arne 243
Hälsingborg's Rowing Club 252
Handbok i friidrott (Athletics Handbook) 88
Handelstidningen 207, 209, 212
Hannam, Edith 266
Hanney, Edward 249
Hansen, Halfdan 253
Hansen, Jörgen 253
Hanson, Pontus 265
Happenny, William 241
Hardwick, Harold 262–3
Hartman, Poul 253
Hasselbacken 10, 24n25, 24n26
Hasselgren, Anders 175
Hatfield, John Gatenby 262
Havslyssnaren 147
Hawkins, Martin 235
Hay, Ebba 106–7, 109, 125, *127*, 130
Healy, Cecil 262–3
Heatherbell (yacht) 253
Hebner, Harry 262

Heje, Arnfinn 253
Helgesson, Carl 223
Hellberg, Carl 30
Hellspong, Mats 9, 23, 275
Hellström, Carl 254
Hellström, Kristian 30, 33, 37, 40, 47, *59*, 60, 64–5, *66*, 67–70, 75, 82–3, 134, 202, *221*, 222
Helsingborg 14, 17
Helsinki 125
Helsinki, local advertising committee 30, 42, 48
Helsinkin Sanomat 37, 46
Hendrickson, John 260
Henner, Robert 248
Henning, Thor 263
Henriques, Emil 254
heritage 52, 171
Hermelin, Sven *59*, 65, 80, 183, 191, 233
Heyman, Bengt 254
Hildebrand, Karl 22
Hill, Arthur 265
Hird, Frederick 257
Hirdman, Yvonne 133
Hirschman, Elisabeth 33
Hjertberg, Ernie 62, 83, *84*, 85–92, 101, 113n18, 181, 211
Hjertberg, Loretta 85
Hjortzberg, Olle 31–5, 141
Hjulsta 251
Hoare, Gordon 249
Hodgson, George Ritchie 262, 273
Högby 113n24
Hohenau,Vilhelm von *see* von Hohenau, Vilhelm
Hohrod, Georges 143, 269
"Holiday in Sweden," Tulebolagen's tourist guide 45
Holland 43–4, 48, 82, 157, 164, 167, 170, 234, 248–9, 272
Holland, local advertising committee 30, 42
Holmér, Gustaf "Gösse" 244
Holmström, Annie 135n51, 267
Holst, Johan Hübner von *see* Hübner von Holst, Johan
Holtermann, Oscar *59*
Horine, George 240
Horn af Åminne, Henric 246
Horsfall, Ewart 251
Hotel Continental 185
Hübner von Holst, Johan 257, 259
Hufvudstadsbladet 160, 168–70
Humby, Harold 260
Humphreys, Frederick 268
Hungary 82, 102, 163, 219, 221, 223, 229, 234, 242–3, 246, 248–50, 255, 262–3, 265, 269–70, 272–3
hunting 138, 270; prize in 270
Hunting Committee 9
Hurley, Charles 62, 122
Huszagh, Kenneth 262
Hutson, George 237
Hvad Nytt 188
Hynes, Mathias 268

IAAF *see* International Amateur
  Athletics Federation
Iceland 234, 271
Icelanders in Denmark 271
Idealist (horse) 246
"Idrotten och Samhället" 95
Idrottsbladet 85, 88
Idrottsparken 5, 12–5, 22, 72, **86**,
  154, 157, 164, 266
Idun 123, 128, 134, 162
IF Sleipner 65
IFK (Idrottsföreningen Kamra-
  terna) 104–5, 113*n*27
IFK Eskilstuna 249
IFK Göteborg 249
IFK Norrköping 249
Ilex (horse) 246
Illustrierte Sportzeitung 62
image of Sweden 50, 192
IMP community 27
information brochure, official 31
insurance 8
International Amateur Athletics
  Federation (IAAF) 225–6, 237;
  see also International Association
  of Athletics Federations (IAAF)
International Association of Athlet-
  ics Federations (IAAF) 60, 67,
  77, 113*n*11; *see also* International
  Amateur Athletics Federation
  (IAAF)
International Olympic Committee
  (IOC) 2, 4–5, 10, 17–8, 20–1,
  53*n*23, 57, 60, 62–4, 69–70, 77,
  100–1, 115–6, 118, 131, 139–41,
  181, 217–20, **221**, 224, 226, 228,
  231*n*42, 231*n*47, 241, 244, 250,
  266, 269; archives, Lausanne 2,
  143; Executive Committee 226
International Skating Federation 122
International Swimming Federation
  20, 118
Inter-Nations Competition 169, 272
Intimate Theater 183
IOC *see* International Olympic
  Committee
Ireland 245
Irish Lass (horse) 246
Irmelin (horse) 246
Isberg, Paul 254
Italy 82, 138, 143–4, 146, 234,
  237, 240, 247–50, 262, 270,
  272–3

Jackson, Arnold 236
Jackson, John 255
Jacobs, David 239
Jacobsson, Sigfrid "Sigge" 85, **86**,
  90, 239
Jacobsson, Skotte 235
Jansson, Eugène 147
Jansson, Johan "John" 264–5
Jansson, Jonas 111
Japan 51, 82, 102, 111, 234, 237
Järva 244
Jebe, Christian 254
Jeffries, Jim 182
Jensen, Søren Marinus 269

Jernström, Verner 255
Johanson, Margareta "Greta" 120,
  121, 123, **124**, 130, 263, 265,
  272, 273
Johansson, Alfred 35
Johansson, Claes 268
Johansson, Hilding 95, 110
Johansson, Hjalmar 96, 264
Johansson, Hugo 255–6
Johansson, Thure 101, 113*n*18
Jöhncke, Axel 248
Johnson, A.E. 41
Johnson, Axel Ax:son 92
Johnson, Folke 253
Johnson, Helge Ax:son 92
Johnson, Jack 182
Johnson, Karl 114*n*32
Johnstone, John 240
Jones, John Paul 236
Jönköping 106, 125, 130
Jönköpings Lawn-Tennis Club
  127, 130
Jönköpings Tennis Hall 130
Jonsson, Carl 268
Jonsson, Gustaf Adolf 256
Jonsson, Martin **166**
Jonsson, Sonja 263
Joy of Effort **145**, 269
Julin, Harald 265
Junsele 96
Just, Jaroslav 267

Kahanamoku, Duke Paoa 262
Kaknäs (shooting range) **17**, **105**,
  157, 212, **218**, 251, 254, **256**
Kaknäs tower 254
Kanakuri, Shizo 51, 237
Kander, Sigurd 253
Karl XII bust in bronze **148**
Karlavägen 269
Karlsson, K. 114*n*32
Karlsson, Ove 233
Keeper, Joseph 237
Kellner, Hanny 122
Kellner, Paul 262
Kelly, Frederick **87**, 235
Kemp, Francis 257
Kempe, Carl 265–6
Kerstin (yacht) 254
Kihlberg, Erik "Kille" 171
Kilman, Gustaf 247
King Gustaf Adolf's Foundation
  for Swedish Culture 1
King of Greece *see* George I
King of Italy 247, 273
King of Sweden *see* Gustaf V
Kinnear, William 253
Kirby, Alister 251
Kiriki (horse) 246
Kitson, Harry 267
Kitty (yacht) 254
Kiviat, Abel 236
Kjellberg, Hans 23, 275
Kleen, Elsa 161
Klefbeck, Ernst 106
Klein, Martin 268
Klerck, Carl-Gustaf 248
Knight, Arthur 249

Kóczán-Kovács, Móric 243
Kolbäck 244
Kolehmainen, Hannes **163**, 169,
  237, 239, 240
König, Claes 119
Konow, Magnus 253
Konstnärsförbundet 140, 142, 147–
  8
Köping 244
Köpings IS 249
Köring, Dorothea **125**, 267
Kornerup, C, Ludvig 30
Koskelo, Kaarlo 268
Kovács, Miklos 80
Kreuzer, Oscar 267
Kristiania Roklub 252
Kristinehamn 120
Kröcher, Rabod Wilhelm von *see*
  von Kröcher, Rabod Wilhelm
Krokstedt, Carl-Gustaf 248
Kronprinsens Lawntennisklubb
  (The Crown Prince's Lawn
  Tennis Club) 126
KSSS 1912 (yacht) 254
Kullerstrand, Karl-Axel 240
Kumfeldt, Torsten 265
Kungliga gymnastiska centralinsti-
  tutet (GCI) 128
Kungsör 244
Kungsträdgården **4**
Kusic, Hugo Maksimilian 253
Kvinnliga föreningen Sveriges
  uppvisning 128

Laboratoriebacken 261
Lady Artist (horse) 246
Låftman, Sven 75, 223
Lager, Gunnar 252
Lager, John 252
Lagergren, Axel 40
Läggesta 244
Lake Geneva 146
Lake Mälaren 21, 50, 158, 244
Lake Värtan 185
Lamby, Nils 253
Landsberg, Karl Josef 190, 245
Lane, Alfred 258–9
Larsen, Alfred 253
Larsen, Edvard 242
Larsen, Niels 256
Larsen, Petter Andreas 253
Larsson, Bernhard 255–6
Larsson, Carl 141
Larsson, Erik 268
Larsson, Karl 261
Larsson, Sam 40
Lasanen, Otto 268
Las-Torres, Béla von *see* von Las-
  Torres, Béla
Laurin, Carl O. 134
Lausanne 2, 146, 222, 224
Lausanne, IOC Session 1913 220,
  222, 224
Laval, Erik de *see* de Laval, Erik
Laval, Georg de *see* de Laval,
  Georg
Laverrière, Alphonse 143, 146,
  270

lawn-tennis 108, 125–6; *see also* tennis
Lawntenniskommittén 126; *see also* Tennis Committee
Lazaro, Francisco 50–1, 93*n*65, 212, 237
Leander Rowing Club 251, **252**
Le Hardy de Beaulieu, Philippe 248
Leister, Karl 252
Lemming, Eric 80, 91, 165, 243
Lessimore, Edward 257
Levidis, Nikolaos 255
Levin, Astley 33, 37, **59**, 62, 71*n*17, 183
Lewenhaupt, Carl Gustaf 247
Lewerentz, Sigurd 155
Lewin, Jacob 249
Lewis, Carl 75
Lewis, Rudolph 21, 245
Lido 155, 251
Lieberath, Ebbe 250, 270
Liesche, Hans 240
Liljeholm Bridge 244
Lilliehöök, Gustaf "Gösta" **119**, 251, 273
Lilliehöök, J. 48
Lind, Carl Johan 243
Lindarängen racetrack 14, 193*n*8, 245
Lindberg, Edward 236, 239
Lindberg, Knut "Knatten" 108, 235, 239
Lindblom, Gustaf "Topsy" 91, 242, 248
Lindh, Sam 130
Lindhagen, Sven 155, 174, 191, 233
Lindholm, Eric 236, 239
Lindman, Arvid 4, 7, 16
Lindqvist, Erik 253
Lindroth, Jan 23, 57, 67, 275
Lindskog, Sven August 261
Lindstedt, Christian 85
Lindstrand, Frans Gustaf 269
Lindström, Herbert 106, 268
Ling, Per Henrik 80, 209
Ling gymnastics *see* gymnastics, Ling
Linnér, Sigfrid Nathanael 37, **59**
Lippincott, Donald 235
liquor licence 182, 186–7
List of Results 235; Athletics 235–45; Concours d'Art (The Art Competition) 269–70; Cycling 244–5; Equestrian Events 245–7; Fencing 247–8; Football (Soccer) 249; Gymnastics 250–1; Hunting 270; Modern Pentathlon 251; Mountain Climbing 270; Rowing 251–3; Sailing 253–4; Shooting 254–61; Swimming (Aquatics) 261–5; Tennis 265–7; Tug-of-War 267–8; Wrestling 268–9
Littlewort, Henry 249
Ljunggren, Jens 174
Ljungström, Gösta 101, 113*n*18
local advertising committees 48

Löfvander, Carl 187–8
Logården 178, 192
Lo-Johansson, Ivar 206
Lomberg, Charles 79, 244
London 154, 156, 169, 219; underground 43
London, IOC session in 1908 4
London, local advertising committee 30, 42–3
London, 1908 Olympic Games 4–5, 22, 48, 58, 77, 91, 97, 118–9, 132, 138, 154, 167, 199
London Olympia diploma 64
Longworth, William 262
Lönn, Algot 245
Lord Iron (horse) 247
Lord Westbury 273
Lowe, Gordon 266
Löwenadler, Carl Oskar 75
Löwenadler, Frederick 59, 63–4
Luber, Hans 265
Lucky Girl (yacht) 254
Ludwigshafener Ruderverein 252
Lukeman, Frank 244
Lund 128
Lundberg, Ivar 108
Lundeberg, Åke 260–1
Lundén, Humbert 254
Lundgren, Karin 120, 263
Lunds Dagblad 203, 205
Luther, Karl August "Charles" 235, 239
Lützow, Wilhelm 263
Luxembourg 82, 234, 250, 267–8
Luxembourg, IOC session 1910 62, 64, 101, 250

Mac Miche (yacht) 254
Macintosh, Henry 239
Madsen, Lars Jørgen 256
Magda IX (yacht) 253
Maggie (horse) 246
Magn. Bergvalls Foundation 1
Magnusson, Emil 80, 242
Maier, Otto 252
Malisch, Paul 263
Mallon, Bill 95, 233
Malm, Ragnar 245
Malmö 104, 113*n*27, 201, 203
Malmö Roddklubb 252
Malmsten, Gustaf 241
Malmström, Gustaf 268
Malmström, Hedvig 68
Marangue, Edouard Marc Mény de *see* Mény de Marangue, Edouard Marc
marathon course 38, **78**
marathon race 21, 50–1, 79, 81–3, 85, 87, 90–1, 96, 154, 158, 161–3, 166, 177, 180, 187, **210**, 212, 234, 237–9, 273
Marble Stadium of Athens 154
March of the Finnish Cavalry 160
Marche Olympique 146
Marga (yacht) 254
Margaret, Crown Princess of Sweden 184
market communication 32

marketing 9, 23, 27–8, 33, 38, 41, 44, 47, 49–52, 53*n*5, 53*n*23
Marseille, local advertising committee 30, 42
Mas Latrie, Jules de *see* de Mas Latrie, Jean
Mattiasson, Edvin 268
Mattson, Per 252
McArthur, Kennedy 90, 239, 273
McDonald, Patrick 242–3
McGrath, Matthew 243
McKenzie, Tait R. **145**, 269
McWhirter, Douglas 249
Medal and Badge Committee 9, 58
Medusa (horse) 247
memorabilia 52
Menaul, Austin 244
Mény de Marangue, Edouard Marc 267
Mercer, Eugene 241, 244
merchandising 49, 52
Meredith, James 236, 239
Meredith, Leon 245
Mészáros, Ervin 248
Metaxas, Anastasios 260
Meyer, Alvah 235
Mignon (horse) 246
Mills, Edwin 268
Milne, William 257
Mina femton olympiader och några till 174
Ministry for Foreign Affairs 42
Minnen (memoirs) 218
Miss Hastings (horse) 246
Mme. G de Montgomery 273
Mme. Jarvis 123
Mme. Pescatore **221**
modern Olympic Games 2, 12, 16–7, 57, 137, 148, 154
modern pentathlon 10, 14, 24*n*26, 67, 83, 97–8, 100, 105–6, 111, 113*n*22, 117–9, 134, 154, 165–6, 170, 203, 205, 213, 217, 223, 225, 227, 230*n*23, 250, 273
Modern Pentathlon Committee 9
Molin, Edvin 30
Möller, Carl 253
Möller, Edvin 241
Möller, Ivan 235, 239
Molzberger, Ansgar 12, 23, 275
Monod, Eugène 143, 146, 270
Montreal 17
Moore, Isabella **122**
Morgen 47
Morgonluft 147
mountain climbing 64, 270; prize in 270
Mountain Climbing Committee 9
Mrs. Holmes 123
Ms. Balck **221**
Ms. Mörk 68
Much Wenlock 17
Mucks, Arlie 242
Mudin, Imre 242
Muller, Emil 242
Munro, Alexander 268
Murphy, Frank 241
Murray, Robert 257

Murray, Walter 33, 37, 59
Muzsa, Jules de *see* de Muzsa, Jules
Myrberg, Herman 249

NA *see* National Archives
Nadi, Nedo 248
national anthem 165–6, 179, 192–3, 203
National Archives 2, 53*n*12, 95, 229*n*11, 233, 235, 270
National Board of Public Planning 14
National Railway Board 40
National Sports Federation 57–8, 69–70, 77, 204; *see also* Swedish Sports Confederation
national symbols 192
Navy's Band 179
Nelson, Frank 241
Neptun 130
Neptun (horse) 246
Nerman, Ture 201–4
Neuendorff, Karin 128
New Collage 252
New South Wales Ladies' Swimming Association 124
New York 18, 40–3, 82, 187
New York Athletic Cub 84
The New York Times 85, 159, 160, 167–8
New Zealand 82, 93*n*22, 111, 157, 234
Nicholson, John 235
Niklander, Elmer 80, 242–3
Nilsson, August 201 203
Nilsson, Einar 242–3
Nilsson, Kristina *see* Countess de Casa Miranda
Nina (yacht) 254
The 1912 Olympic Games 95, 233
"The 1912 Stockholm Olympiad: The Competions–The People–The City" 95, 115
Nobel, brothers 101
Nobelgatan 155
Nobelparken 155, 261
Nordenström, Martin 248
Nordenswan, Arthur 257
Nordic Games 58, 72*n*22, 171, 176, 199
Nordisk Resebureau 30
Nordiska Kompaniet (NK) department store 61, 161, **238**
Nordiskt Idrottslif 72*n*22, 88
Nordlander, Axel 246
Norling, N. 207
Norman (yacht) 254
Norrbro Bridge **190**
Norrköping 113*n*27
Norrköpings Tidningar 209
North West Europe 111, 117
Norway 2, 22, 48, 62, 67, 82, 102, 111, 115, 118, 120, 127, 157, 203, 234, 240, 242–4, 249–56, 267, 270, 272–3
Nurdung II (yacht) 254
Ny Tid 204, 207, 211

Ny Tidning för Idrott 72*n*22, 141; *see also Tidning för Idrott*
Nya Samhället 201
Nyberg, Herman 254
Nybroviken 16, 251
Nykjöbings paa Falster Roklub 253
Nyköping 130
Nylén, Carl Olof 267
Nynäshamn **19**, 96, 157, 253

Öberg, Erik 268
Oceania 82, 111
Ochs, Jacques 248
Ode to Sport 143, 146, 269
Oeffelt 44
Öland 83, 113*n*24
Old Norse theme 214
Olin, Johan 269
Olofsson, Eva 57
Olsson, Robert 75, 243
Olsson, Thorild 240
Olympia, Olympic fairground 184–8, **185**, 192–3
Olympiaboken 233
Olympic Games Challenge Trophies *see* Challenge Trophies
Olympic March 143
Olympic movement 1, 12, 21, 199, 208, 214, 217–20, 224, 226–8, 231*n*46
Olympic News 48
Olympic Stadium 1, 4, 7, 8, 10, **11**, **13–4**, 15–6, 18, 21, 48, 50–1, **60**, 61, 67, 75, 79, 81, 85–7, 90, 96, 129, 144–5, 147, 154, **155**, **159**, 161–4, **166**, 171, 176, 180, 183–5, **186**, 187, **188**, 200–2, 208, 234–5, 237, 239–40, 244–7, 249–51, 262, 265, 267–71; *see also* Stadion
Olympic Summer Games 1
Olympic week 8, 10, 15, 24*n*26, 78, 96, 154, 177, 180, 184, 190, 235; *see also* Stadium week
Olympic Winter Games 1
Omen (horse) 246
opening ceremony 159–61, 182, 234, 270
opening of the games, official 189, 266
Opponent Movement 142
Örebro-Kuriren 206–7
Örgryte IS 108, 149
Orlando, Alfonso 237
Ormsund Roklub 253
Örn (yacht) 254
Örtengren, Ruben 257
OS, Historia & statistik 233
Osburn, Carl 255
Oscar Theater 183, 249
Osiier, Ivan 248
Östberg & Lenhardtson AB 35, 49
Osterley, Friedrich von *see* von Osterley, Friedrich
Östermalm, Stockholm borough 5
Östermalm's Athletic Ground 5, 15, 88, 156–7, 187, 247, 251, 266, 271

Östersund 1
Östra Station 90
Owens, Jesse 75
Oxelösund 113*n*24

Palén, Paul 259
Pan-Hellenic Games 208
Paris 43–4, 54*n*27, 143, 219, 269
Paris, IOC Congress 1914 100, 226–8
Paris, local advertising committee 30, 42, 46
Paris, 1900 Olympic Games 18, 20–1, 97, 154
Paris, 1900 World Fair 18
Paris, 1924 Olympic Games 79
pärk 100, 271
Parton, Mabel 266
Pastorns pojkar 106
Patching, Georg 235
Patent and Registration department 35
Patton, Georg **97**, 98, 251
Pedersen, Carl 253
Pellegrini, Carlo 143–4, 146, 270
Peltonen, Urho 80, 243
pentathlon 50, 58, 79, 102, 148, 241, 243–4, 272–3
Pepé, Joseph 257–8
peripheral activities 174, 192
Person, Ture 235, 239
Personne, Birger 248
Persson, Axel "A.W" 245
Persson, Nils 253
Pescatore, Maurice **221**
Petersburg 101
Petersen, Andrea 139
Peterson, Erik 191, 233
Petre, R. 30
Peyron, Henry 248
Philadelphia 41, 96
Philbrook, Georg 242
Piepes, Felix 267
Pimm, William 257
Plater, Philip 255
police force 105, 154, 189
Polyteknic Roklub 252
Porte du Gymnase Moderne 143
Portland 41
Portugal 50, 82, 93*n*65, 212, 234, 237
Poster Committee 33
poster, official 27–8, 31–3, **34**, 35, 37–47, 49, 52, 54*n*27, 217
Pott, Herbert 265
Poulter, Horatio 258
Powell, Kenneth 235
Prague 125, 273
press badge 48
Press Committee 9, 48
press tickets 28, 48
Pretty Girl (horse) 246
Preuss, Albert 260
Preussianism 206
prize ceremony 50, 144, 273
Prize diploma 31, 46
Program Section 9, 58
programs 9, 29, 38, 40, 43

Prokopp, Sándor 255
public dance 182, 185–6
public order 182, 189
Publicist Club 48
publicity 16, 27–8, 90
punch 181, 189; alcohol free 180
punch patriotism 192
punch song 193

Quebec-Montreal 41

Radmilovic, Paul 265
Rafaelli, Jean-Francois 143
railway tickets 40, 61
Raita, Antti 245
Ramlösa 17
Ramme, Walter 262
Råneå 103
Ranft, Albert 183
Rappe, Signe 184
Rasmussen, Aage 240
Råsta Lake 254
Råsunda IP *18*, 19, 155, 157, 249, 254
Rau, Richard 235
Razo Farbrikerna 41
Reception Committee 9, *63*, 176–7
Regnell, Elsa 135*n*51, 265
Regnell, Lisa *69*, 120, 130, 135*n*51, *200*, 265
Reidpath, Charles 235–6, 239
Reno 182
Residence of the American ambassador 155
restaurants 39, 42, 184, 186–8
Results *see* List of Results
Revue Olympique 142–3, 145, 219–20, 224
Richards, Alma 240
Rieck, Miken 267
Rieck-Müller, Maria 162
Riget 47
right to vote 3, 131
rights for photography 28, 49
Rochow, Friedrich von *see* von Rochow, Friedrich
Roddklubben af 1912 252–3
Rolf, Ernst 171
Romander, Nils 255
Rome 5, 22
rooms, shortage of 48
Roper-Barrett, Herbert 266
Rose, Ralph 242–3
Rosen, Hans von *see* von Rosen Hans
Rosen, Pontus von *see* von Rosen, Pontus
Rosenberg, Margareta "Grete" 263
Rosenblad, Carl 246
Rosencrantz, Fredrik 247
Rosenswärd, Harry 254
Rosvall, Ture 252–3
Rotterdam 42
rowing 10, 13, 16, 62–3, 83, 96, *99*, 100–2, 111, 112*n*4, 113*n*22, 117, 138, 155–8, 178, 225, 227, 230*n*28, 234, 251
Rowing Committee 9

Royal Academy of the Arts, London 138
Royal box 160
Royal Family 4, 11, 15, 46, 157, 160, 170, 177–8, 228*n*2
Royal Lawn Tennis Club of Stockholm (KLTK) 104, 106, 125–6, 187
Royal Palace *4*, 178, 181, 192
Royal Patriotic Society 1
Royal stand 227
Royal Swedish Academy of the Fine Arts 140, 142, 147
Royal Swedish Opera *4*, 50, 178, 183–4
Royal Swedish Yacht Club (Kungliga Svenska Segel Sällskapet, KSSS) 19, 96, 104, 253–4
Royal Tennis Hall 15, 187
Royal tennis pavilion 180, 265; *see also* Tennis Hall
Rudolph, Wilma 75
Runström, Axel 264
Ruskin, John 138
Russia 47, 82, 96, 102, 150, 160, 229*n*14, 234, 247, 249, 253–4, 258–60, 268, 270, 272

Saarela, Yrjö 269, 273
Saaristo, Juho 80, 243
sailing 10, 19, 24*n*26, 96, 100, 102, 104, 107, 111, 112*n*4, 113*n*22, 117, 138, 157, 169, 212–3, 225, 253, 273
St. John 41
St. Louis 219
St. Louis, 1904 Olympic Games 5, 21–2, 68, 77, 91, 154, 219
St. Louis, 1904 World Fair 21
Sällström, Richard 253
Salmon, Gaston 248
Saltsjön 50
Sandberg, Erik 254
Sandberg, Gustaf 249
Sandberg, Harald 254
Sandeberg, Frits af *see* af Sandeberg, Frits
Sándorm, Jósef *166*
Sans Autout (yacht) 254
Sass (yacht) 254
Sassnitz 40, 103
Scandinavia 20, 40, 61, 70, 79, 138, 160, 218
Scandinavia Travel Bureau, New York 43
Scandinavian-American Line 41
Scandinavian tourist agencies, United States 43
Schaesberg-Tannheim, Rudolf von *see* von Schaesberg-Tannheim, Rudolf
Schenker, Zoltán 248
Schnitt, Gustaf Adolf 260
Scholander, Lisa 184
Scholander, Sven 184
Schomburgk, Heinrich *125*, 267
Schonberg, Torsten 33, 35
Schutte, Carl 245

Scotland 245
Scott, Herbert 246
Scott, Rose 69
Seas, Henry 258
Second World War 98, 226, 231*n*44, 251
Segrave, Jeffrey O. 139
Ségura, Louis 250
Selection Committee for Swedish Americans for the Olympic Games in Stockholm in 1912 82, 106
Seligman, Edgar 248
Serafimersjukhuset (Serafimer hospital) 51, 93*n*65
Serbia 82, 102, 207, 234
Setterwall, Gunnar *108*, 125, *125*, 266–7
Sewell, John 268
Shamrock (horse) 246
Sharpe, Ivor 249
Sharpshooter Movement 105
Shepherd, James 268
Sheppard, Melvin 236, 239
Sheridan, Martin *202*
shooting 10, 16–7, 24*n*26, 58, 96, 100–1, 104, 106–7, 108, 110–2, 113*n*22, 117, 135*n*51, 143, 157, 158, 185, 203, 205, 211–3, 218, 225, 227, 251, 254–61, 269, 273
Shooting Committee 9, 230
shooting parties 184
Siikaniemi, Väinö 80, 243
Sirri Bey, Selim *221*
Sjöberg, Gösta 109
Sjöberg, Henrik 77
Sjöstedt, Erik 40, 45–6
Skansen, open-air museum 50, 179
Skatteboe, Gudbrand Gudbrandsen 256
Skogen, Embret 255
Sloane, N. M. *221*
Sloane, William 64
Småland 208
Smålands Folkblad 208
Smedmark, Rudolf 235
Smith, Charles 265
smoking 89
soccer 8, 10, 12, 14, *18–9*, 22, 62, 108, *175*, 193*n*8; *see also* football
Soccer Committee 9; *see also* Football Committee
Social Darwinism 67
Social Democrats 3, 199, 201–8, 211, 213
Social-Demokraten 203–4
Sockalexis, Andrew 239
Söderblom, Bruno 85
Söderlund, Oscar 154, 161
Södertälje 158, 244
Sohlman, Harald 59
Sollentuna 158, 237, 245
Solna 17, 245, 254
Sonja III (yacht) 254
Sörensen, Einar 248
South Africa 82, 90, 111, 162, 234–5, 239, 245, 255–6, 267, 272–3
South America 41, 82, 111

souvenirs 28, 49, 52
Spain 164
Spånga 251
Spanish flu 130
Sparre, Count Louis 107, 111
Speirs, Annie *122*, 263
Die Spiele der V. Olympiade 1912 in Stockholm 95
spokespersons 52
sponsors, official 49
Sports Home 85–6, *175*
sports lottery 4–5, 7, 50, 61
Sportsmen's House *see* Sports Home
Spotts, Ralph 260
Sprout, Warren 255
Staaff, Karl 174, 199
Stadion 61, 154–9, 161, 163, 167–9, 234; *see also* Olympic Stadium
Stadium week 10, 177, 217, 219; *see also* Olympic week
Staib, Fritz 253
Stamper, Harold 249
Stanton, Richard 143
State 12–3; *see also* Government
State grants 4
State land 4
State schools 104
Steer, Irene *122*
Sten Sture Monument 142
Stenborg, Knut 236, 239
Stenroos, Albin 237, 239–40
Steorn, Patrik 23, 275
Stewart, Charles 258–9
Stockholm City Council 3–4, 13, 29, 176
Stockholm City Law Courts 142
Stockholm Cross Country Riding Club 14, 245
Stockholm Exhibition, 1897 40, 175, 189
Stockholm, IOC session 1912 224
Stockholm marriage 131
Stockholm, Old Town 3
Stockholm Rowing Club *16*, 155
Stockholm School of Economics 275
Stockholm Swimming Club 104
Stockholmia 1
Stockholm's Amateur Association 77
Stockholms Dagblad 161, 203, 205–6, 212
Stockholms kappsimningsklubb (SKK) 120, 123
Stockholm's Pistol Club 104
Stockholms Roddförening 155
Stockholm's Sharpshooter Club 104
Stockholms-Tidningen 91, 210
Stocksund 245
Storängsbotten 188
Strand Hotel 175
Strandvägen 156
Strängnäs 158, 244
Stranne, Sidney 251
Stridsberg, Gustaf 203, 205
Strobino, Gaston 90, 239
Ström, Oscar af *see* af Ström, Oscar
Strömbadet 20

Sturegatan 164
Styrelsen i Stockholm för militär idrott (Board of Military Sports in Stockholm) 204
Sullivan, James E 47, 115, 117, 124, 134, 219, 226, 230*n*37
Sundholm, Karl 252
Sundman, Gunnar 262
Sundsvall 201
Sunshine Olympics 12, 23, 52, 57, 90, 154, 174, 191–2, 217
Svanberg, John 84–5, 101, 113*n*18
Svensk-Amerikanska Filmkompaniet 49
Svensk Export 45
Svenska Dagbladet 89–90, 203, 205, 210, 212
Svenska Folkdansens Vänner 50
Svenska Kommunikationer 40
Svenska konstnärernas förening 140, 147
Svenska Morgonbladet 207
Svenska Tidningsagenturen 40
Svenska Utlandstidningen 44
Svensson, Ivar 249
Sveriges Allmänna Exportförening 41
Sverre, Johan *221*
Swahn, Alfred *110*, 260–1
Swahn, Oscar *109*, 110, *212*, 261
Swann, Sidney 251
Sweden's Central Association for the Promotion of Sport 5, 7, 15, 57, 58, 75, 141, 145, 204, 268
Swedish Association of Engineers 140
Swedish Athletic Association 77; Training Committee for the Olympic Games in Berlin 1916 91; *see also* Swedish Athletics Confederation
Swedish Athletics Confederation 226; *see also* Swedish Athletics Association
Swedish Cavalry 273
Swedish clubs in the United States 42
Swedish Consulates 30, 42, 45
Swedish Court 70; *see also* Royal Family
Swedish Football Association 18, 230*n*28
Swedish Gymnastic and Athletic Union of America 82, 106
Swedish House of Parliament 142, 224, 226
Swedish Hymn 160
Swedish Labor Movement 57
Swedish Masterpiece 12, 57, 188
Swedish National Centre for Research in Sports 1
Swedish National Museum 141–2
Swedish News Agency 48
Swedish Olympic Committee (SOC) 226–7, 269
Swedish Olympic Council 83
Swedish Parliament 4, 13, *14*, 50, 142, 170, 200, 222, 229*n*17

Swedish Rowing Federation 62, 96
Swedish School of Sport and Health Science (GIH) 1, 15, 128, 187, 265, 275–6
Swedish Song League 184
Swedish Sports Confederation 58, 69, 77, 93*n*39, 95, 103–4, 204; *see also* National Sports Federation
Swedish Swimming Federation 20, 123
Swedish Tennis Association 118, 132
Swedish Tourist Traffic Association 30, 32, 43, 45
Swedish Travel Agency 44
Swedish Women's National Association 182
Swedish-Dutch Association 42
swimming *6*, 8, 10, 20, 22, 24*n*26, 39, 58, 61–2, 67, 69, 75, 83, 96–7, 101, 103, 111, 112*n*11, 113*n*22, 117–24, 126, 130, 132–3, 134*n*51, 138, 140, 147, 155, 157–8, 160–1, 163, 165, 217, 222, 225, 227, 234, 251, 261–4
Swimming and Athletics Club Hellas 106
Swimming Committee 9, 84, 123
Swimming Stadium 16, *20*, 251, 261
Switzerland 82, 102, 234, 270
Sydsvenska Dagbladet 203, 209
Sydsvenska Gymnastikinstitutet, Lund 128
Sylvén, Sune 233

Taber, Norman 236, 240
Täby 245
Taifun (yacht) 254
Taipale, Armas 80, 242, 273
Tamm, Sebastian 252
Teacher Training College, Gothenburg 120
Technical Section 9, 58
Le Temps 46
tennis 8, 10, 15, 39, 61, 69, 83, 100, 102, 104, 106–9, 111–2, 113*n*22, 115, 117–20, 124–8, 130–4, 135*n*51, 138, 157–61, 163, 170, 178; *see also* lawn-tennis
Tennis Committee 9, 11, 84; *see also* Lawntenniskommittén
Tennis Hall 15, 156, 180, 265; *see also* Royal tennis hall
Tennis Pavilion at Östermalm's Athletic Ground 15, 157, 247, 251, 266
Tennis Restaurant *186*, 187–8, *192*
Ternström, Josef 239–40
Tewanima, Lewis 169, 237
Thames Rowing Club 252
Thaulow, Gustaf 253
Theander, David 262
Thisell, Nore *59*
Thorpe, James "Jim" 50, 75, 79, 87, 91, 97, 102, 180, 231*n*45, 240–1, 244, 272–3
Thubé, Amédée 254

Thubé, Gaston 254, 273
Thubé, Jacques 254
Thulin, Vera 120, 135n51, 263
Thulin, Wilhelmina 135n51
tickets 7–9, *8*, 24n12, 28, 30, 38,
    46, 48–9, 61–2, 154, 157–8, *179*,
    180, 185, 234–5
Tidning för Idrott 57, 158; *see also*
    Ny Tidning för Idrott
Tiel, Alvar 254
Toivonen, Nestor 261
Tornblad, Hjalmar 184–6
Törnmarck, Ivan 259
Törnqvist, Konrad 249
Torstenssonsgatan 156, 251
tossing the caber 271
total experience 175
Tóth, Péter 248
Touring Club 45
Tourist Association 52
tourist associations 39, 43
Tourist Traffic Association's guide-
    book 45
tourists 9, 39–40, 45, 51, 161, 167,
    174, 182–3, 184–5, 190–1
"Tours in Sweden" 31, 40
track cycling 100
Tranebergs IP 18, *19*, 155, 157, 249
travel agencies 35, 38–9, 42, 44,
    51–2
Trelleborg 40, 103
Troilius, Hjalmar 40
Tronner, Hans 242
Trygger, Ernst 170
Tsiclitiras, Konstantinos *80*, 241
tug-of-war 10, 20, 24n26, 91, *105*,
    112n11, 113n22, 165, 169, 205,
    267–8
Tug-of-war Committee 9
Tunesi, Adolfo 250
Tuomisto, Ivari 62, *181*
Tureberg 51, 162, 237
Turkey 111, 234
Turnen, German gymnastics 102, 250
Tuyll, Frederik van *see* van Tuyll,
    Frederik

Uggla, Bertil Gustafsson *59*, 163,
    164, 241
Ultimus (horse) 246
union between Sweden and Nor-
    way 52, 67
Union des Sociétés Françaises de
    Sports Athlétiques (USFSA) 18,
    20
United Kingdom (UK) 118, 120,
    124
United States *see* 40, 41, 64, 77,
    80, 82, 84–5, 87, 89, 102, 106,
    111, 113n18, 117, 130–1, 164, 167,
    169–70, 219, 234–47, 251, 255,
    257–63, 269, 271–3; Olympic
    team 181
Uppsala 120

*V. Olympiaden. Officiell redogörelse
    för olympiska spelen i Stockholm*

*1912 see The Fifth Olympiad.
    The Official Report of the Olympic
    Games of Stockholm 1912*
Valhallavägen 90, 244
Vallentuna 245
van Tuyll, Frederik 220
Varga, Béla 269
Varpa 271
Västerås 120, 130, 158, 207, 244
Västerås Bäsboll Klubb 271
Vaxholms Roddklubb 252
Veirman, Polydore 253
Venningen, von Baron *see* von
    Venningen, Baron
Vienna 47
Vinne, Erling 242
Visby 271
visitors 28, 49, 51 157–8, 178, 181–
    3, 185–6, 190–1, 193, 195n61,
    195n66, 219
von Blixen-Finecke, Hans Sr. 246
von Halt, Karl Ritter 116
von Hohenau, Vilhelm 246
von Kröcher, Rabod Wilhelm 246
von Las-Torres, Béla 262
von Osterley, Friedrich 246
von Rochow, Friedrich 246
von Rosen, Clarence 5, 33, 57, 58,
    59, 61, 63–4, 72n22, 72n53, 141,
    193n8, *221*, 224, 226, 230n28,
    231n41
von Rosen, Hans 247
von Rosen, Pontus 248
von Schaesberg-Tannheim, Rudolf
    246
von Strussenfelt, A. 44
von Venningen, Baron 220, *221*,
    222–4
von Wartensleben, Count *221*
von Zedlitz und Leipe, Franz 260
von Zweigbergk, Otto 206

Wachtmeister, A. 92
Wachtmeister, Schering 252
Waern, Rasmus 142
Walden, Harold 249
walking 79, 102–3, 112n11
Wallenberg, Victor 260
Wallerius, Erik 254
Wallerius, Harald 254
Wäre, Emil 268
Wartensleben, von Count *see* von
    Wartensleben, Count
Wass, Gustav F. 96
Webb, Ernest *103*, 240
Wedholm, Johan Eskil 262
weightlifting 77, 100
welcomming reception *173*, 177–8
Wells, Henry 251
Welt auf Reisen 46
Wendell, James 235
Wennergren, Charles 267
Werkner, Lajos 248
Werner, Helge 248
Westermark, Herbert 254
Westermark, Nils 254
Wetterstrand, Ernst 252

whisky 189
White, Isabelle 122, 265
White City Stadium 22
Whitney, Lawrence 242–3
Wicksell, Ragnar 249
Wide, Ernst 89, 236, 240
Widholm, Christian 71
Widlund, Ture 95, 233
Wieslander, Hugo 79, 91, 102,
    244, 273
Wilding, Anthony 156, 266
Wilhelm, Prince of Sweden 11,
    127, 176
Wilkens, Wilhelm 252–3
Wilker, Herman 252
Wilkinson, George 265
Willems, Victor 248
Williams Affischerings Aktiebolag
    40
Wimbledon Tournament 118, 124,
    156–7, 266
Winans, Walter 143, *144*, 145, 269
Winslow, Charles *156*, 267
winter sports 22, 58, 62, 100, 138,
    144, 146, 240
Winter Sports (painting) 143, 270
Wollert, Carl 260
Women's Gymnastics Association
    for the Swedish Display 106
Woodward, Vivian 249
Worker's Educational Association
    207
world press 50, 218
World War I *see* First World War
World War II *see* Second World
    War
Wormwald, Leslie 251
Worthington, Harry 241
wrestling 10, 14, 24n26, 62, 77,
    82–3, 97, 100, 110–1, 113n22, 117,
    122, 157, 165, 181, 212–3, 220,
    222, 225, 227, 229n14, 230n26,
    268–9, 273
Wrestling Committee 9, 62, 84,
    223
Wright, Edward 249
Wright, Marc 241
Wylie, Wilhelmina 263

Yachting Committee 9
yachtsmen 24n25, 111
YMCA 106
Young, Donnell 235
Yttergren, Leif 7, 23, 57, 111, 276
Yvon, George 264

Zampori, Giorgio 250
Zander, John 240
Zborzil, Arthur 267
Zedlitz und Leipe, Franz von *see*
    von Zedlitz und Leipe, Franz
Zemla, Ladislav 267
Zerling, Paul 236, 239
Zimmerman, Robert 265
Zürner, Albert 264–5
Zweigbergk, Otto von *see* von
    Zweigbergk, Otto